LAW, LIBERTY AND STATE

Hayek, Oakeshott and Schmitt are associated with a conservative reaction to the 'progressive' forces of the twentieth century. Each was an acute analyst of the juristic form of the modern state and the relationship of that form to the idea of liberty under a system of public, general law. Hayek had the highest regard for Schmitt's understanding of the rule-of-law state despite Schmitt's hostility to it, and he owed the distinction he drew in his own work between a purpose-governed form of state and a law-governed form to Oakeshott. However, until now, the three have rarely been considered together, something which will be ever more apparent as political theorists, lawyers and theorists of international relations turn to the foundational texts of twentieth-century thought at a time when debate about liberal democratic theory might appear to have run out of steam.

DAVID DYZENHAUS is Professor of Law and Philosophy at the University of Toronto and a Fellow of the Royal Society of Canada.

THOMAS POOLE is Professor of Law at the London School of Economics and Political Science.

LAW, LIBERTY AND STATE

Oakeshott, Hayek and Schmitt on the Rule of Law

Edited by

DAVID DYZENHAUS AND THOMAS POOLE

CAMBRIDGE
UNIVERSITY PRESS

CAMBRIDGE
UNIVERSITY PRESS

University Printing House, Cambridge CB2 8BS, United Kingdom

Cambridge University Press is part of the University of Cambridge.

It furthers the University's mission by disseminating knowledge in the pursuit of education, learning and research at the highest international levels of excellence.

www.cambridge.org
Information on this title: www.cambridge.org/9781107093386

First published 2015

A catalogue record for this publication is available from the British Library.

Library of Congress Cataloging-in-Publication Data
Law, liberty and state: Oakeshott, Hayek and Schmitt on the rule of law / edited by David Dyzenhaus, Thomas Poole.
pages cm
Includes index.
ISBN 978-1-107-09338-6 (Hardback)
1. Rule of law. 2. Oakeshott, Michael, 1901–1990.
3. Hayek, Friedrich A. von (Friedrich August), 1899–1992.
4. Schmitt, Carl, 1888–1985 I. Dyzenhaus, David, editor. II. Poole, Thomas (Thomas M.) editor.
K3171.L395 2015
340′.11–dc23
2014050248

ISBN 978-1-107-09338-6 Hardback

CONTENTS

CONTRIBUTORS

NEHAL BHUTA
Professor of International Law, Department of Law, European University Institute

DAVID BOUCHER
Professor of Political Philosophy and International Relations, Cardiff University and Senior Associate Researcher in the Department of Political Science, University of Johannesburg

DAVID DYZENHAUS
Professor of Law and Philosophy, University of Toronto

DUNCAN KELLY
University Senior Lecturer, Department of Politics and International Studies and Fellow of Jesus College, Cambridge University

ERIKA A. KISS
Associate Research Scholar, Director of the University Center for Human Values Film Forum, University Center for Human Values, Princeton University

CHANDRAN KUKATHAS
Chair in Political Theory, Government Department, London School of Economics

HANS LINDAHL
Professor of Legal Philosophy, School of Law Tilburg University

MARTIN LOUGHLIN
Professor of Public Law, Law Department, London School of Economics

JAN-WERNER MÜLLER
Professor of Politics, Department of Politics, Princeton University

THOMAS POOLE
Professor of Law, Law Department, London School of Economics

ADRIAN VERMEULE
Professor of Law, Harvard Law School, Harvard University

LARS VINX
Assistant Professor, Department of Philosophy, Bilkent University

1

Introduction

DAVID DYZENHAUS AND THOMAS POOLE

The twentieth century may be said to have witnessed the apotheosis of the state. The state became capable of operating on an unprecedented and potentially all-encompassing scale. It could provide for its subjects in a previously undreamt of manner, taming *Fortuna* to the extent that the vicissitudes of life that at any previous stage of human history would have meant their demise might now be treated as mere inconveniences. But the state could also fight total wars on an intercontinental scale, requiring vast sacrifices from its populations.[1] And, as the century progressed, the state also showed itself capable of controlling its subjects in ways that were deeply troubling to liberals who valued above all the freedom of individuals to decide on the good for themselves.

The rise of the modern state and the possibilities for liberty within it were staple topics of twentieth-century social and political thought. But the subject also had crucial juridical dimensions that are more commonly overlooked. From the turn of the century onwards, theorists realized that the requirements of the modern state put increasing pressure on accepted understandings of law. The dynamism of the new century meant that law, once seen as both relatively settled and stable and protective of individual liberty, was now subject to rapid, sometimes dramatic and unpredictable change. Law increasingly became something made or legislated, connected to functions determined by the organs of the state and as such a 'positive' rather than a 'natural' phenomenon. This development not only reinforced general concerns about the demise of humanistic values in the 'Machine Age', but it also threatened the connection that was previously assumed between the law and the

[1] Historians have begun to argue that the First World War in particular ought to be seen 'not merely as a war between European nation states, but primarily as a war of multi-ethnic, global empires': see Robert Gerwarth and Erez Manela, 'Introduction' in Gerwarth and Manela (eds), *Empires at War, 1911–1923* (Oxford University Press, 2014), 3.

basic values or mores of the community. And this was occurring at a time when, with other traditional forms of social cohesion losing their force, law was being called upon to do more by way of legitimating the government apparatus. This sense of juristic disorientation was heightened by the specificity of the new functional rule making. As law seemed to become regulation, increasingly a matter of detail and of technique, it became unclear what space remained for the image of law as anchor of basic principles and brake on overweening or arbitrary political action. If the *Rechtsstaat* is meant to embody general liberal principles, how can it abide a particularistic core?

This collection examines the response to the problems of law and liberty raised by the modern state of three of the last century's greatest thinkers: Carl Schmitt (1888–1985), Friedrich Hayek (1899–1992) and Michael Oakeshott (1901–1990), whose lives almost spanned the entire century. All were associated with a conservative reaction to the progressive forces of their time, although these reactions took very different forms. Their formative experience was the crisis of European society in the inter-war years. Each was an acute, if controversial, analyst of the juristic form of the modern state and the relationship of that form to the idea of liberty under a system of public, general law. They were also influenced by each other's work, although this occurred as much through the irritant effect one's thought had on another's as through more direct or positive means. Hayek had the highest regard for Schmitt's understanding of the *Rechtsstaat*, despite considering him to be dedicated to the destruction of that form of state. Schmitt, as Perry Anderson observed in an essay on the three thinkers, 'was never far from Hayek's mind – standing for the prime example of a skilled jurist whose sophistry helped to destroy the rule of law in Germany, yet a political theorist whose stark definitions of the nature of sovereignty and the logic of party, at any rate, had to be accepted'.[2] Hayek also acknowledged Oakeshott's influence, notably for the distinction, crucial to his own theory, between a teleocratic (purpose-governed or managerial) form of state and a nomocratic (law-governed or juridical) form.[3] Oakeshott, for

[2] Perry Anderson, 'The Intransigent Right: Michael Oakeshott, Leo Strauss, Carl Schmitt, Friedrich von Hayek', *London Review of Books*, 24 September 1992; republished in Anderson, *Spectrum: From Right to Left in the World of Ideas* (London: Verso, 2005), 15.

[3] F. A. Hayek, 'The Confusion of Language in Political Thought' (1967) in Hayek, *New Studies in Philosophy, Politics, Economics and the History of Ideas* (London: Routledge & Kegan Paul, 1978), 89.

his part, resisted the comparison. Hayek's assault on rationalism, in his view, failed to go far enough. It may have been doctrine against doctrines, but it remained a doctrine for all that. 'A plan to resist all planning may be better than its opposite, but it belongs to the same style of politics.'[4] And although Schmitt seems to have been unaware of Oakeshott's work on Hobbes until the last years of his life, Hobbes was a theorist of cardinal importance to both. Oakeshott's comment about *Leviathan* being 'the greatest, perhaps the sole, masterpiece of political philosophy written in the English language'[5] was a judgement on which Schmitt could wholeheartedly concur.

Despite these points of salient connection and productive contrast, the three writers are rarely discussed together, a gap in the literature which becomes more pronounced at a time when political theorists, lawyers and international relations scholars increasingly turn to foundational texts of twentieth-century thought. This collection considers the juridical aspects of the work of Schmitt, Oakeshott and Hayek and the way that those aspects intersect with their thinking on liberty and the modern state. While some of the essays pay attention to the context in which the theorists wrote, this volume is not primarily historical. Its main aim is to deepen our understanding of the conceptual thinking of the three theorists with a view to identifying what remains useful in the context of contemporary issues and concerns. No strict editorial grand plan has been imposed on the essays. While some authors confine themselves to the thought of one thinker, others discuss linkages and dissonances between two or among all three. The editors have instead devised what they considered the most coherent and satisfying arrangement, one which both places essays that speak most directly to each other wherever possible side by side and also serves to shed the most light on the collection's overarching themes. This has resulted in putting first those essays which have Schmitt as their centre of gravity, then those which concern Oakeshott and finally the essays on Hayek and Hayekian themes. It also means that the collection moves from an initial reflection on the character of the state and sovereignty (Chapters 2–5), through analyses of the theorists' responses to crisis, reason of state and the 'exception' (Chapters 6–8) and their understanding of the rule

[4] Michael Oakeshott, 'Rationalism in Politics' in Oakeshott, *Rationalism in Politics and Other Essays* (Indianapolis, IN: Liberty Press, 1991), ed. Timothy Fuller.

[5] Michael Oakeshott, 'Introduction to *Leviathan*' (1946), collected in Oakeshott, *Hobbes on Civil Association* (Oxford, UK: Basil Blackwell, 1975), 3.

of law (Chapters 9 and 10), to a discussion of more institutional dimensions of their thought (Chapters 11–13).

The collection opens with an essay by Nehal Bhuta (Chapter 2) which brings an important focus on international law and on the enterprise of state building. Bhuta develops a comparative reading of Schmitt's and Oakeshott's diagnoses of the origins and nature of the state, examining in particular their understanding of state concepts and state formation. Noting the two writers' sensitivity towards the fragility of that special kind of liberty which is connected to the modern state form, Bhuta argues that despite their different practical commitments in politics, 'Schmitt and Oakeshott share essential commonalities in their analyses of the state and ... together they leave us with an understanding of the state that has significant implications for how we think about the state and state formation today.'

Hans Lindahl's chapter (Chapter 3) focusses on the systematic relation between state, law and freedom that emerges from Carl Schmitt's discussion of law as a concrete order. Lindahl argues that when legal order is reconstructed as authoritative collective action, a theory of concrete order supports several of Schmitt's objections to normativism while also forcefully rejecting his attempt to ground the validity of legal constitutions in a condition of political normality. Indeed, there is no original normality which lends an independent measure to normativity, no pure 'social type' which could provide the inner measure to which legal norms must correspond if they are to be valid. Constitutional crises reveal that normality is always the outcome of a process of normalization which responds to the abnormal; hence that collective self-restraint is an integral part of the exercise of collective freedom. 'Normality, including constitutional normality', the chapter concludes, 'is always to a greater or lesser extent the outcome of a process of (constitutional) normalization', meaning that the normative domain is never only pre-reflexive but also post-reflexive.

Martin Loughlin's contribution (Chapter 4) looks at the question of origins, a perennial juristic question, here examined through a reading of Carl Schmitt, one of the subject's most important and controversial modern interlocutors. Loughlin does so by illuminating Schmitt's attempt in *The Nomos of the Earth* to recapture the original meaning of *nomos* by going back to its Greek origins, where the term connoted the appropriation, distribution and productive use of land. Schmitt's aim in doing so was not to breathe artificial new life into dead myths but as part of the exercise of following the constitution of political authority to its source. All questions of collective order are to be traced back to the three processes of appropriation, distribution and production. Part of Schmitt's aim in restoring the original meaning of *nomos* thus serves, Loughlin argues, to place in question the authority of the predominant positivism and normativism of modern legal thought.

Lars Vinx's chapter (Chapter 5) asks whether Carl Schmitt's theory of sovereignty manages to establish, as intended, that a sovereign is essential to the very existence of a legal and political system. The concept of sovereignty has come in for a great deal of criticism in legal, political and constitutional theory. It cannot account for a number of key features of developed legal systems, critics argue, such as their continuity through time or the existence of secondary norms. Schmitt's defence of sovereignty, Vinx argues, is at least partially successful. While Schmitt does not manage to show that there must be a sovereign wherever there is an established legal and political system, he does establish that the existence of a sovereign authority in something like the classical sense is not necessarily incompatible with a modern legal and constitutional system characterized by institutional continuity and a rich internal normative structure. Schmitt also succeeds in linking his reformulated understanding of the classical concept of sovereignty, as the power to decide on the exception, to modern notions of popular sovereignty and national independence. His reply to the normative criticism of sovereignty exploits these links by arguing that true popular sovereignty and political self-determination are possible only where sovereignty authority is recognized as the legitimating source of political and constitutional order. Schmitt does not succeed, however, Vinx argues, in showing that sovereignty is politically attractive. Far from being an indispensable condition of the legitimacy of law, the existence of a Schmittian sovereign inevitably undermines the legitimacy of legal order.

David Boucher's contribution (Chapter 6) focusses on the contributions of Schmitt and Oakeshott to the inter-war body of literature on the 'crisis of civilization'. Boucher charts the fascination that Hobbes' political thought exerted upon both writers. As such, it brings to the surface a general sub-theme of this collection: namely, the importance of Hobbes' state theory as an influence on Schmitt and Oakeshott and as a foil for Hayek. Reflecting on the conceptual confusion and the erosion of the theory and practice of authority, Schmitt and Oakeshott identified in Hobbes an individualism that was somehow contributory towards modern liberalism, which they saw as both a cause and a symptom of the modern crisis. Reading Schmitt on Hobbes against Oakeshott on Hobbes sheds light on the sharp differences between them. Thus, while

Schmitt saw politics fundamentally as the ability to distinguish between friends and enemies and thought that modern trends had impaired the state's ability to act decisively in this zone, for Oakeshott, it was the enhancement of the state's ability to act decisively, exacerbated by a propensity to go to war too hastily, that suppressed the individualism of citizens.

Thomas Poole's chapter (Chapter 7) examines the responses of Schmitt, Hayek and Oakeshott to the rise of the modern state and its warping effect on the concept of law by exploring what each had to say about the idea of reason of state. Each may be said to reflect a characteristic response to the years of crisis that beset twentieth-century Europe. For Schmitt, reason of state is connected with the central idea of the exception, tied to a substantive politics of belonging and thus to the basic political question of who counts as friend and who the enemy. Reason of state offers a source of redemption and escape from the humdrum realities of the creeping bureaucratic state. Hayek, by contrast, sees reason of state as the antithesis of his ideal of the common law *Rechtsstaat*,[6] the evolutionary body of law tied closely to the lived experience of the people and which contains the virtues of the many-minds principle in juridical form. His response to the threat presented by reason of state is to try to eradicate it, both normatively and as a matter of institutional design, a move especially evident in his model constitution. Oakeshott shares Hayek's distrust of reason of state but recognizes that the practice of reason of state lies at the heart of one of two conceptions of politics that vie for prominence within the modern European state. Built into the institutional structures and pathways of government, reason of state may be impossible to eradicate, but we may be able to check its more dangerous excesses.

In 'Reconfiguring Reason of State in Response to Political Crisis' (Chapter 8), Duncan Kelly explores what he takes to be a project shared by Oakeshott and Schmitt of understanding the modern state through the emergence of its central ideas in the history of political thought. But, Kelly argues, the commonalities between the two go even deeper. The point of developing an account of the state through an exploration of the history of political thought is, first, to undermine the claim of liberal theory to be able to understand the state as neutral, or non-ideological, or apolitical and, second, to show the political nature of the Western

[6] John Grey, *Hayek on Liberty*, 3rd edn. (London: Routledge, 1998), 69.

secularization process. It is for this reason that both took so much inspiration from Hobbes. Hence, both Oakeshott and Schmitt rejected what one might think of as the rights fetishism of twentieth-century liberal thought and argued for the return of a historically informed sense of the centrality of the 'political' in shaping our contingent practices.

Erika Kiss's chapter (Chapter 9) disinters the philosophical assumptions that drive Oakeshott's rejection of conventional accounts of the rule of law. In part, she suggests, misunderstandings of Oakeshott's argument, which caused him some frustration, are his responsibility, and she seeks to remedy these by reference to his little-known work, *A Guide to the Classics*, an early, jointly authored book on gambling at the horse races. She argues that one can derive from Oakeshott's account in that work an idea of 'stochastic rationality', 'an epistemologically relaxed mode of intellectual engagement, which is somewhat unconcerned with outcomes'. It is akin to the skill involved when people learn their native language. The point for law and the rule of law are that, as 'with a vernacular language, the rule of law will not prescribe what has to be said, and sometimes things can be said that nobody had ever thought could be said in the language at all; as with gambling, we do not know what the outcomes will be – we can just wager as best as we can, using our judgment'. This understanding of the rule of law, Kiss suggests, is apt for a world in which we do not have the certainties that would make it possible for experts and technocrats to lead us.

In 'Dreaming the Rule of Law' (Chapter 10), David Dyzenhaus explores common themes in the accounts of Schmitt, Hayek and Oakeshott of the importance of the rule of law to the liberal state. All three thinkers argued that the rule of law has to be understood as a formal principle of government that is somehow liberty preserving. But, Dyzenhaus argues, the similarities end there. Schmitt thought that the liberal rule-of-law project had been transformed into a politically vacuous, positivistic commitment to granting legitimacy to any technically valid law. In contrast, while both Hayek and Oakeshott considered that the rule-of-law state was in constant danger of being undermined by state forms designed for centralized social planning, they both considered that it remained a viable project. Dyzenhaus focusses mainly on Oakeshott in a bid to show that despite his aversion to instrumental accounts of politics, he developed a natural-law theory of the rule of law that explains why there is a politically valuable connection between legal form and liberty.

Jan-Werner Müller's contribution (Chapter 11) explores Hayek's at first sight rather odd conception of a model constitution for liberal democracy. The conception is odd because Hayek suggested that there should be two assemblies. The Legislative Assembly was to be elected by citizens aged forty-five and older, who would choose candidates of the same generation for a fifteen-year term. It would devise the just rules of conduct for citizens. The Governmental Assembly would be subject to regular election and party political competition. A Constitutional Court would adjudicate conflicts between the two bodies. Müller argues that the Model Constitution does not appear so odd when one takes into account that in times of crisis, people might want to make a fresh start with a different kind of democracy and that it is not uncommon for people to vote to narrow their political choices. He also sketches problems that the Model Constitution encounters in terms of some of Hayek's own central commitments. However, the basic idea behind it retains some allure just because it offers the prospect of 'relief from irrational partisan politics and the burdens of involving oneself in politics and wasting too many evenings'.

In 'Hayek and the State' (Chapter 12), Chandran Kukathas points out that Hayek surprisingly hardly ever refers to the 'state'. His diagnosis of this dearth of reference is that Hayek was in fact torn between two different arguments. The first is that we need to reform and liberalize the institutions of the modern state in order to protect liberty and uphold the rule of law. The second is that liberty and the rule of law cannot prevail unless we get away from a state-centric understanding of political order. Kukathas makes the case that only the second argument, one that repudiates the state as the fundamental institution governing human society, presents Hayek's distinctive contribution to political theory. In a careful account of the development of Hayek's thought, he shows that Hayek constructed an account of the liberal state as an 'abstract order of people who interact with and relate to one another not because they share particular deep ethical commitments but in spite of the fact that they do not'. Hayek thus puts forward an understanding of liberalism whose virtue is that it cannot secure any political unity, one that was opposed to ideas of community and that seeks to transcend, perhaps vainly, political boundaries.

In his contribution (Chapter 13), Adrian Vermeule casts doubt on Hayek's own case for a thoroughgoing hostility to the administrative state. Hayek and Hayekians, he points out, privilege context-specific knowledge about particular economic or regulatory problems, especially tacit or practical knowledge. But this Hayekian position, he argues, overlooks or downplays the fact that 'centralized synoptic regulation is indispensable for epistemic coordination' – the creation of a common knowledge that could not be achieved if everything were left to myopic local actors. In addition, he argues that the administrative state has developed a representative bureaucracy devoted to the gathering and exploitation of local knowledge. While Vermeule regards the distinction between local and global knowledge as of central importance to understanding the scope of the administrative state and its internal organization, his argument exposes deep tensions within the Hayekian position on these issues which require further attention.

As one can see from these brief descriptions, there is much internal disagreement among the contributors about how to evaluate the work of the figure or figures on whom their contributions focus. For example, they differ as to whether one should take the account of law, liberty and state in any of the three figures as foil or as inspiration, or as some mix of both, and, if more than one figure is examined, on whether there are fundamental commonalities in the approaches each adopted to the rule of law. However, all the contributors agree at some abstract level that these figures have much to offer contemporary debates about such themes, and our hope is that readers will find illuminating both the areas of agreement and disagreement that emerge, whether explicitly or implicitly, from the twelve chapters.

2

The mystery of the state

State concept, state theory and state making in Schmitt and Oakeshott

NEHAL BHUTA

Both Schmitt and Oakeshott were antagonists of the rationalist style of thought in politics.[1] Today we might label them 'realists',[2] although the term is anachronistic. Both of them were deeply sceptical (and, in Schmitt's case, ideologically hostile) to the idea that cognitively derived normative principles could be the *foundation* for political orders and the answer to problems of state formation. Both would readily admit that normative reasoning was intrinsic to political practices and indistinguishable from the 'stuff' of politics. But neither accepted that the foundation of state power and authority lies in the voluntaristic assent of citizens persuaded by the best arguments for such authority. Rather, both thinkers approach the modern state and its nature through an historical understanding of the emergence of the state and the determination of its conceptual architecture and normative languages through inherited modes of authority and apparatuses of government, the content and functioning of which are transformed by a series of highly contingent historical developments in Western Europe. And both thinkers also understood the modern state as generating a distinctive kind of freedom, undermined by the dynamics inherent in the emergence of the modern state form itself: Oakeshott's nomocratic civil condition, under threat from teleocratic state action under the shadow of

Helpful comments and criticisms were received from Nida Alahmad, Samuel Moyn, Duncan Kelly, Benjamin Schupmann and Benjamin Straumann.

[1] Carl Schmitt, *The Crisis of Parliamentary Democracy* (Cambridge, MA: MIT Press, 1988), trans. Ellen Kennedy; Carl Schmitt, *The Concept of the Political* (University of Chicago Press, 2007), trans. George Schwab; Michael Oakeshott, *Rationalism in Politics and Other Essays* (Indianapolis, IN: Liberty Fund, 1991); Michael Oakeshott, *On Human Conduct* (Oxford University Press, 1991).

[2] As Terry Nardin does; see Terry Nardin, 'Realism and Right: Sketch for a Theory of Global Justice' in Cornelia Navari (ed.), *Ethical Reasoning in International Relations: Arguments from the Middle Ground* (Basingstoke, UK: Palgrave, 2013), Chapter 3.

mass politics, and Schmitt's bourgeois *Rechtsstaat*, a feeble political and legal form unable to preserve itself from external and internal competitors that have a better understanding of the real sources of political power and the means of generating and wielding it.

In this chapter, I develop a comparative reading of Schmitt and Oakeshott's diagnoses of the origins and nature of the modern state in order better to grasp the implications of their theories for our contemporary understanding of the state. I compare two dimensions of their state theories: their concepts of state and rulership (state concepts) and their understanding of historicity and contingency in the development of the state form and its distinctive kinds of authority and sociology (state formation). In the process, I also touch upon their diagnoses of the fragility of the special kind of liberty generated by the modern state form and the threats to its continuation. Despite very different practical commitments in politics, I suggest that along both of these dimensions Schmitt and Oakeshott share essential commonalities in their analyses of the state and that together they leave us with an understanding of the state that has significant implications for how we think about the state and state formation today.

State concepts: rulership, domination, authority, ethos

A crisis of state authority and deep polemical contestation of how properly to understand the legal and political foundations of the state were formative contexts for both Schmitt and Oakeshott's political writings. Schmitt is an inheritor and radical revisionist of the 'long nineteenth-century' German theoretical preoccupation with the locus of the state's order-generating and order-maintaining capacity, a preoccupation inaugurated by the French Revolution and continued throughout the nineteenth century under the impacts of monarchical restoration, liberal revolt and social transformation. As a theoretical problem, it found expression in various conceptions of the state as an organism or person (Bluntschli) or as dual-sided unity comprising both a unified empirical personality (an organic life order of a people) and a legal unity through which the empirical unity expresses its will and organizes its life.[3]

[3] For extensive discussion, see Duncan Kelly, *The State of the Political: Conceptions of Politics and the State in the Thought of Max Weber, Carl Schmitt and Franz Neumann* (Oxford University Press, 2003); see also Kenneth Dyson, *The State Tradition in Western Europe: A Study of an Idea and Institution* (Oxford University Press, 1980); Ernst-Wolfgang Böckenförde, *State, Society and Liberty: Essays in Political Theory and Constitutional Law* (Oxford,UK: Berg, 1991), trans. J. A. Underwood, Chapters 1–4.

The various positions in this field of conceptual contestation differed in their degree of emphasis on the priority of the empirical-substantial vis-à-vis the legal in characterizing the unity that constitutes a state order[4] – from Gierke's emphasis on Germanic *Genossenschaft* as the true source of national law's binding qualities, to Stahl's attribution of state personality to the real person of the monarch, to Gerber and Laband's attempt to distinguish the ethical-natural person of the state from the legal order of the state that derives its foundation and authority from the self-fulfilling dogmatics of legal concepts and forms (although animated by the real person of the monarch).[5] But, as Böckenförde observes, at stake in this contestation over the theory of the state was also the conflict between contending political forces organized around the poles of ruler sovereignty (monarchical government) and popular sovereignty (parliamentarism), as well as the consequences of the social transformation that characterized nineteenth-century Germany – the dissolution of the traditional authority of estate-based orders, the social emancipation of the individuals and the free movement and ownership of capital.[6]

In Britain, a territorially unified, stable political authority with an integrated legal system had been relatively firmly established since the eighteenth century,[7] with the strengthening and consolidation of state power through 'the achievement of responsible government and of the growth of representative government'.[8] State sovereignty emerged

[4] See Duncan Kelly, 'Egon Zweig and the Intellectual History of the Constituent Power', where Kelly traces meticulously the theoretical dialectic of nineteenth-century theorists concerned to grasp the inner essence of the state, precisely because 'what was at issue was ... the intellectual foundation of the modern nation-state, and on what basis its sovereignty rested' (unpublished manuscript, p. 3).

[5] As Böckenförde points out, the somewhat paradoxical consequence of the Historical School of jurisprudence was that while even as it accepted that law was an emanation of a nation's spirit, formed historically, history was reduced to 'a space within which a natural development [of a *Volksgeist*] unfolds, a development that proceeds organically from an immanent principle ... Law ... is something that is rooted in the natural entity of the nation as understood metaphysically and that itself unfolds historically. It is an autonomous edifice in the intellectual and cultural world ... This makes it possible, in principle, to explain and understand law *in terms of itself* and to adopt or construct and develop legal concepts and legal institutes on the basis of the legal fabric as handed down ... Historical jurisprudence led to an unhistorical understanding of law. Not only was it incapable of erecting a barrier against the abstractly formal conception of jurisprudence of Gerber, Ihering and Laband; it actually paved the way for it.' *State, Society and Liberty*, 10–12.

[6] Böckenförde, *State, Society and Liberty*, 82–3.

[7] Martin Loughlin, *Foundations of Public Law* (Oxford University Press, 2010), 260.

[8] Ibid., 270.

through a process 'by which the powers of the Crown-in-Council were both restricted and extended through the growing legislative authority of the Crown-in-Council-in-Parliament'.[9] As such, it was widely observed that until the nineteenth century, the concept of the state 'played only a marginal role in British political argument . . . [perhaps because] many of the problems which encouraged eighteenth- and nineteenth-century continental theorists to reflect on the nature of the state appeared less acute to the British'.[10] But, as Meadowcroft documents, from the mid-nineteenth century onwards 'the state' becomes a more visible term through which to reflect upon politics, under the impact of the deep transformation of British politics and economy during the 1800s. Civil service reform and expansion of the franchise rationalized bureaucratic institutions and widened participation in the structures of representative government. Modern party government and mass electoral contests unsettled the older structure of rulership and authority dominated by aristocratic and oligarchic political forms, while the intensifying industrial revolution and attendant class conflict undermined traditional community ties and engendered demands for political and legal resolution to the labour question (including challenges to 'freedom of contract') and to the immiseration of newly uprooted rural populations. The idiomatic of 'state' became a means of arguing about the limits of governmental interference in the economy and about the sources of social unity, governing power and political authority in general. The 'movement of theory' about the state in Britain between 1880 and 1914 is helpfully summarized by Meadowcroft:

> During the 1880s, and through the mid-1890s, the primary theoretical concern was with the relation between 'the state and the individual'; a burst of 'individualist' polemic against creeping interventionism was accompanied by the formulation of a range of perspectives emphasizing the broader ethical significance of the state and or justifying greater scope for state action. By the late 1890s the older individualism had obviously decayed, and a more 'positive' conception of the state was broadly taken for granted.[11]

[9] Ibid., 269.

[10] James Meadowcroft, *Conceptualizing the State: Innovation and Dispute in British Political Thought, 1880–1914* (Oxford University Press, 1995), Oxford Scholarship Online (www.oxfordscholarship.com), DOI:10.1093/acprof:oso/978019206019.001.0001, Introduction, 14. See also Dyson, *The State Tradition in Western Europe*, 36–44.

[11] Meadowcroft, *Conceptualizing the State*, 211, 214.

The British Idealists occupied an important intellectual pole in this late nineteenth-century theoretical flourishing of state theory, and their debt to Hegel and nineteenth-century German state theory was no secret. Taking aim at what was decried as an atomizing and overly abstract individualism characteristic of earlier generations of British political theory, Idealists such as Green argued for the mutual determination of individual selves and society, reconciled and perfected through the moral person of the state.[12] Neither contractualist consent nor pure force can justify the authority of the state, but only its status as the emanation and self-conscious regulator of an ethical-political substance produced through the social whole.[13] A state is a 'form which society takes in order to maintain . . . [rights of individuals]. But rights have no being [substance] except in a society of men recognizing each other as . . . [equals]. They are constituted by that mutual recognition.'[14] The foundations of this mutual recognition are other forms of community, such as family, and the state acts as 'sustainer and harmonizer'[15] of the relations grounded in real forms of social existence. Unsurprisingly, Idealist theories of the state, and those influenced by them, had recourse to organicist conceptions of state and society in order to try to capture the essence of the moral and political bond – to other persons, to law and to state authority – engendered and sustained by the state.[16]

Common to both German *Staatslehre*[17] and British Idealism is an idea of the state as at once a comprehensive unity of social life *and* an order of domination (*Herrschaft*) that guarantees the moral relations of this social order and to act as ultimate regulator of competing claims on the purpose of that order. More than an apparatus of government and not exhausted by the activities of governing, the state is nonetheless an organization of rulership that depends upon and reflects the already constituted (or incipiently realizable) social order that it rules. At the same time, the state is also the condition for the possibility of this social order and its values, not a mere framework for the expression of values derived from other forms of association. In other words, in both of these state theories,

[12] T. H. Green, *Lectures on the Principles of Political Obligation* (Kitchener, Canada: Batoche Books, 1999), para. 113.

[13] Ibid., paras. 114–7. [14] Ibid., para. 139. [15] Ibid., paras. 141–3.

[16] Ibid., para. 140.

[17] Even German state-legal positivism had to accept a dualist ontology of the state as composed of two unities – one ethical political, the other legal, even as it subordinated the people to mere subjects of the legal order within a pure juridical account. See Kelly, *The State of the Political*, 87–8.

the state is a concrete social unity in which the normative power of the factual and the factual power of the normative lean upon and implicate one another – and the medium of this mutual implication is law, which cannot be reduced on the one hand to naked coercion or pure command, nor to pure normative legitimacy on the other. On this understanding, a state must be a legal order, but all legal orders – to the extent to which they do *order* a specific social reality – are necessarily concrete orders in which the normative content of law draws upon what Lindahl (in this volume) calls 'the background of a more or less anonymous social order, an order in which "is" and "ought" run over into each other. This is the pre-reflexive order of normal and habitual behavior . . . everything is as it should be, and everything should be as it is.'[18] Put another way, by Bockenförde in his dialectical critique of the German Historical School, the substance of law 'stems from [a total social reality] . . . it flows from beliefs and attitudes of an ethical, legal or political nature that are alive in society, and it flows from living requirements expressed in them . . . The substance of the legal should thus proceed from the social "is" . . . [L]aw is interwoven, right from the outset and by its very nature, with the totality of society and its history.'[19] The authority of the state and law is always a concrete authority anchored in a social whole.

Both Schmitt and Oakeshott are theorists of the state and law as concrete orders in the preceding sense. Each develops his own distinctive and powerful theoretical apparatus, with somewhat different theoretical opponents in view. But, allowing for the idiosyncrasies of their lexicons, some striking convergences can be discerned in their understanding of the state, the sources and nature of its authority and the purposes it might successfully realize.

Oakeshott's Hegelian Hobbesianism: Sittlich foundations of unconditional authority

In his essay for admission to a fellowship at Gonville and Caius, Oakeshott's early debt to the British Idealists is unmistakable.[20] Dismissing

[18] Lindahl, 'Concrete Order: Schmitt and the Abnormality of Collective Freedom', 49–53.

[19] Böckenförde, *State, Society and Liberty*, 19–20.

[20] Michael Oakeshott, 'A Discussion of Some Matters Preliminary to the Study of Political Philosophy' (1925) in Luke O'Sullivan (ed.), *Early Political Writings* (Exeter, UK: Imprint Academic, 2010), 87ff.

with considerable scorn any definition of the state which reduces it to particular features, manifestations or functions (such as territory, government, order, etc.), Oakeshott at once marks his distance from contemporary pluralist, empiricist and positivist theories of the state (Laski, Laband, Zimmern and Russell are all singled out for criticism, along with numerous others)[21] and aligns himself with Hegelian and Idealist authors who, in his argument, grasp that the state 'is not to be defined by a list of its constituent properties, but by a revelation of the law of its life'.[22] The law of its life is nothing less than its character as the 'sum of our social experience',[23] which means 'the whole of moral and social experience'.[24] And to the extent that the state consists of this whole, 'we can neither elevate the "State" ... above the individual self, nor the self above the State, for the two things are not only indistinguishable, but actually the same thing.'[25] As a comprehensive social-ethical (*Sittlich*) reality, the state is not identical to law and government,[26] but the efficacy of the latter depends upon its relationship with the 'wholeness' of the state – the limits of government action and law are imposed *by* the state because 'Government can lay no valid claim to the wholeness which we require of the State.'[27] The identity of the state thus lies in its *status* as a total social unity, a unity of action *and* purpose manifested in 'a tradition and common memory of experience, built up into an individual language, art, culture and social life, so that it can properly be called a "working conception of life"[28] ... For a great state, qua state, is not one which embraces a great population or an extensive territory, but one which achieves a great intensity of social unity.'[29] Individual selves are born into and develop their moral consciousness through this unity, and they join it 'without being previously consulted as to ...[their] willingness to take up membership, from which it is often difficult to withdraw and whose influence over ... [them] it is always impossible to eradicate'.[30] The 'concrete filling' given to individual experience – the very condition of its unity – is nothing less than the unity furnished by the state: 'The self is the State; the State is the self.'[31]

It is tempting to conclude that Oakeshott's mature work is a deflation or rejection of the claim that the state is the social whole and that the self

[21] Ibid., 87–91. [22] Ibid., 90. [23] Ibid., 75. [24] Ibid., 81. [25] Ibid., 111.
[26] Ibid., 118–19. [27] Ibid., 127.
[28] Oakeshott's quotation is from Bernard Bosanquet, *The Philosophical Theory of the State* (London: Macmillan, 1910), 151.
[29] Ibid., 78, 82. [30] Ibid., 72. [31] Ibid., 108.

is the state. Indeed, the *cives* of a *civitas* are defined by their self-chosen satisfactions and self-chosen actions, and they are bound to each other not by their common acknowledgement of some higher social purpose or collective goal, but through a relationship to a common system of *lex* which prescribes only 'moral conditions to be subscribed to in the seeking' of these satisfactions.[32] The language of a social whole, and certainly of social unity, disappears and, if anything, seems more closely associated to the civil condition's counter-concept – the enterprise association or *universitas*. The very idea of collective choices or achievements is rejected.[33] Underlying the common system of *lex* is a system of *practices*,[34] specifically moral practices,[35] which are defined by Oakeshott as

> [T]he outcomes of [human] performances ... a relationship between agents articulated in terms of specific conditional prescriptions ... The intercourse of friends ... the relationship of husband and wife, teacher and pupil, doctor and patient, lawyer and client ... and that of speakers of a common language – each of these is participation in a distinguishable practice, each is a relationship signaled by the names of the *personae* concerned ... in terms of characteristic uses, conventions, rules, or other adverbial considerations, each is an invention of human beings, all are subject to historic vicissitudes and local variations, and none is capable of being participated in except by learning to do so.[36]

A *moral* practice of the kind that is the defining quality of a civil condition, then, is 'neither a system of general principles nor a code of rules, but a vernacular language ... it is made by speakers'.[37] It should be fairly clear that the antecedent of Oakeshott's notion of practice is the Hegelian concept of *Sittlichkeit*, even as Oakeshott abandons any effort at the rational reconciliation of plural *Sittlichkeiten* into a unified *Geist*: 'that there should be many languages [of moral practice] in the world ... is intrinsic to their character. This plurality cannot be resolved by being understood as so many contingent and regrettable divergences from a fancied perfect and universal language of moral intercourse (a law of God, a utilitarian "critical" morality or a so-called "rational morality."'[38] And shortly before this passage, Oakeshott cautions that 'neither changelessness nor perfection is a necessary condition of authority [for moral practices]'.[39]

[32] Oakeshott, *On Human Conduct*, 57–8. [33] Ibid., 87. [34] Ibid., 120–1.
[35] Michael Oakeshott, 'The Rule of Law' in *On History and Other Essays* (Oxford, UK: Blackwell, 1963), 130ff.
[36] Oakeshott, *On Human Conduct*, 56–7. [37] Ibid., 79. [38] Ibid., 80. [39] Ibid., 81.

Consistent with the Hegelianism of his youthful paper, then, self and society remain mutually constitutive. But neither pole of the relationship consists any longer of a *determined* totality. Rather, each develops the *appearance* of determinacy, but on theoretical reflection it becomes clear that both the self (agents) and society (social being, social structures, institutions) are assemblages of a multiplicity of arts and practices. Their apparent solidity and the appearance of unity given to the 'social' and the 'individual' are both the outcomes of an historically contingent suturing of practices through which agents are associated with one another.[40] The 'social' may be more visible and appear more determinate when agents are engaged in the pursuit of a 'common substantive satisfaction,' when they seem to be a 'collective' unity related by a common purpose rather than a 'collected' unity of agents related by common practices. Both *universitas* and *societas* are modes of manifesting the social, but social being is in both cases one of the engagements of reflective consciousness and not 'itself the "determinant of reflective consciousness"'.[41]

The nominalism inherent in this understanding of the constitution of both agents and the social leads to a thorough-going historicism in which all practices are historically contingent and determined only by the adjacency ('touching') of the historical practices and events antecedent to them.[42] Practices are thus only in appearance 'stable compositions of easily recognized characteristics'; they merely 'hold together' rather than 'belong together'.[43] In reality, they are 'footprints left behind by agents responding to their emergent situations ... [They are] compositions of beliefs and sentiments which ... are themselves historic occurrences whose intelligibility is contextual'.[44] Like all occurrences, practices are the outcomes of chains of (other) occurrences (including, but not only, human conduct), 'understood in terms of the meanings they acquire from their evidential contingent relationships'.[45] To try to turn this into a story

[40] Oakeshott, *On Human Conduct*, 87. [41] Ibid., 96–7.

[42] Oakeshott, *On History*, 64, 94: '[An historical event] ... is a by-product of a past composed of antecedent events which have no exclusive characters, no predetermined outcomes and no inherent potentialities to issue in this rather than that ... This antecedent past is not an "incubator" in which subsequent historical events are "hatched" ... It is itself composed of nothing but events, the circumstantial outcomes of conjunctions of events discerned in the same sort of enquiries.'

'Historical events are not themselves contingent, they are related to one another contingently. This kind of relationship is first, one of proximity and of "touch"; an immediate relationship.'

[43] Oakeshott, *On Human Conduct*, 100, 104. [44] Ibid., 100. [45] Ibid., 105.

which shows some exogenous necessity or teaches us a lesson about how to obtain some future state of the world or identifies some essence of social and political being is not to tell a story 'but to construct a myth'.[46]

The state of Oakeshott's civil condition consists of *personae* associated (and recognizing themselves as such) with one another in terms of a practice, a practice composed entirely of rules imposing adverbial obligations (*lex*)[47] and of rules for adjudicating the meaning of these rules, the extent of their jurisdiction, and for making and changing them.[48] These rules are by definition authoritative and derive their authoritativeness not from their reasonableness, efficacy for a purpose or moral rightness, but from the authoritativeness of something else – of the *respublica* and its offices of rulership and adjudication. The civil condition postulates an apparatus of rule and a relationship of ruler and subject[49] – in other words, it postulates an organization of supremacy and subordination, a relationship of *Herrschaft* as the condition *sine qua non* for the maintenance of the association in terms of rules that characterizes the relationship between *cives*. The *activity* of ruling in this kind of association is not unconditional – its authority derives from *lex*, but the authority of *lex* does not derive from itself or from some higher norm of *lex*, as Oakeshott makes clear. No *norm* or *rule* can be the unconditional basis upon which all others derive their authority;[50] the condition of the authority of the items of the *respublica* is 'the authority of the *respublica* itself'.[51] But in what does the authority of the *respublica* consist? Oakeshott is clear about what it does not consist in: not in its ability to provide certain substantive goods, nor in its reasonableness, nor in its identification with a general will, nor in some 'higher law' unless this law 'itself be shown to have *authority*: mere rationality or wisdom will not do'.[52] The authority of the *respublica* is in this sense unconditional – it consists in the social-historical reality of *cives* continuously (habitually and mostly unreflectively) acknowledging that the *respublica* has authority *because it is authoritative*.[53] Authority is the attribute of a concrete social reality

[46] Ibid., 105. [47] Ibid., 128. [48] Ibid., 141. [49] Ibid., 143–4. [50] Ibid., 151.
[51] Ibid. [52] Ibid., 152–3.
[53] Ibid., 154. 'This authority cannot be acquired in a once-and-for-all endowment but only in the continuous acknowledgement of *cives* who [can distinguish between recognizing a rule, its utility and subscribing to its conditions] . . . And should it be asked how a manifold of rules . . . [can be authoritative despite not being capable of obtaining uniform approval and never being more than a very imperfect reflection of prevailing ideas of justice] . . . [T]he answer is *that authority is the only conceivable attribute it could be indisputably acknowledged to have*.'

(as Oakeshott's rather quaint analogy of the Marylebone Cricket Club suggests) and is at once a sociological and normative datum of the kind referred to by Lindahl in this volume. The existence or non-existence of this unconditional authority is the product of a certain kind of social-political unity, not (or not always) a total unity of action and purpose but a 'collected' unity of a concrete order.

Oakeshott describes the civil condition as a 'formal, not a substantive' relationship[54] in which *cives* are related 'solely in terms of their common recognition of the rules which constitute a practice of civility'.[55] But the relationship is formal only in the sense that it is distinguished from a relationship entered into in order to attain a particular satisfaction or common good (the enterprise association). It is my contention that the relationship has (considerable) substance in the same sense that all practices have substance, emerging as they do from particular ways of life, traditions, vernaculars of social and political being and a ceaseless flow of antecedent historical events. The common recognition of the rules is also at the same time a common and unconditional acknowledgement of the authority of the *respublica* and the obligations it imposes and can enforce.[56] This unity-in-authority is a precarious achievement, which Oakeshott explores in greater depth in his essay on the character of modern European state. But the point for present purposes is that the well-ordered civil condition which Oakeshott describes in ideal-typical form rests upon the achievement of this unity as a condition of possibility for the non-substantive relationship that he ascribes to the *civitas*. He makes this clearer in his introduction to *Leviathan*, when he notes that in the Hobbesian system there is no *jus* of *lex* by which the authority of the ruler can be judged and rejected by citizens: 'In civil association the validity of a law lies neither in the wisdom of the conditions it imposes upon conduct, nor even in its propensity to promote peace, but in its being the command and . . . in its being effectively enforced . . . [No] valid law can, strictly speaking, be "unjust"'.[57] In his later essay on the Rule of Law, 'freedom and peace' are described as *characteristics* of this mode of association, but 'not its consequences'.[58] That is, a pacified social order is the antecedent, contingent historical reality upon which the *civitas* rests, and this order – the ethical-practical substance of a

[54] Ibid., 121. [55] Ibid., 128. [56] Ibid., 149; Oakeshott, 'The Rule of Law', 130.
[57] Michael Oakeshott, 'Introduction to the *Leviathan*' in Oakeshott, *Hobbes on Civil Association* (Oxford, UK: Basil Blackwell, 1975), 42–3.
[58] Oakeshott, 'The Rule of Law', 161.

community of *cives* – is the basis for the authority of the *respublica*. The authority of the state of the *civitas* rests on an inner substance in one other sense: its durability requires a particular kind of personality, human beings actually possessed of the dispositions which characterize agents capable of the kinds of performances demanded of *cives* in the civil condition.[59] Described by Müller as an embrace of the aristocratic morality favoured also by Hobbes,[60] these individuals are the historical products of a panoply of European inheritances *and their transformation* under the dynamics of modern state formation. The modern European state as *societas* required the modern European individual, a character 'brought together or held together in a modern European state': 'a substantive personality, the outcome of an education, whose resources are collected in a self-understanding; and conduct is recognized as the adventure in which this cultivated self deploys its resources and enacts itself in response to contingent situations, and both acquires and confirms its autonomy'.[61]

The modern state is an order of domination with absolute authority, but this domination was not antithetical to freedom, provided that it had the characteristics of the right kind of authority – that of the civil condition, in which the absolute authority of the state was expressed in a law that in its formalism preserved 'in every act of obedience an area of unassailable liberty'.[62] This is the liberty of mental activity, as the command must be understood (and interpreted), and the liberty of initiative in order to translate the general command into a particular course of conduct or act.[63] Absolute authority of this kind could be acknowledged 'precisely because it allowed one to belong to oneself – that is, if one as a proper individual, was capable of such a thing'.[64] Here, it seems to me, we have a combination of Hegel and Hobbes in which the possibility of freedom lies in the co-determination of the state as the ground or

59 Oakeshott, *On Human Conduct*, 242.

60 Jan-Werner Müller, 'Re-imagining *Leviathan*: Schmitt and Oakeshott on Hobbes and the Problem of Political Order', *Critical Review of International Social and Political Philosophy*, 13 (2010), 317, 326.

61 Oakeshott, *On Human Conduct*, 236, 237.

62 Michael Oakeshott, 'Introduction' in Thomas Hobbes, *Leviathan* (London: Basil Blackwell, 1946), ed. Michael Oakeshott, 44.

63 Paul Franco, *The Political Philosophy of Michael Oakeshott* (New Haven, CT: Yale University Press, 1990), 90; Oakeshott, *On Human Conduct*, 124–7; Oakeshott, 'The Rule of Law', 129.

64 Müller, 'Re-imagining *Leviathan*: Schmitt and Oakeshott on Hobbes and the Problem of Political Order', 330.

condition of the totality of meanings and values and of individuals whose *Bildung* furnishes them with the arts and practices of agency necessary exercise to concrete freedom within the state.[65] The authority of the state is the ground for the possibility of politics, and in political contention there can be no dissent from the acknowledgement of this authority. The system of rules cannot be put into question nor the worth of the association itself, as this amounts to a notice to terminate the civil association and commence civil war.[66] The authority of the state is not a choice, nor a subjective feeling, but an attribute of its order or perhaps an ethos. This ethos is an expression of the contingent and shifting set of practices that animate it. The practices have the solidity of a 'drywall', held together by a balance of internal and external forces which render the assemblage more or less prone to desuetude, decline or reconfiguration. The whole sum of practices that makes possible the ethos of belief cannot be grasped reflexively, nor can they be cognitively theorized and renovated in some instrumental way. The authority is in a fundamental way arbitrary, neither a product of rational will nor individual reasoning.[67] Unsurprisingly, this renders deeply puzzling (if not insoluble) how one generates this kind of authority in the first place. But before we move to this dimension of Oakeshott's theory, we consider Schmitt's state concept and its parallels.

Schmitt's state: modernity's perpetual crisis of authority

In his essay entitled, 'Ethic of State and the Pluralistic State',[68] Schmitt's understanding of the state as a concrete *Herrschaftlich* order that is the condition of possibility for the content of norms, values and judgements is evident. A state is a 'concrete reality' which is also a unity and puts in place 'the external conditions for ethical life'[69] by creating a normal situation. Only in a normal situation are 'ethical relationships like fidelity and loyalty' possible. The unity that characterizes a real state need not be a homogeneity of its people (although that is one basis); it can also be a

[65] Noel Malcolm, 'Oakeshott and Hobbes' in Paul Franco and Leslie Marsh (eds.), *A Companion to Michael Oakeshott* (University Park, PA: Pennsylvania State University Press, 2012), 217.

[66] Oakeshott, *On Human Conduct*, 164. [67] Malcolm, 'Oakeshott and Hobbes', 226–7.

[68] Carl Schmitt, 'Ethic of State and the Pluralistic State' in Chantal Mouffe (ed.), *The Challenge of Carl Schmitt* (London: Verso, 1999), trans. David Dyzenhaus, 195.

[69] Schmitt, 'Ethic of State', 198–9 (citations omitted in original).

social multiplicity and, in different times and places, internally pluralist 'in a special sense'.[70] Unity in either case may be the product of a power-generating consensus of value (which Schmitt, perhaps with Weber's concept of *Wertrationalität* in mind, calls irrational and ethically repugnant) brought about by various demiurgic techniques, or it could be generated by 'command and power'.[71] With the demise of medieval theological unity, universalist abstractions such as God, world and humanity are incapable of engendering concrete unity, except to the extent that they enter into the 'scuffles of political life' and are too easily transformed into 'an awful instrument of human domination' – one that recognizes none of the limitations inherent in concrete communities.[72] 'Actual order' is a 'human work and task', the product of 'concrete people and social groups', which becomes effective and prescriptive. As such, 'it is rational and sensible to *permit to remain valid* the succession and proximity of peoples and states which have been *put into place by human history*.'[73] This would include states where the ethical content of the concrete order is found in 'the commonly recognized constitutional foundation or of the rules of the game'.[74] But this is an ethos generated by the underlying unity, not a product of reasonableness or justice of the rules themselves. If the normal situation 'falls away' – in cases of civil war or external attack – then the problem becomes one of re-generating the order upon which normality and ethical life depend.

The characterization of the modern state as the first and last ground of political and ethical value brings with it an understanding of the authority of the state as unconditional and as a final reservoir for the state's capacity to create and preserve legal and political order. The historical circumstances under which such a concrete order may in fact come into existence are, for Schmitt, uncertain – at least some such 'real' states come about through the 'succession and proximity' of peoples 'put in place by human history'. The allusion here seems to be towards a contingent succession of political-social forms and formations, starting from the theological unity of the medieval *respublica Christiana*, which is neutralized, secularized and territorially centralized through the (highly conflictual and bloody) emergence of absolutist states and ending in the liberal-democratic and technical-rational evisceration of the foundations of state authority and its presupposed unity. The problem in 1921, much

[70] Ibid., 201. [71] Ibid., 202. [72] Ibid., 204–5. [73] Ibid., 206 (emphasis added).
[74] Ibid., 207.

as in 1521, was that the authority of the state as a concrete political order was in need of fabrication.[75]

But what kind of authority is this? In *Roman Catholicism and Political Form* (1923), Schmitt praises the distinctive, and now forever lost, political form of the medieval Catholic Church. It was at once formal and substantive, concrete and abstract, personal and official.[76] It mediates between and unites a strict juridical formalism and an irrationalist charisma – in other words, it synthesizes *Zweck* – and *Wertrationlität*, the cleavage of which Schmitt accepts leaves us at a loss to choose between gods and demons as the source of authority. The rationalism of the church 'resides *in institutions* and is *essentially juridical*; its greatest achievement is having made priesthood into an office . . . [The] fact that the office is made independent of charisma signifies that the priest upholds a position that appears to be completely apart from his concrete personality . . . In contradistinction, his position is not impersonal, because his office is part of an unbroken chain linked with the personal mandate and concrete person of Christ. This is truly the most astounding *complexio oppositorum* . . . [Such distinctions] remain within and give direction to the human spirit, without exhibiting the dark irrationalism of the human soul'.[77] The kind of concrete order that is 'formed institutionally' in this way is not reducible to functions, norms or rules.[78] Rather, the latter are 'emanations of this substance, as something deriving only from its concrete particular, inner order . . . The cohabitation of spouses in a marriage, family members in a family, kin in a clan, peers in a *Stand*, officials in a state, clergy in a church, comrades in a work camp, and soldiers in an army can be reduced neither to the functionalism of predetermined laws nor to contractual regulations.'[79] The authority of the state as a concrete order, to be 'real,' must be rooted in/derived from a substance proximate to that which anchors and regulates institutions of

[75] Carl Schmitt, *Dictatorship: From the Origin of the Modern Concept of Sovereignty to the Proletarian Class Struggle* (Cambridge, UK: Polity, 2013), trans. Michael Hoelzl and Graham Ward: 'It is rather as L. Waldecker realized in his treatise . . . that the authority of the state was over (at least in 1916)' (p. xlv). Or later, at p. 10: 'By the end of the fifteenth century . . . the power of theology was exhausted and the patriarchal understanding of the origin of kingship no longer satisfied people's appetite for science.'

[76] Carl Schmitt, *Roman Catholicism and Political Form* (Westport, CT: Greenwood Press, 1996), trans. G. L. Ulmen, 14.

[77] Schmitt, *Roman Catholicism and Political Form*, 14 (emphasis added).

[78] Carl Schmitt, *On the Three Types of Juristic Thought*, (Westport, CT: Praeger, 2004), trans. Joseph Bendersky, 54.

[79] Ibid.

the kind enumerated – kinship, a *ständisch* corporatism, a bureaucratic *esprit de corps*, a common God and religious belief and so forth. These are all, to a great extent, historically rooted *ethoi* of belief, and indeed in *Roman Catholicism* Schmitt insists that 'to the political belongs the idea, because there is no politics without authority and no authority without an ethos of belief'.[80] The 'idea' to which Schmitt alludes here is the idea of representation, a concept which for Schmitt is 'completely governed by conceptions of personal authority . . . To represent in an eminent sense can only be done by a person . . . an authoritative person or idea which, if represented, also becomes personified'.[81] Representation is the medium for the generation of authoritative political forms, and these forms generate rhetorics that engender 'the belief in the representation claimed by the orator'.[82] Language, symbols, political forms – together this trinity somewhat alchemically produces the ethos of belief in representative persons that is the essence of authority. The failure of economic and technical thinking – which dominates the modern age in Schmitt's diagnosis – is exactly that it can generate neither representation nor political and juridical forms of this character.[83] Once the state becomes an automaton or leviathan, 'it disappears from the world of representations.' The personalism inherent in the idea of representation is lost or denied, and as such, the fabrication of the authority of the political becomes the central problem.

The state, then, is a condition or status of political unity and order.[84] This status must at the same time take a political form and through these forms constantly renew and maintain itself as a unity.[85] *Sein* and *Sollen* are in this sense co-original constitutive parameters of a state order, dynamically co-producing each other. The political existence of a state is at once an historical product, a factual reality of effective power and a normative system. The agent of its production is the 'bearer' of the constitution-making power, which is the actor (individual or collective) that has the power or authority which renders it capable of producing political unity and generating political forms that represent and maintain

[80] Schmitt, *Roman Catholicism and Political Form*, 17. [81] Ibid., 21. [82] Ibid.

[83] By contrast, the historical greatness of the Catholic Church lay in its capacity to embody 'the aesthetic form of art; the juridical form of law; [and] . . . the glorious achievement of a world-historical form of power . . . [T]he ethos of its own power stands side by side with the ethos of justice': ibid., 21, 31

[84] Carl Schmitt, *Constitutional Theory* (Durham, NC: Duke University Press, 2008), ed. Jeffrey Seitzer, 59–60.

[85] Ibid., 61.

that unity. The production of political unity – and thus the state – presupposes effective power, an actor which engenders and exercises a political will that is 'an actually existing power as the origin of a command. The will is existentially present; its power or authority lies in its *being*.'[86] Beneath, alongside and at the heart of the state is political being, and every political being is 'a concrete and determined existence'[87] – but not every such being arrives at the form of its existence through conscious decision. That is to say, most European states emerged from the historical determinations effected by absolute monarchy, following different paths in different territories; their political unity did not become a matter of decisive choice until the authority of the absolutist state had reached its apogee and entered into an historical decline.

The unity of the state can be 'achieved and held' in two different ways – through an 'unmediated self-identity' of a people who are by virtue of their contingent history (such as natural boundaries) possessed of a 'strong and conscious similarity'. Under this principle of political form, the people are a real entity capable of acting directly and need not be represented. The other – and opposing – political principle under which unity is formed is that of representation, which 'proceeds from the idea that the political unity of the people as such can never be present in actual identity and, consequently, must always be represented by men personally'.[88] Thus, the democratic state as a pure type of status functions under the principle of identity,[89] requiring that unity have its source in the identity of the people: 'The nation *is* there.'[90] The monarchical state as a pure type of status 'rests on the idea that the political unity is first produced by representation through performance'.[91]

Any actually existing state must combine elements of both principles of identity and representation – the principles do not exclude one another but are 'two opposing orientation points for the concrete formation of the political unity'.[92] But in the balance of the *Constitutional Theory* it is apparent that representation plays the more significant role. Whereas representation can never be instituted without the people, it often appears in Schmitt's text that representation is the primary means through which a status of unity and order can be effected: 'In every state, there must be persons who can say, *L'Etat c'est nous* . . . One may even say that in its effect genuine representation is an essential factor of the process of integration [of a people into a unity]'.[93] Consistent with his

[86] Ibid., 64 (emphasis in original). [87] Ibid., 77. [88] Ibid., 239. [89] Ibid., 255.
[90] Ibid., 239. [91] Ibid. [92] Ibid., 240. [93] Ibid., 241.

account of representation in *Roman Catholicism and Political Form*, as intrinsically linked to the production of authority and an ethos of belief, Schmitt maintains in the *Constitutional Theory* that representation is a 'not a norm or procedure, but something *existential* ... Indeed, it presupposes a special type of being.'[94]

> Words like size, height, majesty, fame, dignity, and honor seek to express this peculiarity of enhanced being that is capable of representation ... The idea of representation rests on a people existing as a political unity, as having a type of being that is higher, further enhanced, and more intense in comparison to the natural existence of some human group living together ... That the government of an established community is something other than the power of a pirate cannot be understood from the perspective of the ideas of justice, social usefulness, and other normative elements, for all these normative concepts can apply even to thieves. The difference lies in the fact that every genuine government *represents* the political unity of a people, not the people in its natural presence.[95]

Representation at once presupposes and generates a certain kind of authority, an authority that is inextricably linked to the constitution and maintenance of political unity and thus of the state as a concrete order. In his long footnote to the chapter entitled, 'The Constitution-Making Power,' Schmitt makes it clear that 'both power and authority are, combined with one another, effective and vital in every state'.[96] Citing Victor Ehrenberg, Schmitt observes that authority 'denotes something "ethical-social"', a 'position oddly mixed together from political power and social prestige' that 'rests on and supplements social validity'.[97] Authority rests 'essentially on the element of *continuity* and refers to tradition and duration'.[98] But the *terminus ad quem* of the 'last centuries of European development'[99] is the crisis of this authority almost everywhere in Europe, a crisis in which 'the legitimating foreground [of the present] vanishes in a instant' when the decisive moment arrives. The present leaves no room for the gradual emergence of political unity over centuries unless such unity has not been recently disturbed (as in the case of Britain). What is left in Schmitt's theory, notoriously, is a decisionist production of concrete order through identification with a

[94] Ibid., 243 (emphasis in original). [95] Ibid., 243, 245. [96] Ibid., 458. [97] Ibid.
[98] Ibid., 458 (emphasis in original).
[99] Carl Schmitt, 'The Age of Neutralizations and Depoliticizations', trans. Matthias Konzett and John P. McCormick, in Schmitt, *The Concept of the Political*, 80–96.

powerful representative figure or movement in which political ethos and political form would coincide and replace the teetering political present.[100]

We may step back here for a moment and sharpen some of the parallels and divergences with Oakeshott's concept of the state. Both Schmitt and Oakeshott grasp the state as a unity which cannot rest on abstract principles of reasonableness or justice; it must be an order of domination, and its capacity for domination lies not only in effective power but also in its authority. But authority is not a procedural matter nor (singularly) a matter of normative rightness; it is an historically determined property of the order itself, generated contingently through historical events (Oakeshott) and tendencies (Schmitt). Authority is an ethos generated by real, concrete ways of life and social and political forms. The modern state's authority is (or must be) unconditional in the sense that the final source of the validity of laws and commands must be the state itself; the state is the ultimate arbiter of value and thus the condition for a socially and politically effective value-order; the consequence of conditional authority is a relativization of state authority that can lead only (in both their accounts) to civil war. Schmitt and Oakeshott are in this sense inheritors of an absolutist conception of the state and are concerned with how to grasp and maintain the presuppositions of such an order. But Oakeshott's ultimate preoccupation is less with threats to the maintenance of this order than with threats to the possibilities for civilized life that the order itself holds out – threats I will suggest later that come principally from the dynamics which he identifies as inherent in the creation of such an order. Schmitt's preoccupation is with the maintenance, and, if necessary, re-founding, of state authority, an intrinsically tragic (perhaps even unsolvable) problem under the conditions of modernity as he diagnoses them.

State formation and the sources of the fabrication of state authority: from artifice and will to myth and emergency

In his Introduction to Hobbes' *Leviathan*, Oakeshott explains (and embraces) Hobbes' 'nominalist and profoundly skeptical'[101] doctrine

[100] In *Dictatorship* (p. xlii), Schmitt rather sympathetically ventriloquizes the Leninists: 'Whoever is on the side of things to come is allowed to push against what is already collapsing.'

[101] Oakeshott, *Hobbes on Civil Association*, 23.

concerning both the nature of knowledge and the nature of authority. The former is conditional, yielding provisional and hypothetical propositions reached through reasoning that establishes not truths but working fictions through which to act in and on the world. These artefacts of reasoning are nonetheless powerful and indispensable, to the extent that they also become means of channelling and harnessing passions that propel men to act. The philosophy of civil authority is one such artefact. The civil condition is itself a product of artifice and will, a work of art generated by willing and reasoning.[102] The task of Hobbes in writing a civil philosophy is not only to venture claims about the true nature of the civil condition but also to help realize it by engendering certain kinds of beliefs about its causes, nature and consequences, beliefs which themselves can engender passions that bind humans to that authority.[103] For this reason, *Leviathan* is 'a myth' which attempts to call into being belief in the civil condition by giving us a 'fixed and simple centre' for our political imagination.[104] Like all myth, the purpose of *Leviathan* as civil philosophy is not to break our collective dream but to 'perpetually recall it, to recreate it in each generation, and even to make more articulate the dream-powers of a people'.[105] Reason does not lead to authority, nor does reasoning per se. Producing authority requires means of binding wills and passions, generating not a common will 'but a common object of will ... [Civil association's] unity lies solely in the singleness of the Representative, in the substitution of his one will for the many conflicting wills'.[106]

Man's natural solipsism, his wilfulness and passionate nature, make the generation of civil authority intrinsically difficult and highly unpredictable. Consistent with this Hobbesian scepticism, Oakeshott observes rather casually that most states' attempts to generate civil associations have been unsuccessful, testament to the 'flimsy' foundations of their claims to authority.[107] And claims to political authority advanced in the history of the making of most European states rest on 'implausible and gimcrack beliefs that few can find convincing for more than five minutes together'.[108] So how then can we understand the emergence of civil

[102] Ibid., 27.
[103] See Noel Malcolm, 'The Title Page of *Leviathan* Seen in a Curious Perspective' in *Aspects of Hobbes* (Oxford University Press, 2002), 228–9.
[104] Oakeshott, *Hobbes on Civil Association*, 14.
[105] '*Leviathan*: A Myth' in Oakeshott, *Hobbes on Civil Association*, 150.
[106] Ibid., 61.
[107] Oakeshott, *On Human Conduct*, 190–1.
[108] Ibid., 191.

authority, particularly authority of the very demanding kind required by states which have the character of a *societas*?

Oakeshott's answer is given obliquely in his essay entitled, 'Character of the Modern European State'. The principal concern of the essay is not to identify the historical conditions of possibility for the emergence of the state (although he tells us much about this) but rather to elucidate its two persistent modes of association as ideal types (*societas*/civil, *universitas*/enterprise) and to try to illuminate the determining impact of these dispositions on both the character of political thought about the state and the kinds of conduct that the state is properly capable of undertaking. Nonetheless, Oakeshott's essay does sketch an indirect answer to the question of the historical origins of the civil authority of the modern state, and I suggest that this answer shares certain key insights with Schmitt's diagnosis of the role of emergency and representation in the formation of political order.

Malcolm observes that Oakeshott's principal preoccupation was to 'understand political life as it is lived in a functioning civilized state, where rules are followed and traditions of behaviour are understood'.[109] As we have seen, the foundations for such moral practices – and at bottom, the authority of the civil condition rests only on practices – are a system of behaviour, dispositions and beliefs that develops over time. Where Schmitt's state authority may be a product either of history *or* of decision (states that benefit from relatively unbroken lineages of authority may never have to confront decisionist moments at all), in Oakeshott, there would appear to be only the flow of historical forms and events, which may or may not generate the distinctive authority of the civil condition. But within Oakeshott's historical narrative and despite his disavowal of attempts to recount any social and political essences in history, a structural-conceptual logic of state formation does emerge in which the successful fabrication of the kind of state authority presupposed by the *societas* rests on a material and legal legacy endowed by the *universitas* – a legacy formed through emergency and exception, which constitutes the core of the creation of sovereign power over time and reinforces it through periodic crises of external or internal origin.

The three pillars of the civil condition – authority, obligation and the *cives* capable of the performances required to maintain an association united through *lex* – rest upon the successful creation of effective

[109] Malcolm, 'Oakeshott and Hobbes', 226–7.

sovereign rulership and of the *personae* bearing the necessary dispositions and disciplined imagination demanded by *societas* as a mode of association. But European societies and territories of the Middle Ages hardly seemed promising candidates for the emergence of either of these characteristics. The territories on which states would emerged were composed of

> a variety of ancient communities with undying memories of other allegiances, of independence or of mutual hostility . . . [There were] a mosaic of laws, jurisdictions, and judicial procedures for the settlement of disputes about property and everyday living . . . All European states began as mixed and miscellaneous collections of human beings precariously held together, disturbed by what they had swallowed and were unable to digest . . . And no European state has ever come within measurable distance of being a 'nation state.'[110]

Neither centralized, unconditional authority nor a common *habitus* is possible under such circumstances. To bring them about, several historical changes must transpire: the destruction of intermediate and universal legal orders and parallel claims on fidelity (whether feudal, imperial, *ständisch* or religious), the accumulation and intensification of an apparatus of rule ('the ability to control men and things') and the liberation of persons from the social structures of tradition and religion through the dissolution of the 'self-contained seigneurial estate' and in its place the making of a new *habitus* of individuality. This is essentially the story told by the German historical sociologists of the first half of the twentieth century[111] and a literature with which we have some reason to believe Oakeshott was very familiar.[112] Each of these historical processes is the product of deep and violent conflict[113] or of the victory of one social and political form at the expense or the desuetude of another.[114]

110 Oakeshott, *On Human Conduct*, 187–8.

111 Otto Hintze, *The Historical Essays of Otto Hintze* (Oxford University Press, 1975) Felix Gilbert, ed.; Norbert Elias, *The Civilizing Process [1939]* (Oxford, UK: Blackwell, 1994), Eric Dunning, Johan Goudsblom and Stephen Mennell, eds., trans. Edmund Jephcott; Friedrich Meinecke, *Machiavellism: The Doctrine of Raison d'Etat and Its Place in Modern History* (New Brunswick, NJ: Transaction Publishers, 1998), trans. Douglas Scott.

112 See Kelly's chapter in this volume (Chapter 8). Of course, it was also a literature which was profoundly influential in Schmitt's milieu.

113 Charles Tilly (ed.), *The Formation of National States in Western Europe* (Princeton University Press, 1975).

114 Thomas Ertman, *The Birth of the Leviathan: Building States and Regimes in Medieval and Early Modern Europe* (Cambridge University Press, 1997); Hendrik Spruyt, *The Sovereign State and its Competitors* (Princeton University Press, 1994).

What is interesting for our purposes is that in Oakeshott's narrative these processes are closely connected with moments in which the *universitas* character of a political organization is ascendant or dominant. Thus, a political organization at war has the characteristics of a *universitas* or of teleocratic rule because it must subordinate the actions and transactions of subjects to the substantive purpose of victory against internal or external enemies.[115] This includes measures to intensify the apparatus of rule in order to mobilize resources (human and material) needed for victory, as well as measures to intensify the loyalty of subjects to the political organization. War provokes and deepens the overcoming of competing legal orders, identities and forms of association by providing an existential purpose to which all other competing purposes are subordinated – and in so doing, it structures both state and subject. As Malcolm puts it, a teleological state embodies a higher purpose, and individuals enhance their own value as they align themselves more fully with it. The 'we acting together' and the 'we each'[116] of a concrete community become closely aligned, if not indistinguishable, during such emergencies, and the aftermath leaves both aspects altered.

Another important moment in the forging of stable and absolute sovereign authority also derives from a teleocratic mode of association: the fragmentary and weak authority of medieval kingship – dependent on feudal contract and *ständisch* consensualism – was ultimately conjoined with the spiritual authority of the first great *universitas*, the Roman Catholic Church and its claim to *plenitudo potestatis*.[117] This 'acquisition' established royal authority 'more firmly' and also transformed rulership to include the custody of 'the material, moral and spiritual welfare of a community with a teleology of its own into which that of the individual soul had been assimilated'.[118] The prince's pastoral power authorized deeper administration of social life by sovereign power[119] and paved the way for the insinuation of sovereign authority into all aspects of the *Bildung* of a population. The result was the possibility of generating a 'sentiment of solidarity' and the endowment of 'some semblance of substantive unity' among a territorial people

115 Oakeshott, *On Human Conduct*, 273, 286.
116 Lindahl, this volume.
117 As Schmitt also points out in *Dictatorship* (pp. 34–5), *plenitudo potestatis* was both the conceptual font for modern theories of sovereignty and simultaneously a claim of authority to decide the exception. See also Joseph Canning, *Ideas of Power in the Late Middle Ages* (Cambridge University Press, 2011), Chapter 1.
118 Oakeshott, *On Human Conduct*, 223.
119 Ibid., 222, 279–83.

through the promotion of linguistic, cultural or religious homogeneity 'or, in the parlance of later times, to make them a "nation"'.[120] In this transfiguration of sacred authority into secular authority, Oakeshott sees a strong intimation of developments that ultimately jeopardize civil association, such as Calvinist domination of private life or even National Socialist Germany; he also associates the prince's *auctoritas docendi* with the pernicious tendency of Cameralism and enlightened absolutism to see the state solely as a managerial enterprise. But he cannot entirely avoid the extent to which his idealized individualist subject, bearer of *der Wille* and reflective engagement, is also a product of the secularization of the *potestas docendi*. The 'well-ordered police states'[121] he associates with managerial rule were intensely concerned with producing individuals capable of 'self-conducting' and self-management[122] in part by inculcating (in some places) neo-stoic ethics of self-examination and self-discipline.[123] The 'right to educate' assumed by absolutist states in the seventeenth century was thus an important propaedeutic in many European states for the formation of the autonomous individual that Oakeshott takes as indispensable for the *civitas*. And his arguments place its origins squarely within the legacy of the *universitas* mode of association and its ascendant moments in the history of state formation.

In answer to the puzzle of how the authority necessary for the special kind of freedom characteristic of the civil condition is generated, Oakeshott's narrative of state formation gives us a muted and reluctant dialectic: our wills and passions are forged in relations of domination, intensified through wars and various exercises in subjection, all of which are undertaken by the state as a *universitas*. But in the process, and through the very important residual medium of the language of law, the indispensable conditions of civil peace and unconditional civil

[120] Ibid., 279.

[121] Marc Raeff, *The Well-Ordered Police State: Social and Institutional Change Through Law in the Germanies and Russia, 1600–1800* (New Haven, CT: Yale University Press, 1979).

[122] 'The pastorate had individualizing effects; it promised the salvation of each and in an individual form; it entailed obedience, but as an individual to individual relationship an it guaranteed individuality by obedience itself . . . Western man is individualized through the pastorate . . . Identity, subjection, interiority: the individualization of Western man throughout the long millennium of the Christian pastorate was carried out . . . by subjectivation. To become individual one must become subject.' Michel Foucault, *Security, Territory, Population: Lectures at the College de France 1977–1978* (London: Picador, 2009), 231, note +.

[123] Gerhard Oestreich, *Neostoicism and the Early Modern State* (Cambridge University Press, 1982).

authority are realized, and the teleological orientation of the political association may recede into the background – leaving nonetheless a crucial residuum of substance in the form of common language, some measure of common *Bildung*, common political vocabularies and practices and so forth. The shared ethical-political habitus, the ethical-practical foundations of the state *qua* concrete order, are generated in and through the exception and make possible the *civitas*. But the ethical-political identity remains latent until there arises the risk of war or civil war. At that moment, peace and security *become substantive goods*, and the teleocratic re-emerges and threatens to submerge (and potentially, permanently transform) the nomocratic. This reading seems consistent with Oakeshott's pessimistic observation in his essay on the rule of law that there is 'one unavoidable contingent circumstance of modern Europe for which the rule of law cannot itself provide, namely, the care for the interests of the state in relation to other states, the protection of those interests in defensive war or in attempts to recover notional irredenta'.[124]

The creation and stabilization of new political orders is at the heart of Schmitt's esoterically drawn problematic.[125] How can a new political order be forged and maintained in the aftermath of national defeat and 'under the eyes'[126] of a political force – Bolshevism – which fully understood the constitutive power of political myth against an enfeebled liberal-democratic form? In Schmitt, the dialectic between exception and the realization of normality in a concrete order is also a characteristic of the emergence of modern state authority, an argument perhaps best exemplified by his extended treatment of the state of exception on *Dictatorship*. At the origins of the modern state is a certain kind of orientation towards dictatorship, 'an orientation consisting of the three elements of rationalism, technicality and the executive . . . Historically, the modern state emerged from some kind of political technology or expertise.'[127] The institution of the royal commissar was indispensable to the breaking of indirect and intermediate powers, emanations of the lawful state of the estates.[128] In this very concrete sense, the legal and territorial unification of the state was achieved through the invocation of *plenitudo potestatis*, the originary power of exception and conceptual source of modern sovereign power. The unity of the nation was the work

[124] Oakeshott, 'The Rule of Law', 163.
[125] Most persuasively and carefully argued by Kelly, *The State of the Political*, 165–75.
[126] Schmitt, 'The Age of Neutralizations and Depoliticizations', 80.
[127] Schmitt, *Dictatorship*, 9. [128] Ibid., Chapters 2 and 3.

of absolutism,[129] and absolutism was effected through the authority invoked to respond to the 'concrete situation' – the *telos* of a specific goal or result, such as 'the idea of a concrete enemy whose elimination must be the first circumscribed goal of action'. War makes exception, which makes states. Like Oakeshott,[130] Schmitt also understands the *Polizeistaat* as a mode of teleocratic action that engendered modern sovereign rulership, not technically dictatorship but serving similar functions: 'the police state, through its principle of organization, which is the general task of administration, possesses in principle an element of commissarial character and, as such, is related to dictatorship.'[131]

The specific polemicism of Schmitt's own thinking leads him to emphatically foreground one pole of the dialectic of exception and normality – that which corresponded to his diagnosis of the radical crisis of state authority and the perceived urgency of identifying a contemporary source for its re-fabrication. It should be clear from the discussion in Part II of *Legality and Legitimacy* that Schmitt prioritized the pole of exception, one which in turn finds its concrete contemporary historical form in the *pouvoir constituant*, through a people united in their substantive political decision or in their actual homogeneity, or perhaps through their collective identification with the personalistic authority of a representative person or idea. The re-constitution of a concrete order required a concrete *telos*, which could be a real homogeneity, a representative person or even conceivably a mythicized political idea (for which Schmitt greatly admired the Leninists). Subjects must perforce orient themselves towards this *telos* and forge their ethos accordingly.

> Then the concept of ethic of state acquires a new content, and a new task arises. It is the work of consciously bringing about that unity, the duty to participate to create a bit of concrete and actual order and to make the situation normal once again. Then there comes into being, alongside the duty which resides in its subjection to ethical norms, and alongside the duties against the state, a duty of ethic of state of a completely different kind – the duty towards the state.[132]

Notably, state making and state authority require the making of a *Sittlichkeit*, an 'inner *Gleichschaltung* of beliefs . . . [without which] there could not be any certainty about the association's long-term survival'.[133]

129 Schmitt, *Constitutional Theory*, 99, 101. 130 Oakeshott, 'The Rule of Law', 153.
131 Schmitt, *Dictatorship*, 119. 132 Schmitt, 'Ethic of State', 208.
133 Müller, 'Re-imagining *Leviathan*: Schmitt and Oakeshott on Hobbes and the Problem of Political Order', 322.

States must make subjects – what Foucault would neologize as 'subjectivation' or we might even less elegantly call 'subjectification'.[134] Subjectification, the shaping of inner worlds, may take place gradually or intensively. The exception, the *universitas*, the dictatorship, represent a claim to a higher value (peace, order, the good, the constitution, etc.), a *jus* of *lex*, to which individuals must align themselves (their 'duty towards the state') if a concrete order is to be maintained or created. Without doubt, such a situation places a *societas*/civil condition in deep danger, and it may not survive, as Oakeshott recognized. Whereas some may argue that Schmitt greeted this endangerment with glee,[135] a thoroughly liberal Schmittian such as Böckenförde grasps it as a tragic situation in terms very close to Oakeshott. In a situation where 'everything is "up for grabs" and nothing can any longer be taken for granted' (such as incipient civil war or revolution), a legal state may seek to buttress and defend its authority by claiming to materialize in law a 'higher, material, pre-positive law'.[136] Where there is an attempt to guarantee directly an ethical-practical substance of the individual and the homogeneity of society through the force of law, 'then the liberty of the kind embodied in the *Rechtsstaat* is at an end'.[137] But '*such a defence of this kind might be inevitable to enable a body politic to survive*'.[138]

Conclusion

For both Schmitt and Oakeshott, the state is a product of 'the cunning of unreason',[139] shaped by historical contingencies and unpredictable arbitrary wills formed through intensive processes of domination. Political order of the statist kind is at once highly precarious and ineluctably needed, a form of redemption from an even worse fate – the predicament of being merely natural humans.[140] The generation of the power and authority required to underpin and maintain a state order is best effected

[134] Judith Butler, *The Psychic Life of Power – Theories of Subjection* (Redwood City, CA: Stanford University Press, 1997).

[135] David Dyzenhaus, 'The Concept of the Rule-of-Law State in Schmitt's *Verfassungslehre*' in Jens Meierhenrich and Oliver Simons (eds.), *The Oxford Handbook of Carl Schmitt* (Oxford University Press, 2014).

[136] Böckenförde, *State, Society and Liberty*, 68–9.

[137] Ibid., 69.

[138] Ibid (emphasis added).

[139] To borrow John Dunn's title: John Dunn, *The Cunning of Unreason: Making Sense of Politics* (New York: Basic Books, 2008).

[140] Oakeshott, *Hobbes on Civil Association*, 60.

through path-dependent historical trajectories; Oakeshott simply shrugs his shoulders at the possibility of generating such orders *ex nihilo* as 'absurd'.[141] For Schmitt, the challenge of creating new orders *de novo* cannot be avoided, and the result is an authoritarian decisionism of very dubious plausibility. But both agree that the nomocratic order is a fragile achievement, one whose resilience rests on an underlying social-ethical unity of habitus whether understood as *personae* or ethos of belief. And for each of them, the 'teleocratic' face of the state never disappears but at most lies dormant, emerging as the means of combating existential threats to the political order and, crucially, as the most important means by which the historical substance of the order and its subjects is formed over time.

The implications for our contemporary state-building enterprises are clear: the re-generation or re-creation of state authority is perhaps the most demanding object to which human will and consciousness could ever be directed; by its nature, it almost defies rationalization and requires in equal measures both intensive domination and the fabrication of myths, images and ideals that become the *teloi* for political action and consciousness. It is a profoundly a-legal and a-rational undertaking, although both law and reasoning might well form important propaedeutics in the art of order creation. Yet the understanding of state making as a matter of Will and Artifice, rather than a product of Rational Will, still may help restrain some of the worst errors and pathologies associated with the coercion that is necessary for the creation of new political orders. Both Oakeshott and Schmitt would likely agree that Reason rather than Authority is more destructive of freedom under such circumstances. It also redirects us firmly away from the understanding of state building either as an applied technical knowledge or a matter of right reasoning and normativism. It concentrates our attention on the impossibility of separating the dynamics of order creation from contingent historical determinations and uncontrollable exogenous and endogenous forces; it reminds us that those who wish to create new political orders can neither be wholly inside or outside such forces but are invariably enmeshed within them and thus must interpret and (imperfectly) understand them in order to try to shape what can be shaped and restrain what cannot. The would-be state maker must stand on the shifting sands afforded by *Fortuna* and has only her or his *virtú* as a means.

141 Oakeshott, 'The Rule of Law', 150.

3

Law as concrete order

Schmitt and the problem of collective freedom

HANS LINDAHL

In an important passage of the *Verfassungslehre*, Carl Schmitt argues that '[s]elf-determination inheres in political existence. The constitution in the positive sense is an expression of this possibility of choosing, by virtue of ... [our] own decision, the kind and form of ... [our] *own* existence.'[1] On one level, this passage follows the time-worn interpretation of freedom as collective self-rule. On another level, the passage also highlights the polemical nature of Schmitt's re-appropriation of this concept, a re-appropriation which censures what he calls 'normativism'. He effectively argues that the theory of the relation between state and law espoused by normativism, in particular, the positivist interpretation thereof defended by Hans Kelsen, is incapable of conceptualizing or justifying freedom as collective self-rule. Recovering freedom as a central category for politics and law requires, or so Schmitt argues, thematizing the relation between law and state in terms of what he calls 'concrete order'. I agree. But what renders concrete order an *order*? And what renders concrete order *concrete*? These are questions that Schmitt nowhere directly poses or addresses. My aim in this chapter is to outline a concept of concrete order which brings out into the open the complex relation between the own and the alien at work in collective freedom. My claim is twofold. On the one hand, the orderliness and concreteness of concrete order turn on making sense of legal order and ordering as a specific form of group or collective action. On the other hand, the structure and genesis of group action reveal the complex relation between the own and the alien at the heart of collective freedom. As will become apparent, making sense of law and state in terms of concrete order leads to a very different interpretation of the concept of collective freedom than that envisaged by Schmitt.

[1] Carl Schmitt, *Constitutional Theory* (Durham, NC: Duke University Press, 2008), trans. Jeffrey Seitzer, 120–121 (translation altered).

Three caveats need to be lodged straightaway, before setting out. The first is that this enquiry does not envisage a comprehensive account and assessment of how Schmitt views the relation between state, freedom and law. I am happy to trade in such a study for a quite narrow approach which takes us directly to the fundamentals of Schmitt's thinking about that relation. This entails, amongst other things, that I will eschew an approach that takes its cue from the canonical definition of the state as a political organization in which a monopoly of power is exercised over a population within a given territory. Instead, I am interested in understanding and critically examining what, according to Schmitt, are the fundamental categories that are presupposed, but remain unclarified, in this canonical definition of the state. Secondly, mine is not a primarily exegetical study of key Schmittian texts. While this chapter will scrutinize and engage Schmitt's considerations on concrete order, in particular, his appeal to institutionalism, it does so by putting into place a conceptual framework which draws on two strands of philosophical thinking which have developed independently of Schmitt's thinking: theories of collective action of analytical provenance and a phenomenology of the alien or strange. Finally, I will bracket Schmitt's engagement with National Socialism in his writings about concrete order. My aim is to clarify the concept of concrete order, in a critical discussion with Schmitt, regardless of how he might have pressed it into the service of Nazi politics. Although this point would require development in a separate paper, an adequate conceptualization of concrete order leads to an interpretation of the relation between state, freedom and law that strongly *resists* Nazism.

The critique of normativism

The critical thrust of Schmitt's writings on state and law is oriented to rescuing the priority of the former over the latter, thereby reversing the normativist strategy of subordinating the state to law. This reversal is also key, in his view, to recovering collective freedom as a primordially political category. Kelsen's legal theory represents, in Schmitt's view, the most radical attempt to empty the concepts of state and freedom of their properly political content, to the extent that Kelsen identifies law and state. I will be content to offer a nutshell account of Kelsen's monism and of its implication for the concept of collective freedom before turning to Schmitt's critique thereof.

According to Kelsen, 'the theory of public law assumes that the state, as a collective unity that is originally the subject of will and of action, exists independently of, and even prior to, the law.'[2] This dualistic view of state and law reifies the state by making of it a 'macro-anthropos' which would be anterior to the legal order that it allegedly creates. Yet, notes Kelsen, there is no such collective subject: all state acts are nothing other than acts by individual human beings which are or can be imputed to the state as its acts. To impute an act to the state, to view it as 'its' act, is simply to assert that an act is authorized by a norm. Accordingly, there is no subject 'behind' a legal order, no collective ownership of legal acts: '[t]he state . . . *is* a legal order.'[3] The state is simply the personification of a certain kind of legal order, one which enjoys a certain measure of centralization with respect to the creation and application of legal norms. Conversely, only those acts which are legal acts, that is, which are authorized by a legal order, can be viewed as state acts. In this sense, every state is a *Rechtsstaat*, since '[t]here can be no state that does not have or does not yet have, a legal order, since every state is only a legal order'.[4]

What, then, is a legal order? The unity of a plurality of legal norms, answers Kelsen. Indeed, a manifold of legal norms form a unity 'if the validity of the norms can be traced back to a single norm as the ultimate basis of validity. This basic norm *qua* common source constitutes the unity of the plurality of all norms forming an order.'[5] This account of a legal order implies a regressive strategy which leads from the act of creating a norm to the applied norm and thereon back to the basic norm, which must be presupposed, rather than posited, to make sense of the first constitution as a constitution and of certain social orders as states.

A progressive approach is also possible, which reveals a legal order as an ordering – a dynamic – process whereby a higher-level norm is applied in the act of creating or positing a lower-level norm. This progressive approach to law and state yields the key to the notion of collective freedom available to normativism in its Kelsenian version. Strictly speaking, Kelsen does not outline a theory of *collective* freedom because he explicitly rejects the notion of political unity as flying in the face of the 'national, religious and economic' heterogeneity which

[2] Hans Kelsen, *Introduction to the Problems of Legal Theory* (Oxford University Press, 1992), trans. B. L. Paulson and S. L. Paulson, 97.

[3] Ibid., 99 (translation altered: I render *Rechtsordnung* throughout as 'legal order' instead of as 'legal system'; emphasis added).

[4] Ibid., 105. [5] Ibid., 55.

characterizes society.[6] Self-rule, as the core of the concept of freedom, is *individual* freedom, an aspiration that democracy both facilitates and strongly tempers. In the same way that the state is but the personification of a legal order, so also, for Kelsen, collective freedom, as collective self-rule, has no independent meaning of its own; at most, it simply means that 'the law governs its own creation. In particular, it is a legal norm that governs the process whereby another legal norm is created and also governs – to a different degree – the content of the norm to be created.'[7] Once the identity of law and state has been postulated, the enactment of a constitution can no longer be seen as an act of collective self-rule, for there is no longer a community – a political unity – to which the act of constitution making can be attributed as its owner; collective *self-determination* becomes 'the constantly regenerating process of [the law's] *self-creation*'.[8] The 'self' of legal self-creation no longer speaks to the identity between a legal order and a political unity, such that a community is free to the extent that the legal order corresponds to, or articulates, what joins together the collective's members as a political unity; it becomes a purely legal form of identity in which the legal order remains the same over time to the extent that each new act of norm-creation can be viewed as part of a single, on-going process of legal ordering.

So much for the relation between state, law and freedom in its normativist interpretation. We can now turn to Schmitt's attack on normativism, which develops along at least three fronts, or so I will argue. I have elsewhere staunchly defended Kelsen's account of the emergence of legal orders against Schmitt's critique of the pure theory of law.[9] Thus, while I think that Kelsen's pure theory of law can be defended, at least partially, from Schmitt's objections, I will undertake no such defence in reflecting about the relation between law, state and freedom. Only at a later stage of the argument will I briefly revisit the significance of Kelsen's account of the genesis of legal order for a critique of Schmitt's interpretation of this three-way relation.

[6] Hans Kelsen, *Vom Wesen und Wert der Demokratie* (Aalen, Germany: Scientia Verlag, 1981), 15.

[7] Kelsen, *Introduction to the Problems of Legal Theory*, 63.

[8] Ibid., 93 (emphasis added).

[9] Hans Lindahl, 'Constituent Power and Reflexive Identity: Towards an Ontology of Collective Selfhood' in Martin Loughlin and Neil Walker (eds.), *The Paradox of Constitutionalism: Constituent Power and Constitutional Form* (Oxford University Press, 2007), 9–24.

Schmitt's first objection turns on the internal contradiction at the heart of what might be dubbed (if one follows Schmitt) Kelsen's 'positivistic normativism'. Schmitt notes that a properly normative account of the validity of legal norms, hence of the unity of a manifold of norms, cannot but embrace natural law if it is to be consistent, such that the individual norms composing a legal order are valid if they are correct, and they are correct if their content has certain substantive qualities, that is, if they are derived from certain substantive principles deemed to be valid unconditionally. But Kelsen will have no truck with natural law, instead defending a normativist approach to positive law. This will not do, Schmitt claims. A theory of positive law must acknowledge that law is *posited* law and hence that there is a collective subject in the form of a political unity that enacts the law. Accordingly, and this is key to Schmitt's move to sever the normativist identification of state with law, 'the concept of legal order contains two entirely different elements: the normative element of law and the existential element of concrete order. The unity and order lies in the political existence of the state, not in statutes, rules and whatever other normativities.'[10] By uncoupling order and law, Schmitt seeks to reclaim the dualism Kelsen had sought to supress. The state is anterior to the law as the concrete order – the political unity – which enacts or posits a constitution in the legal sense of the term: a constitutional law (*Verfassungsgesetz*). Prior to this legal sense of a constitution there is a political sense of the constitution which is synonymous to the state. A state does not merely 'have' a constitution; it *is* a constitution (*Verfassung*), 'a particular type and form of state existence'.[11] Legal order as the unity of a manifold of legal norms is unintelligible unless it leads back to and is the expression of political unity – a concrete order.[12] Schmitt effectively argues that the identity of state and constitution is necessarily presupposed and called into question during constitutional crises, about which I will say more later.

Schmitt's second censure of normativism follows from the first, even though it features less prominently than the former. Its gist is that the concept of legal order outlined by Kelsen is incapable of making sense of states as *individual* states. What renders a legal order a particular legal order becomes part and parcel of the *content* of the basic norm which

[10] Schmitt, *Constitutional Theory*, 65 (translation altered). [11] Ibid., 60, 59.

[12] For a careful assessment of the significance of Schmitt's constitutional theory for public law theory, see Martin Loughlin, *Foundations of Public Law* (Oxford University Press, 2010), esp. 209–216.

must be presupposed when making sense of a manifold of legal norms as a unity. While there can be no basic norm absent the presupposition of a normative content, the latter functions as a given for normativistic legal theory rather than as an object of enquiry. In other words, the individuality of states is not part of an enquiry into the statehood of states nor of the orderliness of orders. Schmitt protests: in its fundamental sense, the constitution 'only designates the concrete, individual state, such as German Reich, France, or England, in its concrete political existence'.[13] Concrete-order thinking (*konkrete Ordnungsdenken*) is a type of juristic thought for which the individuality of a political community is the key to understanding the nature of the relation between state and law and, by implication, between state, law and freedom. Schmitt avers that a correct characterization of collective freedom cannot but begin from the recognition that it is, first and foremost, *our* freedom which is at stake in law making and law enforcement, that is, the 'possibility of choosing, by virtue of [our] own decision, the kind and form of [our] *own* existence'.[14] And this individual community's decision, in the twofold sense of a decision by a individual community and a decision about its individuality, has two faces: a *self*-identification and a differentiation with respect to what is *alien* or strange to it. Hence, collective self-rule is, at bottom, a decision about what defines *us* as a concrete order – as an individualized and individualizable community.

There is yet a third line of attack which Schmitt opens up in a later work explicitly oriented to introducing concrete-order thinking. To the extent that normativists pay any attention to the social reality external to the legal order, it is to ask whether that reality corresponds to the legal order. 'For [normativists] . . . an order exists essentially in that a concrete situation corresponds to general norms against which it is measured.'[15] A murder is not a manifestation of social disorder but rather a 'fact' (*Tatbestand*) to which the legal norm assigns certain consequences. Whereas a manifold of legal norms are in order as long as the norms are *valid*, the disorder that befalls a community when an illegal act has been perpetrated is banned from the domain of legal theory, registering only as the sociological problem of the *efficacy* (or lack thereof) of legal norms. While normativism is prepared to accept that efficacy is a condition for legal validity, it denies that efficacy is an

[13] Schmitt, *Constitutional Theory*, 60. [14] Ibid., 120–121 (translation altered).
[15] Carl Schmitt, *Über die drei Arten des rechtswissenschaftlichen Denkens*, 2nd edn. (Berlin: Duncker & Humblot, 1993), 19.

ingredient of the concept of validity, circumscribing the latter to a specific relation between norms. As a result,

> [N]ormativity and facticity remain 'entirely different planes'; ought (*Sollen*) remains untouched by is (*Sein*) and is retained as an invulnerable sphere for normativistic thinking, while in concrete reality all distinctions of lawfulness and unlawfulness, of order and disorder, are transformed, from a normativistic perspective, into the material presuppositions for the application of norms.[16]

Schmitt vigorously pushes back against this reduction of concrete order to legal order, of state to law, and of legal theory to a sociology of law, arguing that

> [T]he norm presupposes a *normal* situation and *normal* types ... The normality of the concrete situation regulated by the norm and of the concrete type it presupposes is not merely an external precondition of the norm which can be neglected by the legal science, but rather an internal, juridically essential feature of the validity of norms and a normative determination of the norm itself. A pure, deracinated and type-less norm would be a juridical absurdity.[17]

By defending the priority of normality over normativity, Schmitt effectively fleshes out more fully the strong thesis that a state *is* a constitution, to the extent that the validity of constitutional laws is only comprehensible to the extent that such laws are the juridical expression of a constitution in the sense of a normal way of being that defines a collective as a political unity. I will return to this point later, when discussing constitutional crises.

Notice, for the moment, that this view involves a remarkable turnabout in Schmitt's appreciation of normality, as compared to his appreciation thereof in *Political Theology*. In this earlier work, Schmitt was concerned to defend the *ex nihilo* character of the decision, for which normality has no value of its own. To the contrary, whereas normal situations cover over a decision *qua* political decision, the exception brings it out into the open. As Schmitt trenchantly puts it in *Political Theology*, for a 'philosophy of concrete life', 'the exception is more interesting than the normal case. The normal proves nothing; the exception proves everything: it confirms not only the rule but also its existence, which derives only from the exception.'[18] In *Three Types of Juristic*

[16] Ibid., 16. [17] Ibid., 19–20.

[18] Carl Schmitt, *Political Theology: Four Chapters on the Concept of Sovereignty* (Cambridge, MA: MIT Press, 1984), trans. George Schwab, 14 (translation altered).

Thought, Schmitt still aims to expose the derivative status of legal norms and rules. But, by contrast with the earlier work, in this later text legal norms are derived from normality, rather than from a decision. More precisely, Schmitt grounds the validity of normativity in normality. This grounding is, at least at first glance, consistent with his insistence on the need to rescue the individuality of states as a constitutive feature of states as such. Indeed, normal behaviour can be construed as the 'manner of existence' – the *Daseinsweise* – of a collective, which allows its members to identify themselves as a group, while distinguishing themselves from other groups.[19] To assert that norms *follow* normality, hence that law is subordinate to the state, means, in Schmitt's view, that legal orders regulate the state in a twofold sense of the term 'regulate': legal norms are valid to the extent that they *articulate* and *preserve* normality.

Authoritative collective action

As should be clear by now, concrete order is of capital importance to Schmitt's thinking about the relation between state, law and freedom. But what is concrete order? More precisely, what determines concrete order as an *order*? And what determines concrete order as *concrete*? Remarkably, Schmitt nowhere addresses these questions directly and in a systematic fashion.[20] A parallel *lacuna* concerns the concept of political unity, which is omnipresent in Schmitt's thinking about the state. Despite Schmitt's insistence that the unity of a political order precedes and is the condition of possibility of the unity of a manifold of legal norms, the reader remains at a loss as to the sense in which a community is a political unity. As Schmitt puts it, the act of constituent power 'constitutes the form and type of the political unity, the existence of which is *presupposed*'.[21] This omission is a source of considerable embarrassment for Schmitt, in light of his critique of Kelsen. For if, as he objects to Kelsen, the unity of a manifold of legal norms rests on a presupposition that is itself beyond the pale of theoretical enquiry, does not Schmitt

[19] Schmitt, *Constitutional Theory*, 59.

[20] Böckenförde notes that Schmitt's account of concrete order is 'impressionistic'. See Ernst-Wolfgang Böckenförde, 'Konkretes Ordnungsdenken' in Joachim Ritter, Karlfried Gründer and Gottfried Gabriel (eds.), *Historisches Wörterbuch der Philosophie* (Darmstadt, Germany: Wissenschaftliche Buchgesellschaft, 1971), vol. 8, 1312–1315, esp. 1313.

[21] Schmitt, *Constitutional Theory*, 75 (emphasis added).

himself fall prey to this very objection insomuch as he rests satisfied with 'presupposing' political unity? What, then, differentiates Schmitt's defence of the priority of political unity over the unity of a manifold of legal norms from Kelsenian normativism?

I will shortly return to the nature of the presupposition of political unity at work in the relation between state and law. But first I would like to prepare the ground for examining the notion of concrete order. Schmitt himself provides the cue as to how to go about this when acknowledging the proximity of his work to the institutionalist theories of law developed by Maurice Hauriou, in France, and Santi Romano, in Italy.[22] In particular, Schmitt draws inspiration from Hauriou, who argues that a legal order can best be understood as an institution. According to Hauriou, an institution is

> an idea of work or of enterprise (*idée d'œuvre ou d'entreprise*) that realizes itself and lasts juridically in a social environment; a power organizes itself which procures organs with a view to the realization of this idea; on the other hand, manifestations of communion come about between the members of the social group interested in the realization of the idea, manifestations which are directed by the power organs and regulated by procedures.[23]

Hauriou parses this definition into three elements. The first and most important is the *idée directrice*, which gathers together a manifold of individuals into a social group the action of which is oriented to realizing that idea. The second is governmental power at the service of and organized with a view to realizing the *idée directrice*. The third is those events in which the members of the social group, as well as its governmental organs, manifest their allegiance to the group as a whole and its guiding idea, such as the spontaneous coming together of individuals at the foundation of new social and political institutions, shareholders' meetings, elections and so on.

[22] See Massimo La Torre, *Law as Institution* (Dordrecht, Netherlands: Springer, 2010), Chapter 4, for an analysis of the institutionalist theories espoused by Hauriou and Santi Romano, as well as a powerful liberal reinterpretation of this approach to law, centred on the idea that law, as an institution, articulates constitutive rules of behaviour to an aspiration to realize justice. See also Neil MacCormick and Ota Weinberger, *An Institutional Theory of Law: New Approaches to Legal Positivism* (Dordrecht, Netherlands: Reidel, 1986).

[23] Maurice Hauriou, 'La théorie de l'institution et de la fondation', *Cahiers de la Nouvelle Journée*, 4 (1925), 2, 10.

I cannot examine here in any detail Hauriou's theory of institution, nor Schmitt's reception thereof.[24] While it contributes to clearing the ground for addressing the questions indicated at the outset of this section, it also has a decisive disadvantage. In effect, it takes for granted, without clarifying, the concept of collective action germane to institutions, hence the perspective whence concrete order can appear as such: the first-person plural perspective of a community. It is telling, in this respect, that Schmitt goes no further than referring to concrete orders as 'suprapersonal' (*überpersönlich*), an expression in which the particle 'supra' names a problem instead of addressing it.[25]

An initial and decisive step is taken if we introduce the concept of collective action into a theory of law as concrete order. Assuredly, whereas Schmitt's notion of concrete order has an unmistakably anti-liberal purport, contemporary philosophers usually conjoin a theory of collective action to a theory of liberal democracy.[26] My interest in this chapter is somewhat different, namely, to explore how collective action could illuminate the concept of concrete order. My purpose therewith is not merely to present Schmitt in his strongest light but also to offer a critique of his understanding of the relation between state, freedom and law in a way that need not take for granted the assumptions of a liberal theory of democracy.

In any case, Margaret Gilbert's adroit distinction between two uses of the pronoun 'we' – we each and we together – offers a good point of

[24] Mariano Croce and Andrea Salvatore have convincingly argued that Schmitt's reception of institutionalism, while fertile in its own right, comes at the cost of rejecting key tenets of these theories, most notably the strong defence of legal pluralism which Santi Romano attaches to his model of institutionalism. They also show how concrete-order thinking allows Schmitt to deal with several fundamental problems besetting the decisionistic model of law developed in his earlier work, including *Political Theology* and *The Concept of the Political*. While there is much of value in their excellent study, the aim of this and the following sections is more limited than theirs; it is also, in an important sense, orthogonal to it. Indeed, drawing on analytical theories of collective action and a phenomenology of the alien, this section puts into place an account of authoritative collective action that will allow me to clarify the notion of concrete order later. See Mariano Croce and Andrea Salvatore, *The Legal Theory of Carl Schmitt* (Abingdon, UK: Routledge, 2013).

[25] Schmitt, *Drei Arten des rechtswissenschaftliches Denken*, 12.

[26] A case in point is Margaret Gilbert, who draws on the notion of 'plural subjectivity' to offer an original interpretation and reconstruction of the concept of social contract. Philip Pettit, for his part, outlines a theory of collective rationality that is in line with his republican interpretation of democracy. See Margaret Gilbert, *A Theory of Political Obligation* (Oxford University Press, 2006) and Philip Pettit, *A Theory of Freedom: From the Psychology to the Politics of Agency* (Cambridge, UK: Polity Press, 2001).

departure for an enquiry into the first-person plural perspective proper to joint or collective action.[27] The first use of 'we' bespeaks an aggregative, the second an integrative, use of this pronoun. Take the example of a manifold of individuals milling around on a platform, waiting to catch a train. An aggregative use of the expression corresponds to a situation in which each of those individuals will take the train to carry on with her or his activities: we each. But suppose that the individuals are getting ready to leave on a joint vacation. Then they are a manifold of individuals who act jointly: we together. While joint action involves the acts of a plurality of individuals, theirs are participatory acts to the extent that their acts contribute to realizing the *point* of joint action, that is, what joint action is about – its *idée directrice*, as Hauriou would put it. The two uses of the pronoun 'we' point to two entirely different interpersonal situations. If, in the second case, one of the vacationers risks being left behind because she hasn't noticed that the train is on the verge of leaving, then she would be entitled to expect and demand of the other members of the group that they alert her to the train's departure so that she can step on board before it pulls out of the station. Doing something together entails mutual obligations and rights, as well as the standing to rebuke members of the group who do not fulfil the obligations derived from joint or collective action.[28] No such mutual obligations and rights ensue when a manifold of individuals are taking the train to continue with their daily chores and activities. If a distracted commuter misses the train, then that is tough luck, but the problem is hers and hers alone; after all, each of us is taking the train on his or her own.

Collective action, thus described, is the genus of the concept of order apposite to politics and law. A further feature must be introduced, however, if we are to distinguish the form of collective agency appropriate to politics and law from, say, walking or playing music together.[29] This is where *structures of authority* come into the picture. In contrast to forms of joint action, such as walking or playing music together, collective agency in the strong sense demanded by politics and law involves a structure of authority whereby certain individuals, acting on behalf of the group, monitor joint action as concerns its point and consistency over

[27] Margaret Gilbert, *On Social Facts* (Princeton University Press, 1992), 168.
[28] Gilbert, *A Theory of Political Obligation*, 147.
[29] See Gilbert's essay, 'Walking Together: A Paradigmatic Social Phenomenon' in Margaret Gilbert, *Living Together: Rationality, Sociality and Obligation* (Landham, MD: Rowman & Littlefield Publishers, 1996), 177–194.

time and take steps to uphold joint action when its point is breached or when the consistency of joint action over time is otherwise undermined or imperilled. Accordingly, collective agency appropriate to politics and law turns on how questions about joint action are dealt with. In effect, questions about its point – about the rights, obligations, entitlements and responsibilities that arise in the light of that point; about the consistency of participatory agency with regard to the point of joint action; and finally, about the consequences that follow from inconsistency therewith – are not left over to the collective's members to decide separately for themselves. These and related questions, especially if they are the source of conflict, are settled by authorities who act on behalf of the group as a whole, such that dissenters are bound by that decision and can, in principle, be forced to comply with it. It is in this way that, to borrow Hauriou's expression, 'power organs' are constitutive features of institutions. The relation between politics and law concerns *authoritative collective action*, as I will call it.

Concrete order

This is, admittedly, a crude and highly abridged formulation of the concept of collective action and of its institutionalized forms, certainly when compared to the extremely refined analyses of these phenomena in the contemporary debate about collective action. But it suffices for our present purposes. The immediate question is how this account of authoritative collective action sheds light on legal order as an *order* and as *concrete*.

Schmitt chides Kelsen for reducing legal order to the unity of a manifold of legal norms. 'An order, including a legal order, is, for concrete-order thinking, not in the first instance a rule or a summation of rules but, inversely, a rule is only an element and a means to order.'[30] Yet Schmitt eludes answering the crucial question: what determines concrete order as an *order*? If, most generally, an order is the unity of a manifold of elements, in what sense is a concrete order the unity of a manifold, albeit not merely a manifold of legal norms, as Kelsen would have it?

Authoritative collective action bespeaks the unity of a manifold in that it is not simply a summation of acts, such as in 'we each', but rather the integration of a plurality of participant acts into a single act. That is to

[30] Schmitt, *Constitutional Theory*, 11.

say, a manifold of acts are unified into *joint* action. In turn, that a plurality of acts can be viewed as an interlocking web of participant acts turns on the fact that each of these acts, even if carried out by different individuals, is oriented to realizing the point of joint action. Accordingly, collective action is the unity of a manifold of agents and of their acts. A point, an *idée directrice*, allows selecting the *who* and the *what* of joint action, both differentiating and relating kinds of agents and kinds of acts. That concrete order is an order means that joint action selects and interconnects different kinds of agency and different kinds of acts which are relevant to realizing the point of joint action.

This preliminary insight can be pushed a step further. In *The Three Types of Juristic Thought*, Schmitt introduced the notion of *nomos* to denote a 'comprehensive concept of law which also includes a concrete order and community'.[31] But he does not further develop this notion in a way that casts new light on the orderliness of concrete order. By contrast, Schmitt's later text, *Nomos of the Earth*, re-appropriates *nomos* in a way that stresses the spatial dimension of concrete order: 'law as the unity of order and emplacement'.[32] Emplacement means here an act of land-taking in the form of a spatial enclosure that draws a boundary separating inside and outside. Emplacement is, quite literally, an act of inclusion and exclusion, which makes room, internally, for the partition of space into different kinds of places which are interconnected as part of a single space, namely, the space a collective calls its *own* territory, over and against an outside. Thus, radicalizing Schmitt's insight, it is not merely the who and the what of behaviour which joint action orders. *Nomos* suggests that concrete order is also always a *spatial* order, hence an order that identifies and apportions a *where* – a proper place – to specific kinds of participant acts by specific kinds of participating agents. We can take yet a further step, albeit one that Schmitt himself does not take, by noting that collective action also involves an ordering of the *time* of participant action, not in the sense of calendar time but rather the appropriate time to engage in a certain act with a view to realizing the point of joint action: the *when* of participant acts.

In short, a concrete order – a *nomos* in a sense of the term which both builds on and radicalizes Schmitt's interpretation thereof – is the unity of

[31] Schmitt, *Drei Arten des rechtswissenschaftlichen Denkens*, 14.

[32] '*das Recht als Einheit von Ordnung und Ortung*'; Carl Schmitt, *Der Nomos der Erde im Völkerrecht des Jus Publicum Europæum*, 4th edn. (Berlin: Duncker & Humblot, 1997), 13ff.

a fourfold manifold that, *qua* unity, (1) *selects* the kinds of places, agents, times and acts which are relevant to realizing the point of joint action and (2) *differentiates and interconnects* the who, what, where and when of joint action into the dimensions of a *single* order. It is in this sense, I submit, that the notion of collective action sheds light on concrete order as an *order*.[33]

The foregoing considerations on the orderliness of concrete order also help us to understand the ways in which law is always a *concrete* order. To begin with, legal orders are concrete in that they appear to those whose behaviour they regulate in the form of a *fourfold unity*: the unity of the time, space, agents and content of participant acts. Secondly, legal orders are concrete in that the integration of these four dimensions of order takes place from the practically oriented, *first-person perspective* of those whose behaviour is regulated. Law appears as a four-dimensional order in which, for example, one finds oneself in a shop (place), as a prospective client (subject), in the course of (time) buying something (content). Only derivatively can a legal order be 'objectified', that is, severed from this first-person perspective, with a view to either isolating the 'meaning' of legal norms as the object of doctrinal analysis and 'interpretation' or establishing from a theoretical perspective under what conditions a manifold of norms can be viewed as a legal unity. Third, a legal order is concrete in that it assigns the *appropriate* places and times for the *appropriate* subjects to do the *appropriate* things. Law is concrete because it provides normative markers for what to do, when and where to do it and by whom, such that we can orient ourselves in each of these dimensions and all of them together. The fourth aspect of concreteness concerns the distinction between legality and illegality. In effect, this distinction is not neutral: the distinction sets up a *preferential differentiation* whereby legality is preferred to illegality, hence whereby legal order is preferred to legal disorder.

There is yet a further and fundamental feature which determines the concreteness of law as a concrete order, for illegal behaviour does not exhaust the disruption of normative orientation by the participants in

[33] I develop these ideas at far greater length in Hans Lindahl, *Fault Lines of Globalization: Legal Order and the Politics of A-Legality* (Oxford University Press, 2013), albeit by way of a revision of Kelsen's analysis of the spheres of validity of legal norms. For an excellent introduction to a phenomenology of the strange, see Bernhard Waldenfels, *Phenomenology of the Alien: Basic Concepts*, (Evanston, IL: Northwestern University Press, 2011), trans. Alexander Kozin and Tanya Stähler.

authoritative collective action. There is a form of the disruption of legal order whereby behaviour not only appears as legal or illegal but also as calling into question how the collective has drawn the very distinction between legality and illegality. Drawing on Schmitt's vocabulary, we can call this a strong form of *abnormality*. It betokens an alien or a strange order, that is, another first-person plural perspective of collective action the realization of which interferes with the realization of collective action from the first-person plural perspective of a given group. In other words, strong abnormality marks the irruption of what is *alien* or strange into what a collective calls its *own* order, that is, what is deemed to be its own way of organizing the who, what, where and when of authoritative collective action. If the legal is preferred to the illegal, and legal order to disorder, the emergence of the alien reveals a *second-level preferential distinction* that is constitutive for the first-person plural perspective of authoritative collective action: the own is preferred to the alien, where 'own' includes both the legal and the illegal. Whereas the qualification of behaviour as legal or illegal involves the (re)affirmation of a collective as a 'we,' abnormality, in its strong manifestation as what is alien or strange, challenges *what* we are as collective and, more or less radically, *that* we are a collective.

An example of this strong form of the alien or strange is the events leading up to the Canadian Supreme Court's famous *Quebec Secession Reference*, and which ended up in a constitutional deadlock between, on the one hand, the Canadian rebuke that the Quebecer secessionists had fallen prey to a performative contradiction by demanding a unilateral right to secession and, on the other, the Quebecer objection that Canadians begged the question when they demanded that Quebec present its claim as a constitutional claim to a right to secession. If, for the Canadians, at stake was the constitutionality or unconstitutionality of a unilateral right to secession (and in that broad sense the legality or illegality of this demand), the Quebecer secessionists rejected altogether the applicability of both terms of this distinction, contesting *that* they ought to be part of the Canadian collective, not merely *what* a Canadian collective that included Quebec ought to be about.[34]

[34] *Reference re Secession of Quebec* [1998] 2 SCR 217. For a detailed discussion of the Court's reference, see Hans Lindahl, 'Recognition as Domination: Constitutionalism, Reciprocity and the Problem of Singularity' in Neil Walker, Jo Shaw and Stephen Tierney (eds.), *Europe's Constitutional Mosaic* (Oxford, UK: Hart Publishing, 2011), 205.

I will revisit the distinction between the own and the strange in the closing section of the chapter. It may suffice to note, for the moment, that all the aforementioned goes into the claim that a state is a concrete order and that a legal order reveals itself as such from the first-person plural perspective of a 'we' in which authorities mediate and uphold who ought to do what, where and when with a view to realizing the point of collective action. Admittedly, I am going considerably beyond what Schmitt himself has to say about concrete order in my reconstruction thereof. But this reconstruction has the advantage of clearly exposing the key strengths and flaws of his thinking about politics and law.

State and law

This reconstruction of the concept of concrete order offers a good vantage point from which to appraise Schmitt's account of the relation between state and law. To begin with, it shows why Schmitt is right to eschew the move to conceptualize the state in terms of its canonical definition as a political organization characterized by the exercise of a monopoly of power over a population within a given territory. Notice that the point is not so much that this canonical definition is incorrect, as far as it goes; the point Schmitt makes is that this definition presupposes, without clarifying, the basic structure which allows one to explain each of the elements into which that canonical definition can be parsed. Indeed, the notions of territoriality, population and monopoly of power are abstractions which presuppose – without clarifying why a state is a concrete order – a *nomos*. No less importantly, and this is what I will now turn to consider, this first-person plural characterization of concrete order helps us to understand to what extent the three objections Schmitt addresses to Kelsen's normativism might be justified.

Schmitt's first line of attack hinges on his refusal to follow Kelsen in viewing a legal order as the unity of a manifold of legal norms. We can now see in what sense his complaint is justified. Kelsen's approach abstracts from the first-person perspective, both singular and plural, whence a legal order can at all appear as a unity. If an order is the unity of a manifold, then the problem of legal order cannot be only, or even in the first instance, the problem about the unity of a manifold of norms, as Kelsen and many others take for granted. It is also, and most fundamentally, the *practical* question about how a legal order manifests itself as a unity with respect to each of the dimensions of behaviour ordered by the law. The conceptualization of legal order as a manifold of legal norms is a theoretical achievement that abstracts from – and hence continues to depend on – the primordially practical interest concerning who ought to do what, where and when with respect to authoritative collective action.[35] Indeed, the disruption of legal order is not normally greeted with indifference by those whose behaviour it regulates. The disruption of legal order provokes a wide range of emotions, ranging from fear, irritation and anger to joy and relief, depending on the stance taken by interested parties in joint action. Perhaps the fundamental reason for this is that, to a lesser or greater extent, the disruption of order concerns our capacity to orient ourselves in the world, thereby exposing our constitutive vulnerability as beings which are not simply 'in' an order but need to take up a relation *to* an order. In short, legal order and its vicissitudes have an *existential* significance which is not merely ancillary to law but is rather constitutive for it. Schmitt's appeal to the notion of a concrete order can be seen as reclaiming this existential significance of legal order for a theory of the relation between state and law, an existential significance from which 'the legal point of view', as Raz calls it, has abstracted, yet which remains its indispensable presupposition.[36]

Kelsen's reticence about conceptualizing legal order as a concrete order is driven by his rejection of the notion of collective subjects. To revisit an earlier citation, 'every state is *only* a legal order' (emphasis added). There is no political unity that needs to be presupposed as antecedent to the unity of a legal order, or so he avers. The foregoing account of authoritative collective action suggests in what way Schmitt's critique of this position is compelling. In effect, Kelsen's methodological individualism blinds him to the fact that collective action is irreducible to an aggregation or summation of individual acts, even though no collective can exist independently of, nor act other than through, the participant acts of its members. There is a meaningful sense in which acts can be viewed as *our* acts and a collective as *owning* an act. Kelsen's identification of law and state is premised on the assumption that all talk of collectives and collective acts amounts to a hypostasis or reification. This assumption is

[35] It can be shown, in particular, that Kelsen's attempt to release legal interpretation of a practical interest in law ultimately fails. See Hans Lindahl, 'Dialectic and Revolution: Confronting Kelsen and Gadamer on Legal Interpretation', *Cardozo Law Review*, 24 (2003), 769.

[36] Joseph Raz, *The Authority of Law: Essays on Law and Morality* (Oxford University Press, 2002), 140–143.

unfounded, even though a reifying reading of collectivity in general, and of states in particular, is of course possible.

In consonance with his defence of collective subjectivity, Schmitt also defends, as we have seen, a dualistic reading of the relation between state and law. Authoritative collective action, as sketched out earlier, reveals in what sense Schmitt is right to postulate a dualistic reading of law and state. In effect, a legal order is a *default setting* of authoritative collective action. By this I mean that a legal order is a provisional determination of who ought to do what, where and when in light of the point of joint action, such that no state is ever exhausted by any of its legal default settings. Indeed, if the emergence of a collective demands the identification of a point of joint action, which includes some kinds of behaviour as relevant and excludes others as irrelevant, it is also the case that a legal order, *qua* default setting of authoritative collective action, operates yet a further inclusion and exclusion: it includes a certain reading of the point of joint action while excluding other possibilities that remain within the compass of the collective's own possibilities. A dualistic reading of the relation between state and law simply points, on one level, to the duality between actuality and possibility, that is, to the fact that more is possible for a collective than what it has actualized as its legal order.

Schmitt's dualistic interpretation of the relation between state and law can be taken a step further: to argue that an extant legal order is a default setting of authoritative collective action is to assert that this legal order is deemed to be a *representation* of a political order or, if you wish, that the unity of a legal order is held to articulate political unity. This means that the validity a legal order demands for itself turns on the claim that law, as posited, gives form (*Gestaltung*) to – that is, expresses – what is deemed to *already* bind together a manifold of individuals as participants in the common enterprise of realizing an *idée directrice*. It is in this sense that we should interpret Schmitt's claim that the unity of a manifold of norms would be unintelligible absent the *presupposition* of political unity. But it is also *only* in this sense that Schmitt's claim about the representational character of legal order should be accepted, for it is one thing to claim that political unity must be presupposed and another altogether to claim that a political unity exists *independently* of the legal order which represents it. Whereas the first claim is part and parcel of a radical interpretation of representation, the second collapses representation into a form of originalism. To argue that political unity must be presupposed is to aver that political unity is perforce a *represented* unity, that is, a unity to which there is no direct accesss. By implication, political unity is never a given but rather always nothing more than a *putative* political unity.[37]

Let us now turn to Schmitt's second objection to Kelsenian normativism, namely, its incapacity to view the individuality of a state as a constitutive feature of legal order. The abstractive move whereby a legal order becomes the unity of a manifold of norms goes hand in hand with an objectifying move that brackets the first-person plural perspective whence a legal order can appear as individualized. As Schmitt puts it, normativistic thinking strives, by its very nature, to be 'impersonal' and 'objective'.[38] Importantly, the critical thrust of Schmitt's objection reaches far beyond Kelsen. In fact, it reveals the blind spot of a wide range of theories which partition the domain of legal theory into the question of 'identity' and the question of 'individuation'.[39] The former, which is taken to be the core problem of legal theory, concerns the features which identify law as such over and against other kinds of normative order. Their acrimonious debates notwithstanding, the defenders and detractors of the so-called separability thesis share the conviction that the identity question is the central question of legal theory. As a result, the question about individuation is forced to play second fiddle to the question about identity, as individuation is deemed to concern a merely factual and contingent feature of legal orders. Schmitt's objection amounts to a defence of the central significance of individuality and individuation for a theory of state and law: 'the state *is* constitution . . . the constitution is [the state's] concrete life, and its individual existence.'[40]

A theory of authoritative collective action offers qualified support to Schmitt's objection against the normativistic move to reduce individuation to a derivative problem, both theoretically and practically. Indeed, to the extent that legal order is primordially a form of collective action, explaining the orderliness of legal order demands accounting for the first-person plural perspective of a 'we' in joint action. In turn, this perspective can only emerge by dint of a *point* of joint action which allows the participants of the collective to identify themselves as a group

[37] This, precisely, is what I take to be the core of Kelsen's brilliant account of the emergence of legal orders and which I have dubbed the paradox of representation. See, to this effect, my 'Constituent Power and Reflexive Identity: Towards an Ontology of Collective Selfhood'.

[38] Schmitt, *Drei Arten des rechtswissenschaftlichen Denkens*, 12.

[39] See, e.g., William Twining, *General Jurisprudence* (Cambridge University Press, 2009), 73–74.

[40] Schmitt, *Constitutional Theory*, 60.

and to differentiate themselves from other groups. In other words, there is a deeper layer of the question about identity and identification which appears as soon as one relinquishes the abstract and theoretical perspective of the scholar to take up the concrete and practical perspective of the member of a group who seeks orientation as to the who, what, where and when of joint action. At this deeper level, the identity question *is* the individuation question. First and foremost, identification is the *self*-identification, individuation the *self*-individuation, of a group. Indeed, who is the 'we' which can be *identified* as a collective act's agent? Well, the group of individuals who refer to themselves as the group committed to acting in certain ways in certain kinds of places and times with a view to realizing the point of their joint action and who, by identifying themselves, can differentiate themselves from other groups.

A theory of authoritative collective action also supports the corollary which attaches to Schmitt's defence of the central theoretical and practical significance of individuation, namely, the meaning of a constitutional crisis. Indeed, what is at stake in such a crisis is the continuation of authoritative collective action. This means, concretely, that what is threatened is its structure as such and in its entirety: collective action and authority. On the one hand, a constitutional crisis imperils the capacity of a manifold of individuals to individuate themselves as a collective, in the sense both *that* they are a collective and *what* they are as a collective. On the other hand, a constitutional crisis announces itself when the ultimate authority to establish which acts count as the collective's own acts is called into question. These two aspects of a constitutional crisis are but the two faces of legal ordering as the on-going political process of collective self-individuation or self-identification.

These considerations on identification and individuation usher in Schmitt's third and decisive censure of normativism, namely, the latter's attempt to relegate the problem of normality to the domain of the factual proper to legal sociology while conceptualizing validity in a way that grounds a legal order in a norm – the basic norm. Schmitt counters that norms follow normality: 'each order, also a legal order, is bound to normal concepts that aren't derived from general norms but rather which bring out these norms from their own order and bring these forth for the sake of their own order.'[41] Normal forms of institutional interaction ground legal orders, which means that a legal order is valid if it articulates

[41] Schmitt, *Drei Arten des rechtswissenschaftlichen Denkens*, 19.

and secures an institution in its normal state, or so he avers. Building on an earlier insight, a constitutional crisis, in Schmitt's view, amounts to a form of abnormality which challenges the capacity of a collective to continue identifying itself as the self-same collective and to distinguish itself from other groups.

In what way might the concept of concrete order enjoined by a theory of authoritative collective action support Schmitt's strong claim about the foundational role of normality vis-à-vis normativity? The crux of the matter is a distinction that needs to be drawn between pre-reflexive and reflexive forms of authoritative collective action. Indeed, in the ordinary course of joint action, legal order as such remains unobtrusive to participant agents. When buying victuals in a shop, I simply select the products I need, walk to the check-out point and so on without interpreting what I am doing as participating in a contract of sale. The hold of law *qua* normative order is at its strongest when it remains unnoticed as an order that opens up and closes down normative possibilities by differentiating and interconnecting four dimensions of behaviour. More pointedly, while the participants understand what it is they ought to do, they do not immediately describe it in specifically legal terms, even if, *ex post*, their behaviour can be shown to be legal (or illegal) and they (and authorities) can qualify it as such. This is important because it suggests that legal orders draw on and *come to stand out* against the background of a more or less anonymous social order, an order in which 'is' and 'ought' run over into each other. This is the pre-reflexive order of normal and habitual behaviour in which one acts more or less blindly and as a matter of course: everything is at it should be, and everything should be as it is. This domain of the normal and habitual is pre-reflexive because it does not require participant agents to take a stance with respect to whether they are a collective and what identifies them as a collective, that is, with respect to who ought to do what, where and when with a view to realizing the point of joint action. The distinction between the normal and the normative only manifests when the ordinary course of joint action is *disrupted*, thereby engendering a reflexive attitude towards joint action: what ought our joint action to be about? Only when social order is disrupted do 'is' and 'ought' fall apart and do a legal order and its claim to validity appear as standing in contrast to the factual. Importantly, the emergent separation between 'is' and 'ought' engenders a reflexive attitude towards joint action and to which law setting is a response: what ought our joint action to be about? The reflexive structure of this attitude, and of the possible responses to which it gives rise, brings into play what Paul Ricœur calls *ipse* identity, which is irreducible to the *idem* identity presupposed in what Kelsen calls the 'self-creation' of a legal order.[42]

Thus, Schmitt's critique of normativism can be taken to mean that this pre-reflexive domain of joint action is not merely a sociological precondition of a state but rather an integral part of a state *qua* state. In short, the pre-reflexive domain of joint action, as summarized in the notion of normality, lends a certain credence to Schmitt's strong thesis that a state *is* a constitution and only derivatively *has* a legal constitution.

Normalization and collective freedom

In the foregoing, I have sought to provide as charitable a reading as I can of Schmitt, a reading which defends his proposal to view law as concrete order, all the while addressing the crucial questions he leaves unanswered. But the time is now ripe to expose the serious – arguably devastating – consequences of this reading for Schmitt's interpretation of the relation between law, state and freedom, for, as we shall now see, a first-person plural reconstruction and defence of the relation between normality and normativity comes at a heavy price for Schmitt.

To begin with, it becomes clear that Schmitt's move to invert the relation of dependency between 'is' and 'ought' such that the latter is derived from the former is no less problematic than the opposite relation of dependency, which he views as characteristic of normativism. In effect, what is characteristic of the pre-reflexive domain of the normal is their *intertwinement*, such that everything is at it should be, and everything should be as it is. Inverting the relation of dependency between 'is' and 'ought', as Schmitt does, is to hold on to their disjunction as original or primordial. In contrast to both normativism and Schmitt's interpretation of concrete-order thinking, the pre-reflexive domain of authoritative collective action reveals this disjunction as derivative, in a specific sense of the expression: the disjunction appears in the event of a disruption of concrete order. In other words, the disjunction between 'is' and 'ought' is abstractive rather than concrete. Authoritative collective action bespeaks, in its pre-reflexive mode, the *indifferentiation* of 'is' and 'ought'.[43]

[42] Paul Ricœur, *Oneself as Another* (University of Chicago Press, 1992), trans. Kathleen Blamely.

[43] This insight offers a critical avenue of approach to Searle's attempt to derive 'ought' from 'is', albeit that I cannot develop this set of issues in the scope of this chapter. See John Searle, 'How to Derive "Ought" From "Is"', *The Philosophical Review*, 73 (1964), 43.

This objection seems to leave intact the main thrust of Schmitt's critique of normativism, namely, the thesis that validity ultimately is grounded in efficacy and that the norm simply *follows* normality. But the model of authoritative collective action also challenges this thesis in a decisive way. Notice that Schmitt's thesis effectively amounts to an *inversion* of the correspondence relation he attributes to normativism, for which order exists to the extent that 'a concrete situation corresponds to general norms, in relation to which it is measured'.[44] It is the other way around, or so argues Schmitt: legal norms are valid to the extent that they correspond to the inner measure of an institution. Thus, although Schmitt describes normativism as 'objectivist', concrete-order thinking is no less objectivist in its purport: the sole difference consists in an inversion of the measure of objectivity. As concerns the state, this means that constitutional laws are valid insofar as they articulate and secure a constitution in its fundamental sense, that is, 'the concrete manner of existence that is given *of itself* with every existing political unity'.[45] That norms follow normality means that legal order is ultimately about the 'restoration (*Wiederherstellung*) . . . of order',[46] an order that has been disturbed by 'abnormal' behaviour. This impinges directly on the notion of a constitutional crisis: to the extent that such a crisis marks the irruption of abnormality into the domain of (constitutional) normality, the task of the guardian of the constitution is to restore normality by way of exceptional measures, where 'restore' means to return to the original condition of normality – the *Daseinsweise* of the collective – as the ground of the validity of the legal constitution.

This line of reasoning amounts to what I earlier dubbed an originalist reading of representation, that is, the reifying assumption that a legal order should merely replicate a pre-given political unity which is independent of its legal representation. Yet to acknowledge that political unity is always a represented unity is to recognize that there is no social order that is simply given prior to and independent of its legal regulation and which provides the latter with an internal measure to which the legal order can correspond (or not) and hence be valid (or invalid). In other words, there is no pristine domain of the normal, unmediated by law, and which the norm simply follows. *Normality, including constitutional normality, is always to a greater or lesser extent the outcome of a process of*

[44] Schmitt, *Drei Arten des rechtswissenschaftlichen Denkens*, 15.
[45] Schmitt, *Constitutional Theory*, 59 (translation altered; emphasis added).
[46] Schmitt, *Drei Arten des rechtswissenschaftlichen Denkens*, 23.

(constitutional) normalization. This means, from the perspective of authoritative collective action, that the social domain of normal and habitual behaviour is never only *pre*-reflexive, such that norms would merely 'follow' normality. It is also always *post*-reflexive, in the sense of a normality that has come about and become consolidated as a result of the reiterated qualification and enforcement of legal behaviour. Normality is always already 'contaminated' by a normativity that has been imposed on it. This is most acutely visible in the case of a constitutional crisis, in which the measures taken by the 'guardian of the constitution' *bring about* a state of normality in the very act of claiming that these measures merely restore normality. In short, it is thoroughly reductive to state, as Schmitt does, that normativity simply follows normality; it is also the case that normality follows normativity.[47] There is no original normality which lends an independent measure to normativity, no pure 'social type' which could provide the inner measure to which legal norms must correspond if they are to be valid.[48]

Therefore, when one fully works out Schmitt's proposal to view law as concrete order, it turns out that this proposal endorses a key – perhaps *the* key – idea of normativism. In effect, the general thesis defended by Gustav Radbruch and Hans Kelsen ultimately carries the day against Schmitt: law is not valid *because* it is effective but rather *when* it is effective.[49] In my reading of law as concrete order, normativity is irreducible to normality because the practical question confronting legal orders – what ought our joint action to be about? – becomes urgent because there is no 'inner measure' in the order of things that could establish *whether* we are a collective and *what* we are as a collective.

How does this insight pan out in terms of the concept of collective freedom? As noted at the outset, Schmitt defends the notion of collective freedom as collective self-rule, where what is at stake therein is the capacity to determine what is 'our [own] kind and form of existence'. Constitution making, as the expression of collective freedom, amounts, in his reading of the relation between law and state, to an act whereby

[47] Compare with Hans Heller, 'The Nature and Function of the State', *Cardozo Law Review*, 18 (1996), 1139 (trans. David Dyzenhaus). I am grateful to David Dyzenhaus for calling my attention to this parallel.

[48] Canguilhem, Foucault's teacher, has drawn analogous conclusions as concerns the normal and the pathological in sicknesses. See Georges Canguilhem, *Le normal et le pathologique* (Paris: Presses Universitaires de France, 1966), 90–91, 139.

[49] Gustav Radbruch, *Rechtsfilosofie*, 2nd edn. (Heidelberg: C.F. Müller, 1999), 83; Kelsen, *Introduction to the Problems of Legal Theory*, 60–61.

constitutional laws are enacted which are the expression of what we already *are* as a collective. This is the constitutional implication of the tenet that normativity must follow normality and hence that 'ought' follows 'is'. At issue here, as noted, is an inversion of the relation of objectivity which Schmitt imputes to normativism: if the latter would have facts correspond to norms, he would have norms correspond to facts. Now, insomuch as a legal order represents a pre-given political unity (the state *as* a constitution), the enactment of a constitutional law is the manifestation of collective freedom; the act is *our own* act, and the enacted law is *our own* constitutional law. In this reading of collective freedom, the 'self' of collective self-rule speaks to identity in terms of what Ricœur calls *idem* identity: the people as ruled (through law) are *the same* as (corresponds or identical to) the people as the ruler. The implication of this account is that, in the face of a constitutional crisis, collective freedom resides in the capacity to preserve what is originally our own *Daseinsweise* over and against the alien or strange and hence the normal and familiar over and against the abnormal. It is in this way, then, that Schmitt clinches his theory about the internal relation between state, law and freedom.

What are we to make of this account of collective freedom and its relation to state and law? With Schmitt, I would defend the thesis that, politically speaking, collective *self-rule* entails the first-person plural perspective of a collective subject, that is, of a manifold of individuals who view themselves as the group which legislates in its own interest. With Schmitt, I would defend the thesis that *collective* self-rule entails that the collective has a mode of existence that is not simply the aggregation of the individuals that compose it. With Schmitt, I would defend the view that collective self-determination amounts to self-*individuation*, that is, to acts which identify what is to count as 'our own' mode of existence and what is to be excluded therefrom as alien or strange. All of this is entailed, I think, by the interpretation of law as a concrete order.

But the implications of this interpretation for the concept of collective freedom do not stop here. If one acknowledges that normality is the outcome of a process of normalization, then the assumptions undergirding Schmitt's concept of collective freedom turn out to be untenable on at least two decisive counts. Against Schmitt, I argue that political unity is perforce a *represented* unity. This means that representation is never merely the reproduction of an original unity but also always the production of unity. Against Schmitt, I would argue that there is no pre-given and directly accessible political unity that could provide the 'inner measure' for the validity of law, no pre-given and directly accessible boundaries that separate an original mode of existence which is our own from what is strange or alien to it.

It is under these conditions that collective freedom can appear as a *response* to the practical problem confronting authoritative collective action: what ought our joint action to be about? In other words, who *ought* to do what, where and when? Freedom is a response to a practical problem because, *contra* Schmitt, there is no inner measure, no original unity that could provide guidance on how to authoritatively draw the boundaries between the own and the strange.

Here is where liberal theories of democracy come into the picture. When there is no prior ground for the validity of law, when normativity does not simply follow normality, when political unity is not given in advance of legal order, then the only way to hold onto an objective grounding for the binding character of a legal order is to locate that objective grounding in the consent of the ruled. Legislation can be viewed as an act of collective freedom, on a liberal reading of authoritative collective action, if and only if all those who are participant agents can grant their consent to the rules that establish what our joint action ought to be about. Only then can participant agents understand themselves as being not only the object of rule but also part of a collective subject that rules over itself. Only then is an act properly attributable to a collective subject as our *own* act; only then can a constitution manifest as *our* constitution; only then has collective freedom become a reality and not merely an aspiration. Collective self-rule, in a liberal reading, becomes the *telos* of an historical process oriented to realizing, at least on principle, an every greater inclusiveness, such that what had been initially excluded as abnormal or alien is progressively integrated into the collective subject. Democratic 'solidarity with the other *as one of us* refers to the flexible "we" of a community that resists all substantial determinations and extends its permeable boundaries ever further.'[50]

Accordingly, the bitter feud between Schmitt and liberal theories of democracy takes place on the ground of a more fundamental alliance between the two positions: both interpret the relation between state, law

[50] Jürgen Habermas, *The Inclusion of the Other: Studies in Political Theory* (Cambridge, UK: Polity Press, 2005), trans. Ciaran Cronin and Pablo de Greiff, xxxv–xxxvi. In the course of critiquing Schmitt's theory of sovereignty, Lars Vinx's contribution to this volume draws on this liberal tradition of democratic theory.

and freedom in terms of a politics of law making in which difference, in the strong sense of the strange or alien, is subordinated to identity. If, for Schmitt, collective self-rule amounts to ensuring that legislation preserves what is originally our own against the alien or strange, for liberal theories of democracy, the alien is only provisionally alien insofar as the task of collective self-rule is 'to make the strange our own'.[51] In both cases, democracy is the celebration of the unity of the self as the ground of the normativity of legal order; in both cases, collective self-rule speaks to the identity between those who are ruled and those who rule.

All of this shows that it is possible to offer a liberal defence of the thesis that concrete order provides the key to the relation between state, law and freedom. I could have concluded this chapter by embracing this defence, but I will not. To recognize that normality is the outcome of a process of normalization of the abnormal is to acknowledge that collective self-rule never only integrates the strange into a legal order at a higher level of generality. In the process of responding to the strange, collective self-rule also always neutralizes the strange, levelling down the extraordinary to a variation of the ordinary. Every collective confronts, in one way or another, normative claims that it cannot integrate in their own terms into its legal order because those normative claims are in contradiction with that collective's normative point. Political difference is never only what-is-not-yet-our-own. It is for this reason that I have eschewed linking a theory of authoritative collective action, and of law as concrete order, to liberal theories of democracy. My aim is instead to preserve the ambiguity of collective self-rule as integration/neutralization, an ambiguity which is neatly captured by the claim that collective self-rule *normalizes* the abnormal. If such is the case, then collective freedom cannot only mean collective self-rule as the progressive integration of the strange into our own collective but also always as a form of *self-restraint* in the face of normative challenges which definitively elude the practical question to which collective self-rule is a response: what ought *our* joint action to be about?

[51] Hans-Georg Gadamer, 'Rhetoric, Hermeneutics, and Ideology-Critique' in Walter Jost and Michael J. Hyde (eds.), *Rhetoric and Hermeneutics in Our Time: A Reader* (New Haven, CT: Yale University Press, 1997), 314 (translation altered).

4

Nomos

MARTIN LOUGHLIN

> On what will man base the economy of the world he wants to rule? If left to each individual's whim, what confusion! If on justice, he knows not what it is. Certainly, if he did know, he would not have laid down that most common of all men's maxims, that a man must follow the customs of his own country. The glory of true equity would have held all nations in its sway. We should see it enacted by all the States of the world, in every age, instead of which we see nothing, just or unjust, which does not change in quality with a change in climate. Three degrees of latitude overthrow jurisprudence. A meridian determines the truth. Law has its periods . . .
>
> From this confusion derives the fact that one man will say the essence of justice is the legislator's authority, another the king's convenience, and a third, present custom. This last is the safest. Following reason alone, nothing is intrinsically just; everything moves with the times. Custom is the whole of equity for the sole reason that it is accepted. That is the mystical basis of its authority. Whoever tries to trace this authority back to its origins, destroys it . . . The art of criticizing and overthrowing States lies in unsettling established customs by delving to their core in order to demonstrate their lack of authority and justice. They say they have to go back to the fundamental and original laws of the State, which unjust custom has abolished. This is a sure way of losing everything; nothing will be just on those scales . . . This is why the wisest of legislators used to say that the good of mankind requires them to be deceived . . . He must not be allowed to be aware of the truth about the usurpation. It was introduced once without reason and has since become reasonable. He must be made to regard it as genuine and eternal, and its origins must be disguised if it is not to come to a swift end.
>
> Blaise Pascal, *Pensées*, (1670) § 94.

Origins

Every jurist seeking to explain the constitution of political authority sooner or later encounters the problem of origins. In order to avoid an infinite regress, theorists invariably try to convert the historical into a normative inquiry, often with unsatisfactory consequences. Expressing his frustration over abstract appeals to 'justice', Pascal places his faith – as have others before and since – in custom. But he recognizes that, if subjected to close analysis, this answer will not satisfy many: custom, it will be suggested, merely bolsters established authority and legitimates a regime that founds itself on an original act of usurpation. Accepting the force of that point, Pascal acknowledges that there is a mystical basis to authority which is unable to withstand intense scrutiny. If measured according to the power of one's 'sovereign reason', every claim to authority will be suspect: puncture the mystical and authority is destroyed. Pascal's warning is directed primarily to the future: modernity, on the threshold of which he stood, is a condition characterized by unwillingness to accept the authority of appeals to the 'eternal past'. Its defining feature is the need to discover a rational basis of political authority.

Many political theorists – Thomas Hobbes and John Locke being prominent examples – have tried to resolve these difficulties by deploying the idiom of a social contract. This converts the question of origins into an exercise of imagination. The challenge becomes that of showing how reason dictates that humans should abandon such freedom as they possess within their 'natural state' and, for the purpose of securing and sustaining freedom, subject themselves to an order of government. There are evident difficulties even before we leave the seminar room. How is it possible for a multitude of strangers to be able to meet, deliberate and rationally agree on a constitution for the common good? Rousseau explicitly recognized the paradoxical character of the exercise. For this to happen, 'the effect would have to become the cause', in that humans would have to be beforehand that which they can only become as a consequence of the foundational pact. How can this entity called 'the people' deliberate and establish a political union if they are identifiable as such only by virtue of the pact?[1]

[1] J. J. Rousseau, *The Social Contract* in his *The Social Contract and Other Later Political Writings* (Cambridge University Press, 1997), trans. V. Gourevitch, 71. Political theorists have enjoyed playing with this paradox ever since: see, e.g., L. Althusser, 'Rousseau: *The Social Contract* (the Discrepancies)' in Althusser, *Politics and History: Montesquieu, Rousseau* (London: Verso, 2007), trans. Marx B. Brewster, 113–60; J. Derrida, 'Declarations of Independence', *New Political Science*, 15 (1986), 7–15; B. Honig, 'Arendt and Derrida on the Problem of Founding a Republic', *American Political Science Review*, 85 (1991), 97–114.

Faced with such difficulties, constitutional lawyers have tended to retreat to the field of positive law. Law, they maintain, is created by the establishment of a constitution, and how and by whom that constitution is authorized are questions lying beyond the boundaries of legal knowledge. By this manoeuvre, legal science is founded only once the authority of a constitution is presupposed. This view, most coherently expressed by Hans Kelsen,[2] has become generally accepted. Constitutional lawyers maintain the purity of their discipline only by accepting that law is a system of norms authorized by a founding norm, the authority of which must simply be assumed. On this account, an autonomous legal order exists when it is not only 'purified of all political ideology' but also of all empirical knowledge, that is, of 'every element of the natural sciences'.[3]

In their distinctive ways, political and legal theorists have sought to retreat to the normative plane in order to avoid having to engage with the actual political circumstances through which constitutional authority is established and maintained. For the discipline of political jurisprudence, however, this is unsatisfactory. While acknowledging the power of normative constructions, political jurisprudence founds itself on the assumption that if existing political conditions are ignored, a distorted view is formed not only of the nature of political authority but also of the concept of law.[4]

The moment we move out of the seminar room, an altogether different narrative presents itself. Rousseau again offers insight. In his *Discourse on Inequality*, he addresses the origins of modern government as a matter of historical fact in order to show that the types of constitutions jurists treat as presuppositions of legal knowledge are invariably deceptive and fraudulent devices. They are documents drafted by the wealthy who have 'invented specious arguments' to win over the people to the established order of things. They exist to transform 'a skilful usurpation into an irrevocable right'.[5] The tricks that political theorists perform, and the

[2] H. Kelsen, *Introduction to the Problems of Legal Theory, B. L. Paulson and S. L. Paulson* trans. of first edition (1934) of *Reine Rechtslehre* (Oxford, UK: Clarendon Press, 1992), 57: 'What is to be valid as norm is whatever the framers of the first constitution have expressed as their will . . . this is the basic presupposition of all cognition of the legal system resting on this constitution.'

[3] Ibid., 1.

[4] For an account of this idea of public law as political jurisprudence, see M. Loughlin, *Foundations of Public Law* (Oxford University Press, 2010).

[5] J. J. Rousseau, *Discourse on the Origin and Foundations of Inequality Among Men* [1755] in Rousseau, *The Discourses and Other Early Political Writings* (Cambridge University Press, 1997), ed. V. Gourevitch, 111–222, at 173.

lines that constitutional lawyers draw, function to uphold and legitimate an order of exploitation.

Rousseau's insights are radicalized by writers such as Georges Sorel and Walter Benjamin, whose general aim is to reveal the violent underpinnings of law that liberal political thought and normativist legal thought shield from view. Sorel and Benjamin claim not only that law finds its origins in violence but also that it achieves reaffirmation in acts of violence.[6] All violence, Benjamin asserts, 'is either law-making or law-preserving'.[7] Although Hobbes conceived life in the state of nature as a perpetual 'war of all against all', he used this image to convince us of the rational need to cede our natural rights and vest authority in the sovereign. In Benjamin's critique, Hobbes's ingenious device of the social contract not only transforms chaos and violence into order, but the office of the sovereign instituted as a consequence of the contract also legitimates the continuation of violence.

Benjamin presents a radical critique of liberal political thought. His challenge cannot be altogether avoided by those who seek to maintain the purity of legal ordering by severing the connection between legitimacy and legality. In ridiculing the tradition of natural law on the ground that it is perennially focussed on 'the eternal question of what stands behind the positive law', for example, Kelsen maintains that those who continue to seek an answer 'will find, I fear, neither an absolute metaphysical truth nor the absolute justice of natural law'. Rather, whoever 'lifts the veil and does not shut his eyes will find staring at him the Gorgon head of power'.[8] This might count as a criticism of the attempt by natural lawyers to fix a connection between law and justice, but Kelsen appears not to recognize that his argument also highlights the problem of presupposing the autonomy – and authority – of an extant legal order since, for many, legal order suggests not merely efficacy but legitimacy.

Pascal tells us that wise lawgivers used to say that 'the good of mankind requires them to be deceived', that these violent origins be

[6] G. Sorel, *Reflections on Violence* [1915] (Cambridge University Press, 1999), ed. J. Jennings; W. Benjamin, 'Critique of Violence' in Benjamin, *Selected Writings* (Cambridge, MA: Harvard University Press, 1996), trans. M. Bullock and M. W. Jennings, 236–52.

[7] Benjamin, *Selected Writings*, 243. For analysis, see J. W. Müller, 'Myth, Law and Order: Schmitt and Benjamin Read *Reflections on Violence*', *History of European Ideas*, 29 (2003), 459–73; S. Weber, 'Taking Exception to Decision: Walter Benjamin and Carl Schmitt', *Diacritics*, 22, no. 3–4 (1992), 5–18.

[8] Kelsen (1927), cited in D. Dyzenhaus, 'Constitutionalism in an Old Key: Legality and Constituent Power', *Global Constitutionalism*, 1 (2012), 229–60, at 229.

masked. But the contemporary situation is different: today, it seems, the 'wise' scholars – the normative political and legal theorists – have come to believe their own myths and, rather than participating in statecraft, are in the business of deceiving themselves. If a sense of reality is to be restored, the discipline of political jurisprudence must be rejuvenated, not least because it tries to ensure that the normative and the factual, the imaginary and the real, reason and history are drawn into an appropriate relationship. It accepts that unless the question of the origins of political order, including its origins in violence or domination, is addressed, a skewed, if not thoroughly ideological, conception of law is likely to result.

In approaching the question of origins from the perspective of political jurisprudence, I examine the topic through a study of one of its most controversial practitioners. Carl Schmitt argues that the basic error of modern legal thought flows from the fact that jurists have systematically ignored the question of origins. This he attributes to the dominant influence of normativism and positivism, the effect of which has been to presuppose and bracket the violence of an original act of acquisition. Schmitt therefore returns to the question of origins for the purpose of restoring a more adequate understanding of the constitution of political authority and setting in place a more realistic concept of law. The core concept in his analysis is that of *nomos*. This chapter examines and evaluates Schmitt's treatment of this concept.

The original meaning of *nomos*

Schmitt investigates the meaning of *nomos* through an exposition in five introductory corollaries and three concluding corollaries to his major work, *The Nomos of the Earth in the International Law of the Jus Publicum Europaeum.*[9] His primary objective is to restore its original meaning. The crux of his argument is that the word has undergone many shifts in meaning over the last 3,000 years and its original meaning has since been overlooked. Although his explanation involves a significant amount of historical and philological analysis, Schmitt's purpose is juristic. The objective is to specify its original legal-constitutional meaning 'in its energy and majesty'[10] in order to demonstrate how jurists who

[9] C. Schmitt, *The Nomos of the Earth in the International Law of the Jus Publicum Europaeum* [1950] (New York, Telos, 2003), trans. G. L. Ulmen.
[10] Ibid., 67.

translate *nomos* simply as law or, if they are to differentiate it from written law, as custom do not get to the root of the matter.

The Greek noun *nomos*, Schmitt explains, derives from the Greek verb *nemein*, and, in common acceptance, *nemein* has three main meanings: these are (in German) *nehmen* (to appropriate), *teilen* (to divide) and *weiden* (to pasture). In its first meaning, it signifies a taking, especially a land appropriation. This process of land appropriation forms the basis of the history of every settled people and 'not only logically, but also historically, land-appropriation precedes the order that follows from it'. This first meaning of *nomos* thus signifies the constitution of 'the original spatial order, the source of all further concrete order and all further law'. Schmitt contends that 'all subsequent law and everything promulgated and enacted thereafter as decrees and commands are *nourished* ... by this source'.[11] Although the first meaning of *nomos* as an appropriation has long been forgotten in jurisprudence, Schmitt notes that the second – the process of division and distribution – has not. This original division and distribution is the basis of property. He shows this with reference to the passage in *Leviathan* in which Hobbes explains that 'the introduction of *propriety* is an effect of commonwealth'; it is the product of the law-making act of the sovereign. This, Hobbes notes, 'they well knew of old, who called that *Nomos,* that is to say, *distribution*, which we call law; and defined justice, by *distributing* to every man *his own*.'[12] *Nomos* in this second sense entails an authorized property distribution, the allotted share of goods within a commonwealth. Schmitt contends that the Earth is connected to law in three ways: 'She contains law within herself, as a reward for labour; she manifests law upon herself as fixed boundaries; and she sustains law above herself, as a public sign of order'.[13]

The third meaning of *nomos*, pasturage, signifies the type of productive activity that normally accompanies ownership. Through this type of activity, the division of land becomes more apparent. The land is 'delineated by fences, enclosures, boundaries, walls, houses and other constructs', and eventually 'the orders and orientations of human social life

[11] Ibid., 48.

[12] T. Hobbes, *Leviathan* (Cambridge University Press, 1996), ed. R. Tuck, Chap. 24.

[13] Schmitt, *The Nomos of the Earth*, 42. With respect to the law as the 'public sign of order', Schmitt notes the relation between this second meaning of *nomos* as *teilen* and the German word for judgement, *Urteil*, which in a literal sense (*Ur-teil*) means original division (p. 326).

become apparent'.[14] This third meaning 'obtains its content from the type and means of the production and manufacture of goods'.[15]

These three meanings of *nomos* are conceived to form a fixed relation: appropriation precedes division, just as division precedes production. Schmitt emphasizes two points. The first is that appropriation is the most fundamental stratum of *nomos*: the constitutive process of a land acquisition 'is found at the beginning of the history of every settled people, every commonwealth, every empire'.[16] No one 'can give, divide and distribute without taking', and in the beginning, 'there was no basic norm, but a basic appropriation'.[17] The second point is that this most basic stratum of *nomos* is the one that has been consistently repressed in modern thought. The sense of *nomos* as 'the first measure of all subsequent measures' and as 'the first partition and classification of space' has been eclipsed.

The shift in the meaning of *nomos*

Schmitt's explanation of the original meaning of *nomos* is corroborated in studies undertaken by classical scholars. Many have analyzed Pindar's Fragment 169, which speaks of *nomos basileus*, that is, *nomos* as king.[18] Although interpretation is notoriously difficult because of the semantic ambiguities of the term, it is commonly accepted that in Pindar's work, *nomos* is 'an all-pervasive power governing with extreme violence the affairs of both gods and men' and that this is conceived as a 'very general concept of a sovereign power governing everything, including the gods'. *Nomos* acts as 'a supreme regulator and an amoral, violent agent'.[19] In this understanding, *nomos* expresses a sense that violence or force is an intrinsic aspect of constitutive power. What results is not a vindication of 'might is right'. Rather, it is an expression of the tragic dimension to the political: political order is the product of necessity.

Classical scholars also explain that the term underwent a shift in meaning during the fifth century BC.[20] Before then, it was acknowledged

[14] Ibid., 42. [15] Ibid., 327. [16] Ibid., 48. [17] Ibid., 345.

[18] See, e.g., H. Lloyd-Jones, *'Pindar Fr. 169' in His Greek Epic, Lyric, and Tragedy* (Oxford, UK: Clarendon Press, 1990), 163–4. For Schmitt's account, see Schmitt, *The Nomos of the Earth*, 72–6.

[19] P. Kyriakou, 'The Violence of Nomos in Pindar fr. 169a', *Materiali e discussioni per l'analisi dei testi classici*, 48 (2002), 195–206 at 198–9.

[20] M. Ostwald, *Nomos and the Beginnings of the Athenian Democracy* (Oxford, UK: Clarendon Press, 1969); P. Cartledge, P. Millett and S. Todd (eds.), *Nomos: Essays in Athenian Law, Politics and Society* (New York: Cambridge University Press, 1991); F. M.

that *nomos* conferred a sense of obligation 'motivated less by the authority of the agent who imposed it than by the fact that it is regarded and accepted as valid by those who live under it'.[21] *Nomos* signified order. It acquired its more conventional meaning as statute only during the fifth century. The significance of this shift has been generally acknowledged, with Martin Ostwald explaining that it 'reflects a deeper change in Athenian thinking about the nature of law and the attitude of the Athenians toward their laws'.[22]

One consequence of this shift is that the original meaning of *nomos* was lost. This was aided by a series of distinctions drawn by the Sophists, the most important of which is that between *nomos* and *physis*. Since *physis* signified nature, drawing the two into antithesis led to a sense of opposition between *physis* (nature) and *nomos* (convention). This stressed the artificial and purely conventional aspect of laws, making *nomos* indistinguishable from mere prescription.[23] By counterposing *nomos* and *physis*, the original meaning of *nomos* was converted from a fact of life (*sein*) into a prescribed ought (*sollen*). As a mere norm, *nomos* could no longer 'be distinguished from *thesmos* (law or legislation), *psephisma* (plebiscite), or *rhema* (command), and from other categories whose content was not the inner measure of concrete order and orientation, but only statutes and acts'.[24]

Schmitt seeks to restore the original meaning of *nomos* 'not to breathe artificial new life into dead myths or to conjure up empty shadows'[25] but as part of the exercise of following the constitution of political authority to its source. All questions of collective order are to be traced back to the three processes of appropriation, distribution and production. The character of every legal, economic and social order is determined by answers to a set of basic questions. Where and how was it appropriated? Where and how was it divided? Where and how was it produced?[26] The Greek concept of *nomos* in its original meaning, as the concrete form of life established in answer to those questions, expresses this most basic grasp of the nature of legal ordering. *Nomos* is an expression of the constituent power to establish order through an original act of appropriation and division.

Cornford, *From Religion to Philosophy: A Study in the Origins of Western Speculation* (Princeton University Press, 1991), esp. 27–34.

[21] Ostwald, *Nomos and the Beginnings of the Athenian Democracy*, 55. [22] Ibid., 6.

[23] H. Arendt, *On Revolution* (Harmondsworth, UK: Penguin, 1963), 186.

[24] Schmitt, *The Nomos of the Earth*, 69. [25] Ibid. [26] Ibid., 327–8.

This philological exercise throws into relief the significance of the constitutive moment. Modern jurisprudence too readily works within the frame of an unquestioned established order that frames legal thought and conceptual practice. In a situation in which 'there is no longer any horizon other than the status quo', normativism and positivism 'become the most plausible and self-evident matters in the world'.[27] Further, once *nomos* becomes the antithesis of *physis* and 'ought' is separated from 'is', 'one could play endlessly on the antithesis of right and power'.[28] It is, for example, only once the shift in the meaning of *nomos* to that of 'mere enactment' has been accepted that Pindar's text can be interpreted as meaning 'nothing more than the arbitrary right of the stronger'.[29] By virtue of this shift, we lose sense of *nomos* as the constitutive act of spatial ordering, as 'the full immediacy of a legal power not mediated by laws' and as 'an act of legitimacy, whereby the legality of a mere law first is made meaningful'.[30] As a consequence, we lose sense of the true meaning of 'the normative power of the factual'.[31]

Restoring the original meaning of *nomos* thus serves the contemporary purpose of placing in question the authority of the predominant positivism and normativism of modern legal thought. Schmitt argues that today the term 'legality' has come to mean only 'the functional mode of a state bureaucracy', with the unfortunate consequence that 'terms, concepts, and conceptual antitheses of our contemporary, completely deteriorated situation are projected into discussions of the genuine and original word *nomos*'.[32] This process was aided by the manner in which the Sophists also made a connection between *nomos* and *logos*. *Logos*, meaning something which lacked passion and which therefore stood for reason, 'was placed above the instinctual and emotional character of the human individual'.[33] Schmitt identifies this move as the source of confusion over the contemporary idea of 'the rule of law'. This is because, recognizing that *nomos* is without passion, Aristotle contended that 'not men, but laws should rule'.[34] This, Schmitt argues, transforms the meaning of

27 Ibid., 341. 28 Ibid., 342. 29 Ibid., 73. 30 Ibid.

31 Ibid., 342. On 'the normative power of the factual' (*die normative Kraft des Faktischen*), see G. Jellinek, *Allgemeine Staatslehre*, 3rd edn. (Berlin: Springer, 1922), 337–44.

32 Schmitt, *The Nomos of the Earth* [1950], 71. 33 Ibid., 342.

34 Aristotle, *The Politics [c. 335–323 BC]* (Harmondsworth, UK: Penguin, 1981), trans. T. A. Sinclair, ed. T. J. Saunders, 226. Schmitt believes that Aristotle did in fact maintain elements of the original meaning of *nomos* but explains that it 'is necessary to read these

Pindar's *nomos basileus*, though the 'intellectual trick' can be identified only if the linguistic shift in the meaning of *nomos* has been grasped.[35]

The first *nomos* of the Earth

In ancient mythology, the Earth was known as the mother of law. The Earth contained within herself an inner measure, her fertility, and as land was cleared and cultivated by human effort, precise divisions were created and subsequently delineated by boundaries and enclosures. The Earth sustained law 'as a public sign of order'.[36] In its original meaning, *nomos* is recognized as the measure by which the land in a specific location is appropriated and divided and thereby determines the form of political, social and religious ordering. Measure, order and form coalesce to 'constitute a spatially concrete unity'.[37] *Nomos* is the unity of *Ordnung und Ortung*, of order and location, or, more euphoniously, of order and orientation.

In this way, law was bound to land. The *nomos* by which 'a people becomes settled, i.e., by which it becomes historically situated and turns a part of the Earth's surface into the force field of a particular order, becomes visible in the appropriation of land and in the founding of a city or colony'.[38] Law is founded on land appropriation: this appropriation is the 'primary legal title that underlies all subsequent law'.[39] Although the specific histories of law formation and settlement are varied, with a rich diversity of property law arrangements emerging in particular regimes, the original law of property derives from a 'common primeval act'. Every land appropriation 'creates a kind of supreme ownership of the community as a whole, even if the subsequent distribution of property does not remain purely communal'.[40]

This primeval act of land appropriation is the basis of all law. It is the 'terrestrial fundament' in which 'all law is rooted'.[41] Land appropriation precedes the distinction between private and public law, it precedes the distinction between *dominium* and *imperium*, and it in fact establishes the conditions in which such distinctions can evolve.[42] That land appropriation precedes the establishment of political order, both historically

passages in Aristotle's *Politics* very carefully, in order to recognize the difference with respect to modern ideologies of the "rule of law"' (Schmitt, *The Nomos of the Earth*, 68).

[35] Ibid., 342. [36] Ibid., 42. [37] Ibid., 70. [38] Ibid. [39] Ibid., 46.

[40] Ibid., 45. [41] Ibid., 47. [42] Ibid., 46.

and logically, has been recognized by many great legal philosophers. Schmitt cites, by way of illustration, Vico's account of the first division and demarcation of the land,[43] Locke's recognition of the significance of 'radical title' which establishes political authority through jurisdiction over the land,[44] and Kant's acknowledgement of the fact that 'supreme proprietorship of the soil' forms the basis of 'territorial sovereignty'.[45]

Since *nomos* is a measure that constitutes a concrete spatial unity, it establishes a boundary which divides internal and external. Originally determined by mythical notions, 'such as the ocean, the Midgard Serpent, or the Pillars of Hercules', the security of these regimes was maintained by 'exclusionary defensive structures, such as border fortifications' whose purpose 'was to separate a pacified order from a quarrelsome disorder, a cosmos from a chaos, a house from a non-house, an enclosure from a wilderness'.[46] From this division between inside and outside, a people is formed. That is, a people is created not by blood ties but by virtue of being situated in a concrete order or *nomos*. This people, attached to a common territory and bound by commitment to a common way of life, constitutes an 'intensity of association' able to form a group organized on a friend/enemy antithesis.[47] Every powerful people considered 'their dominion to be the domicile of freedom, beyond which war, barbarism, and chaos ruled'.[48] The boundary division between internal and external became the boundary division of peace and war, establishing the essential conditions for state formation.[49]

Nomos is an *ordo ordinans*, an order of ordering, which performs the constitutive act of establishing a spatially determined regime of rule.

[43] Vico, *The First New Science* [1725] (Cambridge University Press, 2002), trans. L. Pompa, Chap. XXVI.

[44] J. Locke, *Two Treatises of Government* (Cambridge University Press, 1998), ed. P. Laslett, vol. II, §121.

[45] I. Kant, *Metaphysical Elements of Justice (Part I of the Metaphysics of Morals; known as the Rechtslehre)* (Indianapolis, IN: Hackett, 1999), trans. J. Ladd, Part II: Public Right, Note B (land rights); Schmitt, *The Nomos of the Earth*, 46–8.

[46] Schmitt, *The Nomos of the Earth*, 52.

[47] C. Schmitt, *The Concept of the Political* [1932] (University of Chicago Press, 1996), trans. G. Schwab, 38.

[48] Schmitt, *The Nomos of the Earth*, 352.

[49] In the second concluding corollary, '*Nomos* – *Nahme* – Name', Schmitt also explains how *nomos* is not only the source of the German word *nehmen* (to take) but also *nahmen* (to name). There is, he argues, a close relation between taking and naming: 'A land-appropriation is constituted only if the appropriator is able to give the land a name' (Schmitt, *The Nomos of the Earth*, 336–50, at 348).

Schmitt notes that the Greek term *archy* means 'from the source' and, as monarchy, signals monotheistic power emanating from God. Similarly, *cracy* means 'power through superior force and occupation', as in aristocracy and democracy. *Nomos*, he explains, penetrates both *archy* and *cracy*, and neither can exist without *nomos*.[50] The critical point is that *nomos*, 'even if it were to be raised to the level of a personalized ruler, is something impersonal'.[51] Monarchies, aristocracies and democracies all aim to rule 'in the name of the law'. When Schmitt argues that law 'is certainly power and appropriation, but as pure law it is only pure appropriation',[52] he reveals *nomos* as the fundamental 'law of the political'.[53]

Although land appropriation is the primal act of law creation, there was in a strict sense no '*nomos* of the Earth' before the great Age of Discovery, 'when the earth first was encompassed and measured by the global consciousness of European peoples'.[54] Consequently, no global sense of the planet existed before the fifteenth century. The first phase of *nomos* was entirely land bound, it placed Europe at the centre of the Earth, and its reach was limited to the boundaries of European empires.[55] This first phase of *nomos* was eroded only when the oceans were made accessible for exploration and the Earth was, for the first time, circumnavigated.

The second phase of *nomos*

The second phase of *nomos*, the first global *nomos*, arose because of discoveries made of land and sea by European peoples. This opened up a new spatial order of the Earth as the European powers competed for land appropriations in these newly discovered territories. Through exploration and contest, the European peoples 'appropriated, divided and utilized the planet'.[56]

[50] Ibid., 337–8. [51] Ibid., 338. [52] Ibid., 349.

[53] I develop this point further in M. Loughlin, 'Politonomy' in J. Meierhenreich and O. Simons (eds.), *The Oxford Handbook of Carl Schmitt* (New York: Oxford University Press, 2015), Chap. 21 (www.oxfordhandbooks.com/view/10.1093/oxfordhb/9780199916931.001.0001/oxfordhb-9780199916931-e-004?rskey=S6qDb8&result=3).

[54] Schmitt, *The Nomos of the Earth*, 49.

[55] In *Land und Meer: eine weltgeschichtliche Betrachtung* (Leipzig: Reclam, 1942), Schmitt argues that although pre-modern regimes, such as Athens, Rome and Venice, did develop a sea-faring culture, they remained fundamentally tied to the land, with the 'inland sea' of the Mediterranean remaining a boundary line (at 23–5).

[56] *Schmitt, The Nomos of the Earth*, 352.

In the newly discovered continent of America, this appropriation was achieved by the establishment of colonies in what was characterized as 'free space', 'an area open to European occupation and expansion'.[57] Lands in Asia could not be appropriated in similar manner, and in this sphere of the globe, 'the Eurocentric structure of *nomos* extended only partially, as open land-appropriation, and otherwise in the form of protectorates, leases, trade agreements, and spheres of interest; in short, in more elastic forms of utilization.'[58] And it was only during the nineteenth century that the European powers were able to undertake the task of dividing up the continent of Africa. The essential point, however, is that this second phase of *nomos* was global in reach but entirely Eurocentric in structure.

This phase of *nomos*, lasting for a period of about four hundred years, resulted in a new set of appropriations, distributions and divisions. The on-going struggle between the European powers was stabilized as a result of the emergence of a dual set of balances: between land and sea, on the one hand, and between the land powers on the European continent, on the other. The first involved a balance between land and sea because there was no balance of sea powers: the British alone came to dominate the seas. And the balance of the European land powers, Schmitt maintains, was also underpinned by British sea power.

The emergence of these power balances during this second phase of *nomos* was of considerable legal significance. This is because, within this second phase, a new European spatial order founded on the institution of the state was created. The state, understood as a territorially enclosed organized political entity, was established as a consequence of these power balances. As Schmitt emphasizes, 'statehood' is not a universal category, 'valid for all times and all peoples'. It is 'a concrete historical fact', and the 'singular historical particularity of this phenomenon called "state" lies in the fact that this political entity was the vehicle of secularization'.[59] It became the institution that could neutralize religious conflicts and end 'the European civil war of churches and religious parties'.[60] Recognition of the territorial order of the state – 'spatially self-contained, impermeable, unburdened with the problem of estate, ecclesiastical and creedal civil wars' – was an achievement of the second phase of *nomos*.[61]

The formation of the state became the foundation on which an elaborate set of concepts and practices of modern public law could evolve.

[57] Ibid., 87. [58] Ibid., 352. [59] Ibid., 127. [60] Ibid., 128. [61] Ibid., 129.

Although an entirely European creation, these public law concepts assumed a global significance in the modern era through colonization or other forms of imperialism and hegemonic influence. The pivotal concept of public law is that of sovereignty, which signifies in jural form the essential nature and quality of political relationships that emerge within this second phase of *nomos*. Sovereignty has both external and internal dimensions. One set of relations concerns the position of the state in the international arena. A regime is recognized as a sovereign state when its governing authority is in no way legally dependent on any higher authority, whether that of pope or emperor. Correlating with this external aspect is the internal dimension. From the internal perspective, sovereignty expresses the conviction that the state is the ultimate source of law. There can be no fetter on the law-making authority of the state, whether deriving from divine law or from natural law. The law made by the authorized institutions of the state – the positive law – is supreme. Sovereignty expresses the state's independent status as a political entity in the world and its absolute authority to make law.

The sovereign state is an autonomous entity that acknowledges other similar entities in the sphere of international relations on the basis of formal equality. During this second phase of *nomos*, this status of sovereignty, which was confined mainly to the European powers, created the circumstances for the establishment of public international law. Established within the frame of the *jus publicum Europaeum*, these rules reflected the nature of these balances, not least in drawing a distinction between land and sea with respect to concepts of war, enemy and booty.[62]

Schmitt explains that in international law, land war 'was not conducted between peoples, but only between the armies of European states', and the 'private property of civil populations was not booty according to international law'. Sea war, by contrast, was essentially war over commerce, and in sea war, 'the enemy was any state with which the opponent had commercial dealings'. Consequently, the 'private property of civil populations of warring states, and even of neutrals with whom they had trade relations was fair booty, according to blockade and prize law'.[63]

[62] See Schmitt, *Land und Meer*, note 26, esp. 42–6, where he explains that the sea could never be bounded in the same way as land, and as a consequence, the distinction between trade, conflict and piracy could not be clearly drawn.

[63] Schmitt, *The Nomos of the Earth*, 353.

The event that shapes the form of this new body of law is that of discovery and colonial expansion: 'when an old world sees a new one arise beside it, it is challenged dialectically and is no longer old in the same sense'.[64] The opening up of new worlds provided the exceptional conditions that helped to normalize the rules of interaction in the old. This operated across two dimensions. First, a distinction arose between ordered land and free sea, illustrated by the fact that although the Stuart kings were bound by the *lex terrae* in their domestic affairs, their prerogative powers were considered absolute on the seas.[65] Colonial expansion thus provided opportunities for sovereigns to exercise their prerogative powers 'beyond the seas' untrammelled by the 'law of the land'.[66] Secondly, the significance of the establishment of 'amity lines' became of vital importance in formalizing rules of international law. These amity lines, marked by treaties between European powers, sought mainly to delineate spheres of jurisdiction. By marking the lines at which 'Europe' ended and the 'new world' began, they also established the boundary between norm and exception.[67] In doing so, they helped to

64 Ibid., 87.

65 It might be noted that the boundary line between prerogative (abroad) and law (at home) is the central constitutional question in the case of Ship Money: *R* v. *Hampden* (1637) 3 St.Tr. 825. More generally, note the debate between Grotius and Selden on the question of free or closed seas and the issues of state policy that underpinned it: see H. Grotius, *Mare Liberum* (1609); J. Selden, *Mare Clausum* (1619), discussed extensively in R. Tuck, *Natural Rights Theories: Their Origin and Development* (Cambridge University Press, 1979), 59–63, 86–91; R. Tuck, *Philosophy and Government, 1572–1651* (Cambridge University Press, 1993), 170–9, 212–7; R. Tuck, *The Rights of War and Peace: Political Thought and the International Order from Grotius to Kant* (Oxford University Press, 1999), 90–4, 114–20. Tuck explains that Grotius' work 'had in fact been prepared . . . at the express request of the East Indies Company, who wished to influence the peace negotiations then in progress' (*Philosophy*, 170) and that the first draft of Selden's work was never published until 1635, when it was 'completely rewritten at the request of Charles's government, as part of its anti-Dutch propaganda' (*Philosophy*, 212) and in the context of a fishing dispute between England and Holland and which 'led, incidentally, to Ship Money; the fleet for which the tax was intended was designed to protect English fishing' (*Natural Rights*, 86).

66 This general point is more complicated in British practice since the legal position with respect to colonies depended on whether they had been settled or conquered. If the former, British subjects carried their common-law rights with them, whereas colonies by conquest or cession fell under the Crown's prerogative power without limitation: see, *Calvin's Case* (1608) 7 Co.Rep. 1a, at 17b; *Campbell* v. *Hall* Lofft 655, 741; *Forbes* v. *Cochrane* (1824) 2 B.& C. 448; *Campbell* v. *Kyte* (1835) 3 Knapp 332.

67 See, e.g., A. Pagden, *Lords of All the World: Ideologies of Empire in Spain, Britain and France c. 1500–1800* (New Haven, CT: Yale University Press, 1995); D. Armitage, *The Ideological Origins of the British Empire* (Cambridge University Press, 2000), esp. Chap. 4.

embed the rules of public international law within the 'normal' boundaries of European engagement, leading to a bracketing and formalization of war. But beyond these lines, the conventions of European public law had no meaning: 'the struggle for land-appropriations knew no bounds', there were no legal limits to the conduct of war, and 'only the law of the stronger applied'.[68]

This second phase of the *nomos* of the Earth – the first on a global basis – established a Eurocentric order that left it marked in measurement (think only of the Greenwich meridian), in naming (think only of America, Louisiana, New Amsterdam/New York), but most of all by the distinction between the juridical processes of 'constitutionalization' of the state and formalization of international law within the 'norm' of the European spatial order and colonization through settlement or subjugation (or both) in the 'exceptional' spheres beyond. When Hobbes in the mid-seventeenth century used the device of the state of nature characterized as a 'war of all against all' to resolve the problem of the foundation, he had in mind not only the threat of European religious wars but also the race for land appropriation 'beyond the pale' in the new world. That is, the image of the state of nature could be deployed not only as a temporal heuristic to address the issue of foundational origins but also as a spatial heuristic to differentiate a sphere of civilization from that of chaos. When in the late seventeenth century Locke evokes a more benign image of life in a state of nature to justify the establishment of a liberal constitutional regime, he nevertheless has this distinction between norm and exception in mind. 'In the beginning', he reminds us, 'all the world was America.'[69] And when in 1670 Pascal wrote that 'three degrees of latitude overthrow jurisprudence', 'a meridian determines the truth' and 'law has its periods', he was not dealing with the banalities of differences in the laws of different states. Pascal's meridian, Schmitt suggests, 'is actually nothing but the amity lines of his time, which had created an abyss between freedom (the lawlessness of the state of nature) and an orderly "civil" mode of existence'.[70]

[68] Schmitt, *The Nomos of the Earth*, 93–4.

[69] Locke, *Two Treatises of Government*, note 20, §49: 'thus in the beginning all the World was America, and more so than that is now.' See Schmitt, *The Nomos of the Earth*, 96–7.

[70] Schmitt, *The Nomos of the Earth*, 95. Schmitt notes that Grotius and Pufendorf were similarly influenced. He argues that although some European powers concluded treaties with native leaders, 'no European power considered itself to be the legal successor to the natives.' In asserting their position, he explains, they are not relying on classical sources

Law as institutional order

This Eurocentric *nomos* of the Earth drew to a close as a consequence of the First World War.[71] Schmitt's argument on this point is complicated, but in outline it concerns the relativization of Europe as a consequence of the growth of American power and the influence of other non-European states; the decline of *jus publicum Europaeum* and the conversion of international law into a set of universal norms lacking substance; the consequent growth of a 'normative industry' leading to the 'nihilistic inflation of numberless, contradictory pacts emptied of any content by stated or unstated provisos'[72] and generating 'an illusory science of international law'[73]; and, given the inability to establish a global balance, the emergence of an east-west 'cold war' driven by a dialectic of isolation and intervention.

These developments have resulted in the displacement of the European-centred order established on a land-based balance of power: in place of European powers determining the spatial order of the world, during the twentieth century the world determined the spatial order of Europe. The balance between sea and land was also undermined, not only by the loss of British domination of the seas but also as a result of the emergence of technologies that have 'robbed the sea of its elemental character'[74] and have created a third dimension – airspace – which has established itself as a new battleground and transformed understanding of the *nomos* of the Earth. Schmitt contends that every new age comes into existence as a result of new spatial divisions, resulting in the formation of new spatial orders of the Earth. Writing in the 1950s, he believed that either one of the superpowers would defeat the other and that this would be the staging for the ultimate unification of the Earth or, more

but on the distinction Grotius makes between original and derivative acquisition: *De jure belli ac pacis* (1625), Book II, Chap. 2 (Schmitt, *The Nomos of the Earth*, 136). And Pufendorf recognizes 'a type of original property acquisition that takes the form of a "common seizure by a majority of persons"', which involves the creation of 'general property' and thus to be distinguished from 'the origin of specific private property'. See S. Pufendorf, *De jure naturae et gentium* (1672), Book 4, Chap. 6 (Acquisition by Virtue of the Right of the Initial Occupant). This, Schmitt concludes, is 'very close to actual land-appropriation' (Schmitt, *The Nomos of the Earth*, 137).

71 For a general appraisal, see M. Koskenniemi, 'Histories of International Law: Dealing with Eurocentrism', *Rechtsgeschichte*, 19 (2011), 152–76, at 158: 'Until late-19th century, histories of international law were unthinkingly Eurocentric. Europe served as the origin, engine and *telos* of historical knowledge. In the 20th century, it became more difficult to articulate the normative goal of international law.'

72 Schmitt, *The Nomos of the Earth*, 239. 73 Ibid., 243. 74 Ibid., 354.

likely, that a new equilibrium would emerge constituted by the existence of several relatively independent *Großräume*.

My objective here is not to speculate about these developments but to try to understand the general significance of Schmitt's argument about law as *nomos*. His most basic point with respect to the issue of origins is that order, in the beginning, was not established on the basis of consent or on some universal principle or a basic norm. In the beginning, there was a land grab, and only after the violence of that initial appropriation and division had been completed, 'when the problems of founding anew and of transition have been surpassed', could 'some degree of calculability and security' be achieved and *nomos* emerge as the expression of order.[75] Like Pascal's concept of custom, law evolves; it is not fully formed at the foundation, though it remains 'nourished' by this source.

Nomos founds a concrete spatial entity, but the basis of order continues to evolve in response to answers offered to 'the fundamental question of the problematic sequence of appropriation, distribution, and production'.[76] World history 'is the history of development in the object, means, and forms of appropriation interpreted as progress'. It is a development proceeding from 'the *land-appropriations* of nomadic and agrarian-feudal times to the *sea-appropriations* of the 16th to the 19th century, over the *industry-appropriations* of the industrial-technical age and its distinction between developed and underdeveloped areas, and finally, to the *air–appropriations* and *space-appropriations* of the present'.[77] The concrete form of *nomos* thus alters according to the development of world history.

From this account it is evident that *nomos* carries a rather different connotation to that of the norms of positive law. Law as *nomos* is an expression of the substantive order of a political unity created by the processes of appropriation, division and production. Given this understanding, *nomos* can now be related to other key concepts, such as state and constitution. For Schmitt, the state is 'the concrete, collective

[75] Ibid., 341.

[76] Ibid., 333. See also 330–5, where Schmitt shows the contrasting positions of various liberal and socialist theories. Whereas liberalism 'solves the social question with reference to increases in production and consumption' (331), socialist positions vary: Fourier 'subsumed all problems of appropriation and distribution under a fantastic increase in production', Proudhon's socialism is 'essentially a doctrine of division and distribution' (333) and Marx's launched an attack 'on the expropriation of the expropriators' (334).

[77] Ibid., 347.

condition of political unity';[78] in modernity, it becomes the 'master ordering concept' of this political unity.[79] It is similarly clear that Schmitt's concept of constitution (in its absolute sense) differs from the notion of constitutional law as that enacted in modern documentary form. Since the order that emerges within the state arises from 'a pre-established, unified will',[80] Schmitt argues that the state 'does not *have* a constitution'; rather, 'the state *is* constitution'. In this sense, the state/constitution is 'an actually present condition, a *status* of unity and order'.[81] The basic law of the state finds its authoritative expression not in enacted legal norms but in 'the political existence of the state'.[82]

Once brought into alignment, it would appear that state (the political unity), constitution (the status of unity and order) and *nomos* (the order of a concrete spatial unity) are, to all intents and purposes, synonyms. Schmitt recognizes that, like *nomos*, the state and the constitution continue to evolve: the state expresses 'the principle of the *dynamic emergence* of political unity, of the process of constantly renewed *formation* and *emergence* of this *unity* from a fundamental or ultimately effective *power* and *energy*'.[83] And he recognizes that the 'continuity of a constitution is manifest as long as the regress to this primary appropriation is recognizable and recognized'.[84] If state highlights unity and constitution the form of that unity, then *nomos* accentuates the motive forces that shape the form of that unity: it is 'the full immediacy of a legal power not mediated by laws; it is a constitutive historical event – an act of *legitimacy*, whereby the legality of a mere law first is made meaningful'.[85]

In earlier studies, such as *Political Theology* and *Constitutional Theory*, Schmitt had emphasized the decisionist elements of order maintenance: the sovereign is thus identified as the institution that 'decides' when the norm is displaced in the exceptional moment,[86] and constituent power 'is the political will, whose power or authority is capable of making the concrete, comprehensive decision over the type and form of its own

[78] C. Schmitt, *Constitutional Theory* [1928] (Durham, NC: Duke University Press, 2008), trans. J. Seitzer, 65.
[79] C. Schmitt, 'Staat als ein konkreter, an eine geschichtliche Epoche gebundener Begriff' [1941] in Schmitt, *Verfassungsrechtliche Aufsätze aus den Jahren 1924–1954* (Berlin: Duncker & Humblot, 1958), 375–85, at 375: 'In diesem Zeitalter . . . ist der Staat der alles beherrschende Ordnungsbegriff der politischen Einheit.'
[80] Schmitt, *Constitutional Theory*, note 78, 65. [81] Ibid., 60. [82] Ibid., 65.
[83] Ibid., 61. [84] Schmitt, *The Nomos of the Earth*, 325, note 6. [85] Ibid., 73.
[86] C. Schmitt, *Political Theology: Four Chapters on the Concept of Sovereignty* [1922] (University of Chicago Press, 2005), trans. G. Schwab, 5.

political existence'.[87] By the late 1920s, however, Schmitt started to shift the emphasis of his argument. In place of decision, he accentuated the institutional aspect of unity and order. This is evident in the Preface to the second edition of *Political Theology* in 1933, in which he writes that 'I now distinguish not two but *three* types of legal thinking; in addition to the normativist and the decisionist types there is the institutional one'.[88] 'Whereas the pure normativist thinks in terms of impersonal rules, and the decisionist implements the good law of the correctly recognized political situation by means of a personal decision, institutional legal thinking unfolds in institutions and organizations that transcend the personal sphere.'[89] Institutional thinking seeks to capture 'the stable content' inherent in the political unity.

This institutional argument is most clearly presented in his 1934 book, *On the Three Types of Juristic Thought*.[90] In this work, Schmitt explained that all legal theories comprise three basic elements: norm, decision and concrete order formation. Legal theories may be distinguished according to the emphasis they place on each of these elements, and the type of political regime they envisage is invariably linked to the predominance given to one or other of these elements: 'Every form of political life stands in direct, mutual relationship with the specific mode of thought and argumentation of legal life.'[91] In this work, Schmitt again criticizes normativism, but he also argues against decisionism and in favour of a type of institutionalism that he calls 'concrete-order' thinking.[92]

[87] Schmitt, *Constitutional Theory*, note 78, 125.

[88] Schmitt, *Political Theology*, note 42, 2. [89] Ibid., 3.

[90] C. Schmitt, *On the Three Types of Juristic Thought* [1934] (Westport, CT: Praeger, 2004), trans. J. Bendersky. In his introduction, Bendersky, explains the shift in the following terms: 'It was one thing to advocate sovereign decisionism within the Weimar constitutional framework or even to entrust Paul von Hindenburg, a political figure of proven responsibility deeply devoted to German traditions and western civilization generally, with broad exceptional powers in an *Ausnahmezustand*. It was quite another when such decisions would be made by the leader of a dynamic, revolutionary movement unrestrained by the values, traditions, and institutions that conservatives such as Schmitt cherished' (at 14). This may be right, but there would appear to be more basic theoretical reasons for this shift, and these difficulties were evident even in 1928, when in his *Constitutional Theory* he recognized the importance of homogeneity in democratic order.

[91] Ibid. 45.

[92] This could not be termed institutionalism because Schmitt – for evident political reasons in 1934 – sought to avoid any association with neo-Thomism exhibited in Hauriou's work: see Bendersky's note in *On the Three Types of Juristic Thought* above n. 90, 112 (note 59).

For institutionalism, order is not primarily the product of a set of rules. Norms or rules do not create order; they perform a regulatory function only on the basis of an already-established order. Normativism remains an appealing type, especially in comparison to the personal character of decisionism, primarily because it 'can appeal to being impersonal and objective'.[93] Schmitt argues that in various formulations that emanate from Pindar's *Nomos basileus*, including *Rex*, *Lex* and the idea of a *Rechtsstaat*, normativists promote the 'rule of law' over the 'rule of men'. But he explains that *nomos* 'does not mean statute, rule, or norm, but rather *Recht*, which is norm, as well as decision and, above all, order'.[94] The 'rule of law' cannot mean simply 'the rule of rules'; it must 'contain certain of the highest, unalterable, but concrete ordering qualities'.[95] He emphasizes that one 'can speak of a true *Nomos* as true king only if *Nomos* means precisely the concept of *Recht* encompassing a concrete order and *Gemeinschaft*'.[96]

Normativists promote a purely conceptualistic understanding of law, law as a set of rules and principles. The arguments of decisionists, by contrast, are reduced ultimately to factual analysis. Institutionalism (concrete-order thinking) is Schmitt's attempt to finesse the distinction between normativity and facticity.[97] Rules and decisions are integral parts of legal order, but they carry meaning only as formulations of concrete order. Law as norm does not yield sound jurisprudence because a norm 'cannot apply, administer, or enforce itself', and decisionism is not sustainable because a legal decision does not spring from a normative vacuum.[98] Legal order is maintained as an expression of the underlying order of *nomos*. Rules and decisions achieve regularity by reliance on 'concepts of what, in itself, is normal, the normal type and the normal situation'.[99]

Schmitt's concrete-order thinking has many similarities with the institutionalism propounded by the early-twentieth-century French public lawyer Maurice Hauriou.[100] Hauriou, whose work Schmitt admired,[101]

93 Ibid. 49. 94 Ibid., 50. 95 Ibid., 50 (translation modified). 96 Ibid., 50–1.
97 Ibid., 53. 98 Ibid., 51, 62. 99 Ibid., 54.
100 Hauriou developed a juristic concept of 'directing ideas' (*idées directrices*) that, he claimed, performed a generative role in the shaping and giving meaning to public institutions. Directing ideas give meaning to the basic principles of French public law, which unfold progressively with the power to shape the character of governmental institutions. See M. Hauriou, *Précis de Droit Constitutionnel*, 2nd edn. (Paris: Sirey, 1929), esp. 73–4.
101 Schmitt refers to Hauriou as 'the master of our discipline' (Schmitt, *The Nomos of the Earth* [1950], 210). See also C. Schmitt, *Legality and Legitimacy* [1932] (Durham, NC: Duke University Press, 2004), trans. J. Seitzer, 57 (referring to Hauriou as 'an outstanding French public law specialist').

is particularly helpful in this respect since Schmitt does not specify in much detail what he means by institution. Hauriou argued that the basis of legal order was not social contract, nor the 'rule of law', nor legislative authority, nor even directly the state. The 'real basis' of legal order, he explained, is 'the institution'.[102] Institutions, which stand for 'duration, continuity, and reality', provide the juridical basis of the state.[103]

Hauriou drew a clear distinction between institution and positive law. He emphasized that '[i]nstitutions make juridical rules; juridical rules do not make institutions.'[104] Institutions are generative and provide stability and continuity, whereas legal rules 'only stand for ideas of limitation instead of incarnating ideas of enterprise and of creation'.[105] The distinctive function of the institution is to transform 'an organization of fact into an organization of law' and thereby to transform 'the real into the right'.[106] Hauriou's concept of institution comprises three main elements: the ordering idea (*idée directrice*), the formation of a power able to structure and give effect to the idea, and a widespread acceptance of the directing idea in social and political practice.[107] Schmitt's concept of concrete order is similar to Hauriou's concept of institution. Schmitt also follows Hauriou in taking over his concept of *superlégalité*: super-legality refers to that set of principles and institutions that give form to this concrete order.[108] Super-legality, resting on shared understandings, has affinities with Pascal's notion of 'present custom'.[109] And it can be grasped as an expression of *nomos*.

[102] M. Hauriou, 'An Interpretation of the Principles of Public Law', *Harvard Law Review*, 31 (1918), 813–21, at 813.

[103] M. Hauriou, 'The Theory of the Institution and the Foundation: A Study in Social Vitalism' [1925] in A. Broderick (ed.), *The French Institutionalists* (Cambridge, MA: Harvard University Press, 1970), 93–124, at 93.

[104] Ibid. See also Schmitt, *On the Three Types of Juristic Thought*, note 90, 57: 'a change in the norm is more the consequence than the source of a change in the order.'

[105] Hauriou, 'The Theory of the Institution and the Foundation', 123. See R. Cover, '*Nomos* and Narrative', *Harvard Law Review*, 97 (1983), 4 (on juris-generative and juris-pathic tendencies).

[106] Hauriou, 'An Interpretation of the Principles of Public Law', note 102, 815. He accepts that in the beginning, 'an organization is created simply by force' and then seeks peace. But, to obtain peace, 'the new organization must obtain pardon for its origin . . . peaceful existence is possible only when the demands of law are satisfied' (816).

[107] Hauriou, 'The Theory of the Institution and the Foundation', note 103, esp. 123.

[108] This is analogous to the idea of constituent power: see ibid., 114; Schmitt, *Legality and Legitimacy*, note 101, 57–8. See C. Klein, *Théorie et pratique du pouvoir constituant* (Paris: PUF, 1996), 159.

[109] Schmitt, *On the Three Types of Juristic Thought*, note 90, 86: 'Thus English case law would embody an example of concrete-order thinking, which adheres exclusively to the inner *Recht* of a specific case. The precedent, including its decision, then becomes the

Schmitt's institutionalism brings his legal thought much closer to Hegel's legal and political philosophy, in which 'the state is a "form (*Gestalt*), which is the complete realization of the spirit in being (*Dasein*)"; an "individual totality", a *Reich* of objective reason and morality'.[110] This type of state, he emphasizes, is not an 'order of a calculable and enforceable legal functionalism' (i.e., the product of decisionism), nor is it a 'norm of norms' (normativism). The state 'is the concrete order of orders, the institution of institutions'.[111] Schmitt notes that 'the concrete jurisprudential consideration of an orderly state administration can best provide the element of a general theory of "institutions": jurisdictional authority, hierarchy of offices, inner autonomy, internal counterbalancing of opposing forces and tendencies, inner discipline, honour, and official secrets, and with these the all-important fundamental presupposition, namely a normal stabilized situation, a *situation établie.*'[112] This, it might be noted, is not Hegel's state, in which the universal is willed; it more closely approximates his concept of *Notstaat*, the state based on need, an expression of the form within civil society 'wherein the livelihood, happiness, and legal status of one man is interwoven with the livelihood, happiness, and rights of all'.[113]

Schmitt provides a more specific illustration of his institutionalism in *Staat, Bewegung, Volk* (1933), his highly controversial attempt to sketch a constitutional framework for the Nazi regime.[114] He seeks to show that the entire basis of public law, including those provisions taken over from the Weimar Constitution, is now 'situated in a completely new context'.[115] Relations between offices of state can no longer be determined 'through formalistic ... interpretations of the words of the Weimar Constitution' since public law must 'promote awareness of the fact that the absolute supremacy of political leadership is the effective

concrete paradigm for all subsequent cases, which have their *Recht* concretely in themselves – not in a norm or a decision.' See also C. B. Gray, *The Methodology of Maurice Hauriou* (Amsterdam: Rodopi, 2010), 91: 'Practical direction gives custom a great role in law of creating a system of legal expectations, of "superlegality", since the question of such ends is not the question inside of law.'

110 Schmitt, *On the Three Types of Juristic Thought*, note 90, 78. 111 Ibid., 78–9.

112 Ibid., 87–8.

113 G. W. F. Hegel, *Philosophy of Right* [1821] (Oxford University Press, 1952), trans. T. M. Knox, §183.

114 C. Schmitt, *Staat, Bewegung, Volk: Die Dreigliederung der politischen Einheit* (Hamburg: Hanseatische Verlagsanstalt, 1933).

115 Ibid., 9.

basic law of today's state'.[116] Political unity is the product of a tripartite synthesis of state, movement and people which provides 'the essential structural and organizational policies of the concrete arrangement of the state'.[117] This unity is not determined by positive law (*Legalität*), which has become merely 'the functioning mode of the state administrative apparatus'; rather 'to the law (*Recht*) in a substantive sense belongs the first guarantee of securing political unity'.[118] Every state 'needs a coherent internal logic of its institutions and norms' and 'a unitary form of thought (*formgedanken*) that gives constancy of shape (*Gestalt*) to all the spheres of public life'.[119] However various the rules and regulations may be, a 'consistent main principle must be recognized and maintained'.[120] Though he does not use the expression, Schmitt here contrasts positive law and *nomos*.

Nomos in contemporary jurisprudence

The concept of *nomos* features prominently in the work of Friedrich Hayek and Michael Oakeshott. Both use *nomos* in its post-fifth-century meaning, suggesting an equation between the terms *nomos basileus* and 'the rule of law'. For Schmitt, this usage is an 'intellectual trick', since Hayek and Oakeshott construct their accounts on the distinction between norm and decision, with *nomos* being understood as meaning 'norm' rather than 'concrete order'.

The idea of order plays a key role in Hayek's thought, but it is not conceived as an independent variable. By drawing a sharp distinction between spontaneous order (organism) and constructed order (organization), Hayek effectively absorbs the idea of order into either norm or decision.[121] Spontaneous order is associated with the emergence of an idea of law as evolving rules of just conduct and therefore as a set of norms, and constructed order is tied to an image of law as command (legislation) and consequently is treated as the product of decision.[122] Having identified the distinction between norm and decision as the central tension of legal order, Hayek contends that *nomos*, which he calls 'the law of liberty', yields the true meaning of law. *Nomos* is taken to be an expression of universal rules of just conduct; in its true meaning, law

[116] Ibid., 10. [117] Ibid., 11. [118] Ibid., 15. [119] Ibid., 33. [120] Ibid., 33.
[121] F. A. Hayek, *Law, Legislation and Liberty*, vol. 1: *Rules and Order* (London: Routledge, 1973), Chap. 2.
[122] Ibid., Chaps. 4–6.

acts as a restraint on the exercise of power. Law as legislation, by contrast, conceives of law as an instrument of power.[123] For Hayek, the emergence of the latter conception of law – which consists predominantly of public (as distinct from private) law[124] – has been a retrograde step, is inimical to liberty[125] and must be strictly restrained.[126]

Oakeshott comes closer to sharing Schmitt's view of legal order. Since 'all governments began in violence', Oakeshott acknowledges that the attempt to locate authority in origins will prove fruitless. He is also sceptical of the attempt to convert the question of authority into a philosophical problem that can be resolved by contract and consent.[127] Authority is established not by virtue of a specific historical *event* but from a much more haphazard historical *process* in which force, in order to preserve its own position, is eventually required to yield to customary practice. 'All were aware of anarchy just below the surface', Oakeshott notes, and few modern governments 'have won for themselves anything but a very precarious authority'.[128] He notes that the process by which 'power' is obliged to work through customary ways might be regarded as one in which power is 'moralized'. But he suggests that it is better conceived as being analogous to the rights of squatters, that is, as involving a process in which 'rights' to govern 'grow out of acquiescence and the absence of objection, and they are acquired by prescription, when what was once a demand receives recognition as a "rightful" claim'.[129]

Oakeshott's treatment of political order differs considerably from Hayek's and is much closer to that of Pascal. He recognizes that if, like Hayek, the state is conceived to be analogous to an organism, then, strictly, there is no place for a ruler or for government: 'It would live and move as a vital unit, its vitality being continuously distributed in all its parts.'[130] This, in Oakeshott's view, falls into the category of 'implausible and gimcrack beliefs'[131] – 'the sort of thing only a philosopher would

123 Ibid., 92. 124 Ibid., 132.
125 F. A. Hayek, *Law, Legislation and Liberty,* vol. 2: *The Mirage of Social Justice* (London: Routledge, 1975).
126 F. A. Hayek, *Law, Legislation and Liberty,* vol. 3: *The Political Order of a Free People* (London: Routledge, 1979).
127 M. Oakeshott, *Lectures in the History of Political Thought* (Exeter, UK: Imprint Academic, 2006), 465.
128 M. Oakeshott, *On Human Conduct* (Oxford, UK: Clarendon Press, 1975), 190–1.
129 Oakeshott, *Lectures in the History of Political Thought*, note 127, 466–7.
130 Ibid., 405. 131 Oakeshott, *On Human Conduct*, note 128, 191.

think of'.[132] The ambiguous character of the state can be grasped, he suggests, only by considering two images of the state that manage to incorporate important directions of thought. These are the state as *societas* and the state as *universitas.*[133] In *On Human Conduct*, Oakeshott unpacks these ideal characters in detail, but it might be noted that in his *Lectures* these two images are referred to as *nomocracy* and *teleocracy*: 'government understood as the rule of its subjects by means of law' and government 'imposing on its subjects a substantive condition of things representing a single "purpose" pursued by all'.[134]

Oakeshott here uses *nomocracy* and *teleocracy* as analogies for norm and decision in the constitution of legal order. He recognizes that these terms represent ideal modes of association and explains that these ideal characters of state, government and law have become 'two well-trodden paths' that remain irreconcilably opposed to one another.[135] He accepts that some might reject this interpretation 'on the ground that it leaves an incoherence which, it is thought, should be capable of resolution'. And – in an allusion to Hayek, among others – he notes that some writers 'have tried to make it intelligible to themselves by recognizing one of these dispositions as dominant and the other as recessive'.[136] But this, he suggests, is unconvincing: 'the most one can do is to offer these terms as the most effective apparatus for understanding the actual complexity of a state.'[137]

Oakeshott rightly keeps open the tension between normativism and decisionism in the act of imagining legal order. But, as a consequence of adopting the reformulated conception of *nomos*,[138] he is without a method by which to mediate the gulf between the characters of *societas* and *universitas* and of legal ordering as norm and decision. The great value of Schmitt's restoration of the original meaning of *nomos* and its elaboration in the idea of concrete order is to offer a concept which is able to bridge that gulf. Schmitt's tripartite scheme does not bring resolution to the issue of the equivocal character of the modern state and its mode of legal ordering, but it does follow Oakeshott in recognizing that these dispositions are historical self-understandings and not

132 Oakeshott, *Lectures in the History of Political Thought*, note 127, 405.
133 Oakeshott, *On Human Conduct*, note 128, 198-204
134 Oakeshott, *Lectures in the History of Political Thought*, note 127, 483–4.
135 Oakeshott, *On Human Conduct*, note 128, 317, 319. 136 Ibid., 320.
137 Ibid., 323.
138 Oakeshott, *Lectures in the History of Political Thought*, note 127, 80–2.

universal types. 'Each has to be recognized as a contingent response to a historic situation', Oakeshott emphasizes, and this suggests that 'they should not be so starkly opposed to one another: each is a historic character and a character on the wing continuously exposed to modification in intercourse with the other.'[139] Schmitt would not disagree. All that is needed to enrich Oakeshott's account of the character of the state is Schmitt's understanding of the original meaning of *nomos* as the concrete order that grounds the meaning and variable importance of norm and decision in the constitution of its legal order. And this is not so far removed from Pascal's conception of 'present custom'.

The one scholar for whom *nomos* in its original sense performs a major role in the construction of her political and legal thought is Hannah Arendt. Arendt read Schmitt, agreed with his general critique of the influence of normativism in legal and political thought,[140] and directly followed his account of the original meaning of *nomos*. She relies heavily on Schmitt's work in drawing similar conclusions on the true meaning of *nomos*.

In *On Revolution*, Arendt acknowledges the violent nature of the beginning. 'That such a beginning must be intimately connected with violence', she writes, 'seems to be vouched for by the legendary beginnings of our history as both biblical and classical antiquity report it: Cain slew Abel, and Romulus slew Remus; violence was the beginning and, by the same token, no beginning could be made without using violence, without violating.' She also notes that 'whatever brotherhood human beings may be capable of has grown out of fratricide, whatever political organization men may have achieved has its origin in crime'.[141] Most significantly, Arendt recognizes that 'although the word *nomos* came to assume different meanings throughout the centuries of Greek civilization, it never lost its original "spatial significance".'[142]

Arendt develops the spatial dimension to *nomos* in *The Human Condition*, in which, closely following Schmitt's argument about the

139 Oakeshott, *On Human Conduct*, note 128, 325–6.

140 Arendt's concrete-order thinking is evident, for example, in a research proposal of 1956 in which she stated that her objective would be to 'examine the concrete historical and generally political experiences which gave rise to political concepts. For the experiences behind even the most worn-out concepts remain valid and must be recaptured and reactualized if one wishes to escape certain generalizations that have proved pernicious.' See E. Young-Bruehl, *Hannah Arendt: For Love of the World*, 2nd edn. (New Haven, CT: Yale University Press, 1982), 325.

141 Arendt, *On Revolution*, note 23, 20; see also at 87–8.

142 Ibid., 186.

derivation of *nomos*,[143] she explains that law was originally identified with a boundary line and that in the polis, 'it retained its original spatial significance.' The law of the city-state, she emphasizes, 'was neither the content of political action' (i.e., decision), 'nor was it a catalogue of prohibitions' (i.e., norm). Rather, it was 'quite literally a wall, without which there might have been an agglomeration of houses ... but not a city, a political community'.[144] In a late work, Arendt brings the lines of this interpretation of *nomos* together in a statement that could have been written by Schmitt himself:

> Just as the walls of a city ... must first be built before there can be a city identifiable by its shape and borders, the law determines the character of its inhabitants, setting them apart and making them distinguishable from the inhabitants of all other cities. The law is the city wall that is instituted ... inside of which is created the real political realm where many men move about freely ... The law is ... something by which the polis enters into its continuing life, something it cannot abolish without losing its identity, and violation of the law is an act of hubris, the overstepping of a limit placed on life itself. The law is not valid outside the polis; its binding power applies only to the space that it encloses and delimits ...The crucial point is that law – although it defines the space in which men live with one another without using force – has something violent about it in terms of both its origins and its nature ... The law produces the arena where politics occurs, and contains in itself the violent force inherent in all production.[145]

Arendt's account is of particular interest for two reasons. The first stems from her claim that political power is a phenomenon that is not only distinct from but also directly opposed to violence.[146] Power is generated through the capacity of humans to act in concert. Political power begins in action,[147] but since it is accepted that the beginning requires the use of violence, the relation between power and violence is more complicated

[143] H. Arendt, *The Human Condition* (University of Chicago Press, 1958), 63, note 62: 'The Greek word for law, *nomos*, derives from *nemein*, which means to distribute, to possess (what has been distributed), and to dwell.'

[144] Ibid., 63–4. Arendt also notes (64, note 64): 'The word polis originally connoted something like a "ring-wall".'

[145] H. Arendt, 'Introduction into Politics' in her *The Promise of Politics* (New York: Schocken Books, 2005), ed. J. Kohn, 93–200, at 180–1.

[146] H. Arendt, *On Violence* (New York: Harcourt, Brace, 1970), Part II, esp. at 56: 'To sum up: politically speaking, it is insufficient to say that power and violence are not the same. Power and violence are opposites; where the one rules absolutely, the other is absent.'

[147] Arendt, *The Human Condition*, note 143, Chap. 5.

than Arendt suggests. The second reason concerns law. Arendt makes use of the Roman concept of law: law as *lex*, which is a relational notion. Since *lex* 'was not coeval with the foundation of the city' and could not be conceived as 'pre-political' (i.e., as constitutive of the political), it presupposes the existence of a people.[148] This is evidently a different concept to *nomos*. It signifies what Montesquieu conceived as the 'necessary relations' by which power was sustained: authority is established by 'augmentation of the foundations' (or, in Schmitt's word, 'nourishment').[149] *Lex* presupposes *nomos*. But this concept of *lex* is also more basic than the norms of positive law.[150] Arendt opens up a more complex and layered understanding of law in which positive law presupposes *lex*, which, in turn, presupposes *nomos*.

Conclusions

The most basic insight we obtain from a study of Schmitt's account of the concept of *nomos* is that law is linked to space. The idea of law is tied to the existence of a defined and bounded territory that is able to distinguish inside from outside. Without this boundary, expressed in the concept of *nomos*, there can be no domain of the political. In this respect, it might be said that *nomos* is constitutive of the political. The space that is enclosed is not merely a geographical notion; as Arendt's work highlights, it is also a legal and political concept which relates 'not so much, and not primarily, to a piece of land as to the space between individuals in a group whose members are bound to, and at the same time separated and protected from, each other by all kinds of relationships, based on a common language, religion, a common history, customs and laws'.[151] The space of political freedom is created only through the formation of these relationships. Arendt explains that wherever freedom has existed 'as a tangible reality', it has always been spatially limited: 'if we equate

[148] Arendt, *On Revolution*, note 23, 187.

[149] Montesquieu, *The Spirit of the Laws* (Cambridge University Press, 1989), trans. and ed. A. Cohler, B. Miller and H. Stone, vol. I, 1; H. Arendt, 'What Is Authority?' in her *Between Past and Present* (New York: Penguin, 1977), 91–141, at 121–2: 'The word *auctoritas* derives from the verb *augere*, "augment", and what authority and those in authority constantly augment is the foundation.'

[150] I discuss Arendt's concept of *lex* and its role in the method of political jurisprudence in Loughlin, *The Idea of Public Law* (Oxford University Press, 2003), Chap. 8, esp. 141–2.

[151] H. Arendt, *Eichmann in Jerusalem: A Report on the Banality of Evil*, rev. edn. (New York: Penguin Books, 1965), 262.

those spaces of freedom . . . with the political realm itself', she states, 'we shall be inclined to think of them as islands in a sea or as oases in a desert.'[152] In a political sense, freedom is both an achievement and, from the outset, is ordered.

Nomos gives expression to that concrete order of political freedom. Schmitt, Arendt and Oakeshott all agree that the initial action – the taking – invariably involves an exercise of force or violence. They also agree – though they express this is their own distinctive terminology – that through 'customary practices' (Oakeshott), the emergence of 'intimate connection or relationship' (Arendt), or the establishment of institutional order (Schmitt), force is tamed and 'moralized', and power is thereby generated. Law is neither norm nor decision as such; it is an arrangement of norms and decisions that emerges within a concrete order.

Schmitt may not have been as explicit as other scholars in acknowledging this power-generational aspect of state building, but he was not unaware of this phenomenon. In an essay on pluralism and the state published in 1930, he explains that political unity is never in reality as monistic as jurists, through simplification, or pluralists, for polemical reasons, present it. Even the so-called absolute prince of the seventeenth and eighteenth centuries was obliged 'to respect divine and natural law – that is, to speak sociologically, church and family – and to take into account the manifold aspects of traditional institutions and established rights'. The political unity of the state 'has always been a unity of social multiplicity'.[153]

Elaborating on this theme, Schmitt recognizes that there are many ways of building political unity:

> There is unity from above (through command and power) and unity from below (from the substantial homogeneity of the people); unity through enduring association and compromise between social groups or through an equilibrium achieved somehow by some other means between such groups; unity which comes from within and one which rests only on external pressure; a more static and a permanently dynamic, functionally integrated unity; finally, there is unity by force and unity by consensus.[154]

[152] Arendt, *On Revolution*, note 23, 275.
[153] C. Schmitt, 'Ethic of State and Pluralistic Ethic' [1930] in C. Mouffe (ed.), *The Challenge of Carl Schmitt* (London: Verso, 1999), 195–208, at 201.
[154] Ibid., 201–2.

In this essay, Schmitt notes that pluralists consider that only a unity achieved by consensus can be ethically justified. But this, he explains, is not an unambiguous criterion. Every consensus must, by some means or other, be established. Power is generally required to produce consensus, including 'a rational and ethically justified consensus'. But so too can consensus produce power, including 'an irrational and – despite consensus – ethically repugnant power'.[155] Schmitt here recognizes the complexity, uncertainty and amorality of the processes by which institutional order is capable of being 'nourished' from its original source.

The overall significance of Schmitt's exegesis on *nomos* is to demonstrate that if the originating act of taking/closure is overlooked in legal thought, our grasp of the character of law in modernity will be skewed. Jurists have avoided this question either by treating the foundation as a pure act of representation (as promoted by normativism) or by presupposing some mysterious prior substantive equality of the people (as promoted by decisionism). On this fundamental point, Schmitt surely is correct. But his basic insight needs to be amended and developed. As Lindahl has noted, 'an initiation takes on the form of an accomplishment because the original self-closure of a community only becomes such afterwards, in and through the closures that accomplish it.'[156] That is, the act of foundation can be understood as such only after the event: the original appropriation – the first meaning of *nomos* as the constitution of 'the original spatial order, the source of all further concrete order and all further law'[157] – can be identified as foundational only once the second and third aspects of *nomos* (distribution and production) are institutionalized. This gives *nomos* a reflexive dimension, one that is augmented only with the assistance of Arendt's rendering of the relational quality of *lex*. The authority of the state is established and maintained through a continuous interaction of the modes of ordering that are grasped by *nomos*, *lex* and positive law.

155 Ibid. 202.
156 H. Lindahl, 'Give and Take: Arendt and the Nomos of Political Community', *Philosophy & Social Criticism*, 32 (2006), 881–901, at 897.
157 *Schmitt, The Nomos of the Earth*, 48.

5

Carl Schmitt's defence of sovereignty

LARS VINX

H. L. A. Hart once remarked that a sovereign, according to the classical doctrine of sovereignty, is 'as essential a part of a society which possesses law, as a backbone is of a man'.[1] Not least as a result of Hart's own attack on Austin's theory of sovereignty, analytical legal theorists today agree that a sovereign is not just unnecessary for but incompatible with the existence of legal order. To explain the variety and persistence of legal norms, the continuity of legal order and the evident possibility of legal constraints on legislative power, so goes the contemporary legal-theoretical consensus, legal order must be regarded as rule-based. As a result, sovereignty can at best be an office defined by positive law. There can be no meta-legal, purely political power which is legally illimitable and yet functions as the source of all positive law.[2]

Nevertheless, the doctrine of sovereignty is not without its contemporary defenders. The authors in question, though, rarely address the legal-theoretical worries about sovereignty head on. Rather, they argue that sovereignty is essential to the legitimacy of a modern democratic constitution. To be democratically legitimate, a constitution must, it is argued, be the product of an exercise of a constituent power which is prior to all positive law (including positive constitutional law) and which functions as the legitimating source of all positive legality.[3]

[1] H. L. A. Hart, *The Concept of Law* (Oxford University Press, 1961), 49.

[2] See Hart, *Concept of Law*, 18–76; Joseph Raz, *The Concept of a Legal System: An Introduction to the Theory of Legal System* (Oxford University Press, 1970), 27–43; Pavlos Eleftheriadis, 'Law and Sovereignty', *Law and Philosophy*, 29 (2010), 535.

[3] See, e.g., Dieter Grimm, *Souveränität. Herkunft und Zukunft eines Schlüsselbegriffs* (Berlin University Press, 2009), 99–123; Olivier Beaud, *La puissance de l'état* (Paris: Presses Universitaires de France, 1994), 199–491; Andreas Kalyvas, *Democracy and the Politics of the Extraordinary. Max Weber, Carl Schmitt, and Hannah Arendt* (New York: Cambridge University Press, 2008); Martin Loughlin, *Foundations of Public Law* (Oxford University Press, 2010); Paul W. Kahn, *Political Theology: Four New Chapters on the Concept of Sovereignty* (New York: Columbia University Press, 2011).

However, if the doctrine of sovereignty conflicts with key features of legal order, a constitutional theory based on the concept of sovereignty must be flawed. And if the idea of a sovereign authority as the source of legal order cannot possibly make any sense, we will have to let go of the claim that a constitution must be legitimized by reference to constituent power. Those who want to hold on to the notion of sovereignty because they think it essential to a democratic constitutional theory must first establish that the concept of sovereignty is jurisprudentially meaningful.

Carl Schmitt's theory of sovereignty is the obvious place to look for a defence of the continuing jurisprudential relevance of the concept of sovereignty. Schmitt's famous definition of sovereignty – sovereign is he who decides on the state of exception[4] – offers a surprisingly sophisticated response to the legal-theoretical challenge to sovereignty. Schmitt managed to show, I will argue, that the presence of a legally illimitable sovereign whose decisions condition the applicability of law is not incompatible with the existence of rule-based legal order. Still, Schmitt's theory of sovereignty falls short of a full rehabilitation of the classical doctrine of sovereignty. His argument does not establish that a sovereign is as necessary to law as a backbone is to a man. Like his contemporary followers in constitutional theory, Schmitt claims instead that a sovereign is necessary for the existence of a *legitimate* legal order.[5]

To assess Schmitt's theory of sovereignty, as well as contemporary efforts to defend the relevance of sovereignty for democratic constitutional theory, we therefore have to ask whether there is good reason to hold that a legal order can only be legitimate if it derives from a sovereign power above the law. I will argue that there is not. Schmitt's defence of sovereignty, despite its partial success against the legal-theoretical criticism of sovereignty, is therefore a theoretical dead end.

The positivist challenge to sovereignty

To sharpen our understanding of the aims of Schmitt's defence of sovereignty, it will be helpful to take a brief look at the discussions of

[4] Carl Schmitt, *Political Theology: Four Chapters on the Concept of Sovereignty* (University of Chicago Press, 2005), trans. George Schwab, 5.

[5] Hasso Hofmann, *Legalität gegen Legitimität. Der Weg der politischen Philosophie Carl Schmitts*, 4th edn. (Berlin: Duncker & Humblot, 2002); David Dyzenhaus, *Legality and Legitimacy: Carl Schmitt, Hans Kelsen and Hermann Heller in Weimar* (Oxford University Press, 1997), 38–101.

sovereignty with which Schmitt engaged. Hobbes' theory of sovereignty, which Schmitt presented himself as wanting to revive, is the natural starting point for such an inquiry.

Hobbes' claims about sovereignty arise from a reflection on the nature and function of the state. Hobbes insists that the state will be able to provide peace and security to its subjects only if all its powers are united in the hands of one person or one group of persons. Any form of separation or division of powers, in Hobbes' view, would raise the danger of an irresolvable conflict between different organs of state.[6] Hobbes, moreover, puts emphasis on the claim that the sovereign is not legally accountable to his subjects in any way. Not being a party to the social contract, the sovereign cannot rightfully be deposed, accused of injustice in a court of law or punished.[7]

It would nevertheless be mistaken to conclude that the powers of Hobbes' sovereign are legally unlimited. Throughout *Leviathan*, Hobbes repeatedly emphasizes the claim that the sovereign, as a mere representative of the state, lacks the legal power to alienate any of the essential rights of sovereignty. In particular, Hobbes is very anxious to emphasize the point that a sovereign cannot possibly be legally bound by decisions of previous sovereigns which appear to have granted away sovereign powers, such as the power to tax without seeking consent. Any such grant, in Hobbes' view, is to be regarded as void unless it went along with an explicit renunciation of sovereignty.[8] Sovereignty, for Hobbes, is ultimately an attribute of the state, not a private possession of the sovereign person.

The inalienability of sovereign power in Hobbes illustrates an important feature of Hobbes' theory of the state, a feature which is also evident in the claim that one can draw up a list of essential powers of sovereignty or in the claim that no system of government can possibly accommodate a separation of powers and still fulfil its purpose. In Hobbes' view, the social institution which we call the state has an essence or nature which is determined by its function. The function of the state is to provide peace and security to its members by ending the state of nature between them

[6] Thomas Hobbes, *Leviathan* (Cambridge University Press, 1996), ed. Richard Tuck, 127.

[7] Ibid., 121–9.

[8] Ibid., 127, 153, 222. For some recent work affirming the importance of the rule of law for Hobbes, see Chapters 6–10 in David Dyzenhaus and Thomas Poole (eds.), *Hobbes and the Law* (Cambridge University Press, 2012); Perez Zagorin, *Hobbes and the Law of Nature* (Princeton University Press, 2009) 84–98; Larry May, *Limiting Leviathan: Hobbes on Law and International Affairs* (Oxford University Press, 2013).

and by protecting them against external enemies. Any institution which is to serve this purpose with a degree of success must, according to Hobbes, instantiate the constitutional framework put forward in *Leviathan*. The sovereign is therefore legally limited by what one might call a 'constitution in natural law'. There are certain actions – such as the granting away of essential rights of sovereignty – which a sovereign, though unpunishable, cannot validly perform.

The idea of a constitution in natural law allowed Hobbes to argue that there is no conflict between the claim that sovereignty is an attribute of the state, and thus an essentially public power, and the claim that the existence of legal order requires that there be a sovereign person whose decisions are the sole source of and unbound from all positive law. The constitution in natural law turns sovereignty into a representative and public role defined by natural law, even while shielding it from any limitation grounded in positive law.

Hobbes' theory of sovereignty, however, is clearly no longer tenable. It is motivated by the view that a stable state and a functioning legal order require an extreme concentration of political power. But we now know that states as well as legal systems can exist and be stable without being represented and protected by a sovereign authority which stands above the positive law and which concentrates all political power in its hands. If there is such a thing as a constitution in natural law, an institutional framework which must be instantiated by every functioning state, then Hobbes clearly gave much too narrow a description of it.

Hart's attack on the doctrine of sovereignty can be understood as one possible reaction to this failure of Hobbes' project. Hart, taking his cues from Austin, took the doctrine of sovereignty to claim that wherever there is a legal system, there must be a sovereign person whose legislative decisions are the sole source of law. This view, understandably, no longer made any sense to Hart, given the undoubted existence of modern legal systems which do not contain a sovereign legislator. Austin, in reducing sovereignty to a mere *de facto* power, had already uncoupled sovereignty from natural law.[9] This allowed Hart, who attacked the doctrine of sovereignty in the form which it had been given by Austin, to argue that the attempt to ground law in sovereignty must fail to explain the continuity of the legal system, the diversity of legal norms and the normativity of

[9] John Austin, *The Province of Jurisprudence Determined* (Cambridge University Press, 1995), ed. Wilfrid E. Rumble, 18–37, 164–83 and 211–29.

law. Hart, consequently, rejected the doctrine of sovereignty altogether and replaced it with the theory of the rule of recognition.[10]

Hans Kelsen reacted somewhat differently to the breakdown of the Hobbesian view by adopting a depersonalized reading of the doctrine of sovereignty. Sovereignty, according to Kelsen, is to be understood not as the unlimited power of a person or group of persons but rather as the normative independence of a legal system. What we really mean to convey when we say that a state is sovereign, according to Kelsen, is that the state's law is not derived from any higher source than its own basic norm.[11]

Kelsen, like Hobbes, was interested in the question how it is possible to attribute actions performed by individual human beings to the state and argued that such attribution requires a legal basis. But, since Kelsen rejected the idea of a constitution in natural law, he held that the legal basis for the attribution of individual acts to the state must be sought in positive law. Purported acts of state amount to genuine exercises of public power, according to Kelsen, only if they are properly authorized by positive law. The state, like the sovereign of old, is unable to do wrong; it can act only in the medium of legality. The sovereignty of the state, in the last analysis, thus turns out to be equivalent to the autonomy of positive law. Though the state is, in a sense, properly called 'sovereign', there can be no person or group of persons who act in the name of the state but whose competence is essentially incapable of limitation by positive law.[12]

For our purposes, the differences between Hart's and Kelsen's treatment of the classical doctrine of sovereignty matter less than the commonalities. Both Hart and Kelsen deny that there could be a personal, meta-legal sovereign authority which creates all positive law while being unbound from it. They both concede, of course, that a positive legal system could be structured in such a way as to confer wide-ranging, even materially unlimited powers of law-making on one person or group of persons. However, such a power could not, in either approach, be regarded as being a transcendent source of positive law. Its authority would depend, rather, on the contingent content of a particular rule of

[10] Hart, *The Concept of Law*, 18–76.

[11] Hans Kelsen, *Das Problem der Souveränität und die Theorie des Völkerrechts. Beitrag zu einer reinen Rechtslehre* (Tübingen, Germany: J. C. B. Mohr (Paul Siebeck), 1920), 1–101.

[12] For an overview of Kelsen's development of these themes, see Lars Vinx, *Hans Kelsen's Pure Theory of Law: Legality and Legitimacy* (Oxford University Press, 2007), 78–100.

recognition or basic norm.[13] All public powers, in other words, must be grounded in antecedent positive law.

Schmitt, like Hart and Kelsen, no longer supports the Hobbesian notion of a constitution in natural law. He agrees that all law is positive. Hence, he does not think that the public role of sovereign can be defined in terms of a constitution in natural law. Nevertheless, he wants to hold on to the view that legal order is, or at least ought to be, based on an extra-legal sovereign authority. We can now describe the challenge which Schmitt had to face in developing his defence of sovereignty with greater precision. Schmitt had to show that there is a way to conceive of positive law as being grounded in the decisions of a sovereign person who stands above the positive law while being unbound from it and he had to do so without taking resort to the notion of a constitution in natural law.

Sovereignty as the power to decide on the exception

At first glance, the chances of meeting this challenge appear slim. To meet the challenge, one will have to deny – in order to avoid the legalist implications of Kelsen's analysis – that sovereignty is an attribute of a legal system or of a legally constituted state. One will have to conceive of sovereign authority, instead, as an attribute of a particular individual or group. The only way to do this, presumably, is to understand sovereignty not as a legal competence but as an overwhelming *de facto* power of that individual or group to compel obedience. But then one will have to face the criticisms which Hart levelled against Austin. If it is the mere possession of *de facto* power to issue general commands and to compel obedience which endows a person or group of persons with sovereign authority, it will become impossible, if Hart's argument against Austin is sound, to explain the continuity of the legal system, the diversity of legal norms and the internal normativity of law. It seems that sovereignty must either succumb to legality or remain altogether unrelated to legal order.

Schmitt avoids the first horn of this dilemma by conceiving of sovereignty in purely personal terms. His definition of sovereignty states that the sovereign is he who decides on the state of exception.[14] This defines sovereign authority as the power to take a decision on the exception. In addition, the definition carries the implication that sovereignty must

[13] See Hart, *Concept of Law*, 66–8; Kelsen, *Das Problem der Souveränität*, 27.
[14] Schmitt, *Political Theology*, 5.

inhere in a particular individual or group. If there is to be a sovereign, there must be a real or concrete will capable of taking an actual decision on the exception. A rule-based, impersonal institution cannot be the primary bearer of sovereignty. The power of sovereignty, according to Schmitt, ultimately belongs to him or to them who can in fact take the decision on the exception, not to a legally constituted artificial person of the state which is merely represented by a sovereign.[15]

Schmitt explicitly argues that the power to take a decision on the absolute exception is not to be understood as a power conferred by law but rather as a *de facto* power. Constitutional law, to be sure, may contain acknowledgements of the existence of such a power (or it might, for that matter, try to deny the existence of such a power), but the power exists wherever there is someone who can in fact take a decision on the total exception, and it is not bound to any legal form.[16] It is a misinterpretation of Schmitt's definition of sovereignty to read it as though it claimed that one ought to look to who is made competent by a positive constitution to decide on the state of emergency to find out who is sovereign. The existence of such a constitutional provision, for Schmitt, is neither a necessary nor a sufficient condition for sovereignty: it is not necessary because there obviously may be an agency that can bring about a decision on the total exception even without being formally authorized to do so. It is not sufficient because constitutional emergency provisions, for rather obvious reasons, will typically fail to confer a power to declare an absolute exception. Their usual aim, after all, is to tame and domesticate the power to decide on the exception.[17] What is more, the claim that Schmittian sovereignty is a competence conferred by a positive

[15] To be sure, Schmitt suggests, in *Political Theology*, that sovereignty is an attribute of the state. For instance, he says that in the state of absolute exception, 'the state remains, whereas law recedes' and that it is 'the state that suspends the law' (Ibid., 12). But the term 'state', in this context, cannot refer to an institution structured by any kind of law if, as Schmitt makes clear, the decision on the exception is at least potentially a decision that suspends absolutely all law, perhaps with the view of establishing an altogether new constitution. In his *Constitutional Theory*, Schmitt defines the state as 'the political unity of the people', which manifests itself in legally unregulated acts of constituent power. See Carl Schmitt, *Constitutional Theory* (Durham, NC: Duke University Press, 2008), trans. Jeffrey Seitzer, 75. Schmitt's talk of the state, then, is perhaps best understood as referring to a Schmittian political community, that is, to a group of people united only by a shared disposition to distinguish between friend and enemy in the same way. See Carl Schmitt, *The Concept of the Political. Expanded Edition* (University of Chicago Press, 2007), trans. George Schwab, 19–25. However, to call such a group a state is misleading at best, if it is essential to the state to be an artificial person or an organized community.

[16] Schmitt, *Constitutional Theory*, 125–35.

[17] Schmitt, *Political Theology*, 12.

constitution also conflicts with Schmitt's theory of popular sovereignty. If the people are to be sovereign, and if popular sovereignty is to be understood as an inalienable power of constitution-making, then popular sovereignty (or sovereign dictatorship exercised on behalf of the people) cannot be a power or a competence conferred by a positive constitution.[18]

Note as well that the power to take a decision on the total exception is not a legislative or adjudicative authority. It does not create legal norms or modify legal relationships between legal persons. Neither does it apply norms. All it does, so to speak, is to switch the law as a whole on and off.[19] Despite its nature as a *de facto* power, however, the power to take a decision on the total exception is a power that affects the law: it conditions the law's applicability. The decision on the exception, then, is

[18] Martin Loughlin claims that when Schmitt's sovereign takes a decision on the exception, 'positive law recedes, but *droit politique* remains' (Loughlin, *Foundations of Public Law*, 401). He goes on to argue (Ibid., 402) that *droit politique* is manifest, for instance, in the fact that 'in the Weimar Republic that power [to take a decision on the exception] was vested in the president under Article 48 of the Constitution, a common arrangement under modern constitutions'. Schmitt, however, denies that the dictatorship of the president under Article 48 is a power of sovereignty precisely because the former, but not the latter, is a competence allocated (and limited) by positive constitutional law. See Carl Schmitt, 'The Dictatorship of the President of the Reich According to Article 48 of the Weimar Constitution', in Schmitt, *Dictatorship: From the Origin of the Modern Concept of Sovereignty to Proletarian Mass Struggle* (Cambridge, UK: Polity Press, 2014), trans. Michael Hoelzl and Graham Ward, 180–226. Hence, the positive constitutional rules which confer circumscribed powers of dictatorship to a president (or some other constitutional office) cannot be the order that Schmitt, in *Political Theology*, claims will remain even in a state of total exception. What remains in the state of total exception, according to Schmitt, is not a legal order but the distinction between friend and enemy. In George Schwab's translation of *Political Theology*, Schmitt is made to say, on p. 12, that in a state of exception 'order in the juristic sense still prevails, even if it is not of the ordinary kind'. However, what Schmitt really wrote (in my translation) is that 'since the state of exception is still something other than a mere anarchy or chaos, an order in the juristic sense still exists, *though not a legal order*'. See Carl Schmitt, *Politische Theologie. Vier Kapitel zur Lehre von der Souveränität*, 7th edn. (Berlin: Duncker & Humblot, 1996), 18: 'Weil der Ausnahmezustand immer noch etwas anderes ist als eine Anarchie oder ein Chaos, besteht im juristischen Sinn immer noch eine Ordnung, *wenn auch keine Rechtsordnung*'. What Schmitt wants to say here is clear enough. What still exists in the state of exception is the state, understood as a political community (see the discussion in note 15), which, according to Schmitt, is a subject of juristic thought, but not the law, political or otherwise. Schwab's translation simply drops Schmitt's explicit statement that there is no longer a legal order in the state of exception. Loughlin's view that, according to Schmitt, '*droit politique* remains' in the state of exception appears to be based on Schwab's incomplete translation. See Loughlin, *Foundations of Public Law*, 401.

[19] Schmitt, *Political Theology*, 12.

jurisprudentially relevant, even though it does not legislate or adjudicate. Every ordinary application of the law, according to Schmitt, presupposes a prior decision to the effect that the situation is normal and not exceptional and that it is therefore possible and appropriate to rely on legality for the solution of social conflict.[20]

These observations explain how Schmitt avoids the second horn of the dilemma outlined earlier. Hart's attack on Austin's notion of sovereignty is an attack on the claim that a mere *de facto* power can become the source of all positive legal norms by assuming the role of an uncommanded commander. Schmitt, however, is clearly not guilty of the mistake of conceiving of laws as sovereign commands. A sovereign who does not legislate obviously does not issue commands which claim legal authority. Hart convincingly argues that Austin's conception of a sovereign legislator fails to explain the continuity of legal system, to account for the diversity of legal norms and to explain the internal normativity of legal rules. But since Schmitt's sovereign is not a legislator and does not enact positive legal norms, Schmitt's theory simply is not vulnerable to the objections that Hart levelled against Austin.

Let me explain these claims in a little more detail. Schmitt's sovereign is perfectly able to coexist, in times judged non-exceptional, with a working positive constitutional order, perhaps even a liberal-democratic one.[21] Such an order would determine a procedure of legislation for the production of legal norms, norms which, in turn, guide the activity of the courts and of administrative agencies. Hence, no positive legal norm, under circumstances of normality, need be validated by recourse to sovereign authority. A norm's validity, rather, will rest on the fact that it has been enacted in accordance with the rule of recognition determined by the constitution. Since there is no need for Schmitt to portray positive laws so validated as commands, his theory is well able to accommodate Hart's rule-centred description of the legal system.

Of course, Schmitt argues that the operation of the legal system presupposes that the sovereign judges the general situation to be non-exceptional so that law can apply. He also takes it that legal norms, though validly enacted, will not apply as long as the sovereign judges the situation to be exceptional. Thus, perhaps a Hartian might argue that there is still room for a continuity puzzle of the sort which Hart deploys against Austin to arise. Imagine that the sovereign suspends legality

[20] Ibid., 12–3. [21] Schmitt, *Constitutional Theory*, 145–6.

altogether, in a global state of emergency, and that legality is later re-established, after the sovereign, through the use of *de facto* force, has managed to produce a situation which he judges to be normal. Should we say that the legal system after the state of emergency is the same as the one which was in force before the emergency? Or should we say that a new legal system has been created? Questions of this sort will not embarrass Schmitt, for the simple reason that Schmitt will answer such questions in line with the criteria which a Hartian would apply to judge of questions of continuity.

A sovereign's actions in a state of exception, presumably, could lead to two different results. A sovereign might re-establish the social condition which underpinned the old constitution so as to make it possible, once again, to apply the law of the old constitution. Otherwise, a sovereign's actions could lead to the establishment of a new constitution. This, presumably, will happen if the old constitution has been made obsolete by social change so that it is no longer possible to preserve the condition of normality which underpinned it. In the first of these two scenarios, Schmitt would claim that there is legal continuity, while he would deny continuity in the second.[22] Hart will arrive at exactly the same result because, in the first case, judges and officials are going to continue to apply the old rule of recognition, while in the second they will follow a new rule.

Let me draw a preliminary conclusion of our discussion of Schmitt's theory of sovereignty so far. Schmitt's theory of sovereignty seems to offer a coherent response to the legal-theoretical claim that a sovereign authority above the positive law, an authority which conditions the law's applicability, is incompatible with a continuous, rule-based legal order. However, Schmitt's argument clearly does not establish that a meta-legal sovereign authority is as necessary to the existence of legal order as a backbone is to a man. There would appear to be no good reason to deny that a society characterized by the absence of a Schmittian sovereign could have a functioning rule-based legal system. Schmitt, then, has fought the legal-theoretical criticism of sovereignty to a standstill. But where does that leave us?

It is crucial to Schmitt's argument, as we have seen, that the power of deciding on the exception – though it is not legislative or adjudicative – be seen as a power which conditions the applicability of positive law.

[22] Of course, Schmitt thinks that the continuous existence of political community is not tied to legal continuity. See ibid., 140–6.

If sovereign power is not interpreted as conditioning the applicability of positive law, Schmitt's conception of sovereignty risks becoming purely political and jurisprudentially irrelevant.

A Kelsenian would press Schmitt on precisely this point. The Kelsenian will admit that a society might contain a person or group of persons who have a *de facto* power altogether to suspend legality, to completely interrupt the normal operation of the law. But why should this fact be jurisprudentially significant? As long as the law does not recognize the power to take a decision on the exception, the existence of that power, or its successful exercise, will be no more than a mere fact of political sociology. In making this claim, one does not have to deny that politically powerful groups attempt, from time to time, to interrupt the application of law and that they sometimes succeed in breaking legal continuity. Neither does one have to contest that a legal system can exist and operate only where it is sufficiently effective, that is, where its operation is not successfully challenged by *de facto* powers aiming to suspend or block its application. If the view that the power to take a decision on the exception conditions the applicability of law boils down to the banal insight that law must be sufficiently effective to exist, how can that power be portrayed as any kind of legal power, as a power which is of jurisprudential concern?

To meet this challenge, Schmitt adds an important qualification to the view that the sovereign decision conditions the applicability of law. He claims that it is the *legitimate* applicability of the norms which belong to some positive legal system which presupposes a sovereign who can decide on the exception.[23] This response, if defensible, opens a way out of the impasse we just pressed on Schmitt. The power to take a decision on the exception obviously must be regarded as jurisprudentially relevant if the existence of that power is a necessary condition of the legitimate applicability of positive law. But, of course, Schmitt will now have to explain why a sovereign who can take a decision on the exception is necessary for the existence of legitimate positive law.

Schmitt's answer to this question, in a nutshell, is that the sovereign's decision on the exception expresses the political existence of a people. The sovereign decision, in other words, is the only form in which popular sovereignty can be actualized, and popular sovereignty, Schmitt argues, is

[23] Ibid., 136; Carl Schmitt, *Legality and Legitimacy* (Durham, NC: Duke University Press, 2004), trans. Jeffrey Seitzer.

the only modern basis for the legitimacy of law.[24] It is the assessment of this normative claim to which we must turn to resolve the standoff.

Schmitt on sovereignty and the legitimacy of legal order

Schmitt's claim that a sovereign authority is necessary to secure the legitimate applicability of law makes a first appearance, at least implicitly, in Schmitt's early work, *Gesetz und Urteil*, which was published in 1912.[25] In this book, Schmitt is concerned to outline the conditions of legal determinacy in judicial decision-taking. The starting point of the argument is a rejection of a formalist picture of adjudication. The application of statutes to particular cases by the courts, Schmitt argues, cannot be portrayed as a process of logical deduction in which general statutory rules clearly determine their applicative instances. Rather, application will, in many instances, require a judgement to the effect that a case can be brought under a concept, a judgement which is not itself guided by the legal rule which is to be applied.[26]

Schmitt does not think, however, that the rejection of formalism should lead a judge to embrace the self-conscious use of judicial authority as an instrument of social reform. Schmitt holds that judicial decision-taking is legitimate only as long as it does not depend on potentially controversial moral or political judgements on the part of the judge.[27] The fact that legal determinacy cannot be ensured by a judicial commitment of fidelity to statute does not imply, in Schmitt's view, that legal determinacy cannot be achieved at all. Judicial practice, Schmitt claims, has developed an alternative means of ensuring legal determinacy: a shared sense of appropriateness, grounded in the common educational background of legal officials, in the common experiences of those who hold judicial office and in the convergent ethical assumptions of members of the judiciary.[28]

If it is the social homogeneity of the judiciary which ensures legal determinacy, and if legal determinacy is desirable, we will have to conclude that a justifiable judicial decision is one which conforms to the expectations of other legal officials. This is why Schmitt claims that a

[24] Schmitt, *Constitutional Theory*, 126–30.
[25] Carl Schmitt, *Gesetz und Urteil: Eine Untersuchung zum Problem der Rechtspraxis*, 2nd edn. (München: C. H. Beck, 1969).
[26] Ibid., 21–43. [27] Ibid., 42, 99. [28] Ibid., 68–114.

legal decision is correct if and only if we can assume that another judge would have taken the same decision.[29]

Schmitt's argument in *Gesetz und Urteil* does not yet explain why legal determinacy is desirable – so desirable, in fact, as to be declared the sole basis of a standard of the correctness of judicial decision. It is possible, however, to gather an answer to this question from Schmitt's later works. A legal decision not determined in advance by a shared practice would amount to an instance of domination or, as Schmitt prefers to put the point, to a form of 'indirect rule'.[30]

The authority and institutional independence of the judiciary, Schmitt insists, depends on the presupposition that it does no more than to apply the law. A judge who takes decisions conditioned by his or her personal moral or political judgement, under the guise of applying the law, exercises a form of arbitrary and unaccountable political rule. Not surprisingly, Schmitt harbours a strong suspicion against judicial review.[31] At the same time, though, he argues that an unrestrained parliamentary legislator is in danger of becoming a mere instrument of the illegitimate rule of partial interests which have found ways to corrupt the legislature.[32] From Schmitt's point of view, both the fundamental positions in contemporary normative constitutional theory – a rights-oriented constitutionalism arguing for judicial review and a political constitutionalism concerned with protecting the democratic legislature from judicial interference – fall equally short of preventing domination.

The reason, according to Schmitt, is that both positions overlook the importance of legal determinacy as a condition of the legitimate applicability of law, including constitutional law. Liberal constitutionalism will have to admit that judicial decisions which enforce constitutional rights have the character of un-democratic judicial impositions as they will often turn out to be controversial, unexpected and not grounded in an

29 Ibid., 68–9.

30 See for the notion of 'indirect rule', Carl Schmitt, *The Leviathan in the State Theory of Thomas Hobbes: Meaning and Failure of a Political Symbol* (University of Chicago Press, 2008), trans. George Schwab and Erna Hilfstein, 65–77.

31 Carl Schmitt, *The Guardian of the Constitution*, part I, in *The Guardian of the Constitution: Hans Kelsen and Carl Schmitt on the Limits of Constitutional Law* (Cambridge University Press, 2014), trans. Lars Vinx, 79–124; Carl Schmitt, 'Das Reichsgericht als Hüter der Verfassung' in Schmitt, *Verfassungsrechtliche Aufsätze aus den Jahren 1924–1954* (Berlin: Duncker & Humblot, 1958), 63–109.

32 See Carl Schmitt, *The Crisis of Parliamentary Democracy* (Cambridge, MA: MIT Press, 1985), trans. Ellen Kennedy, 33–50; Schmitt, *Hüter der Verfassung*, 73–91; Schmitt, *Legality and Legitimacy*, 17–36.

established judicial practice which is already accepted as appropriate by the community at large.[33] Political constitutionalism, or what Schmitt calls the legislative state,[34] must own up to the fact that parliamentary decision-taking, especially in a pluralist society, need not reflect the will of the people and that it may well come to benefit partial interests over the common good. In either case, the appeal to the constitutionality of the decision – be it judicial or legislative – is merely going to paper over the fact that genuine democratic self-determination remains unrealized.

Schmitt does not hold that such a failure of self-determination is an inevitable result of judicial review or of parliamentary legislation. However, if there is no failure, he argues, the reason must be that the judicial or legislative decision takes place in the context of a shared social understanding of what is appropriate that makes decisions both expectable and acceptable. Legal determinacy, in other words, indicates the absence of conflict between social groups and hence the absence of domination of one social group by another. Determinacy, however, is based on the presupposition of social homogeneity, a presupposition which cannot be taken for granted under modern social conditions and which cannot be guaranteed or protected by the law itself.[35] Once a decision is controversial, we must conclude that determinacy, as the condition of the legitimate applicability of the law, no longer obtains. And whenever the condition of homogeneity is unfulfilled, decision-taking under legal or constitutional procedures must turn out to be dominating to some. The rule of law will become an instrument of the indirect rule of a part over the whole and veil it at the same time. Where decisions which take place within the constitutional system have become deeply controversial, social homogeneity must first be restored to make the law legitimately applicable. This restoration, Schmitt argues, requires a sovereign decision on the exception as well as dictatorial action in the state of exception.[36]

We already know what the sovereign decision on the exception does. It declares the law as a whole to be non-applicable. As Schmitt makes clear, the decision on the exception thereby opens the space for a sovereign dictatorship which operates without any legal restraints of any kind and

[33] Carl Schmitt, 'Grundrechte und Grundpflichten' in Schmitt, *Verfassungsrechtliche Aufsätze*, 181–231, at 217–24; Carl Schmitt, 'Die Auflösung des Enteignungsbegriffs' in Schmitt, *Verfassungsrechtliche Aufsätze*, 110–23.

[34] Schmitt, *Legality and Legitimacy*, 17–26.

[35] Schmitt, *Political Theology*, 5–15.

[36] Schmitt, *Dictatorship*, 80–147.

which uses its unbounded discretion to create a situation of normality or homogeneity – if necessary by the use of force which eliminates dissent. This activity need not be conservative. It may well turn out to be revolutionary. He who decides on the absolute exception also decides what is to be regarded as normal or exceptional and thus defines what kind of homogeneity is to be brought about.[37]

It would be wrong, however, to think of the sovereign's decision as a top-down imposition of authority. For the sovereign to be successful in the attempt to define normality, the decision must express some widely shared substantive identity which is prior to the law and to the state as a legal expression of community. This identity will become political, Schmitt argues, only if a sufficient number of members of a society are willing to fight and die for the defence of that identity against those whom they perceive as its internal and external enemies.[38]

Schmitt's famous criterion of the political is motivated by the aim to portray the constitution of political community as a process which does not involve legality. Schmitt insists that we cannot define 'the political' with reference to the state, for example, as the fight for control over the state.[39] The state is inextricably bound up with law; it is an institution constituted by rules of legality. If sovereignty and political community are to be prior to law, then sovereignty and political community must be explicable in terms which do not make reference to the state. It must be possible to explain what a political community is, what distinguishes it from other kinds of community, without taking resort to the implicitly legal notions which are the building blocks of our idea of the state: representation, authorization or the idea of a social contract. This is why Schmitt claims that political community is defined by a pre-legal distinction between friend and enemy.[40] In successfully dividing society into those who support or reject a decision on the exception, and the definition of normality implied by it, the decision on the exception proves that some shared identity has political quality. It does this by forcing people to take sides, to reveal themselves as friends or enemies in a space outside the law relative to the identity highlighted by the sovereign as a marker of political community.[41]

[37] Schmitt, *Political Theology*, 13.
[38] Schmitt, *Concept of the Political*, 25–7.
[39] Ibid., 19–25.
[40] It is also why Schmitt emphasizes that an exercise of constituent power is not bound to any particular legal form. See Schmitt, *Constitutional Theory*, 130–5.
[41] Schmitt, *Concept of the Political*, 46–7, on the internal enemy.

A group exists as a political community, Schmitt concludes, as long as (and only as long as) it remains capable of taking a decision on the exception and thus to determine its own political identity.[42] The decision must be the group's own, not one imposed on the group, whether by force or fraud, by its internal or external enemies. Since every decision on the exception draws a boundary between insiders and outsiders, we can also conclude that a group will enjoy existence as a political community only as long as it has the power to determine its own membership. It follows that those who would attempt to subject a political community to some normative standard of inclusion must be seen as attacking its very existence. And a political community, Schmitt argues, must take itself to have a right to reject and to repel their proposals.[43]

In making this claim, Schmitt does not put forward a view about the instrumental value of political community to its members. He does not argue, say, that membership in a political community which enjoys unrestricted self-determination, including the right to redraw its boundaries as it sees fit, is necessary to realize the good life of individuals and that we should therefore recognize each political community's right to determine its own identity. Any such argument would raise the obvious question of why it should be morally permissible for the decision on the exception to pre-emptively exclude those who are defined by the sovereign as internal enemies from the community.

Schmitt addresses himself only to those who already see each other as the true members of some pre-legal political community, or who can be brought so to see themselves, and who already accept the claim that nothing should be allowed to thwart that group's political existence.[44] Schmitt's aim is simply to raise awareness, amongst readers or listeners who fit that description, of the danger that an unconditional commitment to legality may threaten the existence of the political community to which they take themselves to belong and which they hold to be supremely valuable. Or, to put the point slightly differently, Schmitt is trying to stop his audience from confusing their political community with their state. The latter is a legally constructed entity whose rules are likely to give some sort of standing, perhaps even citizenship, to some who do not truly belong to the political community and who undermine the homogeneity which is the necessary condition of legal determinacy.[45]

[42] Ibid., 50–3. [43] Ibid., 45–50. [44] Ibid., 26–7. [45] Schmitt, *Leviathan*, 41–52.

Hence, one should recognize that the concrete will of the political community, as manifested in the decision on the exception, must have the power to prevail against the rule-based authority of the state.

In raising awareness of the conditions of preservation of the political community, Schmitt takes himself to be defending democracy. Pretending to take his cues from Rousseau, Schmitt defines democracy as the identity of ruler and ruled, and he argues that the successful sovereign decision on the exception is the most perfect realization of that identity.[46] In taking a decision on the absolute exception, a pretender to sovereign authority proposes to a group of people to define their political identity in a certain way. He or she will be successful, though, as already pointed out, only if a sufficient number of the addressees concur with his or her distinction between friends and enemies and are motivated to draw the requisite practical conclusions from it. Hence, the sovereign decision on the exception is really a communal decision. Through that decision, a group manifests its existence as a political community in the willingness of its members to treat some characteristic which they share as a political identity, an identity for which one must be willing to fight and die.

A successful sovereign decision on the exception, Schmitt suggests, is the paradigmatic case of collective self-government. The sovereign, in taking the decision on the exception, is not a representative whose will is imputed by fiction to all those who are regarded as members of an artificial social body, though their individual wills may differ from that of the sovereign. The successful sovereign decision, rather, is the concrete manifestation, according to Schmitt, of the real, the unanimous will of a people – the only one there can be.[47] And it is only as long as the identity which finds political expression in it is preserved, in the day-to-day business of constituted, legally regulated politics, that the law remains legitimately applicable.[48]

[46] For Schmitt's theory of democracy, see Schmitt, *Crisis of Parliamentary Democracy*, 8–15, 22–32; Schmitt, *Constitutional Theory*, 255–67.

[47] Ibid., 75–7, 125, 130–2, 136; Schmitt, *Concept of the Political*, 27.

[48] Schmitt's critique of the Weimar constitution claims that the revolution of 1918 had failed to bring about homogeneity. See Schmitt, *Constitutional Theory*, 82–8, 154–6. Once the Weimar Republic entered its political crisis, Schmitt argued that a renewed exercise of sovereign authority might be called for to solve the problem. See Schmitt, *Legality and Legitimacy*, 85–94.

The failure of Schmitt's normative argument

We are now in a position to offer an assessment of Schmitt's normative claim. Does Schmitt present a convincing argument for the claim that the legitimate applicability of law requires the existence of a sovereign authority?

It is not difficult to see why Schmitt's theory of popular sovereignty is problematic. Schmitt claims that the sovereign's decision on the exception perfectly realizes the democratic identity of ruler and ruled. But this is so only for the trivial reason that any successful decision on the exception draws the boundaries of political community in such a way as to remove from the polity all those who do not follow and support the sovereign's interpretation of its identity. The identity of ruler and ruled which is manifest in the successful decision on the exception is an artefact of antecedent exclusion, in a space outside of law, of all interesting political difference and all deep dissent.

The view that democracy is the identity of ruler and ruled is normally understood to raise a more interesting claim. Rousseau, for instance, argues that democratic institutions, attitudes and practices will allow citizens who differ in their private interests and their social identities to benefit from the realization of common interests and to do so in a way that ensures a proper respect for the individual freedom of each. For Rousseau, democratic identity results from the reasonable acceptability to all of laws produced by a legal and constitutional system which successfully implements the ideal of civic equality.[49] In Schmitt's view, on the other hand, the identity of ruler and ruled is no longer a goal to be pursued through the instrumentality of settled democratic political practice. Rather, a democratic legal and constitutional system is said to presuppose a political identity which it cannot itself establish or protect and which therefore must be created through the prior dictatorial homogenization of society. The identity of ruler and ruled is no longer realized in a general will but in a particular will which is opposed to the 'crust' of rule-based legality.[50] For Schmitt, democratic politics in the state of normality does little more than to raise a danger of the corruption of the people's antecedent identity. The most we might ever be able to claim in its favour, in circumstances where the sovereign sees no need to take a decision on the exception, is that it does no harm.

[49] See Joshua Cohen, *Rousseau: A Free Community of Equals* (New York: Oxford University Press, 2010).

[50] See Schmitt, *Political Theology*, 14–5.

What seems to start with the laudable aim to achieve non-dominating law thus turns into a paean for a collectivist version of the right of the stronger. It may well be true that judicial or legislative decisions, in a society that has been made perfectly homogeneous by sovereign dictatorship, would no longer imply a danger of a domination of the ruled for the simple reason that judicial and legislative decisions could no longer be very controversial among the rulers and the ruled. But this result, to repeat, is achieved only through the prior violent repression and exclusion of all ethical and cultural diversity in the space of exception. The determinacy which results from perfect homogeneity does not make law legitimate as much as it turns the legitimacy of law into something which now can be dispensed with for the reason that all those who are addressed by law, as well as those who make it, share a political identity and will never disagree about the wisdom of any important decision. All others, by definition, are enemies who are outside the polity. The question of how to treat them is not one of legitimacy but of power politics.

Let me emphasize that this critique of Schmitt's theory of popular sovereignty is not primarily a moral critique. The point is not that Schmitt's conception of popular sovereignty is to be regarded as morally incorrect because it licenses disregard of individual rights or minority rights, however true that may be. The point is that Schmitt's argument, though it claims to ground the legitimacy of law in an appeal to popular sovereignty, is self-defeating as an account of the legitimacy of law.

Imagine that you question the legitimacy of the laws of your society, laws which the sovereign, together with the majority of the members of your community, holds to be legitimately applicable. It would be useless, presumably, for someone to tell you that the laws are legitimate because they express the identity of the people. The fact that you raise a complaint already establishes that you do not belong to the people. If you did belong to the people, on the other hand, you would not raise the complaint, and no explanation of the legitimacy of the law would have to be given to you. Appeals to the legitimacy of the law or the constitution, even if based on the notion of constituent power, become meaningless in Schmitt's framework. Thus, whatever Schmitt thinks he has shown, he cannot have shown that the existence of a sovereign authority is a condition of the legitimate applicability of law.[51]

[51] For a fuller statement of this argument, see Lars Vinx, 'The Incoherence of Strong Popular Sovereignty', *International Journal of Constitutional Law*, 11 (2013), 101.

It will likely be objected that this criticism misunderstands Schmitt's claim that the legitimate applicability of law requires a sovereign authority. Schmitt, it might be argued, is not concerned with a situation in which the positive law does express the people's identity but with a case where it does not. If law does not express the identity of the people, it will run counter to and frustrate the people's collective self-determination and thus be illegitimate. This is what happens, for instance, when a parliamentary legislature is captured by partial interests which have the power to bring about legislative decisions that frustrate the true will of the people, as expressed in a past decision on the exception. The claim that the legitimate applicability of law requires the existence of a sovereign authority is to be understood as the claim that such a situation can only be prevented where there is a sovereign who can switch the law off.[52]

This re-interpretation of the claim that sovereignty is a pre-condition of the legitimate applicability of law concedes that Schmitt is not concerned to offer reasons to a dissenting minority why it should defer to the law though it rejects the law's content. He is now portrayed as concerned, rather, to warn the majority against accepting the deliverances of the positive legal system's procedures as final. In doing so, the majority would alienate its collective autonomy to a positive legal system that provides legal and perhaps political standing and influence to minorities or interest groups which do not share the majority's political identity. The reason why a sovereign authority is needed, then, is not that a sovereign is necessary for the constitution of authoritative law, of law that binds even those who criticize its content. Rather, a sovereign authority is necessary to make sure that the results of legal procedures cannot prevail against the will of the majority of those who claim that they truly belong to the people.

One is inclined to reply that, strictly speaking, it makes no sense for Schmitt to argue that the positive law might frustrate the political self-determination of a people. According to Schmitt, a political community exists if and only if it has the capacity to take a decision on the exception. In this case, though, the law cannot be an impediment to self-determination because the sovereign's decision on the exception can switch it off. If, on the other hand, a group is unable to bring about a decision on the exception, it simply does not exist as a political

[52] For this perspective, see Kahn, *Political Theology*.

community or a people, and it consequently cannot make any sense to complain that the group's self-determination is impeded by law.

Admittedly, this reply is a little too quick. Schmitt's writings on sovereignty during the Weimar era address a situation in which it is unclear, not least to Schmitt himself, whether there still is a sovereign authority. Put differently, they address a situation in which it is unclear whether the German people still exist as a political community in Schmitt's sense. The answer to these questions must depend on whether the German people, suitably led, are still capable of bringing about a decision on the exception which will, if necessary, prevail against the corrupted positive legality of the Weimar constitution – and whether the German people are still capable of bringing about a decision on the exception depends, in turn, on whether they are willing to support such a decision in light of the conviction that to do so is a pre-condition of the preservation of their collective autonomy. Schmitt's theory of sovereignty, then, is perhaps best seen as an exhortation to Germans to be willing to take the decision on the exception.[53]

This alternative reading of Schmitt's claim that the existence of sovereign authority is a condition of the legitimate applicability of law, in contrast to the one we already rejected, is not self-defeating. But it is also devoid of jurisprudential interest.

We can admit that if political existence is understood in Schmitt's way, it will follow that a political community must always be ready to put aside its commitment to legality if it wants to preserve itself. We can also admit that if political existence, as Schmitt defines it, is desirable, we should fight against an ideology of legalism which wishes to make the law out to be the final arbiter of all social disputes. But what is all that to the law? Why should the law, faced with Schmitt's conception of political existence, abandon its own claim to normative finality? Why should it recognize the Schmittian sovereign's decision on the exception as a legally relevant decision, as a decision about the legitimate applicability of the law? The law, as far as I can see, would have to recognize the sovereign's decision as legally relevant only if the existence of an authority that can take a decision on the absolute exception were necessary for the law to be able to achieve its own essential purposes. But is this the case?

Arguably, a system of law must be backed up by a state to be sufficiently effective to achieve whatever essential purposes it might have.

[53] See Schmitt, *Crisis of Parliamentary Democracy*, 65–76, on the need for a nationalist political myth.

This was one of the key claims of the classical doctrine of sovereignty. But, as should be clear, the law may very well have the backing of a state even where there is no sovereign capable of taking a decision on the absolute exception. The presence of a sovereign, moreover, is not just unnecessary to secure the law's effectiveness, but it is also likely to frustrate the law's essential purposes on some of the most plausible accounts of what these might be. In recognizing the sovereign's decision as legally relevant, the law would, for example, have to betray the aim which is peculiarly its own according to the classical discourse of sovereignty: namely, the aim to subject social conflict, as far as possible, to peaceful arbitration and to suppress the employment of violence not licensed by the law. We arrive at the same result, obviously, if we follow Fuller and take the law's essential purpose to be the establishment of an inviolable rule of law which will make exercises of power predictable to those affected.[54] To maintain the claim that the existence of a Schmittian sovereign is necessary to allow the law to achieve its essential purposes, one would, it seems, have to adopt the rather silly view that the essential purpose of law consists in not getting in the way of the decision on the exception.

Legal positivists who question the claim that the law has essential purposes are unlikely to arrive at a different conclusion. In recognizing the legal relevance of the Schmittian sovereign, the law would, for instance, betray its claim to authority because the law, to claim authority, must take its own decisions to be final.[55] And if we deny that the law necessarily claims authority, or perhaps that it has any nature at all, there is simply nothing left to build on in trying to establish the jurisprudential relevance of the decision on the absolute exception. Schmitt is not in a position to adopt an instrumental conception of law and to argue that the law's essential purpose is to serve whatever goal the sovereign decides to pursue. The sole purpose of sovereign action, according to Schmitt, is to create homogeneity, and Schmitt is firmly committed to the view that this goal can only be achieved through dictatorial action freed of all legal restraints. Schmitt's conception of sovereignty, I conclude, turns out to be too purely political to be of any jurisprudential relevance.

[54] See Lon L. Fuller, *The Morality of Law*, rev. edn. (New Haven, CT: Yale University Press, 1964).

[55] See Joseph Raz, 'Authority, Law, and Morality' in Raz, *Ethics in the Public Domain. Essays in the Morality of Law and Politics*, rev. edn. (Oxford University Press, 1995), 210–37.

Schmitt's basic claim is that legality can never make any positive contribution to the legitimate settlement of profound social conflict. He holds, as we have seen, that whenever the answer to a political question is not determined by a background of social agreement, its arbitration in a legally regulated form must involve a hidden exercise of domination under the guise of the rule of law. The liberal idea that suitably constructed legal procedures could ever lead to the fair settlement of political conflict consequently must be a form of false consciousness – a consciousness which must be fought because it might stop the majority, those who truly belong to the people, from asserting their identity against a minority which relies on the rule of law to thwart the strong and subject them to the 'indirect rule' of the weak. Schmitt's point, of course, is not that the rule of the strong is more justifiable, from a moral point of view, than the rule of the weak. His point is simply that as a member of the majority, one should reject the constraints of legality on the majority's power once one has seen them for what Schmitt thinks they are: the impositions of alien groups whose members ought to be regarded as enemies and be done away with in the interest of securing substantive homogeneity.

I hope it is clear that it would be a grave mistake to regard Schmitt's purported rehabilitation of the doctrine of sovereignty as a continuation of the classical discourse of sovereignty. In that discourse, sovereignty and law are seen as essentially arbitrative. Hobbes' sovereign creates unity, and thus peace and security, through representation, not through antecedent exclusion.[56] His will displaces the wills of those who enter into a social contract; it must be owned, as Hobbes says, even by those who disagree with the wisdom of the sovereign's decisions.[57] But this displacement, as Schmitt himself complained in his book about Hobbes,

[56] Hobbes, *Leviathan*, 117–21. It might be objected that Hobbes is not as concerned with peaceful arbitration as I am suggesting. Note, however, that there is not the slightest indication, in Hobbes, of the view that only those who share a certain antecedent identity may become members of the state. Hobbes, admittedly, does not deny that those who violate the social contract may legitimately be treated as enemies. But he clearly takes the view that the default stance of the state must be to extend an offer of inclusion to all who are willing to give peace in exchange for protection, a view that is in stark contrast with Schmitt's views on the constitution of political community. Hobbes also holds – as he makes clear in Chapter 28 of *Leviathan* – that those who have entered into the social contract are entitled not to be treated as enemies as long as they do not violate the law in outer act. This, again, is a demand of the rule of law that Schmitt is concerned to reject.

[57] Hobbes, *Leviathan*, 120, 124.

does not destroy the individual will by fusing it into a true collective identity based on a friend-enemy distinction.[58] It only excludes or pre-empts it for the time being, for as long as an individual has reason to prefer sovereign protection to the danger of the state of nature. Sovereign representation thus turns plurality into unity without eliminating difference. A modern liberal-democratic state, despite the fact that it does not contain a personal sovereign, does much the same, provided that it has the capacity to finally settle all social conflict.

In Schmitt's theory of sovereignty, by contrast, sovereign representation, as a principle of political unity, is replaced with pre-legal exclusion, and the very possibility of political difference within a legally constituted and pacified political unity is denied. To be more precise, Schmitt's legal theory deliberately attempts to create an attitude, in those to whom it addresses itself, which will make political difference within legal unity impossible. This political project, if I am correct, has little to teach us about the nature of law and the conditions of its legitimacy.

Schmittian sovereignty and the foundations of public law

The critique of Schmitt presented in this chapter, I hasten to add, is not meant to suggest that we ought to get rid of the notion of popular sovereignty or that we ought to abandon the project of explicating the proper foundations of democratic public law. What I have tried to show is only that Schmitt's attempt to conceive of sovereignty as a personal or 'concrete' authority, prior to both state and law, is unhelpful. Contemporary defenders of popular sovereignty, as well as those searching for foundations of modern public law, are well advised to look for a different source of inspiration. To illustrate this conclusion, I would like to end with a brief discussion of Martin Loughlin's recent attempt to found modern public law on a Schmittian notion of sovereignty.

According to Loughlin, 'the public realm now presents itself as autonomous, it cannot be anchored in either divine law or natural law. The public realm must function according to laws that we have given ourselves.' Loughlin holds, in other words, that the foundations of modern public law cannot and must not be sought in a constitution in natural law. Any such attempt, apart from running the danger of failing

[58] Schmitt, *Leviathan*, 53–64.

to convince denizens of a post-metaphysical age, would be exposed to the suspicion of being un-democratic, as it would apparently have to deny the people's power autonomously to determine the conditions of its own political life.

It would be wrong, Loughlin goes on to argue, to react to the failure of the idea of a constitution in natural law by embracing positivism, that is, 'to follow Hobbes' and to conclude that 'law means simply the command of the established law-making authority'. To do this, Loughlin holds, would imply that 'the conditions under which . . . law-making authority is exercised are matters of politics that lie beyond juristic knowledge.'[59] Loughlin accuses modern positivists such as Hart and Kelsen of the same mistake which he attributes to Hobbes. They are said to be unable to reflect on the legal constitution of law-making authority because they allegedly hold the constitution of that authority to be 'beyond juristic knowledge'. Schmitt's theory of popular sovereignty, Loughlin suggests, provides a way out of this impasse. It will allow us to understand a democratic constitution as the product of the validating choices of a perfectly autonomous constituent power.

It is not quite clear whether Loughlin's critique of positivism is meant to be theoretical or normative. On a theoretical reading, Loughlin complains that positivism provides an incomplete understanding of public law. However, if the critique of Schmitt presented in this chapter is sound, then this theoretical criticism begs the question. Loughlin assumes that Schmitt's theory of (popular) sovereignty contributes to juristic knowledge and extends it beyond the limits implied by Hartian or Kelsenian approaches. But it is far from clear, as should by now be obvious, whether Schmitt's theory of sovereignty really does this.

Note that Loughlin's attack against Hobbes is confused, since Hobbes acknowledges that the valid exercise of legislative authority is conditioned by a constitution in natural law that, in Hobbes' view, surely is not beyond juristic knowledge. More importantly, Loughlin also misunderstands the legal positivism of Kelsen (or, for that matter, of Hart). According to Kelsen, for instance, laws are not mandatory commands issued by an un-commanded commander. They are rules that authorize organs of state to employ legitimate force. As such, they lay down the conditions, among other things, of the rightful exercise of legislative power. It is therefore plainly false to claim, with Schmitt, that the Pure

[59] Loughlin, *Foundations of Public Law*, 158.

Theory of Law is unable to reflect on the conditions of the rightful exercise of legislative authority.[60]

Loughlin is in a position to chastise modern positivists for not recognizing that there is a law that enables and conditions the exercise of political power only because he wrongly attributes an Austinian picture of law to Kelsen.[61] This manoeuvre is made all the less convincing by the fact that Loughlin himself seems implicitly attached to an Austinian picture of law. While he attacks Austin's claim that all law is sovereign command, Loughlin at times seems to express his agreement with the view that, in a modern legal order, all *positive* law is sovereign command.[62] He also holds, like Schmitt, that *droit politique*, the meta-positive law which is said to constitute the state, is not judicially enforceable and that its content, since it cannot be drawn from a science of public right, is wholly subject to the materially unrestricted choices of the (popular) sovereign.[63] In substance, this is an Austinian picture of the relation between the sovereign and the law, veiled by the rhetorical choice to refer to what Austin would have called constitutional morality as *droit politique*.

This rhetorical choice, however, begs the question why *droit politique* deserves to be recognized as a species of law. The only convincing answer I can think of is that it consists of rules which – while they are not commands backed by threats – condition the valid exercise of public power. But if that is what makes *droit politique* into law, it is perfectly possible, as Kelsen, in particular, has shown, to conceive of it as part and parcel of the system of positive law – since the system of positive law as a whole is best understood as a system of authorizations for the use of force – and to make it judicially enforceable by giving judges the power to void purported acts of public power which lack adequate legal authorization.[64]

The real issue here, I submit, is not that modern, 'normativist' positivists have no coherent story about the foundations of public law or that

[60] See Hans Kelsen, 'Who Ought to be the Guardian of the Constitution?' in *The Guardian of the Constitution*, 174–221.

[61] For Kelsen's relationship to Austin's command theory, see Lars Vinx, 'Austin, Kelsen and the Model of Sovereignty: Notes on the History of Modern Legal Positivism' in Michael Freeman and Patricia Mindus (eds.), *The Legacy of John Austin's Jurisprudence* (Dordrecht, Netherlands: Springer, 2013), 51–71.

[62] Loughlin, *Foundations of Public Law*, 186, 196, 209–16.

[63] See, e.g., ibid., 229.

[64] Hans Kelsen, 'The Nature and Development of Constitutional Adjudication' in *The Guardian of the Constitution*, 22–78.

they cannot offer any substantive discussion of the problem of the legality of acts of state. What really bothers Loughlin (and others) is that modern positivist approaches to public law deny the jurisprudential relevance of a certain kind of popular sovereign. Kelsen refuses to admit that a popular sovereign transcendent to all law, and completely unbound from it, could be more than a *de facto* power. He denies that the decisions of such a sovereign could ever be regarded as a validating source of constitutional legality. The claim that this stance leads to an incomplete understanding of the law rests on a normative criticism, on the claim that rule-based positivism systematically obscures the ground of the legitimacy of law. Authors who, like Loughlin, are concerned to resurrect Schmitt's strong notion of popular sovereignty hold that there can be no true collective freedom unless the established legal and political system is made subject to the legally untrammelled choices of a meta-legal popular sovereign.[65]

Loughlin, then, must establish, like Schmitt, that his adaptation of a strong notion of popular sovereignty is required from a normative point of view, that reliance on that conception of sovereignty is necessary to explain the *legitimate* constitution of legal order, that it is necessary to allow us to conceive of legal order as the product of a legitimating collective choice. In the absence of a constitution in natural law, however, it is difficult to see what could constitute a constituent power prior to all law, other than Schmitt's distinction between friend and enemy. And that distinction, as we have seen, apart from implying a rather problematic understanding of democracy, systematically fails to account for the legitimacy of law.

The reason for this failure, I suspect, is not that Schmitt did not understand the limitations of his own theory. It is that Schmitt was not really trying, despite his protestations to the contrary, to explain the legitimacy of law. Schmitt's clever and inventive theory of sovereignty is a tactical deception, designed to misdirect those who are interested in understanding the foundations of a democratic constitution on to an authoritarian path. It is time for theorists of public law to stop falling for it.

[65] See also Hans Lindahl's contribution to this volume (Chapter 3); Panu Minkkinen, 'Political Constitutionalism versus Political Constitutional Theory: Law, Power and Politics', *International Journal of Constitutional Law*, 11 (2013), 585. It should go without saying that Schmitt's project of resurrecting the absolutist *Obrigkeitsstaat* in pseudo-democratic garb is not the only way to understand popular sovereignty.

6

Schmitt, Oakeshott and the Hobbesian legacy in the crisis of our times

DAVID BOUCHER

Thomas Hobbes, Carl Schmitt and Michael Oakeshott were theorists of crisis, and all located its epicentre in the conceptual confusion and erosion of the theory and practice of authority and its relation to power. During the 1930s, Schmitt in Germany and Oakeshott in England developed an admiration for Hobbes. Schmitt and Oakeshott admired Hobbes' ingenuity but were ambivalent about his legacy. Each identified in Hobbes an individualism that was somehow contributory towards modern liberalism, which was both a cause and a symptom of the modern crisis. They differed on whether this individualism was a good thing. Schmitt considered Hobbes an instigator of the crisis. For Schmitt, Hobbes undermined the power-authority nexus by allowing a place for conscience which was embryonic of the public and private divide that facilitated liberal challenges to state authority. For Oakeshott, Hobbes' exclusive tying of authority to the control of men's actions rather than their intellects or conscience was one of his crowning achievements.[1] The key to understanding the different perspectives of Schmitt and Oakeshott on Hobbes is the different emphases they gave to power and authority and the relation of each to legitimacy.

Bertrand de Jouvenal makes an important distinction against those who wish to conflate authority and power. Power, or force, is a relationship that may pertain irrespective of agreement, whereas the distinguishing feature of authority is that it is exercised only over those who consent to it.[2] De Jouvenal argued that the contribution of ancient Rome to our understanding of authority had been lost. Practically and theoretically,

[1] Michael Oakeshott, 'Thomas Hobbes', 4 *Scrutiny*, (1935), 263; reprinted in Michael Oakeshott, *The Concept of a Philosophical Jurisprudence* (Exeter, UK: Imprint Academic, 2007), ed. Luke O'Sullivan, 117.

[2] Bertrand de Jouvenal, *Sovereignty: An Enquiry into the Political Good* (Cambridge University Press, 1957), trans. J. F. Huntington, 32.

we no longer know what authority really is. Part of the problem was the conflation of its modern forms with power and dominion.[3]

Authority was always related to a particular context and was internal to a set of arrangements which provided the explanation of how the elements cohered and functioned. Authority was not restricted to the political sphere. The key distinction to be made is between executive authority, of which political authority is a species, and epistemic authority, which is non-executive. Unlike political authority, epistemic authority does not imply a right to command or rule, nor a correlative duty on the part of others to obey. Knowledge does not give anyone the right to impose his or her considered conclusions on others. This is something that Hobbes made clear in his characterization of the state of nature. Reason obliges no one, and it is only by an act of will that we may authorize others to rule over us, that is, to exercise political authority.

The perceived danger in modern democracies, by those who fear the unaccountable influence of the 'expert', is not so much that epistemic authorities will impose their designs upon society, in the manner of philosopher kings, but that they will come to wield overbearing influence over legitimately elected executive political authorities who defer to their 'superior' knowledge.[4]

The crisis of civilization

Schmitt and Oakeshott, in their different ways, contribute to a significant body of literature evident in the 1920s and 1930s whose subject matter may be characterized as the 'crisis of civilization'. Schmitt and Oakeshott subscribe to a theory of degeneration. The degeneration was attributable to faulty ways of thinking. Ultimately, the state and politics had somehow become the victim of false conceptions and inappropriate expectations. In essence, we labour under misconceptions about the nature and purpose of the state and sovereignty and misunderstand the character of the rule of law, authority and its relation to power and legitimacy.

[3] Hannah Arendt, 'What Is Authority' in Arendt, *Between Past and Future* (New York: Viking Press, 1968).

[4] Particularly sophisticated warnings against this appeared in the early 1980s. See Ronald Beiner, *Political Judgement* (London: Methuen, 1983) and Hans-Georg Gadamer, *Reason in the Age of Science* (Cambridge, MA: MIT Press, 1982). For a perceptive and neglected discussion of such distinctions, see Richard de George, *The Nature and Limits of Authority* (Lawrence, KS: University of Kansas Press, 1985).

Both Schmitt and Oakeshott turn to Hobbes as an epistemic authority, but each portrays him in his own image. For Oakeshott, Hobbes is the philosopher of authority, who teaches us about legitimate governance, while Schmitt skates around the issue of authorization, preferring instead to offer practical success, or power, as the criterion of authoritative legitimacy. In essence, for Schmitt, Hobbes is the philosopher of politics *par excellence*, while for Oakeshott, Hobbes is the philosopher of governance *par excellence.* Schmitt and Oakeshott identified trends evident for centuries, manifesting in the most pernicious ways in modern Europe. For Schmitt and Oakeshott, the crisis was the affliction of liberal democracy and the erosion of sovereign legitimacy.

The threats to civilization they perceived constituted an undermining of the myths that peoples tell themselves about the nature of their communities and the ties that bind them. Neither used the idea of myth in a pejorative manner. For each, myths play an essential role in bolstering the state apparatus and sustaining order. For Schmitt, Hobbes' genius was to recognize the necessity of myth,[5] and for Oakeshott, Hobbes' ingenuity lay in retelling or reconstructing the Western civilizational myth.

Schmitt's crisis

The First World War and its aftermath marked, for Schmitt, a humiliation for Germany and a decisive turn in European history. In the postwar settlement, Germany was treated like a criminal to be punished, marking the *de facto* abandonment of the public law of Europe and its concomitant principle of the just enemy that had regulated foreign policy and wars between states since the Peace of Westphalia in 1648.[6] The weight of reparations and foreign control of the Reichsbank and German railroads served to undermine sovereignty even further, with the Rhineland bearing the brunt of the burden.[7]

[5] For Schmitt's imaginative but ultimately manipulative and distorted interpretation of Hobbes' imagery, see Tomaž Mastnak, 'Schmitt's Behemoth' in J. Tralau (ed.), *Thomas Hobbes and Carl Schmitt: The Politics of Order and Myth* (London: Routledge, 2011), 17–38.

[6] Gabriella Slomp, *Carl Schmitt and the Politics of Hostility, Violence and Terror* (London: Palgrave, 2009), 6.

[7] Carl Schmitt, 'The Status Quo and the Peace' (1925); reprinted in Arthur J. Jacobson and Bernard Schlink (eds.), *Weimar: A Jurisprudence of Crisis* (Berkeley, CA: University of California Press, 2002), 291.

Schmitt saw himself as contributing to the literature of crisis which emerged around the issue of the modern state, and he was in particular critical of pluralistic conceptions, such as those of Gierke, Maitland, Figgis, Barker, Cole and Laski, which he saw as undermining the state by demoting it to one of many associations within the body politic.[8] In his *Political Theology*, Schmitt accused the bourgeoisie, the espousers of liberalism, of the same sort of weakness he detected in romantics, namely, indecisiveness, preferring to defer decisions with a motion to adjourn or refer them to an investigative committee.[9] He developed a critique of parliamentary democracy, the institution most closely associated with liberalism.[10] The principles of openness and discussion, intrinsic to parliamentarianism, with the advent of modern mass democracy rendered public discussion a mere antiquated formality.[11] The myth upon which parliamentary democracy was based had been exposed. No right-thinking person could any longer be deluded into thinking that rational debate, open discussion, a free press and free competition of ideas resulted in the 'truth' or better legislation and policies. The opposing myths which rejected peaceful negotiation and agreement were, in his view, more intellectually vibrant, particularly the concept of a Marxist rationalistic dictatorship of the proletariat and the irrationalist dictatorship of direct force proposed by Georges Sorel.

Schmitt rejects Sorel's substantive political conclusions, but he extols the virtues of the irrationalism of myths and their intellectual power to sustain our political practices and institutions. Myth, which need not be expressive of a reality, supplies the vital strength for national enthusiasm, legitimizes great causes and harnesses the energy of the nation to reach heroic heights. Mussolini well understood the irrational power of myth in creating the myth of the Italian nation, a nation that was yet to be made into a concrete reality. In its creation, he swept aside the democratic parliamentarianism of Italy, which had been grounded in the traditional ideology of Anglo-Saxon liberalism.

8 Carl Schmitt, 'State Ethics and the Pluralist State' (1930); reprinted in Jacobson and Schlink, *Weimar: A Jurisprudence of Crisis*, 303–12.

9 Carl Schmitt, *Political Theology: Four Chapters on the Concept of Sovereignty* (University of Chicago Press, 2005), trans. George Schwab, 53.

10 See Ellen Kennedy's 'Introduction' in Carl Schmitt, *The Crisis of Parliamentary Democracy* (Cambridge, MA: MIT Press, 1988), trans. Ellen Kennedy, xvi.

11 'German romantics possess an odd trait: everlasting conversation ... a product of a gruesomely comic fantasy' (Schmitt, *The Crisis of Parliamentary Democracy*, 49).

The immense power of myth, the strongest political tendency of the day, had been realized in the face of the decline of the relative rationalism of parliamentary thought. The danger was the proliferation of such myths which served to destroy the 'last remnants of solidarity' that held a community together.[12] Hobbes, in Schmitt's view, recognized this but ultimately failed to invoke the right type of myth to harness enthusiasm for the political arrangements he proposed.

For three hundred years there had been a degenerative process which had ended in 'the age of neutralizations and depoliticizations'.[13] The triumph of liberalism constituted the demise of the political, that is, the ability decisively to distinguish friends and enemies. The celebration of the individual embedded in the principles of 1789 and 1848 and somewhat stifled under the Reich of Bismark in 1870 were resurrected in the Weimar constitution. The substance of the constitution of 1919 was the imposition by the West of the liberal rule of law tradition on Germany. The foundational principles of states built on the idea of the liberal rule of law were the sanctity of the rights of the individual and the separation of powers. Schmitt contended, 'In this context, the freedom of the individual is essentially unlimited, the state and its powers limited.'[14] The underlying assumption was that there was an unlimited sphere of opportunities for individuals and a comprehensive system of checks on the activity of the state.

The liberal rule of law, however, embodied fundamental misconceptions about law, exemplified by the confusion of Hans Kelsen's legal positivism, in which the formality of the law assumes impartial application. It is the elimination of anything arbitrary and personal with reference to an objective norm in which the impersonal validity of the legal order rests on a will-less impersonal norm.[15] This, in Schmitt's view, fails to grasp the fundamental indeterminacy of law.[16] Liberal democracies operate according to an incoherent logic which tries to eliminate all elements of the personal from the legal order.[17] Law cannot completely specify the circumstances of its applicability, and conformity of the law to

[12] Schmitt, *The Crisis of Parliamentary Democracy*, 68–76.
[13] Carl Schmitt, 'The Age of Neutralizations and Depoliticizations' (1929) in Schmitt, *The Concept of the Political* (Chicago University Press, 2007), trans. George Schwab, 80–96.
[14] Carl Schmitt, 'The Liberal Rule of Law' (1928); reprinted in Jacobson and Schlink, *Weimar: A Jurisprudence of Crisis*, 296.
[15] Schmitt, *Political Theology*, 29. [16] Schmitt, *Political Theology*, 30.
[17] Tom Sorell, 'Schmitt's UnHobbesian politics of Emergency', *Rechtsphilosophische Hefte*, 11 (2005), 130.

particular circumstances is always subject to discretion or judgement. In other words, law is always under-determined. Schmitt further distinguishes between the rule itself and the act of judgement. Application of the rule requires judgement by a human will and is categorically distinct from the rule or norm itself. Law is only fully realized in a judgement and not in a norm.[18]

Typically, the rule of law is manifest in parliamentary democracies, a mixture of forms including monarchy and democracy, essentially the creation of the bourgeoisie to protect itself from the state. Just as the liberal bourgeoisie were apolitical, the liberal state was anti-political. The secret ballot itself served to isolate people from each other at the very moment they bore public responsibility, and majority rule necessarily minimized the political decision.[19]

The problem with Weimar and liberal democracies in general was their heterogeneity. They were socially divided by class, culture, race and religion and were inconsistent with a political state because of their inability to distinguish between friend and enemy.[20] From at least 1923, Schmitt believed that a fundamental presupposition of sovereignty was a homogeneous body politic. Every democracy, he argued, needed a homogeneous unified people because only then could it assume political responsibility.

Influenced by his reading of Hobbes, Schmitt took the state of nature, the natural condition of man, to be composed of collectivities poised to do battle with each other. It was not in the battle that politics consisted 'but in the mode of behaviour which is determined by this possibility, by clearly evaluating the concrete situation and thereby being able to distinguish correctly the real friend and the real enemy'.[21] Leo Strauss suggested that the fundamental difference between Schmitt and Hobbes in this regard was that in Hobbes' state of nature everyone is the enemy of everyone else, and the purpose of the characterization is to motivate people to deliver themselves from the predicament. In Schmitt, all political behaviour is oriented to friends and enemies.[22]

[18] See Iain Hampsher-Monk and Keith Zimmerman, 'Schmitt's Critique of Rule-of-Law Liberalism', *Rechtsphilosophische Hefte*, 11 (2005), 113.

[19] Schmitt, 'The Liberal Rule of Law', 296–8.

[20] Schmitt, 'The Liberal Rule of Law', 299.

[21] Schmitt, *Concept of the Political*, 37; Leo Strauss, 'Notes on The Concept of the Political'; reprinted in Schmitt, *Concept of the Political*, 105. Also see Heinrich Meier, *Carl Schmitt and Leo Strauss: The Hidden Dialogue* (University of Chicago Press, 2006). It also includes Strauss's 'Notes' and in addition three letters from Strauss to Schmitt.

[22] Strauss, 'Notes on The Concept of the Political', 107.

In essence, then, Schmitt's diagnosis of the crisis afflicting modern society was expressive of his opposition to individualism, liberalism, parliamentarianism, modern democracy and the rule of law, all of which were the drivers behind the trends culminating in the modern malaise of state authority and the undermining of state power.

Oakeshott's crisis

All societies, Oakeshott tells us, are founded upon imaginative myths. A myth is not strictly speaking philosophy but may include elements of philosophy. Hobbes' *Leviathan*, for example, was described by Oakeshott as a work of philosophical literature, a genuine work of art and a masterpiece of English literature, expressive of the collective dream of civilization. The substance of the collective dream was a myth, 'an imaginative interpretation of human existence, the perception (not the solution) of the mystery of human life'.[23] A myth or legend serves the practical purpose of reminding a people of its origin, heritage and traditions. It is not history but may have historical elements. It differs from history because history is a disinterested activity released from considerations of conduct. Nor is it a political doctrine, or ideology – that would make it too rationalist for comfort. A legend or myth is a vital aspect of the self-understanding of any society which has been awakened to political self-consciousness in that it constructs for itself an imaginative story of how it came to be what it is, including that society's imagined conception of its manner of government and of being governed.[24] Oakeshott tells us, 'In legend, all that is casual, secondary, unresolved, unmediated, obscure or uncertain is absent. There is a clear outline; men act from fear and simple motives; there is a unity of feeling. It is a pattern; there are repetitions, types. Exact time and place absent, but everything else is exact and nothing is confused.'[25] 'Every people', Oakeshott argued, had 'some beliefs about the kind of community they compose, and usually they are among its

[23] Michael Oakeshott, '*Leviathan*: A Myth' in *Hobbes on Civil Association* (Oxford, UK: Blackwell, 1975), 150. Schmitt appears to have been unaware of Oakeshott's work on Hobbes until 1979. Carl Schmitt to Ellen Kennedy, 6 November 1979 and 4 January 1980. Oakeshott papers, British Library of Political Science, London, Oakeshott, 1/6/3.

[24] Michael Oakeshott, *Lectures in the History of Political Thought* (Exeter, UK: Imprint Academic, 2006), 208.

[25] Michael Oakeshott, 'Notebook', dated Sept. 1958, Oakeshott papers, British Library of Political Science, 2/1/16 XVI, p. 18.

more important beliefs.'[26] Myths and legends are not necessarily untrue. What is important about them is that they represent a people's own self-awareness of its politics and are expressive of its confidence in itself.[27] Understanding oneself as belonging to a particular kind of community necessarily involves beliefs about the sort of person one is. Not all myths, however, are the genuine article. Counterfeit myths have been manufactured from time to time which are enemies of civilization.[28]

The myths we construct in coming to understand the modern European state are contingently related to each other, the outcome of human choice and refined under the guise of different, but barely disguised, dualisms whose features are portrayed in different lights and whose unity is made up of diverse characteristics. They are 'ideal characters', never found in a pure form, but which coexist with each other in intimate connection. In an early formulation of the binary divide, Oakeshott referred to them as discussions about the function of governing, relating to 'activity of a primary order', or substantive activity, and 'activity of a secondary order', or 'simply regulative' activity.[29] The latter understanding is variously labelled 'civil association', 'societas', 'nomocracy', the 'politics of scepticism' and 'libertarianism'. This, for Oakeshott, is undoubtedly the self-perception compatible with the myth of civilization. The alternative vision, which appears to be a counterfeit myth, is variously designated 'enterprise association', 'universitas', 'rationalism', 'teleocracy' and 'collectivism'. Oakeshott points to a number of synonyms, of which by implication he disapproves. They are 'managed society', 'communism', 'national socialism', 'socialism', 'economic democracy' and 'central planning'.[30]

The first – civil association and its synonyms – was associated with the emergence of the 'individual' in early modern Europe and the flourishing of personal freedom, most noticeable at first in renaissance Italy with the demise of medieval communal life. It was distinguished not by subservience to a master or lord but by the ability to make one's choices for oneself.[31] In this respect, 'Every practical undertaking and every

[26] Oakeshott, *Lectures in the History of Political Thought*, 209. [27] Ibid., 45–6
[28] Oakeshott, '*Leviathan*: A Myth', 153.
[29] Michael Oakeshott, *The Vocabulary of a Modern European State* (Exeter, UK: Imprint Academic, 2008), ed. Luke O'Sullivan, 99.
[30] Michael Oakeshott, *Rationalism in Politics and Other Essays* (Indianapolis, IN: Liberty Press, 1991), ed. Timothy Fuller, 398.
[31] Oakeshott, *Rationalism in Politics and Other Essays*, 364.

intellectual pursuit revealed itself as an assemblage of opportunities for self-enactment.'[32]

Simultaneously with the emergence of the individual who took responsibility for making moral choices arose the anti-individual, unaccustomed to making such choices and who longed for life in the community where such decisions were made for him or her. Oakeshott suggested that 'the "anti-individual" had feelings rather than thoughts, impulses rather than opinion, inabilities rather than passions, and was only dimly aware of his power.'[33] Individuality and moral choice were not valued and instead subsumed under the conception of the common good in a form of association understood on the analogy of a *universitas* and in which substantive goals and purposes were imposed by the rulers. The anti-individual, collectively known as the masses not on account of their numbers but because of their rejection of individuality and the longing for the security of the community, required leaders to direct them. They required a discourse not of persuasion but of demonstrative, or scientific, proof. In other words, the sort of authority they craved was both epistemic and executive.

It was the 'rationalist' in politics who epitomized the leader of the masses. To approach political problems with preconceived systems of principles or rights as criteria of and guides to conduct was typically rationalist. The rationalist conceived ruling as a problem-solving activity and believed that he or she began with a *tabula rasa*. Starting from first principles, solutions to problems were devised and pursued as substantive purposes, with laws enacted instrumental to the achievement of the desired ends. The rationalist believed in certainty and the sovereignty of reason. It was politics as the crow flies, relying heavily on technical knowledge, or the politics of technique and the mistaken belief that the practical knowledge embedded in practices may be profitably ignored.

The binary oppositions informed the business of governing, ruling or engaging in political discourse. Oakeshott argued that they enable us to understand far better the complex character of the modern European state than any of the moribund conceptually vacuous political labels that today have become shrouded in confusion. Oakeshott was averse to attaching labels to himself on the grounds that the current vocabulary of politics had become debased and that categories such as left and right, liberal and conservative, totalitarian and egalitarian had degenerated into

[32] Michael Oakeshott, *On Human Conduct* (Oxford University Press, 1975), 240.
[33] Oakeshott, *Rationalism in Politics*, 370–1.

an 'artless muddle'.[34] He contended that the political doctrines evident in continental Europe during the 1930s were the result of a 'deep and natural dissatisfaction' with liberal democracy, whose allure had fascinated Western Europe since before 1789 and had become so embedded in the modern psyche that its profundity could not save it from the fate of all things which became intellectually boring. He disparaged liberalism for having two afflictions: an inability to discriminate its true friends and 'the nervy conscience which extends a senile and indiscriminate welcome to everyone who claims to be on the side of "progress"'.[35]

Each of the newer doctrines was a reaction to the doctrine of liberal democracy as a whole or some specific aspects of it.[36] Oakeshott saw merits in aspects of the doctrine of representative democracy because it included certain elements he valued, including modification of the extreme individualism associated with liberal democracy. While rationalism, or managerialism, has become almost irresistible as the term in which the modern state was conceived, there was a commensurate corruption of the vocabulary of politics, a blurring of distinctions and a detachment of concepts from their proper place, and a grafting of them on to places they did not belong. He complained particularly of the abuse of the vocabulary of authority, which 'has generated a fatal indifference to the authority of an office of rule and has persuaded many that the principle of association in a state is to be sought not in the authority of its government but in a consensual approval of its performances – which, of course, in a modern state is always lacking'.[37]

There had been an unhealthy tendency to conflate power and authority. Power, as Oakeshott conceived it, was a relationship among humans which assumed the ability to bring about with certainty a desired response in the conduct of another and the ability and disposition in the respondent to act appropriately. Neither could there be absolute certainty, nor was power ever completely irresistible. Oakeshott maintained: 'Power, then, is categorically distinguished from authority. To have power does not, itself, endow a man or an office with authority; to be acknowledged to have authority does not in itself endow a man or an office with power; and to recognise the power behind a demand, although it may be a good reason for complying with what is demanded, cannot be

[34] Ibid., 439. [35] Ibid., 385.

[36] Michael Oakeshott (ed.), *The Political Doctrines of Contemporary Europe* (Cambridge University Press, 1947), xi–xii, xvii.

[37] Oakeshott, *Rationalism in Politics*, 444–5.

a reason for acknowledging an obligation to do so. Thus, a well-informed blackmailer and his fearful subject may be said to stand to one another in a transitory relationship of power.'[38]

Oakeshott attributed the relative dominance of teleocracy, or managerialism, in the development of the European state to modern warfare.[39] Once the state intruded so pervasively, it was difficult to roll back the frontiers. The development and intensity of industrialization were the basic explanation. The modern era, Oakeshott claimed, was dominated by the ever-present threat of war, necessitating provision of security against foreign foes. Accompanied by the success of the Baconian technocratic conception of the state, war provided the conditions favourable to the adoption of a managerial conception of governing. With greater and lesser efficiency, each state busied itself with building the capacity to attack or defend itself against other states. The total mobilization of the state in the twentieth century during and leading up to two world wars, with accentuated levels of destruction and the use of propaganda to achieve hitherto unheard of levels of homogeneity, required heightened levels of exploitation and managerial acumen which were decisive in the development of the view that the state was an enterprise invested with a common purpose, to be managed by government. In early 1941, the attitude was exemplified in a British government memorandum: 'war is now a highly mechanised form of economic activity requiring very heavy capital investment. It is now waged on a "totalitarian" scale involving a diversion of the entire national economy to a single purpose.'[40]

The main difference we are able to discern in the analysis of crisis between Hobbes and Schmitt is fundamental and completely at odds. For Schmitt, successful politics is the ability permanently to distinguish between friends and enemies and the perpetual readiness of the sovereign to respond decisively. Modern trends had impaired the ability of the state to act decisively. For Oakeshott, it was the enhancement of the state's ability to act decisively, which was exacerbated by the propensity to go to war too hastily, which suppressed the individualism of citizens, the very individualism Schmitt abhorred.

[38] Ibid., 445–6. [39] Oakeshott, *On Human Conduct*, 146–7, 272–4.

[40] Public Records Office, CAB 117/39, 'Memorandum on Economic Demobilisation' (19 February 1941), p. 1. Cited by W. H. Greenleaf, *British Political Tradition: The Rise of Collectivism* (London: Methuen, 1983), 49.

Hobbes: a miserable comforter?

In what did Hobbes' originality consist for the German and the Englishman, and to what extent is he contributory to the modern crisis or a potential saviour in resisting it? For Schmitt and Oakeshott, it was not as important to remain faithful to the logic of *Leviathan* as it was to pursue its significance and implications for understanding political action, in Schmitt's case, and governing, in Oakeshott's. Because of the precarious conditions in which he wrote, Hobbes was forced to be circumspect. Both Schmitt and Oakeshott follow Leo Strauss in maintaining that Hobbes, like all the great thinkers of that time, had a taste for esoteric messages, revealing his thoughts only partially, as if opening a window for a moment and closing it 'quickly for fear of a storm'.[41]

Schmitt's Hobbes

Schmitt recognized Hobbes as a potential ally. All genuine political theories, Schmitt suggested, presuppose that man is dangerous. It is the postulate that underpins both Hobbes' and Schmitt's theories.[42] In his book *Dictatorship*, Schmitt subscribed to the standard interpretation of Hobbes as a philosopher influenced by the scientific method, whose importance was that he expressed with absolute clarity the idea that there is no law prior to nor outside of the state. The state decided what was right and wrong and granted all honours and distinctions. The state, for Hobbes, Schmitt contended, was 'by constitution, essentially a dictatorship'.[43] Hobbes' version of natural law, 'the natural law of science', unlike that of Grotius, was concerned not with the content of a decision, or its justness, but with the fact that a decision had been made. Schmitt contended that in Hobbes there was no room for private conscience, a view which he was later to retract. One ought to obey the official law, which was the highest moral obligation. On this basis, he was able to portray Hobbes as the anti-individualist in whose version of natural law 'the individual was stripped of its concrete individuality'.[44]

[41] Carl Schmitt, *The Leviathan in the State Theory of Thomas Hobbes: Meaning and Failure of a Political Symbol* (University of Chicago Press, 2008), trans. George Schwab and Erna Hilfstein, 26.
[42] Schmitt, *The Concept of the Political*, 61.
[43] Carl Schmitt, *Dictatorship*, (Cambridge, UK: Polity, 2014), trans. Michael Hoelzl and Graham Ward, 17.
[44] Schmitt, *Dictatorship*, 99.

In his initial formulation of *The Concept of the Political* in 1927, the importance of Schmitt's Hobbes was to bring to the fore the primacy of the political and lead the offensive against one of the most corrosive tendencies of the age, 'de-politicization'.[45] The key nexus was 'protection-obedience'. Schmitt made the bold claim that '[n]o form of order, no reasonable legitimacy or legality can exist without protection and obedience.'[46] The state machine guarantees my physical security and in return demands 'unconditional obedience to the laws by which it functions'.[47]

This, for Schmitt, was the central lesson to be drawn from Hobbes, describing it as the 'cardinal point of Hobbes's construction of the state'.[48] Hobbes was praised for understanding the necessity for the qualitative total state and for opposing any division of power into discrete spheres of religion and politics. The *Leviathan* was not the defender but the creator of peace. If protection ceases, the obligation to obey ceases, and the individual's natural freedom reverts back to him or her. In January 1933, in his 'Strong State, Sound Economy', days before Hindenburg appointed Hitler Chancellor of Germany, he distinguished two types of state: the qualitative total state and the quantitative total state. The significant difference between them was the former's ability to distinguish the state, that is, the sphere of politics, from the non-political sphere, namely, society. The qualitative total state is in possession of a monopoly of the political, distinguishing between friend and enemy because it stands above society. The quantitative total state is drawn into every aspect of society, unable to resist the numerous and competing social forces and consequently incapable of distinguishing friend from enemy, the victim of antagonistic ideologies organized into a multi-party system.[49]

In Schmitt's view, religious, moral, economic, ethical and other entities, however, may potentially become transformed into political entities if they form such strong groupings that they position themselves according to friends and enemies.[50] The state possesses the right of war,

[45] Tracy B. Strong, 'Foreword' in Carl Schmitt, *The Leviathan in the State Theory of Thomas Hobbes* (University of Chicago Press, 2008), x.

[46] Schmitt, *The Concept of the Political*, 52. See also Carl Schmitt, 'The State as Mechanism in Hobbes and Descartes' (1937); reprinted as an appendix to Schmitt, *Leviathan in the State Theory of Thomas Hobbes*, 96.

[47] Schmitt, *Leviathan in the State Theory of Thomas Hobbes*, 45.

[48] Ibid., 72.

[49] George Schwab, 'Introduction', in Schmitt, *Leviathan in the State Theory of Thomas Hobbes*, xxxii–xxxiii.

[50] Schmitt, *The Concept of the Political*, 37.

the power to require of its citizens that they are ready to sacrifice their lives and without reservation kill its enemies. It is in this respect that 'the political community transcends all other associations or societies.'[51] Hobbes' sovereign stands above society, is able to make genuine decisions about the exceptional, can distinguish friends from enemies and has the monopoly on the right of war.

Schmitt elaborated on and departed from his early interpretation by giving greater emphasis to the myth of Leviathan, a myth which Schmitt thought ultimately failed; the idea of an artificial man; and the introduction of a destructive crack in the theory, namely, religious conscience. Hobbes made juristic positivism possible by envisioning the state as a great artifice created by man and which in its performance and function realized right and truth in itself. In other words, legal and 'state-theoretic' thinking were placed on a new foundation, namely, juristic positivist thinking. The integrity of the state was based on its inclusive organization and calculable ability to function rationally as a mechanism of command. It was in the sphere of international relations that the Leviathan, a huge animal and machine, reached its highest level of mythical force. Constant danger characterized the sphere in which the mighty Leviathans wrestled with each other. The state and the sovereign representative were not one and the same. The latter was the soul or animating force of the former, depicted as a huge man comprising multiple small men. As a totality, the state was an artificial man, body and soul mechanized, engineered by men. The soul, Schmitt contended, became 'a mere component of a machine artificially manufactured by men', designed to ensure the physical protection of the governed.[52] It was a technically neutral state in which the values of truth and justice were absorbed by abolishing the distinction between *auctoritas* and *potestas*. The supreme power became the supreme authority. *Auctoritas non veritas facit legem* – authority and not truth makes the law. Truth and values were subordinate to the authority of the law, whose source was the Leviathan.[53] In essence, there was no punishment and no crime without law. It was no longer feasible to distinguish between power and authority, *summa potestas* and *summa auctoritas*, because authority for Hobbes was not equated with truth. In so far as a decision emanates from the recognized authority, its rightness or wrongness was not a consideration.[54]

[51] Ibid., 47. [52] Schmitt, *Leviathan in the State Theory of Thomas Hobbes*, 34–5.
[53] Schmitt, *Political Theology*, 33, 52.
[54] Schmitt, *Leviathan in the State Theory of Thomas Hobbes,* 44–5.

Schmitt highlighted fear in Hobbes' theory as the originator of reason which delivered humans from their predicament. Anguished and terrified, with fear at fever pitch, a 'spark of reason (*ratio*) flashes, and suddenly there stands in front of them a new god'.[55] In emphasizing the power of the state, Schmitt accentuated and equated legitimacy with power. The purpose of the state was to put an end to civil war and to protect citizens from external threats; in so far as it did that, it might legitimately lay claim to the title of 'state'. Schmitt asserted, '[A] state is not a state unless it can put an end to that kind of war.'[56] This was not Hobbes' reasoning but was what many believed to be the logical implication of his argument, and indeed, theorists such as T. H. Green praised Spinoza for being much more explicit about equating legitimacy with power.[57]

In Hobbes' theory, the state was God-like only in a juristic sense, not metaphysically. It failed to achieve the unity of a person and allowed private beliefs, and this rendered the state mostly a mechanism falling short of totality. Its soul was merely a component of the machine. The image of the sea monster failed to achieve the un-problematic immediacy necessary for such myths to gain uptake: '[w]hat could have been a grand signal of restoration of the vital energy and political unity, began to be perceived in a ghostly light and became a grotesque horror picture.'[58] In making the state into a vast mechanism, the creature and creation of man, the force of his own myth was undermined. Hobbes did not appreciate that it was beyond his control to limit what the myth evoked in the present from its past incarnations.

Given Schmitt's emphasis on power, he naturally focussed on a feature of Hobbes' argument that was potentially destructive of the technical character of the state's functions and commands. He detected a flaw in Hobbes which was to become fatal for the political and which opened the door to liberalism. The mortal God of the Leviathan had power over miracles as well as confession, giving unity to religion and politics. However, in leaving belief in miracles to the individual conscience, he introduced a crack in the argument which admitted of the division between inner faith and public confession. Hobbes' 'non-eradicable, individualist proviso' was the liberal element in Hobbes that potentially

[55] Ibid., 31. [56] Ibid., 47.
[57] T. H. Green, *Lectures on the Principles of Political Obligation* (London: Longmans Green, 1917), ed. Bernard Bosanquet, §42.
[58] Schmitt, *Leviathan in the State Theory of Thomas Hobbes*, 81.

undermined 'the otherwise so complete, so overpowering unity' of the state.[59] This was a serious flaw which acknowledged a sphere into which the state could not enter. Such an idea, Schmitt contended, 'contained the seed of death that destroyed the mighty leviathan from within and brought about the end of the mortal god'.[60]

Hobbes had unwittingly prepared the ground for liberal politics by introducing this crack into his argument which allowed for freedom of religious thought (but not expression or action), which Jews such as Spinoza, Moses Mendelssohn and Friederich Stahl-Jolson (who had converted to Lutheranism at the age of nineteen) were to exploit fully. The corrosive distinction between inner and outer, public and private, became integral to juristic thinking and was consistent with the thinking of all educated people.[61]

However, Schmitt may be accused of over-reacting to Hobbes' concession. At no stage whatsoever did Hobbes concede a right to civil disobedience on grounds of religious belief. All are equally obliged to obey the law, irrespective of what they believe. Hobbes undermined his theory of sovereignty, however, in a different way. If the sovereign is the person who decides upon the exception and makes the decision, then the reason Hobbes gives for joining political communities, namely, self-preservation, has inherent in it a politically fatal flaw. It is logically inconsistent to give up the right to self-preservation, along with all other rights, when we enter civil society.[62] In retaining this right, that is, the right to decide when our lives are in danger, and to disobey the sovereign, if necessary, it is the individual and not only the sovereign who decides on the exception.[63] In other words, the fatal flaw is not conscience, upon which we are not able to act, but the retention of the right of self-preservation, upon which we can act. It is this, and not conscience, which makes Hobbes an individualist, and for Oakeshott, it makes him the individualist *par excellence*.

In summary, although Hobbes had his faults, he was attractive to Schmitt because he had highlighted the importance of fear as a motive force in the establishment of political authority and had understood what

59 Ibid., 56. See also Steinvorth, 'On Schmitt's Interpretation of *Leviathan*', 103.

60 Schmitt, *Leviathan in the State Theory of Thomas Hobbes*, 57.

61 Tracy B. Strong, 'Foreword: Carl Schmitt and Thomas Hobbes: Myth and Politics' in ibid., x.

62 Hobbes, *Leviathan*, 98, 153, 214, 230; see also 484–5, 491.

63 For an excellent formulation of this argument, see Gabriella Slomp, *Thomas Hobbes and Carl Schmitt: The Politics of Order and Myth* (London: Routledge, 2011), 99–111.

was intrinsically political about the arena of political action, namely, the ability to distinguish between friends and enemies. Conflict played a vital role in establishing the state and guaranteeing its validity. The legitimacy of the state lay in the eternal principle of protection-obedience, and failure to uphold it was fatal to any nation. Of particular importance, Hobbes identified the crucial distinction between the political and all other particular interests in civil society, excluding them in his qualitative conception of the state from political interference. He saw the need of the sovereign to exercise a form of authority unconstrained by rules in moments when decisiveness was of the essence, in circumstances for which there were no rules for guidance.

Oakeshott's Hobbes

Oakeshott contended that philosophical reasoning, for Hobbes, was limited to knowledge of causes and effects in order to determine either 'the conditional causes of given effects, or to determine the conditional effects of given causes'.[64] Philosophy differed from science in that it was not concerned with knowledge of things as they appear but enquired into the fact of their appearance. Nor was philosophy concerned with knowledge of the phenomenal world as such but with the theory of knowledge.[65] Oakeshott contended that there was nothing in Hobbes that betrayed anything other than the view that philosophy is conditional knowledge: 'knowledge of hypothetical generations and conclusions about the names of things, not about the nature of things'.[66]

Leviathan, while a philosophical masterpiece, was something more, in that it recognized that civilization was a work of imagination, something that natural science was incapable of comprehending. The aspiration of

[64] Michael Oakeshott, 'Introduction to *Leviathan*' reprinted in Oakeshott, *Hobbes on Civil Association* (Oxford, UK: Blackwell, 1975), 7, 17. In *The Elements of Philosophy*, Hobbes suggests that all men can 'reason to some degree, and concerning some things: but where there is need for a long series of reasons, there most men wander out of the way, and fall into error for want of method', Thomas Hobbes, *The Elements of Philosophy: The English Works*, vol. 1, (London: John Bohm, 1839), ed. William Molesworth, 1. Oakeshott based his account on pp. 65–6 and 387. Hobbes contended, 'METHOD, therefore, in the study of philosophy, is the shortest way of finding out effects by their known causes, or of causes by their known effects' (vol. 1, p. 66).

[65] Oakeshott, 'Introduction to *Leviathan*', 19. Also see Ian Tregenza, *Michael Oakeshott on Hobbes* (Exeter, UK: Imprint Academic, 2003), 25.

[66] Oakeshott, 'Introduction to *Leviathan*', 25. Oakeshott is here alluding to Hobbes, *Levaithan*, 47.

science was to solve the mystery of life, to wake us from the dream, but instead it substituted a nightmare destructive of the myth. A work of philosophical literature, such as that of Hobbes, through its imaginative power, accentuated and did not abate the dream. Its force was to dream more profoundly, in that it retold the myth upon which Christian civilization was built, namely, the Creation and Fall. The *Leviathan*, Oakeshott believed, was a powerful retelling of the Augustinian tragedy of the fall of man against the Pelagian heresy which denied the doctrine of original sin and affirmed human perfectability. Oakeshott, then, detected a very different myth projected by Hobbes from that which Schmitt apprehended.[67]

Hobbes represented, for Oakeshott, an important conceptual advance in early modern Europe because it was he who was the first 'to take candid account of the current experience of individuality'.[68] Oakeshott did not subscribe to the conventional wisdom that Hobbes began with a theory of radical individualism and destroyed it with his authoritarian theory of civil association. For Oakeshott, Hobbesian authority was at the heart of civil association, individuals united in a common recognition of the 'authority of the rules of civil association' and the preservation of freedom encapsulated in this common recognition.[69]

The authorization of a sovereign substituted law for freedom, or liberty, and obligation for right, but it did not entail the creation of a general will. Both the will of the sovereign and the wills of the subjects remained separate.[70] Oakeshott wanted to deny Schmitt's view that Hobbes equated authority with power. All authority, whether established by institution or by conquest, was the product of an act of consent, something that Schmitt played down. Diminishing the importance of the compact and consent in the idea of the collective authorization of the state, Schmitt contended that the contract was the occasion but not the instrument of state creation. It was the accumulated fear of individuals, who with trembling solicitude and in trepidation summoned the Leviathan, a power hitherto unimaginable, but it was invoked rather than created by the contract.

[67] Michael Oakeshott, 'Thomas Hobbes'; reprinted in Michael Oakeshott, *The Concept of a Philosophical Jurisprudence* (Exeter, UK: Imprint Academic, 2006), ed. Luke O'Sullivan, 110–21.

[68] Oakeshott, *Rationalism in Politics*, 367; Oakeshott, 'Introduction to *Leviathan*', 7.

[69] Paul Franco, 'Oakeshott, Berlin and Liberalism', *Political Theory*, 31 (2003), 502, 503.

[70] See Ian Tregenza, *Michael Oakeshott on Hobbes* (Exeter, UK: Imprint Academic, 2003).

Oakeshott's insistence on distinguishing power and authority in Hobbes may best be illustrated with an example. In his discussion of slavery, Hobbes understood the relationship between master and slave as one of power. It was the ability of the master to force the slave to act on the master's instructions which was the basis of the relationship. There was no obligation on the part of the slave to submit to the will of the master, and the slave could attempt to escape at any time. The relationship changed into one of master and servant as soon as the slave consented to obey the master, converting it from a relationship based purely on power or force into a moral relationship in which obligations are incurred as a result of compact or consent.[71]

Oakeshott believed that Hobbes' lasting legacy was to re-state what had been crucial to the political experience of the Romans. The whole idea of authority was central to Oakeshott's political philosophy, and it was one of the features of Hobbes' philosophy that he admired most. In Oakeshott's view, we are united as *cives* in civil association, not in terms of a common enterprise, but in terms of our common acknowledgement of the authority of the rules, and this is what he understood Hobbes to be telling us.

Oakeshott, unlike Schmitt, emphasized the passion of pride rather than fear as the master conception in Hobbes' retelling of the civilizational myth. The passion of pride was the impetus to honour, while fear made us apprehensive of dishonour. Pride, however, was a disruptive and untamed passion with a propensity to lapse into vainglory, deluding man into believing his own superiority over his fellows. Pride, the overestimation of one's own powers, was a hindrance to choosing the best course of action when one was alone. When in the company of fellow human beings, 'pride is more dangerous and death more likely.'[72] The predicament of humanity is unenviable: '[t]here is a radical conflict between the nature of man and the natural condition of mankind: what the one urges with hope of achievement, the other makes impossible . . . and it is neither sin nor depravity that creates the predicament; nature itself is the author of his ruin.'[73] Reason holds out the possibility of deliverance from this dangerous tension. However, as Oakeshott contended, '[o]n no plausible reading of Hobbes is the Law of nature to be considered obligatory because it represents rational conduct . . . because

[71] It is the covenant between the two that establishes the right to obedience. Until then, the slave may justly escape from prison (*Leviathan*, 128).

[72] Oakeshott, 'Introduction to *Leviathan*', 35.

[73] Ibid., 36.

"reason" (except where he is being unmistakably equivocal) has no prescriptive force.'[74]

The obligation did not arise because of the wisdom or rationality of the law, but because it was backed by the requisite authority. Hobbes was enough of a philosophical sceptic to propose that the foundation of political authority, or obligation, was nothing more than the opinions of those who gave their consent.[75]

All law must have a law-giver who is the sovereign instituted by compact or conquest or acknowledged by those subject to obey his commands because 'all men are by nature free'; no man may acquire an obligation 'which ariseth not from some act of his own'.[76] As Oakeshott maintains, '[i]t is in their acknowledgement of him as their ruler that he comes to be known as the author of law properly speaking; this acknowledgement is the necessary "act" from which all obligation "ariseth" because it is the act without which the ruler remains unknown.'[77]

Every natural person is the author, owner or lord of his or her action. In laying down our natural right to govern ourselves by our own reason in the unconditional pursuit of our own felicity, we do much more than authorize another individual to govern on our behalf. What one does is to give up one's authorship or agency to a representative who personates the people in all matters that concern the public safety. The representative cannot be a natural person from among the contractees who surrendered their right to govern themselves. This would simply be to place the governance of the community in the hands of one of their number 'moved only by his appetite to satisfy his own wants'.[78] What the covenanters create and authorize to act is an Office, which bears the person of each and every one of them. This office, or artificial man, although occupied by one or more office holder, or holders, remains a single sovereign when acting in an official capacity.

Oakeshott argues that Hobbes' understanding of individuality or personality owed much to that of the late medieval nominalists, who emphasized the primacy of the will, the separateness, incommunicability, irrationality and eccentricity of the individual. Hobbes' solipsism made him not an egoist, of which he is commonly accused, but an individualist.

74 Oakeshott, 'The Moral Life in the Writings of Thomas Hobbes', 94–5.
75 Tregenza, *Michael Oakeshott on Hobbes*, 178. 76 Hobbes, *Leviathan*, 150.
77 Oakeshott, 'The Moral Life in the Writings of Thomas Hobbes', 108.
78 Oakeshott, 'Introduction to *Leviathan*', 40. This was originally published in 1946 and reprinted with some of the more obvious blemishes removed by the author.

There is no hint in Hobbes of an argument based on the value and sanctity of the individual. His individualism is based instead on a view of the world comprising substantive individuals, unavoidably isolated within worlds of their own sensations.

Hobbes' individualism was far too robust to allow the merest hint of a general will or indeed collectively comprising anything like the 'people', or *volk*. Oakeshott contended that all of Hobbes' individuals had relationships which were purely external, and no degree of addition or subtraction to their number was capable of modifying or compromising a collectivity in which their individuality was lost.[79] To authorize a representative to make choices for me does not destroy or compromise my individuality. It is clear in Hobbes, Oakeshott argued, that there was no confusion of wills. My will, for example, is in the authorization of the actor or representative. The choices he or she makes are not mine, but his or her own made on my behalf. Individuals are agreeing not only to transfer their right of governing themselves but also to transform themselves into subjects and to confer all their strength and power to the office in order to discharge whatever duties are necessary for it to maintain the peace. Whereas the transfer of right is a single act, the supply of power in support of its exercise is deemed continuous. The effect is not designed to compromise the individuality of each agent.

How, one may ask, is individuality preserved when the absolutism of the sovereign severely curtails individual freedoms? The answer, as far as Oakeshott is concerned, is that the sovereign is absolute in strictly circumscribed areas relating to the pursuit of felicity, and where the law is silent, the individual is free to exercise his or her will in whatever way he or she desires. Hobbes' sovereign is not an absolutist in the sense of being totalitarian, precisely because he or she is authoritarian.[80] Although the sovereign Leviathan is absolute, it is only so in two respects, neither of which is destructive of individuality or freedom. In the first place, the surrender of natural right to the sovereign is absolute, and secondly, the legitimacy of his or her command is unquestioned.

In Oakeshott's view, Hobbes is merely specifying the minimal conditions for any association among individuals to subsist. Liberty or freedom is equated with the absence of impediments to motion, and man is properly free when he is not prevented from performing the actions he has willed to do. As a subject who has authorized a sovereign, however,

[79] Ibid., 60–2. [80] Ibid., 63.

individuals have willed certain impediments, namely, civil laws, which may restrict their freedom by compelling them to do certain acts they may not wish to do.[81] These impediments were authorized by them, and therefore chosen, and on balance, they anticipate that the restrictions will be far fewer than those encountered in the natural condition. The whole of any person's conduct cannot be prescribed by law. Rules may only be observed by choosing to observe them, and there is always an indeterminacy in which freedom is exercised, the judgement of the applicability of the rule to the situation we find ourselves in. Where the law is silent, the greatest degree of freedom is enjoyed. Furthermore, the covenant cannot compel the individual to do anything that endangers that for which he entered into civil association, that is, the preservation of his life. He is not obliged to implicate himself in a crime without assurance of pardon; if found guilty, he is not obliged to kill himself or any other man; and he retains the right to protect himself and his interests with all his ability should the authorized sovereign no longer be able to protect him.[82] As Oakeshott argues, 'it is Reason, not Authority, that is destructive of individuality . . . What, indeed, is excluded from Hobbes's *civitas* is not the freedom of the individual, but the independent rights of spurious "authorities" and of collections of individuals such as churches, which he saw as the source of the civil strife of his time.'[83]

In essence, Hobbes allows for a considerable degree of freedom, which preserves the individual will and resists any notion of a general will. The mode of association most appropriate to the idea of a general will is what Oakeshott believed characteristic of *universitas*, teleocracy, Cartesian and Baconian rationalism or enterprise association, in which governing is a managerial activity, citizens are united in a common purpose and laws, instead of being adjectival, are substantive instruments in the achievement of a purpose.

Oakeshott was convinced that contrary to what we might associate with a purported absolutist state, there is nothing in Hobbes' cosmology to accommodate civil society conceived on the analogy of an enterprise association. Hobbes does not conceive of human beings surrendering themselves to a *telos*, 'joined in terms of a singular substantive purpose'. They are associated instead in terms of their recognition of the authority of the rules of conduct in terms of which civil association is constituted.[84]

[81] Ibid., 44. [82] Ibid., 46. [83] Ibid., 63.
[84] Michael Oakeshott, 'Logos and Telos' in *Rationalism in Politics*, 358.

No one more ably than Hobbes in the early modern period explored the postulates, that is, the conditionality, of the emergence of the ideal character of individuality. Furthermore, *Leviathan*, in imaginatively retelling the myth of Western civilization, attained the level of philosophical literature and, unlike poetry, which increases our imaginative power, it did more than this in increasing our knowledge by prompting and instructing us, reminding us of the common dream that unites us, and in making the myth more intelligible.[85]

What is to be done?

Schmitt and Oakeshott claimed to be engaged in analysis, or diagnostics, and not in recommendation. Schmitt disingenuously disavowed recommendation in defending himself at Nuremberg.[86] His business, he claimed, was to identify the problems and not offer solutions. For Oakeshott, philosophy was released from considerations of conduct, having nothing to offer practical life by way of recommendation.[87] Despite these protestations, both do offer prescriptions.

In Oakeshott, there is a certain resignation to the fate of mankind. He was an unrepentant Augustinian who believed that the 'real grievances of mankind are incurable'.[88] Politicians play on our pride and our insecurities, 'manufacturing curable grievances', seducing us into believing that our problems are collectively resolvable. For those who have no desire to rule others, 'politics is an uninteresting form of activity'.[89] It may be uninteresting but, by implication, necessary in the face of the crisis he identified. Oakeshott gave considerable emphasis to authority, which he equated with ruling, and distinguished from politics, as categorically distinct from acknowledgement of authority. Politics is the activity of questioning the desirability of the laws, not of questioning their authority, and of attempting to persuade others of the merits of alternative laws. In this context, Oakeshott's characterization of the rule of law and of nomocratic governance may be viewed as a political act, or intervention, in so far as he is questioning the desirability not of any particular law but

[85] Oakeshott, '*Leviathan* A Myth', 151.
[86] J. Bendersky, 'Carl Schmitt at Nuremberg', *Telos*, 17 (1978), 91.
[87] See Oakeshott, *Experience and Its Modes*.
[88] Oakeshott, 'Notebook', 2/1/16 XVI, dated Sept 1958, pp. 52–3, Oakeshott Papers, British Library of Political Science.
[89] Ibid.

of all laws that are instrumental and which do not have the character of being adjectival to human purposes and interests.

Schmitt, on the other hand, at least for a while, had aspirations that the Nazi Party would deliver his prescriptions but was disappointed that it failed to fulfil its end of the bargain in the obedience-protection nexus. For Schmitt, the solution to the crisis of authority and constitutionalism had to be the introduction of a large element of illiberalism into the polity. Only a substantive homogeneity among the people was able to provide the basis for the transition from a condition of political chaos to stability and certainty. He wanted an illiberalism which was also democratic, grounded in a morality that was nothing more or less than what a people happened to believe at particular times and places. It was, indeed, a peculiar notion of democracy which was certainly not participatory but limited to the affirmation or rejection of concrete proposals. As an admirer of Mussolini's decisiveness and exploitation of the myth of the Italian nation, it is well to remember that he believed fascism to be a pure form of democracy in which *il Duce* expressed the will of the whole.[90]

Schmitt's solution

Schmitt's political philosophy comprised historico-philosophical analyses which purported to identify postulates or features of the state and its related activities, which he then used as the criteria against which he measured the political condition of Germany in its relation to other European states.[91] Sovereignty, the agency that constituted the body politic and which lay at the heart of Hobbes' political theory, remained a pre-occupation of Schmitt's throughout his life. In his *Political Theology: Four Chapters on the Concept of Sovereignty*, written in 1922 and republished with a few revisions in 1933, the year he joined the Nazi Party, he famously defined sovereignty, or the sovereign, as 'he who decides on the exceptional case'.[92] Exceptional cases may include economic or political crises or disturbances, inviting extraordinary

[90] Benito Mussolini, 'The Doctrine of Fascism' in Michael Oakeshott (ed.), *The Social and Political Doctrines of Contemporary Europe*, 164–79.

[91] In his conception of political theology, Schmitt was not suggesting that modern politics is fundamentally religious in character. What he meant was that all the significant concepts in modern politics are secularized theological concepts imported from theology into the theory of the state. The idea of the omnipotent God, for example, became the omnipotent law-giver (Schmitt, *Political Theology*, 36).

[92] Ibid., 5.

responses. In essence, then, just as the liberal rule of law is found wanting because it fails to incorporate the personal in its account and operation of the legal system, the idea of sovereignty too must incorporate the personal. Just as personal judgement bridges the gap between the generality of a norm, or rule, and the situation to which it is applied, personal judgement also must decide on the exception and save the state in ways the constitution did not anticipate. In a strong state, the decision on whether enmity threatens the existence of the state is not determined by a norm but by the personal decision of a dictator or sovereign. And this is the lesson Schmitt believed Hobbes taught us.

The exception, by definition, is not codified in the present legal system, and action should not be hampered by checks and balances, as in a liberal constitution. The exception is a situation in which the norms and constitutional arrangements that constitute a given political system are suspended. In a normative vacuum where the people are deemed incapable of conceiving and transcending the abnormal or chaotic, a decision is required which is neither grounded in a pre-existing code of norms nor amenable to discussion or criticism.[93] The sovereign decides what the emergency is and what must be done about it. Schmitt adds, 'Although he stands outside of the normally valid legal system, he nevertheless belongs to it, for it is he who must decide whether the constitution needs to be suspended in its entirety.'[94]

The political, for Schmitt, had to be distinguished from the relatively autonomous forms of human thought, such as morals, aesthetics and economics. What distinguishes the political from other forms of human activity is that political actions and motives could be reduced to the distinction between enemies and friends.[95] Here he offered a criterion of the political and not an account of its substantive content. Strictly speaking, politics precedes the state. He was referring purely to public enmity when two collectivities potentially confront each other. It is the state as an organized political entity which must be decisive in relation to the friend-enemy distinction. Implicit in Hobbes' characterization of the state of nature was not only the infamous relationship of the war of all against all but also the ability to gain for oneself 'friends', or auxiliaries of

[93] R. Farneti, 'Paradoxes of Normativity: On Carl Schmitt's Normative Scepticism', *History of Political Thought*, 34 (2013), 118.
[94] Schmitt, *Political Theology*, 7. From the point of view of political theology, the exception in jurisprudence is equivalent to a miracle (Schmitt, *Political Theology*, 36).
[95] Schmitt, *Concept of the Political*, 26.

war, for mutual protection. Schmitt contended, 'The political entity presupposes the real existence of an enemy and therefore coexistence with another political entity.'[96] The enemy as well as the friend plays a crucial role in that the political is not wholly equated with enmity. Gabriella Slomp suggests, 'The enemy is, for Schmitt, the standard against whom we measure ourselves and come to know who we are. If we have no enemy or if our enemy is the absolute other, our identity remains unknown to us.'[97]

What is required is a dictatorship in the name of the people, consistent with democracy, in that a considerable element of the people assent. The democratic role is limited, however, to saying 'yes' or 'no'.[98] Democracy had to be rescued from the liberal elements that were dysfunctional within it, particularly the rule of law. Schmitt recommended that the secret ballot and parliamentary decision-making procedures be replaced by the authentic democratic constituents of the assembled crowd signifying acceptance or rejection by acclamation.

His answer was for the state to rescue back the sphere of the political from the forces of depoliticization which challenged its monopoly of political power. Technological advances, such as radio and film, which could be used to manipulate the masses had to be controlled by the state, and political parties had to be banned because they had exploited the rules of liberal democracy to acquire power legally, with a view to denying the same right to other parties.[99] On his own account, he became complicit in the work of the National Socialist Party between 1933 and 1936 in the mistaken belief that he could influence the structural composition of the Third Reich. Hitler provided for him, Schmitt believed, the opportunity to realize the ideal of the qualitative total state that embodied the fundamental competence of distinguishing friends and enemies.[100]

[96] Ibid., 53. [97] Slomp, *Carl Schmitt and the Politics of Hostility*, 13.

[98] Ellen Kennedy in her introduction to *The Crisis of Parliamentary Democracy* (p. xx) highlights this distinction, which Habermas picks up in his review, accusing Schmitt of making a mockery of democracy by enlisting it to bolster an authoritarian cause (Jürgen Habermas, 'Sovereignty and the *Führerdemokratie*', *Times Literary Supplement*, 26 September 1986, 1054). Renato Cristi wants to emphasize that Schmitt was committed to reforming parliamentary politics and that in 1923 he wished not to attack liberalism but to enlist it in order to neutralize democracy ('Carl Schmitt on Liberalism, Democracy and Catholicism', *History of Political Thought*, 14 (1993), 284).

[99] See Carl Schmitt, *Legality and Legitimacy* (Durham, NC: Duke University Press, 2004), trans. Jeffrey Seitzer.

[100] Ulrich Steinvorth, 'On Carl Schmitt's Interpretation of Hobbes', *Rechtsphilosophische Hefte*, 11 (2005), 99.

Oakeshott's solution

Oakeshott does not say that political philosophers do not engage in recommendation, merely that when they do, they are no longer doing political philosophy.[101] It is clear that Oakeshott believed that the myth that had become dominant in contemporary Europe was a counterfeit myth. We were deluding ourselves about the kind of community to which we belong and the sorts of persons we are. This constitutes a serious threat to civilization and individual freedom. When he contends that 'recently we seem to have sunk so low as to believe that the community we compose is an "economy"', he is alluding to enterprise association in which ruling is conceived as managing. The counterfeit myth, that is, the story we tell ourselves about the nature of government and governing in terms of a teleocracy, constitutes the most pressing threat. By implication, to counter it most effectively, we need to be reminded of the dangers by retelling that counterfeit myth, just as Hobbes retold the genuine myth.

Oakeshott's way of responding to the crisis was to give a graphic warning of the consequences of the destructive conflation of governing with managerialism. It is to be found in an allegorical morality tale, or myth, based on the story of the Tower of Babel. The story exemplifies, for him, a universal predicament. It is a lament composed to reconcile a passionate people to contingent misfortunes, expressive of the sufferings and sorrows endured since the beginning of time by mankind in pursuit of Sangrael. The Babelians were inventive and ambitious in their aspiration, but were of limited resources. The Babelians were capable of immense envy and resentment, but what united them was their profound feeling of deprivation. Nimrod exploited their frustrations by persuading them that God was the author of their predicament. Nimrod revealed his ambition to realize their dreams. He would lead them to the gates of heaven, force them open and seize the wealth God had kept from them. This would require the building of a tower from which to launch the assault. Work commenced immediately, and very quickly private convenience gave way to public good, the 'sovereignty of the *utilitas publica*'.[102] The enormity of the project gradually subordinated all the resources of Babel to its completion. The supply of bricks could not keep

[101] Oakeshott, 'Thomas Hobbes', 111.

[102] Michael Oakeshott, *On History and Other Essays* (Indianapolis, IN: Liberty Fund, 1999), 181.

up with demand, and the houses of the inhabitants were demolished and the bricks used to sustain the building programme. All value became measured in terms of the project, and the only occupations that were honoured were those relating to bricklaying and serving the needs of bricklayers. The inhabitants resided in squalid conditions, living in tents and enduring appalling deprivation, in the knowledge that their dreams of wealth would soon be realized. On hearing the rumour that Nimrod had commenced the ascent without them, the Babelians surged up the tower, trampling the very young and infirm who could not keep up. The weight of the panic-stricken inhabitants as they surged into the upper regions of the tower caused it to sway and groan under the pressure, collapsing into a huge pile of rubble which destroyed the Babelians and their ambitions. This, then, is Oakeshott's elaboration of the counterfeit myth, a morality tale that clearly betrays Oakeshott's preference for nomocracy, or civil association, and acts as the extreme against which any move to governing as the crow flies could be judged.

Conclusion

Both thinkers, Schmitt and Oakeshott, engaged in extensive diagnostics, and in their different ways offer, or imply, resolutions to the problems detected. For both it is largely a procedural problem. Something has gone wrong with the mechanisms, the way politics and the political are conceived and practiced, and the solution is to assert, or re-assert, procedures that more adequately enable authority to be identified and exercised – and rescued from erosion. For Schmitt, what was required was decisionism, substantive action in face of the exceptional; for Oakeshott, a pulling back from the imposition of desired projects on the polity and the establishment of a framework which did not allow of exceptionalism. The rule of law plays a part in both their solutions. In Schmitt's theory, law is a fugitive from the political, the decider on the exceptional. It may be placed in abeyance, ignored or eliminated in an emergency, decided not by the people but by the ruler. Schmitt's constitutional theory puts the state and the rule of law in confrontation. The rule of law is in fact anti-political in that it undermines the state and may be manipulated by parties and groups, as Schmitt claims it was in the Weimar Republic, to further their own interests.[103] The unity of the state

[103] Renato Christi, *Carl Schmitt and Authoritarian Liberalism: Strong State, Free Economy* (Cardiff: University of Wales Press, 1998), 123–5.

takes priority over the people who comprise it in that the president is almost unconstrained by law.

For Oakeshott, the rule of law is a safeguard against the rationalist who seeks to impose substantive designs on a community. The rule of law is the guarantor of individuality. The rule of law specifically refers to non-instrumental rules which befit the relationship in which individuals stand with each other in civil associations. This has been interpreted to mean that for Oakeshott, non-instrumental rules do not have purposes or that they are neutral in their effects. The counter against him has been that all legislation has a purpose and that no law is neutral in its effects.[104] Substantive purposes are for Oakeshott specific requirements of action, and therefore, some general aims do not in themselves qualify as substantive purposes. Such aims as security, peace and prosperity are not substantive purposes.[105] The reason for this is that action is responsive to understood contingent situations and appraised in terms of wished-for or imagined outcomes. The end chosen is implicit in the situation, and there is no trans-situational scale in terms of which to convert un-alikes into fractions of a common currency, such as degrees of pleasure and pain. What this means is that a situation is not found intolerable because it lacks a measurable degree of a homogeneous satisfaction, such as happiness. Oakeshott maintains, 'I cannot *want* "happiness"; what I want is to idle in Avignon or to hear Caruso sing.'[106]

Both Oakeshott and Schmitt, one may argue, abandoned political philosophy. Schmitt denied the very possibility of political philosophy and offered instead political theology, which was to be the central thread that held his work together. Schmitt's doctrine is itself a theology in which not argument but revelation of the truth that the sovereign demands the complete obedience of the collective. Although Schmitt did not publish his book on Hobbes until 1938, in which he proclaimed himself the self-appointed heir to Hobbes, the Englishman had a pervasive influence in shaping Schmitt's political thinking. Schmitt turned to Hobbes to assist him in providing a theology, as a ground for authority, to combat liberal scepticism. Political authority is made to depend upon epistemic authority, that is, the unquestioned knowledge of the sovereign, which Schmitt conflates with executive power or authority. In Oakeshott, we find a concerted effort, at least conceptually, to distinguish executive

104 See, e.g., David Mapel, 'Purpose and Politics: Can There Be a Non-Instrumental Civil Association', *The Political Science Reviewer*, 21 (1992), 78.

105 Oakeshott, *On Human Conduct*, 119.

106 Ibid., 53.

authority from epistemic authority. In this respect, we have much to learn from the Romans, who believed that they comprised a 'civil association'. They were united not in a common enterprise but in respect for their ancient customs and the rule of law. What Oakeshott meant by civil association in this context was the belief that law was not conceived as the organization of an enterprise but instead as the terms in which the Roman people kept faith with one another.

What, then, does this tell us about the crises Schmitt and Oakeshott identified and how Hobbes is related to the diagnoses and solutions? Here we have two twentieth-century thinkers, each stigmatized by the label of being intransigent right, but representing very different positions, which make the left-right nexus redundant in this context. Schmitt was an extreme collectivist; Oakeshott, an extreme individualist. The world appeared differently to them through the conceptual spectacles they wore. The 'crisis', or at least the way it was conceived, was manufactured by each in the image of the desirability of where they stood on the collectivist-individualist spectrum. For Schmitt, too much individualism undermined and threatened the necessity for collectivism in his vision of the political; for Oakeshott, too much collectivism was the problem and constituted the treat to individualism and the proper governance of civil society. Hobbes was invoked by both as an epistemic authority, and what they saw in Hobbes tells us more about their own political preferences than they do about Hobbes. He is at once the philosopher of both collectivism and individualism. It was suggested earlier that Oakeshott contended that the business of the politician was to manufacture problems and peddle the mistaken belief that they are resolvable. The irony is that both Schmitt and Oakeshott manufactured their own peculiar crises which required their own idiosyncratic solutions.

7

The mystery of lawlessness

War, law and the modern state

THOMAS POOLE

A pervasive, if relatively undramatic, feature of the juristic and political thought of the first half of the twentieth century was a preoccupation with the rise of the administrative state. The topic provided a focus for humanistic concerns about the automatizing of political and social life that the arrival of the 'machine age' seemed to augur. For those interested in the juridical dimensions of the state – a category which includes all three thinkers under consideration in this volume – a central worry was the displacing or warping effect of the modern state on law and legality. The post-1918 state was a 'positive state', as Laski called it, which 'through the agency of government, has directly undertaken the control of national life'.[1] Society became an object that the state might manage and transform with a view towards perfecting it. An Enlightenment belief in the self-improvement of man had become a 'high modernist' belief in the perfectibility of social order: '[i]t was possible to conceive of an artificial, engineered society designed, not by custom and historical accident, but according to conscious, rational, scientific criteria. Every nook and cranny of the social order might be improved upon.'[2] Law within the state so conceived was understood principally as a social technique, subordinate to politics, whose purpose was primarily functional: to provide a framework for the effective realization of the social goals specified by legislation through an often fragmented and complex administrative sphere.[3]

This development had profound consequences. The increased demands on the state, in part a response to the sacrifices made by

[1] Harold Laski, *The Foundations of Sovereignty* (New York: Harcourt, Brace & Co., 1921), 30, 33–4.

[2] James C. Scott, *Seeing Like a State: How Certain Schemes to Improve the Human Condition Have Failed* (New Haven, CT: Yale University Press, 1998), 92.

[3] Martin Loughlin, 'Modernism in British Public Law, 1919–1979', *Public Law* 56 (2014), 58–66.

ordinary citizens during the First World War, disrupted existing patterns of government.[4] The inter-war years saw a transformation of the function of parliaments. Parliaments across Europe increasingly resorted to broad delegations of power to executive or administrative bodies.[5] On the back of their control over a purportedly technocratic administrative apparatus, executives increasingly claimed normative authority in their own right.[6] As Max Weber was among the first to observe, the evolution of the West had produced a bureaucratic state, an industrial capitalist economy characterized by means-end rationality and a formally rationalized legal system.[7] Within such a state, the *Rechtsstaat* ideal was threatened as demands for redistributive justice induced a move away from general statutes to more specific measures and decrees aimed at particular situations or groups of citizen. Offering only an emotionally and spiritually unsatisfactory 'mastery' through 'calculation', the 'mass state' and its 'rule by officials' had the potential to produce, Weber argued, 'the greatest form of collective enslavement the world had ever known', the 'steel-hard casing' of universal rationalization and bureaucratization.[8]

This chapter examines the response of Schmitt, Hayek and Oakeshott to these developments. It does so by exploring what each has to say about the idea of reason of state. Reason of state presupposes a situation in which state action moves from one register, based on law and right, to

[4] The situation tended to be more pronounced in those states which had been restructured in the aftermath of the war or following the Treaty of Versailles. On Germany, see, e.g., Arthur Jacobson and Bernhard Schlink (eds), *Weimar: A Jurisprudence of Crisis* (Berkeley: University of California Press, 2002) and, on the inter-war European situation more generally, the essays in Robert Gerwarth (ed.), *Twisted Paths: Europe 1914–1945* (Oxford University Press, 2007).

[5] A development not just feared by those on the right: see, e.g., Harold J. Laski, *Liberty in the Modern State* (Harmondsworth, UK: Penguin, 1937), 73: 'There has accreted today about the departments of State a type of discretionary power which seems to me full of danger unless it is exercised under proper safeguards.'

[6] Peter L. Lindseth, 'The Paradox of Parliamentary Sovereignty: Delegation, Democracy, and Dictatorship in Germany and France, 1920s-1950s', *Yale Law Journal*, 113 (2004), 1341, 1344; Edward L. Rubin, 'Law and Legislation in the Administrative State', *Columbia Law Review*, 89 (1989), 369.

[7] Dana Villa, 'The Legacy of Max Weber in Weimar Political and Social Theory' in Peter E. Gordon and John P. McCormick (eds), *Weimar Thought: A Contested Legacy* (Princeton University Press, 2013), 75–6.

[8] John P. McCormick, *Carl Schmitt's Critique of Liberalism: Against Politics as Technology* (Cambridge University Press, 1997), 39; Jan-Werner Müller, *Contesting Democracy: Political Ideas in Twentieth-Century Europe* (New Haven, CT: Yale University Press, 2011), 28.

another, based on interest and might.[9] The condition for such a shift is normally the assertion that the state's vital interests are at stake. In the course of acting in its own interest, the state might face the prospect of violating moral and legal norms in protecting its overriding interests or security.[10] While the phenomena of modern reason of state politics and the rise of the administrative state might seem unconnected, they are in fact anything but. On the contrary, as Weber observed, 'the relationship of the state to violence is particularly close at the present time.'[11] Understanding the inter-war state was very much a matter of getting to grips with the sharp end of state action of the type long associated with the category of reason of state: war, crisis, diplomacy. The twentieth century saw plenty of action on all these fronts. The earlier part of the century in particular made manifest the new 'massification' of both war and politics. Preparing for and waging mechanized and global warfare now necessitated a vast state apparatus. The heightened coordinating functions accrued by the state during wartime were substantially carried over in to its constitutional structure during the peace.[12]

Schmitt, struggling to make sense of the juridical challenge presented by these years of turmoil and change, characteristically resorted to theology. Drawing on one of the most enigmatic of apocalyptic texts, St Paul's second letter to the Thessalonians, Schmitt turned repeatedly to the phrase the 'mystery of lawlessness' as if that – and the need to find an earthly Restrainer (*katechon*) while we awaited the Redeemer on Judgement Day – was the defining problematic of the age.[13] While they would have rejected the apocalyptic language, the basic sentiment was one that

[9] Carl J. Friedrich, *Constitutional Reason of State* (Providence, RI: Brown University Press, 1957).

[10] Gianfranco Poggi, *The State: Its Nature, Development and Prospects* (Cambridge, UK: Polity, 1990), 84.

[11] Max Weber, 'Politics as a Vocation' in Weber, *The Vocation Lectures* (Indianapolis, IN: Hackett Publishing, 2004), ed. David Owen and Tracy B. Strong, 33.

[12] Poggi, *The State*, 112. In the United Kingdom, government spending accounted for 8.9 per cent of gross domestic product in 1890 but 20.2 per cent by 1920. See also Chris Thornhill, *A Sociology of Constitutions: Constitutions and State Legitimacy in Historical-Sociological Perspective* (Cambridge University Press, 2011), 275. The same pattern emerged after the Second World War. See Ross McKibbin, 'Great Britain' in Gerwarth, *Twisted Paths*, 56.

[13] 2 Thessalonians 2: 'The mystery of lawlessness doth already work; only there is one that restraineth now, until he be taken out of the way; and then shall be revealed the lawless one, whom the Lord Jesus will slay with the breath of his mouth, and bring to nought with the manifestation of his coming.'

Hayek and Oakeshott shared.[14] They, too, were alarmed at the prospect of the masses, manipulated by a demagogue or elite interest, unleashing the vast destructive capacity of the modern state and viewed 'with horror the swallowing up of other values in the all-consuming interests of the society which is considered to be identical with the state'.[15] They searched for someone, some institution, some conceptual scheme that might contain the risks of unbridled democracy, 'seen and feared through the prisms of their theories of law, as the abyss of its absence: *to misterion tes anomias*, the mystery of lawlessness'.[16] The problem had a political specification: Europe groping for a new form of governance and a new legal order, internal and external – a *novus ordo seclorum* to replace the one that had died in the trenches in 1914–18. It also had a conceptual specification: rescuing the normative in law out of the modern idea of law as technique, as that which the machine of state wills.

'Now the machine runs itself': Schmitt versus the law

Schmitt saw himself as the 'cleric of post-neutralization Europe',[17] his self-appointed task being to make contemporaries aware of the dangers of technicity inherent to the twentieth-century 'total state'.[18] His message to a post-war generation full of complaints 'about a soulless age of technology in which the soul is helpless and unconscious' is that their romantic pessimism 'has been carried to an end'.[19] In his early book, *Political Romanticism* (1919), the target was a certain style of nineteenth-century romanticism that Schmitt thought now dominated politics. Those who accepted the liberal, bureaucratic and technocratic status

[14] Perry Anderson, 'The Intransigent Right: Michael Oakeshott, Leo Strauss, Carl Schmitt, Friedrich von Hayek' in Anderson, *Spectrum: From Right to Left in the World of Ideas* (London: Verso, 2005), 26–7.

[15] Ernst Fraenkel, *The Dual State: A Contribution to the Theory of Dictatorship* (New York: Oxford University Press, 1941), trans. E. A. Shills, 60.3.

[16] Anderson, 'The Intransigent Right', 26.

[17] McCormick, *Carl Schmitt's Critique of Liberalism*, 103.

[18] Carl Schmitt, *The Concept of the Political* (University of Chicago Press, 1996), trans. George Schwab, 23. See also Carl Schmitt, *Dictatorship* (Cambridge, UK: Polity, 2014), trans. Michael Hoelzl and Graham Ward, 9: 'This orientation towards dictatorship – an orientation consisting of the three elements of rationalism, technicality and the executive – is at the origins of the modern state.'

[19] Carl Schmitt, 'The Age of Neutralizations and Depoliticizations' (1929), trans. Matthias Konzett and John P. McCormick, *Telos*, 96 (1993), 130, 140.

quo were charged with 'effeminate passivity', an 'inability to decide' and 'subjective occasionalism'. People of this sort lived not 'a kind of lyrical paraphrase of existence'.[20] As such, they were incapable of engaging in politics other than as a spectacle for gossip and idle criticism.[21] Schmitt offers instead the image of the 'romantic politician', pointing (quite bizarrely) to Don Quixote as a model. He was a man, we are told, with 'the enthusiasm for a real knight of his rank', who 'was capable of seeing the difference between right and wrong and of making a decision in favour of what seemed right to him'. The battles he fought may have been fantastically absurd, but at least they were real battles in which he exposed himself to personal dangers.[22]

In little of this was Schmitt original. He was one of a group of reactionary modernists that included Oswald Spengler, Ernst Jünger, Martin Heidegger and Werner Sombart.[23] This 'masculine cult of action and will' saw decision as good, deliberation ('endless talk') bad. Its associates were existentialists who used the same 'jargon of authenticity' and espoused what Goebbels was to call 'steel-like romanticism'. Positivism, liberalism, Marxism and parliament they hated as inimical to life. They wanted for the future not more of the same *Entseelung* (de-souling) but a renewal of the soul in a modern setting.[24] Walter Benjamin captured some of the spirit of this movement when he wrote in his essay, 'The Work of Art in the Age of Mechanical Representation', that 'fascism

[20] Carl Schmitt, *Political Romanticism* (Cambridge, MA: MIT Press, 1991), trans. Guy Oakes, 128, 117, 140, 159. Ellen Kennedy describes the 'romanticism vs. politicism dilemma' as 'the major question for his [Schmitt's] generation' (Ellen Kennedy, '*Hostis* Not *Inimicus*: Toward a Theory of the Public in the Work of Carl Schmitt' in David Dyzenhaus (ed.), *Law as Politics: Carl Schmitt's Critique of Liberalism* (Durham, NC: Duke University Press, 1998), 93.

[21] Schmitt, *Political Romanticism*, 159: 'following political events with marginal glosses, catch phrases, viewpoints, emphases and antitheses, but always without making its own decision and assuming its own responsibility and risk. Political activity is not possible in this way. But criticism is.'

[22] Schmitt, *Political Romanticism*, 147–8.

[23] See also F. A. Hayek, *The Road to Serfdom* (University of Chicago Press, 2007), ed. Bruce Caldwell, 189, note 27, where Schmitt is listed alongside Sombart, Spengler, Jünger, Arthur Moeller van den Bruck, Othmar Spann and Hans Freyer as the 'intellectual leaders of the generation which has produced nazism'.

[24] Jeffrey Herf, *Reactionary Modernism: Technology, Culture, and Politics in Weimar and the Third Reich* (Cambridge University Press, 1984), 23, 27. See also Eric D. Weitz, *Weimar Germany: Promise and Tragedy* (Princeton University Press, 2007), 332–41, discussing the broader social and political context and shared language of the 'conservative revolution', naming Schmitt as one of its leading intellectual figures.

sees its salvation in giving [the] masses not their rights but instead a chance to express themselves.'[25]

Schmitt pushed the rightist critique of Weimar more deeply into the field of jurisprudence than anyone else and became the most important conservative critic of liberal constitutional theory. His route to what he called the 'political' – that is, authentic politics which is substantive rather than procedural, decisionistic not deliberative, existential as opposed to just muddling through – was through the 'exception'. Whereas liberals were scared of the exception and so shied away from it,[26] the philosopher of concrete life 'must not withdraw from the exception and the extreme case, but must be interested in it to the highest degree'.[27] Reason of state, seen traditionally as a central problem for constitutional politics, becomes the route to solve the apathy and stagnation of the West.[28] Concentrating on the steely edges of *raison d'état* is a prerequisite, Schmitt maintains, for identifying the dynamic flow of power through state institutions,[29] the source of state power in notions of community and identity,[30] the true relationship between politics and public law and the connection between the internal and external faces of the state. It is in relation to the exception and not the rule, he says, that we must look to uncover the secrets of constitutional theory: '[i]n the

[25] Walter Benjamin, 'The Work of Art in an Age of Mechanical Representation' in Benjamin, *Illuminations* (London: Pimlico, 1999).

[26] Carl Schmitt, *Political Theology: Four Chapters on the Concept of Sovereignty* (University of Chicago Press, 1985), trans. George Schwab, 13–15. Oakeshott also thought that liberalism, due to its obsession with the threat of the re-appearance of absolute monarchy, was blind to other threats and 'lacked appropriate doctrinal weapons for combating what has turned out to be the real danger': Oakeshott, *The Social and Political Doctrines of Contemporary Europe* (London: Basic Books, 1940), 4.

[27] Schmitt, *Political Theology: Four Chapters on the Concept of Sovereignty*, 15.

[28] See also Carl Schmitt, *The Crisis of Parliamentary Democracy* (Cambridge, MA: MIT Press, 1985), trans. Ellen Kennedy, 37–8, suggesting that *Arcana rei publicae* 'belong to every kind of politics', not just absolutism.

[29] Schmitt's most extensive analysis of reason of state and the development of constitutional theory is to be found in the first chapter of *Dictatorship*, where he connects the growth of the concept with the spread of the technical conception of the state, derived from a reading of Machiavelli's *Il Principe* and refracted through the state theory of Hobbes and Bodin.

[30] Carl Schmitt, *Constitutional Theory* (Durham, NC: Duke University Press, 2008), trans. Jeffrey Seitzer, 61: 'constitution = the principle of the dynamic emergence of political unity, of a process of constantly renewed formation and emergence of this unity from a fundamental or ultimately effective power and energy . . . Political unity must form itself daily out of various opposing interests, opinions, and aspirations.'

exception the power of real life breaks through the crust of a mechanism that has become torpid by repetition.'[31]

Schmitt observes that 'the exception' refers to a general concept in constitutional theory and not merely a construct applied in situations of emergency.[32] The exception is internally related to the norm, not just its dirty little secret. Although a 'limit case', it is part of a constitutional order rather than somehow outside or in a straightforward sense opposed to it. 'Although he [the sovereign] stands outside the normally valid legal system, he nevertheless belongs to it, for it is he who must decide whether the constitution needs to be suspended in its entirety.'[33] Schmitt argues that his analysis of the exception enables him to get closer to sovereignty than liberal and neo-Kantian jurists such as Hans Kelsen, who obfuscate or 'radically suppress' the idea.[34] Close attention to the prerogative zone also enables Schmitt to make connections between the state and the people. The contrast is again with Kelsen and those for whom the state was an entirely normative – that is, in this context, formal – structure. Schmitt, by contrast, insists that 'the state is a specific entity of people'.[35]

The exception is vital because it connects with the creation, renewal and sustenance of an individual political community. It is necessarily, Schmitt thinks, the world unstructured by prior norms and so marked by the absence of constrained legalistic thinking. 'What characterizes an exception is principally unlimited authority, which means the suspension of the existing order . . . The decision frees itself from all normative ties and becomes in the true sense absolute.'[36] This is the realm of decision, of might rather than right, and so the space where a real choice can be made about the goals and ambitions of the nation. The exception allows the nation to determine its *raison d'être* – literally so, since Schmitt sees the political properly so-called to be a matter of the survival and flourishing

[31] Schmitt, *Political Theology: Four Chapters on the Concept of Sovereignty*, 15.

[32] Ibid., 5. [33] Ibid., 7.

[34] Ibid., 21. Also, Schmitt, *Constitutional Theory*, 187: 'A logically consistent and complete *Rechtsstaat* aspires to suppress the political concept of law, in order to set a "sovereignty of the law" in the place of a concrete existing sovereignty. In other words, it aspires, in fact, to not answer the question of sovereignty and to leave open the question of which political will make the appropriate norm into a positively valid command . . . [T]his must lead to concealments and fictions, with every instance of conflict posing anew the problem of sovereignty.' See also Lars Vinx's critical analysis of Schmitt's treatment of the question of sovereignty in this volume (Chapter 5).

[35] Schmitt, *The Concept of the Political*, 19.

[36] Schmitt, *Political Theology: Four Chapters on the Concept of Sovereignty*, 12.

of this particular community, a condition understood existentially[37] as being defined according to its fundamental enmities: that is, its readiness to fight against those it constructs as its enemies.[38] 'Political democracy, therefore, cannot rest on the inability to distinguish among persons, but rather only on the quality of belonging to a *particular people.* This quality of belonging to a people can be defined by very different elements (ideas of common race, belief, common destiny, and tradition).'[39] Alternative models of the modern state (liberal, parliamentary, positivist) attempt a 'formalist-functionalist hollowing out' of the state; pluralism is a recipe for chaos and anarchy.[40] Their effect is to remove from the state all sense of substantive value and with it any sense of community and meaning. As Dyzenhaus observes, Schmitt's feared that Hobbes' description of Leviathan as a great machine might supplant all other meanings that animated the state. 'The product of [this] rationalist impulse was the destruction of the state's soul which rendered the state insubstantial and thus open to enemy capture.'[41] This is not only a problem at the socio-psychological level, in that it produces effete political romantics helpless against the modern state machine. It also removes the bedrock of values with which that a system of law sustains itself. Legality is thus deprived 'of its persuasive power' and rendered incapable of distinguishing between justice and injustice.[42]

Prioritizing the exception in this way enables Schmitt to specify a hierarchy in which law is subordinate to the political – politics, that is, in its 'authentic' sense as normatively unconstrained decision. One reading of this position emphasizes the relatively conventional nature of Schmitt's theory, maintaining that Schmitt is claiming no more than

[37] McCormick, linking Schmitt to Nietzsche, calls the former the 'infamous, early-twentieth-century political existentialist' and the latter 'the renowned, late-nineteenth-century philosophical existentialist' (*Carl Schmitt's Critique of Liberalism*, 85).

[38] Schmitt, *Constitutional Theory*, 76: 'The constitution does not establish itself. It is, rather, given to a concrete political unity . . . Every existing political unity has its value and its "right to existence" not in the rightness or usefulness of norms, but rather in its existence. Considered juristically, what exists as *political* power has value because it exists. Consequently, its "right to self-preservation" is the prerequisite of all further discussions; it attempts, above all, to maintain itself in its existence, "*in suo esse perseverare*" (Spinoza); it protects "its *existence*, its *integrity*, its *security*, and its *constitution*", which are all existential values.'

[39] Ibid., 258. [40] Schmitt, *The Concept of the Political*, Chapter 4.

[41] David Dyzenhaus, '"Now the Machine Runs Itself": Carl Schmitt on Hobbes and Kelsen', *Cardozo Law Review*, 16 (1994), 1, 8.

[42] Carl Schmitt, *Legality and Legitimacy* (Durham, NC: Duke University Press, 2004), trans. Jeffrey Seitzer, 29.

what many political theorists before him would have thought obvious, namely, the lexical priority of order over justice and the truth of the maxim *auctoritas non veritas facit legem*. Andreas Kalyvas sees Schmitt's aim as being to combine 'Hobbes's absolutist concept of sovereignty and Emmanuel Sieyès's notion of *le pouvoir constitutant*, that is, the power of a political subject to create a new constitution'. Schmitt's concern throughout his Weimar works, Kalyvas maintains, was to theorize a two-level constitution not all that different from Bruce Ackerman's theory of dualist democracy,[43] capable of protecting 'the general will of the popular sovereign from the particular wills of ephemeral majorities'.[44]

This revisionist reading has the virtue of making us pause before making too quick a move from extraordinary to ordinary when interpreting Schmitt's theory. It is true that Schmitt's writings offer a theory of constitutional change and dynamism. As such, they can be seen as an attempt to inject life into a situation that their author feared was becoming torpid. In this sense, Schmitt's theory may be seen as a characteristic response to a classic early twentieth-century predicament. But the attempt fully to normalize Schmitt fails to convince. The reading does not do justice to the tone and conceptual vocabulary Schmitt deployed. His choice of language is that of a reactionary modernist of the Weimar period, inclined to embrace the existential and extraordinary at the expense of the normal and quotidian. Even the closest thing Schmitt wrote to a standard legal treatise, his *Constitutional Theory* (1928), is largely taken up with considerations of constituent power and the prioritization of the 'positive' concept of the constitution, 'the constitution as the complete decision over the type and form of the political unity', over the constitution in the normative sense, referred to dismissively as the 'bourgeois *Rechtsstaat*'. The book does show considerable sophistication in its handling of deep-lying historical trends, for instance, in analyzing the liberal constitutionalist paradigm. But its real interest lies in emphasizing and prioritizing the idea of systematic constitutional change. This is at odds with standard theoretical and doctrinal treatments, although its

[43] Bruce Ackerman, *We The People: Foundations* (Cambridge, MA: Harvard University Press, 1991).

[44] Andreas Kalyvas, *Democracy and the Politics of the Extraordinary: Max Weber, Carl Schmitt, and Hannah Arendt* (Cambridge University Press, 2008), 88. See also Martin Loughlin's (Chapter 4) and Duncan Kelly's (Chapter 8) contributions to this volume and Adrian Vermeule, 'Our Schmittian Administrative Law', *Harvard Law Review*, 122 (2009), 1095.

unorthodox position arguably makes sense in an era of radical instability, revolution and counter-revolution.

The role the extraordinary plays in Schmitt's theory is far more extensive than an account of a process in which epoch-making constitutional moments end up shaping public law for a generation and more.[45] One of the most consistent themes within Schmitt's work, an essential part of his critique of liberal legalism and positivism, was his insistence on the penetration of the ordinary by the extraordinary. Existential moments 'bleed into the quotidian', as Nomi Claire Lazar puts it, 'in part because every quotidian moment is potentially existential'.[46] Schmitt envisages a situation in which normal juridical relations are always and everywhere subject to and structured by the political (i.e., the substantive decision on the basis of friend/foe). 'The political decision, which essentially means the constitution, cannot have a reciprocal effect on its subject and eliminate its political existence. This political will remains alongside and above the constitution.'[47] Anything less pervasive would lack the redemptive quality Schmitt seeks in the political and would amount to an acceptance of the status quo. As John McCormick observes, Schmitt consistently presents the normal liberal political order as being 'so utterly corrupted by science and technology that it is actually *redeemed* by the exception and the sovereign dictatorial action for which it calls'.[48] The exception is juris-generative and life affirming, while an excess of normativity leads to civic death. It is only by virtue of this primacy of the prerogative, not just during exceptional moments but at all times, that the 'power of real life' can constantly break through 'the crust of the mechanism'.

The exception also enables Schmitt to connect the internal constitution of the state with its external manifestation. The friend-enemy distinction, the definition of the political, is the attribute of a sovereign power that is itself determined in the exceptional moment. The pre-eminent act of sovereign power is the decision that fixes the nature and

[45] Schmitt, *Constitutional Theory*, 77: 'Prior to the establishment of any norm, there is a fundamental *political decision by the bearer of constitution-making power*' (Schmitt's italics).

[46] Nomi Claire Lazar, *States of Emergency in Liberal Democracies* (Cambridge University Press, 2009), 41.

[47] Schmitt, *Constitutional Theory*, 125–6.

[48] John P. McCormick, 'The Dilemmas of Dictatorship: Carl Schmitt and Constitutional Emergency Powers' in Dyzenhaus, *Law as Politics*, 225. (Italics in the original.)

frontier of any community.[49] Internally, it defines community and constitution, stipulating who counts as 'friend' and on what basis. Externally, it is enmity constructing and pregnant with the possibility of conflict. 'War is neither the aim nor the purpose nor even the very content of politics. But as an ever present possibility it is the leading presupposition which determines in a characteristic way human action and thinking and thereby creates a specifically political behavior.'[50] We have already met a precursor of this position in the figure of the romantic politician Don Quixote, who made a decision on what was right and wrong and lived by it, as exemplified by his preparedness to do battle, even where to do so was seen by others as absurd. His later writings on war and international law are equally illuminating, not least in that they reveal a different dimension of the destabilizing force of Schmitt's commitment to decisionist politics. Here, we see the state almost bursting at the seams. In 'The *Großräum* Order of International Law' (1939–41), Schmitt seems prepared to subordinate the state to the political decision, whereas before it was the decision that gave the state its shape and animating purpose.[51] He argues in this essay for a new order of international law to reflect new political realities, chief among which was the expanding *Großdeutsche Reich*. 'Today we think planetarily and in *Großräume* [large spaces].' The new international law should be 'grounded in concrete *Großräume*' and not the 'universalistic-humanitarian world law' that currently dominates. Within this order, states are obsolete. They are to be replaced by *Reich*s as the central legal subject, *Reich*s being 'the leading and bearing powers whose political ideas radiate into a certain *Großräum* and which fundamentally exclude the interventions of spatially alien powers into this *Großräum*'. The immediate political message is clear. The new *Deutsches*

[49] On the way, Schmitt connects this primary move of boundary fixing to the normative (*nomos*); see his *The Nomos of the Earth in the International Law of the Jus Publicum Europeaum* (New York: Telos Press, 2003) and Nehal Bhuta's (Chapter 2) and Martin Loughlin's (Chapter 4) contributions to this volume.

[50] Schmitt, *The Concept of the Political*, 34.

[51] It is at least arguable, though, that in his slightly earlier work, *The Leviathan in the State Theory of Thomas Hobbes: Meaning and Failure of a Political Symbol* (University of Chicago Press, 2008), trans. George Schwab and Erna Hilfstein, Schmitt is making the case against the 'quantitative total state' that Germany had become under the Nazis and reiterated his argument in favour of the 'qualitative total state' comprising of a strong authoritarian state and an unrestricted economy. See also his address 'A Strong State and Sound Economics' before the *Langnam Verein* (literally the 'Long Name Association' or northwestern industries) in 1932 in R. Cristi. (1998), *Carl Schmitt and Authoritarian Liberalism* (Cardiff: University of Wales Press, 1998).

Reich, spreading its control across increasing parts of the European continent, 'has the holy honour of defending a non-universalistic, *völkisch* order of life with respect for the nation'.

> Today, however, a powerful German *Reich* has arisen. From what was only weak and impotent, there has emerged a strong centre of Europe that is impossible to attack and ready to prove its great political idea, that respect of every nation as a reality of life determined through species and origin, blood and soil, with its radiation into the Middle and European space, and to reject the interference of spatially alien and un-*völkisch* powers.[52]

Schmitt was only one of a number of German lawyers to press this geopolitical case.[53] What is noteworthy, though, is Schmitt's preparedness to sacrifice the state on the altar of the political. The decision is now the property of the nation (*Volk*) rather than the state and may have expansionary properties – certainly where the nation is strong and decisive enough for its political idea to radiate and take on continental proportions. We see here a reasonably comfortable alliance between Schmitt's prerogative-dominated state theory and Nazi race imperialism. (Incidentally, the anti-Semitism in 'the *Großraum* Order' is as apparent as it is odious.[54]) In Schmitt's hands, Franz Neumann observed, 'the exception becomes the rule. There is no one international law but as many as there are empires, that is, large spaces. The *großdeutsche Reich* is the creator of its own international law in its own space.'[55]

Schmitt's relentless exploration of the prerogative zone brings insight into the dynamic energy that underpins constitutions, orients them and flows through and outside them. It is nonetheless problematic, not least because in paying insufficient attention to the normal juridical sphere, Schmitt's theory is radically unstable. Schmitt's obvious and increasing relish throughout the Weimar period for the use of quasi-dictatorial powers to enable an authoritarian president to bypass the liberal/parliamentary

[52] Carl Schmitt, 'The *Großraum* Order of International Law with a Ban on the Intervention for Spatially Foreign Powers: A Contribution to the Concept of Reich in International Law' in Schmitt, *Writings on War* (Cambridge, UK: Polity, 2011), trans. Timothy Nunan, 96, 101, 102, 111.

[53] Franz Neumann, *Behemoth: The Structure and Practice of National Socialism, 1933–1944* (Chicago: Ivan R. Dee, 2009), 150–71.

[54] Schmitt, 'The *Großraum* Order', 108 ('the Jew Laski') and 121–2: 'The relation of a nation to a soil arranged through its own work of colonization and culture and to the concrete forms of power that arise from this arrangement is incomprehensible to the spirit of the Jew.'

[55] Neumann, *Behemoth*, 158.

framework of checks and balances is indicative, for in this context practice and theory come together. The idea of a continuing or floating sovereignty that pervasively inhabits normal constitutional and legal structures combines with a streamlined model of supposedly authentic political activity – of myth-encrusted political life, existentially freighted decision, popular acclamation, immediate enactment. The state, Schmitt writes, 'intervenes everywhere. At times it does so as a *deus ex machina*, to decide according to positive statute a controversy that the independent act of juristic perception failed to bring to a generally plausible solution; at other times it does so as the graceful and merciful lord who proves by pardons and amnesties his supremacy over his own laws.'[56] This is a theory of the sovereign as Old Testament God. Its dynamism is capable of undermining a framework of 'settled, stable law'. The theory folds the realm of law into the world of the exception, the artificial reason of law into the political reason of state.

Schmitt's antinomian position glories in the image of the statesman-sovereign cut free from the baggage of parliamentary democracy and constitutional laws who acts authentically in what he takes to be the interest of state. This transition is sketched with mesmerizing skill in a chapter in *Legality and Legitimacy* on the President's decree powers under Article 48 of the Weimar Constitution. It starts solidly enough, with the text itself and an account of the settled practice that even refers to two court cases. Soon, though, these conventional legal trappings disappear, submerged by Schmitt's *modus operandi* of 'categorical elision and rhetorical manipulation'.[57] The 'simple truth of legal scholarship becomes evident through all the normative fictions and obscurities', we are told, and is 'that norms are valid only for normal situations, and the presupposed normalcy of the situation is a positive-legal component of its "validity"'. And who gets to decide whether normality exists? 'By his own discretion, the extraordinary lawmaker determines the presupposition of his extraordinary powers (danger for public security and order) and the content of "necessary" measures.' It is thus 'evident' that the President is superior to the Reichstag, 'that is, to the ordinary, national legislature in regard to the scope and content of its recognized legislative power'.

This position is reached despite it being the opposite of the constitutional text on which the analysis supposedly rests. We are left with

[56] Schmitt, *Political Theology: Four Chapters on the Concept of Sovereignty*, 38.
[57] McCormick, 'The Weimar Crisis of Law', 67.

something that looks very much like bare power – as straightforward, untrammelled and de-institutionalized as possible.

> The practice that was only a groundless theory in parliament becomes self-evident in the dictator, and the legislative power becomes the weapon useful for completing his mission. Instead of issuing a general decree, therefore, the dictator can issue an individual order, even immediately and directly . . . In this way, he renders practically meaningless the entire system of legal protections that was built up with great artistry to counter the orders of the executive . . . But for the extraordinary law-maker of Article 48, the distinction between statute and statutory application, legislative and executive, is neither legally nor factually an obstacle. The extraordinary lawmaker combines both in his person.[58]

In passages such as this one, it is almost impossible to identify when Schmitt is talking about normal constitutional operations and when he is talking about emergency ones.[59] As Gopal Balakrishnan notes, echoing Fraenkel's contemporaneous analysis of Schmitt's role in fashioning the Nazi prerogative state,[60] 'the distinction between the normal and the exceptional had become so thoroughly effaced that the question of

[58] Schmitt, *Legality and Legitimacy*, 67, 69, 70–1. Schmitt's earlier article, 'The Dictatorship of the President of the Reich According to Article 48 of the Weimar Constitution', developed from a keynote address given in 1924 to the conference of German Constitutional Jurists and which appeared as an appendix to the second edition of *Die Diktatur* in 1928, is somewhat more nuanced, less obviously an endorsement of sovereign dictatorship, for instance, in its discussion of the difference between true 'laws' and executive (emergency) 'measures'. But the thrust of the piece is identical to that pursued more decisively in later works such as *Legality and Legitimacy*, arguing for the maximum possible reach and the minimum possible interference with the president's use of Article 48 emergency powers. See *Dictatorship*, 183, 185, 208, 225: '[T]he truth is that in 1919, in view of the incredibly difficult situation, the National Assembly was concerned first to give as far-reaching authorisations as possible [to the president]; and it left the fulfilment of the constitutional requirements to a later, "detailed" regulation, which was not forthcoming.'

[59] John P. McCormick, 'From Constitutional Technique to Caesarist Ploy: Carl Schmitt on Dictatorship, Liberalism, and Emergency Powers' in Peter Baehr and Melvin Richter (eds.), *Dictatorship in History and Theory: Bonapartism, Caesarism, and Totalitarianism* (Cambridge University Press, 2004), 208.

[60] Fraenkel refers to Schmitt's *Über die drei Arten des rechtswissenschaftlichen Denkens* of 1933 as the 'most influential juridical study of recent years' (*Dual State*, 142). See also *Dual State*, 25: 'Schmitt's theory has been adopted by the *Gestapo*.' There are more references to Schmitt in the index of the book than to any other figure. See also Neumann, *Behemoth*, 43, 49, where Schmitt is referred to as 'the ideologist of this sham' and 'the most intelligent and reliable of all National Socialist constitutional lawyers'.

what the normal procedures were could no longer be answered except politically.'[61] To an extent, such a move is perfectly understandable for a jurist trying to make sense of the inter-war crisis years.[62] The exception has unquestionably become a much more common feature of political life. Older conceptions of law are threatened by social and political developments and by other ideas of what (modern) law really is. There is a concern, which Schmitt shared, about the deadness of modern life, at one extreme, and a Leftist revolutionary culture that seems the most obvious alternative, at the other. Redemption from the former is sought in authentic political life. Protection from the latter is sought in the unity of the nation at the level of political will – the state as a 'specific entity of people' – and a lack of squeamishness about protecting that unity from internal and external enemies. One of the problems, though, with Schmitt's vision is that it saves law – or what Schmitt liked to call the 'persuasive power' of the juridical – almost at the expense of law itself, for in his scheme it is not law or legality that acts as a binding agent. That role is taken by the popularly acclaimed decider, who represents the unity of the people. The subordination of norm to exception and the juridical to the political deprives law of its autonomous capacity, its characteristic of providing a settled framework of rights and duties capable of operating coherently and at arm's length from the ministrations of those in power. Contrary to his intentions, then, Schmitt's theory threatens to make law instrumental to the needs of the political unit as perceived by the decider. This, as it turned out, was precisely the fate of law within the Nazi dual state, where prerogative, understood as the will of the decider, was always and everywhere capable of trumping law. Just as troubling, Schmitt's theory also reduces law and constitutional politics to a game, played without much rhyme or reason. The essential qualities of law and politics are made mysterious, myths designed simultaneously to shroud and prop up the authority of an imagined central decider. We are left with a 'huge cloak-and-dagger drama', as Schmitt called it, to be marvelled at by a largely uncomprehending people, in whose name, we should remember, the whole thing is said to take place.

[61] Gopal Balakrishnan, *The Enemy: An Intellectual Portrait of Carl Schmitt* (London: Verso, 2002), 158. See also Ellen Kennedy, *Constitutional Failure: Carl Schmitt in Weimar* (Durham, NC: Duke University Press, 2004), 85: Schmitt's claim that sovereignty *is* order 'introduces an apparently unlimited space of legal indeterminacy in which sovereignty is that very aspect of law that is not determined. Schmitt seems to remove all law.' Schmitt, *Political Theology*, 38.

[62] For more on this subject, see David Boucher's contribution to this volume (Chapter 6).

Hayek: dethroning politics

Hayek's constitutional theory was not just written against the background of the twentieth-century crisis of law and the administrative state but also and more specifically against Schmitt's solution to that problem, which he saw as offering the pathological elements of a legal system as the cure of its present ills.[63] Schmitt's theory of concrete-order formation, he wrote, provided 'the instrument of arrangement or organization by which the individual is made to serve concrete purposes. This is the inevitable outcome of an intellectual development in which the self-ordering forces of society and the role of law in an ordering mechanism are no longer understood.'[64] Arguing against precisely such a formulation, Hayek's theory is a self-conscious attempt to re-invigorate older strands of liberal thought, particularly the British tradition made explicit by the Scottish moral philosophers 'led by David Hume, Adam Smith, and Adam Ferguson, seconded by their English contemporaries Josiah Tucker, Edmund Burke, and William Paley', all of whom drew on a tradition rooted in the jurisprudence of the common law in which the key figure is Matthew Hale.[65] By contrast, Schmitt's decisionist theory, which sought to narrow decision making and to de-institutionalize political decision, was a particularly egregious case of synoptic delusion, the 'fiction that all relevant facts are known to some one mind, and that it is possible to construct from this knowledge of the particulars a desirable social order'.[66] The idea that an authoritarian leader might present the truest form of representative government Hayek would have dismissed as spectacular nonsense. Schmitt was 'in the grip of a picture', the relevant picture being the theological one within which one credulously accepts the 'argument from design'.[67]

Hayek's work sits squarely within a broader liberal tradition, a characteristic of which is its 'distrust of determinate, personal authority,

[63] Friedrich A. Hayek, *Law, Legislation and Liberty: A New Statement of the Liberal Principles of Justice and Political Economy*, vol. I: *Rules and Order* (London: Routledge, 1982), 71.

[64] Ibid.

[65] Friedrich A. Hayek, *The Constitution of Liberty* (London: Routledge, 2010), 50; Hayek, *Rules and Order*, 22. As a number of commentators have noted, the evolutionary liberal dimensions of Hayek's theory often sit uneasily next to its more Kantian liberal elements. See Chandran Kukathas, *Hayek and Modern Liberalism* (Oxford University Press, 1989), 17.

[66] Hayek, *Rules and Order*, 14.

[67] Edna Ullmann-Margalit, 'The Invisible Hand and the Cunning of Reason', *Social Research*, 64 (1997), 181, 183.

authority whose power was visible and traceable to a specific person, such as a pope or monarch'.[68] One way of reading his constitutional analysis is as a systematic attempt to do away with reason of state altogether, to fade even the idea of a moment of decision into a system of laws understood as non-purposive social rules that have evolved over time. The image of common-law development as the epitome of law understood as *nomos* (the law of liberty) is crucial to this enterprise. Historically, the common law provided the anchor of the eighteenth-century liberty that Britain enjoyed and the rest of Europe admired.[69] Theoretically, the common law is a demonstration of how 'rules that have never been deliberately invented . . . have grown through a gradual process of trial and error in which the experience of successive generations has helped to make them what they are.'[70] The common law shows how an order of laws can develop largely in the absence of design, with very little commanding intelligence[71] or substantive purpose beyond peaceful coexistence.[72]

This account of the common law as a model for the free society corresponds to a sceptical account of human intelligence. There is no other theme that Hayek emphasizes more 'than the need for human reason to recognize the limitations of human reason'.[73] Man's 'unavoidable ignorance' is for Hayek a 'fundamental fact'.[74] Indeed, it becomes all the more so as people and the societies they inhabit become more complex. 'The more civilized we become, the more relatively ignorant must each individual be of the facts on which the working of his civilization depends.'[75] Counter-intuitively, then, the seemingly archaic common law is perfectly adapted to modern conditions. Seen as a collective intelligence device, a vast system of trial and error on matters of law and coordination, it is a near-perfect way, so Hayek argues, of aggregating experience and transmitting the accumulated stock of knowledge through time. Admittedly, Hayek's use of the term 'common law' is

[68] Sheldon Wolin, *Politics and Vision: Continuity and Innovation in Western Political Thought* (Princeton University Press, 2006), 311.

[69] Hayek, *Rules and Order*, 85. [70] Hayek, *Constitution of Liberty*, 138.

[71] Ibid., 140: 'Much of the opposition to a system of freedom under general laws arises from the inability to conceive of an effective co-ordination of human activities without deliberate organization by a commanding intelligence.'

[72] Hayek, *Rules and Order*, 112: 'to conceive as a goal an abstract order, the particular manifestation of which no one could predict, and which was determined by properties no one could precisely define'.

[73] Ullmann-Margalit, 'The Invisible Hand and the Cunning of Reason', 185.

[74] Hayek, *Constitution of Liberty*, 21. [75] Ibid., 25. Also, Hayek, *Rules and Order*, 14.

imprecise. His conception of *nomos* conflates two distinctive types of law, customary law and common law. While at one point in the long history of English common law there would not have been all that much that separated the two, certainly by the nineteenth century, common-law courts applied 'both procedural and substantive rules of law consistently with the rules announced in prior judicial decisions' and aimed to developed and maintain 'a consistent and coherent body of rules'.[76] It is arguably customary law, rather than common law as it developed into the modern era, that better reflects Hayek's idea of spontaneous order. Still, we might modify the claim and suggest that (modern) common law nonetheless offers a model different from and preferable to legislation, one that is interstitial, evolutionary, both backward- and forward-looking and in which authority is depersonalized and dispersed.[77]

In fact, Hayek presses his objection to rationalist accounts further, arguing that reason is significantly shaped by culture. Intelligence and the pathways reason takes in the human mind are themselves products of the social order in which they have evolved. 'Man is as much a rule-following animal as a purpose-seeking one', he argues, and 'his thinking and acting are governed by rules which have by a process of selection been evolved in the society in which he lives.'[78] Society is in essence a 'social order of actions' that arises from a system of rules.[79] What identifies a society – and differentiates it from other societies – is the particular set of rules

[76] John Hasnas, 'Hayek, the Common Law, and Fluid Drive', *New York Journal of Law and Liberty*, 1 (2005), 79, 94.

[77] T. R. S. Allan makes precisely this argument, drawing upon Hayek in order to do so, in *Law, Liberty and Justice* (Oxford University Press, 1994). For a defence of the position from a law and economics perspective, see George L. Priest, 'The Common Law Process and the Selection of Efficient Rules', *Journal of Legal Studies*, 6 (1977), 65. Others are sceptical of claims for the superiority of common law, given the pace of social change; see Giacomo A. M. Ponzetto and Patricio A. Fernandez, 'Case Law vs. Statute Law: An Evolutionary Comparison', *Journal of Legal Studies*, 37 (2008), 379; Adam J. Hirsch, 'Evolutionary Theories of Common Law Efficiency: Reasons for (Cognitive) Skepticism', *Florida State University Law Review*, 32 (2005), 425; Adrian Vermeule, *Law and the Limits of Reason* (New York: Oxford University Press, 2009), 109–12.

[78] Hayek, *Rules and Order*, 11. Also, 17: '[M]ind is an adaptation to the natural surroundings in which man lives and . . . has developed in constant interaction with the institutions which determine the structure of society.'

[79] Friedrich A. Hayek, 'Notes on the Evolution of Systems of Rules of Conduct: The Interplay between Rules of Individual Conduct and the Social Order of Actions' in Hayek, *Studies in Philosophy, Politics, and Economics* (University of Chicago Press, 1967). See also Douglas Glen Whitman, 'Hayek contra Pangloss on Evolutionary Systems', *Constitutional Political Economy*, 9 (1998), 45.

that it has developed (really the rules that have developed as that society has developed) and the way that it relates to and identifies with those rules.[80] To describe this process, Hayek uses an analogy to evolutionary theories in biology. Rules are to orders of action as genes are to organisms. In essence, 'in Hayek's account rules play a role analogous to genes in biological evolution; whereas individual organisms are constituted by following the instructions of genes, a Great Society is constituted by following the instructions of rules.'[81] Complex societies in particular are apt to be self-maintaining. It might be possible synoptically to control a warrior band or village community. Aspiring to do the same thing in a social order as complex as the modern state is quite a different proposition,[82] especially if you want that society to be even remotely free. Complex societies are characterized by constant novelty, so all the relevant data could never be given to single mind. Their operating principle is the natural selection of traditions.[83] Social evolution specifies a mechanism of selection according to which certain social traits are selected in a competitive environment over others. As Hayek sees it, 'evolutionary accounts provide the real alternative to design theories, and they articulate precisely the "explanations of principle" that are appropriate to complexity.'[84]

Reason of state, seen from this perspective, is twice damned. First, conceived as the reflection of the reason of the individual or relative small group of individuals who happen to be at the helm of state at a given time, it is necessarily limited, certainly when set against the accumulated

[80] Hayek, 'Notes on the Evolution of Systems of Rules of Conduct', 68; also, Friedrich A. Hayek, *The Fatal Conceit: The Errors of Socialism* (University of Chicago Press, 1988), ed. William W. Bartley III, 6.

[81] Gerald F. Gaus, 'Hayek on the Evolution of Society and Mind' in Edward Feser (ed.), *The Cambridge Companion to Hayek* (Cambridge Univesity Press, 2006), 238, 243. Note, however, that Hayek argued that the idea of evolution is older in the humanities and social sciences than in the natural sciences and suggests that Darwin, who was reading Adam Smith when formulating his own theory, 'got the basic ideas of evolution from economics' (Hayek, *The Fatal Conceit*, 24).

[82] Hayek, *The Fatal Conceit*, 113.

[83] John Gray, *Hayek on Liberty*, 3rd edn. (London: Routledge, 1998), 55. See Hayek, *Rules and Order*, 18; Hayek, *The Fatal Conceit*, 43: An evolutionary account of customs must show the 'distinct advantages by those groups that kept to such customs, thereby enabling them to expand more rapidly than others and ultimately to supersede (or absorb) those not possessing similar customs.'

[84] Gaus, 'Hayek on the Evolution of Society and Mind', 237. See also Gerald F. Gaus, *The Order of Public Reason: A Theory of Freedom and Morality in a Diverse and Bounded World* (Cambridge University Press, 2011), 415–24.

knowledge gains of generations embodied in the evolved law (*nomos*). It is even more limited than the law of legislation (*thesis*), which is at least refracted through a series of institutions (i.e., more and larger groups) before becoming law.[85] Institutionally speaking, reason of state represents an attenuated structure of decision making and is as such even more subject to Hayek's observations about the limits of individual human intelligence. Secondly, reason of state often presents itself as operating in a certain sense outside time. The moment of decision interrupts the normal flow of social intercourse and development.[86] The sort of intelligence that this kind of action presupposes is antithetical to Hayek: 'any attempt to use reason to control or direct the social process threatens not only to impede the development of our powers of reason but also to bring the growth of knowledge to a halt.'[87] The exception, understood as a kind of caesura in constitutional time, was for Schmitt the nation's potential saviour, perhaps even a reflection of the voice of God. For Hayek, the same phenomenon, not all that dissimilarly understood,[88] threatens the evolution of the spontaneous order of freedom and is, as such, necessarily problematic.

So much for the 'reason' part of reason of state. What Hayek says about the 'state' side of the equation is also important. His interpretation of the constitutional maxim *salus populi suprema lex esto* is particularly illuminating. The principle is historically linked to reason of state, providing a justification for agents of government to act on their own initiative outside and sometimes even against the requirements of the ordinary law.[89] This is exactly the sort of action that Hayek wants to foreclose. 'Correctly understood', Hayek argues, *salus populi* 'means that the end of the law ought to be the welfare of the people, that the general rules should be so designed as to serve it, but *not* that any conception of a particular social end should provide a justification for breaking those

[85] Hayek, *Rules and Order*, Chapter 6, esp. 129–31.

[86] See Vermeule, *Law and the Limits of Reason*, 33–6, which points to the necessarily diachronic aspect of Hayek's evolutionary theory.

[87] Kukathas, *Hayek and Modern Liberalism*, 61.

[88] Hayek says of Schmitt: 'It has been contended with some plausibility that whoever has the power to proclaim an emergency and on this ground to suspend any part of the constitution is the true sovereign' (Hayek, *Rules and Order*, 125).

[89] For an important discussion of the history of the idea of *salus populi* and its connection to changing understandings of reason of state, see Duncan Kelly's contribution to this collection (Chapter 8).

general rules.'[90] This passage is a reminder that the relevant unit of his theory is the group – or, rather, the order of actions of a group.[91] A group is defined not by the will of a group of living agents (a people) but through shared identity with a system of non-positive laws (a public). 'This means that our units are systems of cooperation – arising out of a system of rules – and for Hayek this means that the rules actually regulated peoples' actions.'[92] This entails that there is nothing either special or mysterious about the state – it is just the form that a system of co-operation under rules tends to take in modern politics. Certainly, there is no cause to reify or personify the state, nor any justification for imbuing it with any special notion of agency.[93] The rules that are contained within the state's legal order (or, perhaps better, the rules that as a system define the state) ought to serve the welfare of the people and should do so where law making operates as *nomos*. Breaking these rules is highly unlikely to benefit the public, as opposed to a powerful group within it.

This conception of state and law is remarkable in how far it goes to deny agency on the part of the state or its officials. Hayek's model constitution is designed to enclose the decision-making capacity of individual agents within dense institutional structures whose purpose is to remove agency from government as far as possible.[94] We are entitled to ask whether this position is plausible, especially in the conditions of modernity that Hayek acknowledged. In normal conditions, the ideal of legal development that Hayek presents, modelled on the common law understood as a species of customary law and resting on an organic selection between competing traditions, seems too slow to accommodate the pace of change that occurs in modern societies.[95] In this environment, as Vermeule notes, statutes (and other types of directive legislation) 'can

[90] CoL, 139. [91] Hayek, 'Notes on the Evolution of Systems of Rules of Conduct', 72.
[92] Gaus, 'Hayek on the Evolution of Society and Mind', 241.
[93] This dimension of Hayek's thought is explored systematically in Chandran Kukathas's contribution to this volume (Chapter 12).
[94] Friedrich A. Hayek, *Law, Legislation and Liberty: A New Statement of the Liberal Principles of Justice and Political Economy*, vol. iii: *The Political Order of a Free People* (London: Routledge, 1982), Chapter 17. See also Jan-Werner Müller's contribution to this volume (Chapter 11).
[95] As Richard Bellamy points out, the pluralism of contemporary societies also challenges the possibility of the well-ordered, co-operative society based upon the sort of shared universal principles that Hayek defends: Richard Bellamy, '"Dethroning Politics": Liberalism, Constitutionalism and Democracy in the Thought of F. A. Hayek', *British Journal of Political Science*, 24 (1994), 419, 434.

innovate more rapidly and completely than the common law, when there is an abrupt change of circumstances'.[96] In respect of exceptional conditions, Hayek's escape from reason of state is not complete. In his more engaged political writings, Hayek was not afraid to use reason-of-state-type arguments to justify, for instance, a proposal for 'real political and economic union with France' at the outset of the Second World War.[97] In his theoretical work, reason of state emerges briefly from the shadows in a short passage in his discussion of the model constitution in *Law, Legislation and Liberty*. Hayek here recognizes that the basic principles of a free society may have to be temporarily suspended when the long-run preservation of that order is itself threatened:

> Though normally the individuals need be concerned only with their own concrete aims, and in pursuing them will best serve the common welfare, there may temporarily arise circumstances when the preservation of the overall order becomes the overruling common purpose, and when in consequence the spontaneous order, on a local or national scale, must for a time be converted into an organization.[98]

This way of conceptualizing emergency action is unconvincing not least because there are few resources within Hayek's theory that might account for it. He presents the shift in the register of the state – from common law to reason of state – as a natural thing, like 'a wounded animal in flight from mortal danger'. Hayek is elsewhere very critical of the application of animistic vocabulary and imagery to describe large societies such as the state. Such extended orders are formed into a concordant structure through observance to similar rules of conduct and do not correspond to a model of intimate fellowship. It is misleading, he says in *The Fatal Conceit*, to treat the state 'animistically, or to personify it by ascribing to it a will, an intention, or a design'.[99] But here, for an instant, he moves into the territory of the Schmittian exception, adopting Schmitt's conceptual scheme, even parroting his rhetoric. But Schmitt had extensively, even excessively, laid the groundwork for this in his theory of the exception and its prime importance to juridical order, the necessity of sovereign authority to legal system and an account of substantive popular unity and representation which focusses on

[96] Vermuele, *Law and the Limits of Reason*, 109.

[97] Friedrich A. Hayek, 'War Aims', letter to *The Spectator*, 17 November 1939, in Bruce Caldwell (ed.), *The Collected Works of F. A. Hayek – Socialism and War: Essays, Documents, Reviews* (Indianapolis, IN: Liberty Fund, 1997), 162.

[98] Hayek, *Law, Legislation and Liberty*, 124.

[99] Hayek, *The Fatal Conceit*, 113.

exceptional moments. Hayek has done the opposite. He has tried to eradicate even the conditions that make the Schmittian exception possible. In Hayek's vision, there is no sovereign. There is little by way of individual or small-group political agency. There is only an attenuated notion of the state.[100] This makes the theory of emergency powers have the feel of a drop-in. As such, it has a similar conceptual logic to Schmitt's exception but the opposite normative logic. The exception in Hayek has the same *deus ex machina* structure as in Schmitt, but here the descending gods are figured as would-be tyrants rather than welcomed as potential redeemers.

Hayek's is a second characteristic response to twentieth-century conditions, one that steers a very different path from Schmitt's embrace of the idea of reason of state as a rejuvenating and purifying force. On this second account, reason of state becomes an illegitimate exotic, aberrant and dangerous, to be distinguished sharply from normal juridical conditions and pushed to the margins as much as possible. But Hayek does not tell us why reason of state should present itself differently from all other aspects of political life. If the pattern of development within a complex order of action proceeds in the way Hayek imagines, then reason of state, too, must be subject to evolutionary development and must develop a particular and complex institutional, conceptual and rule-bound shape over time. We choose between competing traditions of reason of state politics just as surely as we select from competing traditions of ordinary rule.

Oakeshott's dual state

In exploring Michael Oakeshott's contribution to the idea of reason of state, I proceed by way of an exploration of two somewhat different layers within his work. The first, most clearly visible in his more polemical writings, connects reason-of-state thinking straightforwardly to the

100 Hayek faces parallel difficulties in relation to that important area in which reason of state operates: international relations. As he wrote in *The Road to Serfdom*, if 'the resources of different nations are treated as exclusive properties of . . . nations as wholes, if international economic relations, instead of being relations between individuals, become increasingly relations between whole nations organized as trading bodies, they inevitably become the source of friction and envy between nations' (p. 224). The only legitimate option this leaves is a universal state, with no restrictions on movement or, alternatively, national states with no redistribution. Neither option is plausible in the world as it exists today. See Harold James, *The Roman Predicament: How the Rules of International Order Create the Politics of Empire* (Princeton University Press, 2006), 37–8.

errors of Rationalism. The second, based on a reading of *On Human Conduct*, reluctantly accepts the inclusion of reason-of-state politics within the state understood as a complex and conflicted whole.

At first sight, reason of state seems to fit neatly within Oakeshott's scheme as one of the errors of Rationalism. He is deeply antagonistic to the Schmittian (or indeed Lockean[101]) exception, regarding it as belonging to a political imagination that is both revolutionary and perfectionist. As such, it adopts a view of politics which takes wartime or other moments of national crisis as the norm and attempts to use them as a model for times of peace.[102] This model mistakenly views politics and statecraft as a science of 'technique'. Machiavelli, writing a crib on politics for the new prince, inadvertently invented a species of political thought (Machiavellianism, *raison d'état*, Rationalism) whose founding tenet was the 'sovereignty of technique' epitomized by the belief that 'government was nothing more than "public administration" and could be learned from a book.'[103]

Oakeshott finds this perspective, which he calls the 'politics of the book', both specious and dangerous. To think of politics as a purposive endeavour is to conceive of the state as an instrument of its rulers. It thus reflects the 'unpurged relic of "lordship"'[104] within the modern state. To apply this model in practice endangers the continuity of otherwise stable political traditions and the moral practices out of which they arise. It also has massive destructive potential. Providing a kind of genealogy of the practice of reason of state in the last chapter of *On Human Conduct*, Oakeshott links the disposition to consider the state as an enterprise (or purposive) association[105] with the history of colonialism and commercial empire. 'What is important for us is that the notionally uninhabited lands

[101] Michael Oakeshott, 'Rationalism in Politics' in Oakeshott, *Rationalism in Politics and Other Essays* (Indianapolis, IN: Liberty Fund, 1991), 30–4, where the Second Treatise of Civil Government is described as 'as valuable a political crib' as there has ever been, responsible in part for the rationalistic errors of the early history of the United States.

[102] Steven B. Smith, 'Practical Life and the Critique of Rationalism' in Efraim Podoksik (ed.), *The Cambridge Companion to Oakeshott* (Cambridge University Press, 2012), 138.

[103] Oakeshott, 'Rationalism in Politics', 29–30.

[104] Michael Oakeshott, *On Human Conduct* (Oxford University Press, 1975), 268.

[105] Ibid., 315: 'An enterprise association is composed of persons related in terms of a specified common purpose or interest and who recognize one another in terms of their common engagement to pursue or to promote it. Each associate knows himself as the servant of the purpose being pursued . . . This mode of association is, then, substantive; it is association in co-operative "doing".'

of the New World were understood to belong, by right of conquest or occupation, to the rulers of the states whence the settlers came. They were extensions of a royal domain.'[106] The activities of expansionary colonialism, in the first instance typically undertaken by private enterprises backed by rulers of states such as East India Company rule in India, ended up fostering the sense that government was a matter of both law making and human management:

> They were enterprises, promoted directly or indirectly by the rulers of states, in which government and management were indistinguishable engagements. And the consequence of this colonial experience was to familiarize modern Europe with states which were, in some significant respects, enterprises and with governments which were managers of enterprises.[107]

The argument, here channelling Adam Smith and Edmund Burke, is that jealousy of trade and competition for colonial possessions – the imperatives of enterprise association played out *in foro externo* – led inevitably to war. Not only did the perspective of politics as technique lend itself to risk-tasking behaviour among rulers and ruling groups, who tied the destiny of the state to their own self-interest, but it also produced complex feedback effects that tended to embed the same associational model *in foro interno*. 'War is the enemy of civil association; belligerence is alien to civil association.' In war, the subject of the law gives ground to the agent performing tasks prescribed by the state. The word 'public', Oakeshott adds, 'loses its meaning as considerations of civility to be subscribed to by *cives* in pursuing their chosen satisfactions and comes to stand for the now compelling corporate purpose of the association'.[108] Preparing for war and repairing the ravages of war became the normal condition of the European state. The instantiation of the managerialist and purposive political culture in peacetime as well as times of war produced a near despotism that required 'not only a "poor" who neither had nor could have any incentive to resist the intrusive management of their lives, but a whole people who had been, in this sense, pauperized: that is, persons deprived of their status as "subjects" obligated to subscribe to conditions of civility and transformed into the servants of a compulsory corporate enterprise.'[109] The corruption of civil association naturally also had an institutional dimension: parliaments became 'markets where private interests clamour for awards from patron governments' and laws are degraded into 'instruments of managerial policy'.[110]

[106] Ibid., 271. [107] Ibid., 272. [108] Ibid., 273. [109] Ibid., 305. [110] Ibid., 312.

This first-blush reading of Oakeshott, in which reason of state is simply a core aspect of an impoverished conception of civil life – *universitas* or enterprise association – is consistent with many aspects of his writings. And it is true that, in full polemical mode, Oakeshott's emphasis on the traditional character of human conduct can reach an extraordinary pitch. He comes close to doubting even the possibility of exceptional moments of political crisis and revolution, for instance, when dismissing the French and Russian Revolutions as themselves tradition bound.[111] His Manichean rendering of European history and politics also sometimes can border on the maniacal. In the essay, 'The Masses in Representative Democracy', Oakeshott splits the history of Europe from the twelfth to the twentieth century into two. The good part – which began with the emergence of human individuality in Renaissance Italy – produced a new image of human nature distinguished by its multiplicity and endless self-transformative power and generated a governing structure combining sovereign power, representative legislatures and the rule of law in which individuality could flourish. The bad part – the counterpart to the individual – comprised the mass man or individual *manqué*, scared of modern life and resentful of the individual, banding together out of cowardice and seeking a leader to relieve them of the burden of freedom and impose their misery on the whole population.[112]

It is hard to take this just-so story, iced with patrician disdain, entirely at face value. Were we to, it would represent an even more radical attempt than Hayek's to eradicate reason of state and as sweeping an attack on modern parliamentarism as Schmitt's.[113] To insist on the triumph of *societas* (civil association) over the idea of the state understood as *universitas* (enterprise association) is not so much a window into reason of state and like political concepts as a flat denial that it should exist at all. Such an outcome is distinctly odd coming from a philosopher for whom the deep historical currents of European political life were so important. These traditions of thought are all that we have, he insisted:

[111] Michael Oakeshott, 'Political Education' in *Rationalism in Politics*, 59, note 6: 'The Russian Revolution … was a modification of *Russian* circumstances. And the French Revolution was far more closely connected with the *ancien regime* than with Locke or America.'

[112] Michael Oakeshott, 'The Masses in Representative Democracy' in *Rationalism in Politics*.

[113] Compare Oakeshott's 'The Masses in Representative Democracy', 377–80, and *Social and Political Doctrines of Contemporary Europe*, xvi–xvii, and *On Human Conduct*, 312, with Schmitt, *Crisis of Parliamentary Democracy*, 6–8, 48–50.

'each of them is an expression of something in our civilization, in some cases of what were better forgotten, in others of what to our loss we have failed to remember, and in all of what we cannot merely ignore. And we cannot merely regret them without regretting our civilization – a fruitless, if heroic, act.'[114] It is true that Oakeshott sometimes seems to offer a pure and austere constitutional theory which leaves no room for collective purpose and state action other than the operation of a structure of general laws that specify conditions of conduct. His essay on the rule of law, for instance, attributes 'a *persona* to the occupant or occupants of this office which reflects the engagement of enacting authentic rules: a *persona* without interests of its own and not representative of the interests of others. That is, a *persona* which is the counterpart of the *persona* of those related in terms of the rule of law.'[115] The theory, when generalized, threatens to produce an account of political life that is shapeless, stripped of meaning. As Perry Anderson observes, 'For if their association was void of purpose, why should individual agents ever accept a public authority at all? In Oakeshott's construction, government without goal yields what looks very much like an *état gratuit*. His famous image of politics – a vessel endlessly ploughing the sea, without port or destination – is all too apt. For why then should any passengers want to board the ship in the first place?'[116]

A second reading of Oakeshott is available which is to be preferred not just because the first reading is so problematic but also on the ground that Oakeshott himself provided in his early book, *Experience and Its Modes*, namely, that a unified interpretation is to be preferred since 'pluralism or dualism are not, as we are frequently invited to believe, the final achievement in experience with regard to some ideas.'[117] The reading builds on the fuller rendition of the history of the European state in *On Human Conduct*, the filigree of liberty within which now being connected to the *civitas peregrina* – 'an association, not of pilgrims travelling to a common destination, but of adventurers each responding as best he can to the ordeal of consciousness in a world composed of others of his kind'.[118] This account retains the same set of binary

[114] Oakeshott, *Social and Political Doctrines of Contemporary Europe*, xii.
[115] Michael Oakeshott, 'The Rule of Law', in Oakeshott, *On History and Other Essays* (Indianapolis, IN: Liberty Fund, 1999), 150. See also Oakeshott, *On Human Conduct*, 128–9. For discussion, see David Dyzenhaus's contribution to this volume (Chapter 10).
[116] Anderson, 'The Intransigent Right', 19.
[117] Michael Oakeshott, *Experience and Its Modes* (Cambridge University Press, 1933), 33.
[118] Oakeshott, *On Human Conduct*, 243.

distinctions, enterprise and civil association, *societas* and *universitas*, and the same astringent attitude towards weakness.[119] The state understood as *universitas* models itself on one of its versions as 'an association of invalids, all victims of the same disease and incorporated in seeking relief from their common ailment – and the office of government is remedial engagement. Rulers are *therapeutae*, the directors of a sanatorium from which no patient may discharge himself by a choice of his own.'[120] Even so, Oakeshott is here prepared to recognize, albeit grudgingly, that both understandings of association – *societas* and *universitas* – are inescapably part of the character of the state structures we inhabit. We see this first in the analysis of state action initially at the margins, particularly in situations of emergency. In such situations, the 'invasion of "public" by "private", of ruling by lordship, may indeed be recognized (somewhat equivocally) as a contingent situation which may emerge in the history of a civil association, and not as a direct denial of the civil condition, when the common concern that the prescriptions of *lex* shall be acknowledged is circumstantially transformed into a substantive purpose.' Thus, in cases where the civil association is threatened or in lesser emergencies to which judicial remedies are unable to restore the situation, 'the common concern may become a common purpose and rulers may become managers of its pursuit.'[121]

Given the way the European state has developed, though, the margins are not just marginal. Oakeshott says that the use of the word 'state' to identify the emergent associations of early-modern Europe was a 'masterpiece of neutrality' in that it could encompass both types of association to which he refers.[122] There is no plausible way of eradicating the aspects of enterprise association from the modern state not least because they are intertwined not just within our cultural and institutional practice but even at the level of our concepts. Indeed, it is hard to imagine what a state so reconstructed might look like. A world of pure *lex* seems more like a theoretical postulate, a kind of philosophical glass bead game, than a remotely viable constitutional idea. In his essay on the topic, Oakeshott calls power the third condition of association in terms of the rule of law. Rather embarrassed by the idea, he devotes just one sentence to the

[119] See, e.g., ibid., 276: 'The relatively weak are apt to seek safety in the protection of the relatively more powerful and are usually gratified if they can find an adequate and not over-exacting patron'; also, 308: 'Here, a state is understood to be an association.'

[120] Ibid., 308. [121] Ibid., 146. [122] Ibid., 233.

matter.[123] Under what conditions is that power to be retained, but for some sense of allegiance to the political community understood in some sense or other as purposive community? Even the adjective 'European' – as in 'The Character of the European State', the title of the final chapter in *On Human Conduct* – connotes some state of belonging, some sense of community that is not purely or even primarily formal or juristic.

Even if crafting such a hollow state were plausible, it is hard to see it as desirable. Internally, what would glue it together? Externally, it is hard to imagine it surviving long in a world where other states are just not made this way. These points are given added weight by Oakeshott's renunciation of Rationalist reform projects. The type of reason Oakeshott sees as appropriate in relation to the state – practical knowledge as opposed to technical or scientific knowledge, *mētis* rather than *techne* – is contextual and particular. While this perspective acknowledges that something can be said about state, revolution or constitution in general, this will only take us so far in understanding *this* state, *this* revolution, *this* constitution. As James C. Scott observes, such local knowledge is by its nature '*partisan* knowledge as opposed to generic knowledge', the holder of such knowledge typically having 'a passionate interest in a particular outcome.' In as much as Oakeshott can be read as extolling local knowledge while seeking to give various localities (states) the identical core based on generic knowledge (*lex*), he stands accused not only of muddled contradiction but also of advocating a state theory doomed to fail. 'A mechanical application of generic rules that ignores these particularities is an invitation to practical failure, social disillusionment or, most likely, both.'[124] Besides, if all that passed for government within a state were the maintenance of an abstract framework of rules granting entitlements and imposing obligations, then it really would not be all that hard to teach and understand it by means of a treatise or crib.

The only way Oakeshott can escape this trap is to accept that state and government contain both dispositions, towards *societas* and towards *universitas*, neither of which is able to predominate. He reaches just such a conclusion in the closing pages of *On Human Conduct*: '[i]t may be true that, hidden in human character, there are two powerful and contrary dispositions, neither strong enough to defeat or to put flight the other.'[125] In this way, Oakeshott manages to reconcile the historian and the political philosopher within him. Given how we got here, he argues, it

[123] Oakeshott, 'The Rule of Law', 160–1. [124] Scott, *Seeing Like a State*, 318.
[125] Oakeshott, *On Human Conduct*, 323.

is inconceivable that the state will suddenly model itself in terms of pure civil association, even assuming that such an option is possible. We are the inheritors of a deeply imperfect, confused and fractured political condition, at the base of which lies a never-ending conflict between the liberty-supporting framework of *societas* and the community-supporting idea of *universitas*. Given the state we find ourselves in, some sense of community-giving purpose seems to be essential to the political condition and even to the maintenance of the liberty-protecting dimensions of the state. But this does not mean that we need to accept them as equals. On the contrary, whereas it is right to cherish and protect those strands within our associational life which relate to *civitas pelegrina*,[126] our stance towards manifestations of *universitas*, including reason of state, ought to be nearly the opposite, regarding it as something like a necessary evil and particularly open to abuse. Reason of state is part of a tradition with deep cultural and institutional roots and which connects to a larger conception of the state as a purposive entity. The pathways of *lex* and reason of state are ineluctably intertwined in the history of the state. As reason of state flows through the same channels as the rule of law, it has the capacity to warp those channels from the inside as well as from the outside. Repeated recourse to reason of state leads to an infantilized subject. Man is the subject of the rule-of-law state; mass man, the subject of the security state, the individual *manqué* who demands security like a comfort blanket.[127]

Oakeshott's final position thus reflects a third characteristic twentieth-century reaction to modern reason-of-state politics. This can be seen as either a pragmatic response, in the Burkean mold, to the existence of pathways of political and legal thought and action that have a very deep heritage. Or it works in a tragic register: the way we have developed makes it impossible now to re-cast political life in a way that would allow us to be truly free. This response, in its pragmatic mode, is arguably the most common reaction to the crisis years of the early and mid-century, and one might link it with the rise of Christian democracy in Europe in

[126] See, e.g., ibid., 241–2: The idea of individuality 'although, later, it was almost buried under a mountain of rubbish, confused with trivial liberations, romanticized, mistaken for the exercise of "subjective will", confounded with a "sacred inner light" and with a banal individualism, and finally corrupted in being confused with "sentience" (a capacity for feeling pleasure and pain) or with so-called "libidinal instinct", it has remained the strongest strand in the moral convictions of the inhabitants of modern Europe.' The passage refers to Pico della Mirandola, Rabelais, Luther, Cervantes and Pascal.

[127] Ibid., 275.

particular after the Second World War.[128] But, at least as Oakeshott presents it, it is deficient on a number of fronts. It threatens to leave law and legality in its twentieth-century limbo, perched uncomfortably between conflicting accounts – law as normative order versus law as managerial technique. And, while the theory provides at least the outlines of a discernible normative position, it is one that we are told is unrealizable. Although this is not part of Oakeshott's immediate theoretical objectives, it leaves us short of answers to some of the most pressing questions concerning reason of state. When ought you to trade off the demands of *societas* (rule of law) for the needs of *universitas* (reason of state)? Who makes this choice and under what institutional conditions?

Conclusion

The writers considered in this chapter present three contrasting accounts of reason of state and the role that it plays within modern constitutional politics. For Schmitt, reason of state is connected with what is for him the central idea of the exception, tied to a substantive politics of belonging and thus to the basic political question of who counts as our friend and who the enemy. Reason of state offers a possible source of redemption and escape from the humdrum realities of the creeping bureaucratic state. Hayek, by contrast, sees reason of state as the antithesis of the common-law *Rechtsstaat*,[129] a constitution of liberty fashioned out of the crooked timber of *nomos*, the evolutionary body of law tied closely to the lived experience of the people and which contains the virtues of the many-minds principle in juridical form. His response to the threat presented by reason of state is to try to eradicate it, both normatively and as a matter of institutional design, a move especially evident in his model constitution. This attempt is problematic in several respects, not least because it allows reason of state to re-emerge as part of an animistic (non-cognitive, deinstitutionalized) account of emergency politics. Oakeshott shares Hayek's distrust of reason of state, even deepening some of the criticisms, but he recognizes that the practice of reason of state lies at the heart of one of two conceptions of politics that vie for prominence within the modern European state. Built into the institutional structures and

[128] Müller, *Contesting Democracy*; Stathis N. Kalyvas, *The Rise of Christian Democracy in Europe* (Ithaca, NY: Cornell University Press, 1996); Wolfram Kaiser, *Christian Democracy and the Origins of the European Union* (Cambridge University Press, 2011).

[129] John Grey, *Hayek on Liberty*, 3rd edn. (London: Routledge, 1998), 69.

pathways of government, reason of state may be impossible to eradicate, but we may be able to check its more dangerous excesses.

The differences between the three writers, stated in this way, are marked. Each may be said to reflect a characteristic response to the crisis-ridden decades of the first half of the twentieth century. But it is important to acknowledge what the three writers share. In each, there is a palpable yearning for wholeness – to become one again after the fracturing and dehumanizing experiences of what Eric Hobsbawn called the 'age of catastrophe'.[130] The juridical dimension is of paramount importance to all three, notably in the need to make sense of the 'ordinary' and 'extraordinary' at a time when the difference between the two categories had become increasingly blurred. Here again, though, the precise strategies diverge in revealing ways. Schmitt seeks to infuse the ordinary with the extraordinary. Hayek looks to make the extraordinary properly extraordinary so as to ring-fence and reinforce the ordinary. Oakeshott regards the categories as at least partially redundant – both the ordinary and extraordinary have, in a sense, become ordinary now through long use and interbreeding. However, while Oakeshott comes closer than the others to a recognition of the developmental lines of reason of state, noting its evolutionary and institutional aspects, he fails to develop a reflexive account of the relationship between the ordinary and extraordinary within constitutions of the type that Hans Lindahl identifies elsewhere in this volume (Chapter 3), in which normality is always the outcome of a process of normalization.

[130] Eric Hobsbawm, *The Age of Extremes: The Short Twentieth Century, 1914–1991* (London: Michael Joseph, 1994), Part 1.

8

Reconfiguring reason of state in response to political crisis

DUNCAN KELLY

Politics and the state

In his last major book, *On Human Conduct*, Michael Oakeshott presented the final iteration of a claim he had been making for nearly fifty years, namely, that 'a concern to understand politics is a concern with the considerabilities of political deliberation and utterance'.[1] Politics, that is to say, is concerned with practices of deliberation about political things, expressed in and through language. Furthermore, and at least since the medieval period, he wrote, the predominant ways in which languages of politics and deliberation have been conducted in Europe generally, and Britain particularly, have revolved around the idea of the state as a particular sort of association.[2] This association took two well-known general forms in Oakeshott's work. One considered the state as a procedural, rule-governed civil association, a *nomocratic* form of *societas*, while another considered the state as a purposive and rationalist form of enterprise association, or a *teleocratic* form of *universitas*.[3]

Reflection upon this civil condition properly understood as *societas* took the form of reflection upon 'ascertainable' and 'circumstantial practice', where practice is understood broadly as the series of conventional rules and norms expressed in conventional idioms and vocabularies.[4] Thus outlined, politics is reason of state understood as conventional practice described through reflection upon that practice. For Oakeshott,

[1] Michael Oakeshott, *On Human Conduct* (Oxford University Press, 1975), 177.

[2] Michael Oakeshott, 'Contemporary British Politics', *Cambridge Journal*, 1 (1948), 474, 489.

[3] Oakeshott, *On Human Conduct*, 201, 203–5, 215, 233, 257; Michael Oakeshott, *Lectures in the History of Political Thought* (Exeter, UK: Imprint Academic, 2006), ed. Terry Nardin and Luke O'Sullivan, 471, 483f.

[4] Oakeshott, *On Human Conduct*, 177.

particularly during his time as a Cambridge don, Hobbes stood as a model for this form of understanding. He did so, Oakeshott thought, because of his account of the relationship between philosophy and politics, not on account of his politics. For Oakeshott, politics and freedom require a diffusion of power within society, and if there is surely one thing which Hobbes neither discussed nor countenanced, it was the diffusion of power within society.[5]

The inherent danger of thinking about this civil condition under the modern state as an enterprise or purposive association is that it requires a transposition of politics into administration and management. Rather than being an alternative form of reason of state and thus a practice-based form of politics, administrative management is instead a form of anti-politics.[6] The danger of rationalism in politics is therefore that it is really a form of de-politicization, an attempt to go beyond the civil condition where politics happens and to focus on planning and policy outcomes.[7] To counteract this move, Oakeshott's political writings came down heavily on any hint of excessive rationalism, optimism or self-confidence about the possibilities of planning, guiding and directing policy in a self-conscious manner. For example, although Oakeshott agreed with the sentiments behind Friedrich Hayek's post-war attack on collectivism, *The Road to Serfdom*, he thought that Hayek failed to go far enough in resisting this de-politicizing trend.[8] Both upheld a sceptical critique of planning as epistemologically impossible and politically dangerous, but Hayek's book still constituted a plan in Oakeshott's mind, even if it was a plan to resist planning.[9]

Resisting the planned imposition of a post-war welfare state was exactly the point at issue for Oakeshott, but his attack was not just an attack on a developmentally 'despotic' Labourism.[10] It was also an attack

[5] See Michael Oakeshott, 'The Political Economy of Freedom', *Cambridge Journal*, 2 (1948), esp. 222–4.

[6] See Maurizio Viroli, *From Politics to Reason of State* (Cambridge University Press, 1991), for an account of the rise of reason of state itself as anti-politics.

[7] Oakeshott, *On Human Conduct*, 183f.

[8] Friedrich A. Hayek, *The Road to Serfdom* (London: Routledge, 1944); the condensed version of this text that was published in *Reader's Digest* of 1945 has been reprinted as Bruce Caldwell (ed.), *The Road to Serfdom: Text and Documents, The Definitive Edition* (University of Chicago Press, 2007).

[9] Michael Oakeshott, 'Rationalism in Politics', *Cambridge Journal*, 1:2 (1947), 81-98; 1:3 (1947), esp. 146; Oakeshott, 'Contemporary British Politics', 484–5.

[10] Oakeshott, 'Contemporary British Politics', esp. 476–8, on the 'legends' and 'experience[s]' of 1945 for British social democracy; 480–2, rhetorically bemoaning Labourism for making

on the so-called delusions of rationalism in politics, which blind its advocates to the fact that there never are secure philosophical (as opposed to conventional, historical and practical) foundations from which to direct politics. The modern rationalist is the 'enemy' of traditional authority and custom, with a 'touch of intellectual equalitarianism'. He brings existing conventions to bear at the 'tribune of his intellect', replacing tradition with ideology and promoting a politics of either 'uniformity' or 'perfection'. Rationalism is the 'politics of the politically inexperienced'.[11] In fact, it is precisely the thought that there might be secure foundations for politics that leads directly to administrative anti-politics, and part of Oakeshott's equal antipathy towards post-war British conservatism can be seen in its attempt to sign up to a European charter on human rights, another token of political rationalism in his view.[12] For in seeking secure technical knowledge from outside the only credible sources of knowledge about politics, namely, history and local practices or vocabularies, rationalism undercuts the only possible foundations there are.[13] And only history could show this, as Oakeshott's criticism of Hans Morgenthau's contemporary conflation of parliamentarism with rationalism suggested.[14] This formed part of a broader scepticism about knowledge which had emerged in Oakeshott's major early work, *Experience and Its Modes*, and which remained clear in his polemical interventions about modern politics. Throughout, he vowed to show that 'a genuinely *laissez-faire* society has *never* existed anywhere on earth at any time, and that what through all the centuries has prevented its existence is not central planning, but a rule of law which has emphasized duties at least as much as rights between private individuals.'[15]

the British Parliament into a merely 'executive body' for carrying out the wishes of the party conference; 484–6, on the tyrannical and despotic character of the Labour Party.

11 Oakeshott, 'Rationalism in Politics', 81, 83f, 147, 152, 154, 157; see Oakeshott, 'Contemporary British Politics', 489: 'British democracy is not an abstract idea. It is a way of living and a manner of politics which first began to emerge in the Middle Ages'; Oakeshott, *Lectures in the History of Political Thought*, 321; Michael Oakeshott, *Morality and Politics in Modern Europe* (1958) (Cambridge, MA: Harvard University Press, 1993), 23.

12 On which, see M. Duranti, 'Curbing Labour's Totalitarian Temptation: European Human Rights Law and British Postwar Politics', *Humanity* (2010), 361.

13 Michael Oakeshott, 'Review of Hannah Arendt, *Between Past and Future*' (1961) in Oakeshott, *What Is History? And Other Essays* (Exeter, UK: Imprint Academic, 2004), ed. L. O'Sullivan, 315; Oakeshott, 'Rationalism in Politics', 88–92.

14 Michael Oakeshott, 'Scientific Politics', *Cambridge Journal*, 2 (1948), 357.

15 Michael Oakeshott, *Experience and Its Modes* (1933) (Cambridge University Press, 1991), 214ff; Oakeshott, 'Contemporary British Politics', 479 (emphasis in original).

Ironically, contemporary political theorists inspired by Hannah Arendt, when considering the rise of 'administration' and the decline of 'politics' in the post-war period, and for whom democracy has become a form of 'inverted totalitarianism', are on almost exactly the same terrain as Oakeshott.[16] And although Oakeshott was ambivalent about Arendt, a similarity of concern is evident in his immediate post-war essays on contemporary British politics. In ways similar to those assayed by Alasdair Macintyre, Oakeshott bemoaned what he saw as a collectivist attempt to deduce a science of political behaviour and action. Neither was remotely possible, he thought, and of course, his rejection was a rejection of the mainstream of contemporary democratic theory in the wake of the Second World War, particularly in America.[17] His was an attempt to maintain a sense of politics as a practice, focussing on the language and vocabulary used to deliberate about that practice from within shared traditions and conventions of discourse and meaning. This was his sense of understanding politics through a conservative disposition, and it required the rejection of what he took to be the fatuous distinction between 'continental' and 'rationalist' ideas of 'left and right' as binaries of modern politics.[18] For these reasons, he has often been thought to embody an aesthetic, rather whimsical and ultimately romantic rejection of the realities of politics.

This certainly forms part of Perry Anderson's celebrated polemic concerning Oakeshott's place in the pantheon of the 'instransigent right' alongside Carl Schmitt, Leo Strauss and Friedrich Hayek. In particular, Anderson attacks what he sees as Oakeshott's wilful flattening out of Hobbes's argumentative edges, when pressed into the service of an apparently romantic account of the origins of the state.[19] By contrast, Luke O'Sullivan suggests that such a general opposition between rationalism and Hobbesian man progressively dissipates in Oakeshott's post-war

[16] Sheldon S. Wolin, *Politics and Vision*, rev. edn. (Princeton University Press, 2006), Chapter 9; Sheldon S. Wolin, *Democracy Incorporated* (Princeton University Press, 2010), Chapter 3.

[17] See Michael Oakeshott, 'Scientific Thinking about Politics' (1930) in Oakeshott, *Early Political Writings*, 172–82; Alasdair MacIntyre, 'Is a Science of Comparative Politics Possible?' in Peter Laslett, W. G. Runciman and Quentin Skinner (eds.), *Philosophy, Politics and Society* (Oxford, UK: Basil Blackwell, 1972), 8; Edward Purcell, *The Crisis of Democratic Theory* (Lexington, KY: University Press of Kentucky, 1973), esp. 260–72.

[18] Oakeshott, 'Contemporary British Politics', 479.

[19] Perry Anderson, 'The Intransigent Right at the End of the Century', *London Review of Books*, 24 September 1992, 7–11.

work, becoming instead more of an opposition between the 'mass man' of representative democracy with his 'anti-individualist' morality and the independent gentleman of the *ancien régime*.[20] Both accounts seem to me overstated because it is surely the case that Oakeshott's focus on European uniqueness in the development of a particular vocabulary appropriate to the 'character' of the modern state remained consistent. He continually worried about the necessary component parts that might explain the 'authority' of a state.[21]

A sharp perspective nevertheless emerges from Anderson's mapping of Oakeshott's co-ordinates within the framework of political romanticism, particularly when he considers Oakeshott alongside Schmitt. When Schmitt wrote in Germany just as the Versailles treaty was being negotiated and in the aftermath of a crushing military defeat, he offered a coruscating critique of political romanticism as a form of anti-politics. He termed political romanticism a form of 'subjectified occasionalism', an idea that took politics as a subject for the free play of romantic intellect, a form of conversation rather than decision. Indeed, Schmitt wrote of a clear disjuncture between politics as regular, prudential and power-based practices governed by established norms and the anti-politics of romantic intellectualism. This, he suggested, was the truly reactionary moment of post-revolutionary politics, where romanticism and historicism combined to make possible a new form of modern liberalism. That liberalism was a part of what he tried to rail against and against which he constructed alternative genealogies of politics and crisis that offered contemporary lessons. In moments of crisis (i.e., siege, war, dictatorship or revolution), basic norms of political authority are illuminated through the very process of their transgression. Different historical forms of reason of state could help to illuminate this recurrent problem, and in his visionary lecture on

[20] Luke O'Sullivan, *Oakeshott on History* (Exeter, UK: Imprint Academic, 2002), 22; Michael Oakeshott, 'The Masses in Representative Democracy' (1961) in Oakeshott, *Rationalism in Politics and Other Essays* (Indianapolis, IN: Liberty Fund, 1991), 376; Oakeshott, *Morality and Politics*, 26f.

[21] Michael Oakeshott, 'The Authority of the State' (1929) in Oakeshott, *Religion, Politics and the Moral Life* (New Haven, CT: Yale University Press, 1993), ed. Timothy Fuller, 74–90; Michael Oakeshott, 'The Concept of a Philosophy of Politics' (1946) in Oakeshott, *Religion, Politics, and the Moral Life*, 122, 126, 136. At 122: '[A] philosophy of politics, that is, an analysis of political concepts, which itself became genuinely philosophical would at once defeat its own end'. See Michael Oakeshott, 'Political Philosophy' (1946) in Oakeshott, *Religion, Politics, and the Moral Life*, 152–4; Michael Oakeshott, 'The Idea of "Character" in the Interpretation of Modern Politics' (1954) in Oakeshott, *What Is History?*, 255–77, at 269, 276.

the so-called 'Age of Neutralizations and De-Politicizations', the connections were clarified. The geopolitical situation of Russian and European relations was dissected through an account of the transition from theological to secular politics from the sixteenth century onwards, where liberalism had become the modern form of anti-politics.[22]

That transition framed a counter-history of liberalism, presenting it as an on-going attempt to neutralize conflict (the raw material of politics) through the use of bureaucratic management or economic and technical calculations of political possibility. As Schmitt famously suggested, '[A]ll significant concepts of the modern theory of the state are secularized theological concepts.'[23] Oakeshott's concerns were broadly congruent, and for both men, the rise of liberalism signalled the victory of economic and administrative management as part of a trend towards the de-politicization of conventional 'politics'. In the ten years between Schmitt's attack on political romanticism and his updated critique of the tendency towards neutralization, his critique of liberalism became more pointed. Similarly, in the immediate aftermath of the Second World War, Oakeshott's rejection of liberalism and concern with the philosophical foundations of contemporary politics also became more acute. The move began with Oakeshott's edition of Hobbes' *Leviathan* in 1946, celebrating Hobbes for his distinctive 'conception of the nature of philosophical knowledge' rather than the exact political commitments that flowed from the text, moving quickly towards an attack on contemporary scientific and British politics in 1948.[24] Then came his celebrated lectures, *Morality and Politics in Modern Europe*, a decade later, culminating in the final iteration of his argument. Throughout his writing, though, Oakeshott's work is a continuous and continual revision and reworking of a rejection of liberalism and representative democracy as ultimately anti-political.

[22] Carl Schmitt, 'The Age of Neutralizations and Depoliticizations' (1929), trans. J. McCormick, *Telos*, 96 (1993), 130.

[23] See Carl Schmitt, *Political Theology* (Cambridge, MA: MIT Press, 1985), trans. George Schwab, 37; Carl Schmitt, *The Concept of the Political* (University of Chicago Press, 1996), trans. George Schwab, 23.

[24] Michael Oakeshott, 'Introduction to Leviathan' (1946) in *Hobbes on Civil Association* (Oxford, UK: Blackwell, 1975), 25; Oakeshott, 'Scientific Thinking about Politics', *passim*. See Noel Malcolm, 'Oakeshott and Hobbes' in Paul Franco and Leslie Marsh (eds.), *A Companion to Michael Oakeshott* (University Park, PA: Penn State University Press, 2012), 217–31, esp. 228–9, on Hobbes's peace-seeking political rationalism, which stands opposed to Oakeshott's rendition of Hobbes as a political philosopher whose civil association has no substantive purpose to fulfil.

It was also a rejection of any attempt to think that 'political action' is something that any more than a few should participate in and a rejection of various attempts to incorporate the demands of philosophy, art or literature into the specific field of politics. Oakeshott's concern remained with the demarcating of boundaries, even (or perhaps especially) in moments of acute crisis. With the outbreak of war in 1939, he wrote 'The Claims of Politics' for a symposium on that subject for *Scrutiny*. He did so in such a way as to claim that although there is a 'special temptation' to prioritize 'political activity' for the purposes of protection, the 'work of protection is never of primary importance'. As with Plato's more famous account, secular politics was always a secondary or second-best activity. Even if political action might be the only thing that could save a society, on its own it cannot 'make it live'.[25] To understand the claims of politics in modern civil associations was therefore to understand that in times of crisis what is necessary is an appropriate recognition and reconfiguration of politics as conventional reason of state. In times of crisis, particularly in post-revolutionary and post-war Germany and England in the early twentieth century, both Schmitt and Oakeshott pursued such a reconfiguration of reason of state with recourse to the history of political thought.

If normal politics here simply means reason of state, it is also clear that this is neither Machiavellian expediency nor the pursuit of a singular enterprising policy. In fact, both writers rather dethrone Machiavelli from the pinnacle of reason-of-state theory, defining it instead with reference to the historical experience and practical techniques of state theory since the early-modern era.[26] Reason of state on their account refers to the terminology and techniques of statecraft, explained with reference to the vocabularies of modern politics that have become normal or routine and whose development can be traced through the history of modern political thought. Herbert Butterfield taught Oakeshott as much, and we might reasonably assume that Weber taught the same to Schmitt whether through his writing directly or through Schmitt's attendance at Weber's late seminars in Munich.[27]

[25] Michael Oakeshott, 'The Claims of Politics', *Scrutiny*, 8 (1939), 146, 149, 150.

[26] Carl Schmitt, *Die Diktatur* (1921) (Berlin: Duncker & Humblot, 2006), xivff; Carl Schmitt, 'Macchiavelli. Zum 22. Juni 1927' in G. Maschke (ed.) *Staat, Großraum, Nomos: Arbeiten aus den Jahren 1916–1969* (Berlin: Duncker & Humblot, 1995), 102–7; Carl Schmitt, 'Diktatur' (1926) in *Staat, Großraum, Nomos*, 33–7; Schmitt, *Political Theology*, 9.

[27] Herbert Butterfield, *The Statecraft of Machiavelli* (London: G. Bell & Sons, 1940), 16f; Herbert Butterfield, *Raison d'État* (University of Sussex, 1975), 9, 11f, 17; Michael

Dictating reason of state

By reinterpreting historically prudential political thinking as foundational for any realistic appraisal of contemporary politics, Schmitt rejected romanticism and liberalism, often conflating both. In 1919, this could easily be read as a sideways blow aimed at Friedrich Meinecke, whose account of the centrality of German romanticism to the ultimate development of a unified German nation-state he scorned.[28] On occasion, Schmitt also directly and at length engaged with Meinecke's treatise on the intellectual origins of reason of state.[29]

By avoiding the neo-Roman or imperialistic freedom that led to Napoleonic tyranny, Meinecke suggested that a moral understanding of reason of state and cosmopolitanism, filtered through Goethe, Hegel and Fichte and allied to the Prussian wars of liberation, provided a pathway for German reason of state to build a bridge between coldly utilitarian reasoning about state interest, on the one hand, and rampant nationalism, on the other. Modern, post-restoration romanticism and liberalism offered the possibility of cultivating a particularly German idea of freedom, one congenial to Meinecke's historicist model of intellectual history. The moralizing of key political doctrines it entailed, however, was precisely what Schmitt refused. In Schmitt's review, he outlined the need for a more starkly Weberian ideal-typical method of historical writing in the service of contemporary political and legal theory.[30] Where Meinecke opposed *ethos* and *kratos*, or good and evil, Schmitt claimed that politics was simply more ordinary and symmetrical in terms of its conceptual oppositions. Friend or foe is the principal opposition, and although it can

Oakeshott, 'Political Philosophy' (c. 1925) in Oakeshott, *Early Political Writings 1925–1930* (Exeter, UK: Imprint Academic, 2010), ed. Luke O'Sullivan, 68–9; Oakeshott, 'Rationalism in Politics', 148, suggests that Machiavelli is another 'crib to politics, a political training in default of a political education, a technique for the ruler who had no tradition'. See Max Weber, 'Politik als Beruf' (1919) in Weber, *Gesammelte Politische Schriften* (1921) (Tübingen: J. C. B. Mohr, 1988), ed. J. Winckelmann, 517–8, 524, 555, 558; Carl Schmitt, *Die Militärzeit 1915 bis 1919: Tagebuch Februar bis Dezember 1915* (Berlin: Akademie Verlag, 2005), ed. E. Hüsmert and G. Giesler, 51, 495. See also Reinhard Mehring, *Carl Schmitt Aufstieg und Fall* (Munich: C. H. Beck, 2012), 118.

28 Friedrich Meinecke, *Weltbürgertum und Nationalstaat* (1907) (Berlin: Oldenbourg, 1911), esp. Chapters 3–5 and 7.

29 Friedrich Meinecke, *Die Idee der Staatsräson* (Berlin: Oldenbourg, 1925), 24–7, 31–60, 461–8.

30 Carl Schmitt, 'Zu Friedrich Meineckes Idee der Staatsräson' (1926) in Schmitt, *Positionen und Begriffe im Kampf mit Weimar-Genf-Versailles 1923–1939* (Berlin: Duncker & Humblot, 1988), 51–9, esp. 54.

take different historical forms, he assumes symmetry if a political relationship is to obtain. This is why political disputes and conflicts are decided by power or force under conventionally understood procedures and practices. The claim was the fulcrum of his account of the specificity of the political, and it lay behind his post-war history of the idea of a *nomos* of the Earth under which a peculiarly European *jus publicaeum* had arisen but which was now threatened by the rise of America.[31] Where symmetry is absent, moralism quickly enters, and that moral asymmetry has structured, he suggests, a high-minded but utopian form of European politics since the French Revolution, namely modern liberalism. The language of politics as cosmopolitan and universal threatened to undermine conventional mechanisms for reconciling political disputes through law and force, because there is no symmetry in the idea of a friend or enemy of humanity, and therefore no obviously political resolution to a conflict between them. Reinhart Koselleck would later also make much of this claim in his early work on the crisis of the absolutist state. He too was openly antipathetic towards Meinecke's *Ideengeschichte*.[32]

Strict conceptual boundaries were, in Schmitt's rendering, the *sine qua non* of historically informed research that wants to engage with contemporary politics. Yet, at the same time, he presented politics as the kind of practice that defied strict moral or cultural boundaries such as those Meinecke placed around it. The autonomy of the political in Schmitt's mind always resists such *a priori* limitations, a claim that finds resonance both in his concern with the historical and cultural particularities of state formation and in the responsibility and authority of political leadership in practice.[33] Here, it was the supposedly liberal figure of John Locke who provided intellectual ballast, even if Hobbes had the stronger intellectual position. Locke clearly recognized the anti-parliamentary implications of his recourse to prerogative, but contemporary liberalism which took its

[31] Carl Schmitt, *The Nomos of the Earth* (1955) (New York: Telos Press, 2003), trans. G. L. Ulmen, 130f, 144f, 146ff.

[32] See Reinhart Koselleck, *Kritik und Krise* (Berlin: Suhrkamp 1973), 124, 156; Reinhart Koselleck, *Futures Past: On the Semantics of Historical Time* (New York: Columbia University Press, 2004), trans. K. Tribe, 58–71, 119–25, esp. 56f, 62f; Reinhart Koselleck, 'A Response to Comments on the *Geschichtliche Grundbegriffe*' in Hartmut Lehmann and Melvin Richter (eds.), *The Meaning of Historical Terms and Concepts: New Studies on Begriffsgeschichte* (Washington, DC: German Historical Institute, 1996), 59–70, at 61–2, 69.

[33] Schmitt, *Political Theology*, 5f.

cue from Locke did not. In fact, it sought to neutralize prerogative in favour of rationalism and parliamentarism. By putting his analysis in these terms, moreover, Schmitt was free to attack both the development of parliamentary democracy in general and forms of German liberalism associated with the nineteenth-century *Rechtsstaat* in particular. He did so first by considering the ways in which liberal constitutional theory had neglected the importance of dictatorship as a technique of conventional political management. Second, he argued that the principles of modern politics (identity or representation) in nation-states were grounded in nationalism but that nationalism was simply an updated form of reason of state.[34]

Dictatorship took different forms in Schmitt's work depending on whether it was seen as a tool for administering or for transforming politics. His frame of reference spanned Bodin's distinction between sovereignty and government, to contemporary Marxism on the dictatorship of the proletariat. It bounded an issue he had been trying to be clear about since the time of the First World War concerning a distinction between dictatorship and the military state of siege.[35] Returning to Munich after the First World War with the help of one of his principal academic benefactors, Moritz Julius Bonn, in October 1919 Schmitt gave a lecture on the history of political ideas since the Reformation. Here, he built upon the account of modern political theory outlined in *Politische Romantik*, moving towards a consideration of the rise of political absolutism in the form of the modern unified state (*Einheitsstaat*) as considered by Bodin, Hobbes and Montesquieu. This would form the bedrock of his most considered early work of political and legal theory, *Die Diktatur*, which appeared in 1921. Over the course of that year, he taught classes on political ideas since the French Revolution, constitutional law, the foundations of the social welfare state, labour law and legal forms of economic administration.[36] He quickly developed a reputation as a sharp critic of liberalism, indicated early on not only in his searing attacks on parliamentarism but even earlier in the précis of his critique of political romanticism published in the *Historische Zeitschrift*, Germany's

[34] Carl Schmitt, *Die Diktatur, xiv, xv, xvi; Verfassungslehre* (1928), 8th edn. (Berlin: Duncker & Humblot, 1993), 32–4; Carl Schmitt, *Constitutional Theory* (Durham, NC: Duke University Press, 2008), trans. Jeffrey Seitzer, 85–6.

[35] Carl Schmitt, 'Diktatur und Belagerungszustand' (1916) in Schmitt, *Staat, Großraum, Nomos*, 3–23, 20; Schmitt, *Verfassungslehre*, 58–60; Schmitt, *Constitutional Theory*, 108–11.

[36] Mehring, *Carl Schmitt*, 119, 612, notes 21 and 26.

leading academic history journal and edited by Meinecke.[37] All this work developed from his prior analysis of dictatorship.[38]

His analysis was conducted on the terrain of the history of political thought, particularly focussing on the pivotal moment of the French Revolution and differentiating between 'commissarial' and 'sovereign' models of dictatorship.[39] What Schmitt suggested, as did Oakeshott, was that self-styled liberals misunderstood the origins as well as the historical construction of their own form of politics, which was really a series of reflections on the rise of the modern European state best outlined in the writings of Bodin, Hobbes and Montesquieu and later redeployed in restoration debates after the French Revolution. These were the true sources, he thought, of debates about popular sovereignty and cosmopolitan nationalism in the nineteenth century. Neglecting this, he wrote, led to a misguided attempt to disassociate politics from prudence and history whose roots once again lay in proto-liberal forms of political romanticism.[40]

For Schmitt, political romanticism relies upon a 'conscious rejection of every adequate causal relationship' (*bewußter Ablehnung jedes adäquaten Kausalzusammenhanges*) that matters in politics. A romantic, 'subjectified' and 'occasional' response to politics turns it into a form of intellectual 'production'.[41] In Oakeshott's corresponding rendition, liberal or socialist political rationalism typically assumed something akin to a guidebook for politics that goes beyond experience. For him, this assumption made the subject of politics into a play of intellect, and just as Schmitt attacked the conflation of liberalism with romanticism, so too did Oakeshott reject romanticism as nothing more than an artifice of historical production. Like an early publication (a guide to picking the

37 Carl Schmitt-Dorotic, 'Politische Theorie und Romantik', *Historische Zeitschrift*, 123: 3 (1921), 377–97; Carl Schmitt-Dorotic, *Politische Romantik* (Berlin: Duncker & Humblot, 1919), 109–62; Carl Schmitt, *The Crisis of Parliamentary Democracy* (1922) (Cambridge, MA: MIT Press, 1985), trans. Ellen Kennedy; Mehring, *Schmitt*, 119f.

38 See Duncan Kelly, 'Carl Schmitt's Political Theory of Dictatorship' in Jens Meierhenrich and Oliver Simons (eds), *The Oxford Handbook of Carl Schmitt* (Oxford University Press, 2015).

39 Franz L. Neumann, 'Notes on the Theory of Dictatorship' in Herbert Marcuse (ed.), *The Democratic and Authoritarian State* (New York: Free Press, 1957), 233–256, at 254, note 1.

40 See Luke O'Sullivan, 'Introduction' in Michael Oakeshott, *The Vocabulary of a Modern European State* (Exeter, UK: Imprint Academic, 2008), ed. Luke O'Sullivan, 12f.

41 Schmitt-Dorotic, 'Politische Theorie', 392; also Schmitt-Dorotic, *Politische Romantik*, 160.

Derby winner) had suggested, practice and understanding are the keys to good judgement, and rationalist theories get you nowhere in this regard because any recourse to rationalism signifies an overall decline in political experience. Politics once more simply was presented as a 'fact of experience'.[42] Technical knowledge cannot provide practical knowledge based on experience, although it can occasionally be useful to political practice, much as Schmitt's analysis of dictatorship suggested.

In its own terms, Schmitt's theory and history of dictatorship simply continued his interest in explaining the rise of the modern state as unified, centralized power. He looked to Bodin as the originator of a view about the commissarial dictatorship of the public person and saw Rousseau as the progenitor of the sovereign dictatorship of the people. Bodin provided Schmitt with a distinction between the commissar and the official and between the different practical legal techniques available to them.[43] With this distinction in mind, Schmitt presented a vision of the dictator first as analogous to the legally bound commissar.[44] Next, moving towards the unified modern nation-state, Bodin's limiting framework of commissarial action laid conceptual foundations which were developed, according to Schmitt, in the writings of both Locke and Sidney. Indeed, Lockean prerogative on this account looks structurally similar to the defence of political sovereignty Schmitt proposed under the Weimar Republic.

Schmitt then moved to discuss what he saw as princely commissarial dictatorships down to the eighteenth century. Beginning with a discussion of papal *plenitudo potestatis*, he considered Catholic political philosophy alongside judicial activity. His related analysis of Catholicism and political representation stems from this moment too, and it would find an early audience in England through a rather poor translation in the hard-headed series, *Essays in Order*, edited by Christopher Dawson.[45] Dawson, a celebrated Catholic intellectual and historian of the Church, was another contributor to the *Scrutiny* symposium entitled, 'The Claims of Politics'. There, like Oakeshott, he had written of the ways totalitarianism threatened claims of traditional culture with 'mass civilization',

[42] Oakeshott, 'Rationalism in Politics', 97, note 2; more generally, Michael Oakeshott and Guy Griffith, *A New Guide to the Derby* (London: Faber & Faber, 1936); Oakeshott, *On Human Conduct*, 246ff; Oakeshott, *Lectures in the History of Political Thought*, 465f.

[43] Schmitt, *Die Diktatur*, 33ff. [44] Ibid., 38–9.

[45] See Christopher Dawson (ed.), *Essays in Order No. 5: The Necessity of Politics* (London: Macmillan, 1931).

differentiating professional from merely ideological politics and focussing on the singular task for the modern statesman of what he termed *salus reipublicae*. This task had no other substantive end than itself.[46] Equally, when discussing dictatorship, Schmitt's first aim was to focus on 'general' political activity taking place under the heading of *salus populi*. This encompassed techniques of prerogative or commissarial, and hence powerful but strictly limited, political authority.[47] The history of legal and political thinking about this, he wrote, suggested lessons for liberalism that had largely been forgotten.

In the next part of his book, Schmitt outlined the transition to what he called 'sovereign' dictatorship, a move away from the use of legal means to restore an extant constitutional structure and towards the use of legal means to create a new legal and political order. It was a transition towards a technical or rationalist form of political sovereignty, and there were three stages to its development, beginning first in France in the movement from absolutism to revolution. Schmitt presents the quasi-dictatorial *auctoritas* of a figure occupying a commissarial office but shows that such authority nonetheless stems from the king. This was part of a wider account of the complex system of intermediary powers (*pouvoirs intermédiares*) buttressing the monarchy, similar to that which Montesquieu had outlined.[48] But if this first stage related to the power of *auctoritas*, the second concerned the eighteenth-century development of dictatorship from a term of opprobrium towards a philosophical 'dictatorship of reason'. This would coalesce around Mably and Voltaire.[49] Such a view would be opposed and refracted by Rousseau most famously, and Rousseau's political theory was the third and crucial hinge in Schmitt's account of sovereign dictatorship.

Schmitt referred to Mably, glossing his radicalism to note that a sovereign dictator not bound by representation would be 'more like a king' (*mehr als ein König*). For Schmitt, this hinted at the transition towards a 'new concept of dictatorship'.[50] Rousseau, however, was the main protagonist for the ideal of a sovereign dictator both above and beyond the law, where 'the dictator is total power without law' (*die Diktatur ist Allmacht ohne Gesetz*).[51] Of course, one can easily show that the Jacobin Terror actually opposed Rousseau's attempt to keep the

[46] Christopher Dawson, 'The Claims of Politics', *Scrutiny*, 8 (1939), 138f.
[47] Schmitt, *Die Diktatur*, 48. [48] Ibid., 95, 97.
[49] Ibid., 100f, and note 14, 107, 110f, and more generally, 101–11. [50] Ibid., 114.
[51] Ibid., 126.

public and private spheres separate and that Schmitt did not really produce a single pre-revolutionary writer to adequately support his claims.[52] Like much more recent scholarship, however, Schmitt's account of Rousseau's political theory related it back to debates about representation in Hobbes and then forward into the work of Sieyès.[53]

Schmitt's account in *Die Diktatur* saw Hobbes's *Leviathan* as the 'substantial bearer of all rights' and suggested ways in which Hobbes might be allied to Locke's 'less systematic' system. Schmitt thought the rationalization of society and individuality was made possible under a particular and representative form of sovereignty. Moreover, by combining Hobbesian representation and Lockean prerogative as part of the history of this process, he was able to provide another way of thinking about the politics of a potentially incoherent liberalism. For Rousseau, of course, there could be no representative sovereign, only representative government, and his argument claimed that modern politics could only resolve the problems raised by the non-representative quality of sovereignty in two ways – either the austerity of submission to law or a perfect form of Hobbism. Neither appealed very much, but to think that other alternatives were possible would be, he thought, like trying to square the circle.[54] Sieyès subsequently tried to pursue such an alternative with his account of the social division of labour, the nation as the source of constituent power and representation as the mechanism through which all indirect and direct political agency takes place.[55] And when Schmitt noted the similarity between aspects of Hobbes' presentation in *De Cive* and Rousseau's analysis of sovereignty, he came to quite a dramatic conclusion by aligning his interpretation of Rousseau as a Hobbesian absolutist with an idiosyncratic interpretation of Sieyès.[56] He argued first that Rousseau's focus on the 'direct self-government of a free people' (*unmittelbare Selbstherrschaft des freien Volkes*) supported sovereign

52 Alfred Cobban, *Dictatorship: Its Theory and History* (London: Jonathan Cape, 1939), 339.

53 See Istvan Hont, *Jealousy of Trade* (Cambridge, MA: Harvard University Press, 2009), 486; Schmitt, *Verfassungslehre*, 76f, 79f, 208–17; Schmitt, *Constitutional Theory*, 126ff, 242–52.

54 Jean-Jacques Rousseau, 'Letter to Mirabeau', July 26, 1767, in Rousseau, *The Social Contract and Other Later Political Writings* (Cambridge University Press, 1997), ed. Victor Gourevitch, 268–71.

55 See Schmitt, *Die Diktatur*, 116–17; Olivier Jouanjan, 'La suspension de la constitution de 1793', *Droits*, 17 (1993), 125, 137.

56 Schmitt, *Die Diktatur*, 117, 119f; see Richard Tuck, *The Rights of War and Peace* (Oxford University Press, 1999), 197–207.

dictatorship. Just as Rousseau had hinted when writing to Mirabeau about the choices available to modern politics (either Hobbism or the despotism of law), for Schmitt, Rousseau's politics was nothing more than the 'justification of a dictatorship' that took the form of a 'despotism of freedom' (*diente so zur Rechtfertigung einer Diktatur und lieferte die Formel für den Despotismus der Freiheit*).[57]

Second, according to Schmitt's analysis the dictator in Western politics operated either under a form of commission or was sovereign unto itself. Sovereign dictatorship arose through Rousseau's vision of a legislator who exists both outside of and prior to the constitution, such that sovereign dictatorship is a tool by which the general will might transform the structures of politics altogether.[58] Reflecting upon this sovereign dictatorship, Schmitt also paid attention to the idea of constituent power derived from Sieyès. Thus, in a third move, he agreed that the very idea of the constituent power of the people had transformed the concepts of modern politics, but claimed that in practice such power could only be controlled with resort to something like a Hobbesian sovereign as the artificial person who brings unity to an otherwise disordered multitude through the complex mechanisms of representation.[59] He did so, moreover, in the context of a thorough-going critique of the development of nineteenth-century liberalism, whose realization in the 'dilatory formal compromise' of the Weimar constitution he attacked.[60] In order to reconfigure reason of state and dramatize the shape of a possible response to the crises of the Weimar Republic, his analysis of dictatorship was necessary background.

Histories of political thought

If Schmitt recognized Montesquieu as a hinge figure in this narrative, someone who grounded his account of the state on the idea of practice and experience by focussing on intermediary powers, so too did Oakeshott. Alongside figures such as Aristotle and Hegel, who gave direction to his thinking about sociability and civil society, Montesquieu

[57] Schmitt, *Die Diktatur*, 121. [58] Ibid., 123, 125.

[59] Ibid., 143; Duncan Kelly, 'Carl Schmitt's Political Theory of Representation', *Journal of the History of Ideas*, 65 (2004), 113–134. See Ulrich Thiele, *Advokative Volkssouveränität* (Berlin: Duncker & Humblot, 2003), esp. 165–395, for the sheer range of Schmitt's idiosyncratic interpretation of Sieyès.

[60] Schmitt, *Verfassungslehre*, 32–5; Schmitt, *Constitutional Theory*, 84–8.

provided for Oakeshott an account of the 'character' of the state and the 'spirit' of its law.[61]

Crucially, Montesquieu offered a way out of what Oakeshott saw as the muddle of Kant's arguments about republicanism and peace: '[w]ar in a modern European state', he writes, 'is the enemy of civil association,' not its helpmeet.[62] And if war is the enemy of civil association, two interesting issues arise. Firstly, this provides one obvious response to Anderson's critique of Oakeshott's turn to Hobbes in order to ground a theory of the state as civil association or *societas*. What Oakeshott proposed about Hobbes, of course, is that he was a theorist of anti-war, not of war, and that *Leviathan* in particular was designed to help avoid war, reduce uncertainty and meet the challenge of scepticism head on. It is, in fact, rather like the model of Hobbes proposed by Michel Foucault in contemporaneous lectures at the Collège de France, which is also to say that it is the same thought about the primacy of Hobbesian *salus populi* that Kant himself had defended.[63] Secondly, if war is the enemy of civil association, then is democracy under the modern European nation-state an appropriately updated solution to this Hobbesian problem? Here, Oakeshott's answer was ambivalent.

With reference to Montesquieu's terminology, modern democracy for Oakeshott is a sort of despotism without fear, where public administration has become a science of politics. Democracy as a form of government (rather than a form of state) is a 'confidence trick' pertaining to authority, an 'emblem of ambiguity which has infected the vocabulary of all political discourse', and such an 'authority' word 'escapes corruption only when it is safely laid to rest'.[64] Democracy, like other modern social and political doctrines or theories, is an attempt to arrest experience and give it temporary political shape.[65] Oakeshott's focus on political theories as forms of doctrine, or ideology, also offered a way out of some thorny methodological problems.

According to Oakeshott, a 'history of thought' can discern meaning in experience, but it certainly cannot present a 'social history of ideas'. That

[61] See Michael Oakeshott, 'On Misunderstanding Human Conduct: A Reply to My Critics', *Political Theory*, 4 (1976), 353, 364f.
[62] Oakeshott, *On Human Conduct*, 273.
[63] Michel Foucault, *Society Must Be Defended* (1976) (Basingstoke, UK: Macmillan, 2000), ed. M. Betani and A. Fontana, trans. D. Macey, 270.
[64] Oakeshott, *On Human Conduct*, 191; Oakeshott, *The Vocabulary of a Modern European State*, 17.
[65] Oakeshott, *Experience and Its Modes*, 332f.

was just the 'unredeemed relic of the intellectual legend of the Enlightenment'. Materials for the history of thought are not ideas but 'human artefacts [and] expressions', which means that they are reflections expressed about practices or forms of concrete-order thinking. The legacy of the social history approach hypostatized thought as action, and was unable to recognize the peculiarities of practise. In fact, such an argument lay behind Oakeshott's consistent critique of Harold Laski's political pluralism, which he had railed against since his first lectures to undergraduates on the impossibility of a purely philosophical approach to politics in the 1920s.[66] For Oakeshott, the state precisely was not an association like any other, and although he might be able to agree with pluralist claims about divided sovereignty in the modern world, he could only do so if that was understood as the result of a natural historical development. In Oakeshott's mind, Laski completely mistook the connections between philosophy and politics, whether or not he was right about the question of sovereignty, because the state is not a 'thing' but is instead a 'unifying principle in political life'. It was almost precisely the same attack upon Laski's political pluralism as that made by Schmitt, when he had suggested both that the state 'is the political unity of a people' and a vehicle of 'secularization'.[67]

Equally, Oakeshott supplemented his attack on pluralism by aligning it to his critique of romanticism and Whig history. He wrote, '[N]o course of historical events exists until it has been constructed by historical thought,' and to avoid the problems of romanticism and tunnel vision when writing about politics would require a radically historicist approach.[68] Yet, this move towards radical historicism could easily slide into relativism or moralism or, worse, still flounder in the same category mistake of failing to recognize that the past is always a construct of historical writing. It is not the case that concepts are indefinable, rather that concepts structure historical writing and historical writing constructs a past upon which or through which we think about politics as a form of conversation. In other words, ones that equally resonate with Schmitt's account, Oakeshott wrote that 'all concepts are definable in the sense that all concepts whatever belong to the totality of experience.'[69] For both, this means focussing on the

[66] Oakeshott, 'Conclusion' in Oakeshott, *Early Political Writings*, 133–5.

[67] Carl Schmitt, 'Staatsethik und pluralistischer Staat', *Kant-Studien*, 35 (1930), 28; Schmitt, *Verfassungslehre*, 90; Schmitt, *Constitutional Theory*, 97; Schmitt, *Nomos*, 127.

[68] Oakeshott, *Experience and Its Modes*, 137.

[69] Ibid., 342.

concept of the state within the totality of European experience and reflecting upon politics since the medieval period.

Oakeshott's motivations here surely lay in his engagement with the work of a Cambridge colleague Herbert Butterfield. Oakeshott's awareness of what constituted Whig history, made famous by Butterfield, also came in part from the aspects of the Historical Tripos which he had enjoyed in Cambridge (as opposed to those he famously did not, namely, the comparative politics component).[70] Alongside his attack on Whig historical writing, Butterfield also worked on the Anglican foundations of modern historiography.[71] Yet Oakeshott's account of the role of historical writing in constructing the historical past first of all offered a devastating critique of political romanticism. Butterfield's own early attempt in his *The Historical Novel* (1924) had been a poor attempt to get around such problems, according to Oakeshott, but the challenge moved both to develop their own claims about the importance of history to politics.[72]

For Oakeshott, another (hitherto largely unknown) figure who must have influenced his thinking about politics was someone who lectured most explicitly on German political thought in Cambridge and who was one of the referees for his fellowship at Gonville and Caius. Ernest James Passant was a Fellow at Sidney Sussex College, and later officer in the Ministry of Propaganda during the Second World War. Although his only listed publication is a collection on German history from the Vienna Congress to the end of the Second World War, several of his own books remain in the Cambridge University Library, in particular, those of Carl Schmitt on the political, on theology and on the guardian of the constitution, all from early editions. Passant had lectured on German political thought in Cambridge in the later 1920s in a manner that looks altogether modern. He was also slated to teach mainstream European history, from Richelieu to the French Revolution in broad outline, and his notes for those lectures remain intact. As the political situation in Germany worsened, however, first under Weimar and then during the rise of Hitler, his teaching of German political and social ideas came

[70] Michael Oakeshott, 'The Cambridge School of Political Science (April, 1924)' in Oakeshott, *What Is History?*, 45–66, at 48, 50, 57–9, 64.

[71] Michael Oakeshott, 'Review of Herbert Butterfield *The Whig Interpretation of History*' (1951) in Oakeshott, *What Is History?*, 219–23, esp. 221.

[72] Michael Bentley, *The Life and Thought of Herbert Butterfield: History, Science and God* (Cambridge University Press, 2011), 47.

presently to the fore. Moving beyond the basic outlines of nineteenth-century German history and its focus on Bismarck, Passant channelled that background as a way into an understanding of the broad arc of political theory from the utopian socialists to National Socialism, with Treitschke, Schmitt and even Max Weber as his polestars.[73] Oakeshott was fully aware of such a genealogy, and his own account of the distinctive character of the modern European state, although grounded in Hobbes, has a distinctively Germanic cast.

Histories of political thinking

Oakeshott's interest in German-inspired theology and philosophical idealism was a definite presence in his work of the 1920s and 1930s. Oakeshott's father had been in touch with William Beveridge, as head of the London School of Economics, trying to get an introduction for his son to Tugendhat and other Heidelberg theologians. At the time of his relevant sabbatical leave, Oakeshott was clearly reading Hegel, Nietzsche and Heidegger extensively and focussing on the British Idealists, particularly Green and Bosanquet simultaneously.[74] He also took forward specific dimensions of German theories of the state and incorporated them into his claims about politics and experience. He was keen, for example, not to essentialize the German 'character' whether in peace or war. Thus, when he wrote of the way in which all Germans in the early 1940s could not be thought of as a 'nation of Fichtes', he distinguished the guilt of a nation from its national character.[75] His friend and colleague Butterfield had done the same in the first number of the *Cambridge Journal*. There, Butterfield worried about the 'disinherited' classes from the Great War to

[73] Faculty of History Lecture List: *Cambridge University Reporter*, 1930–1931 (1 October 1930), 75; 1931–1932 (9 October 1931); 1934–1935 (2 October 1933), 58; 1935–1936 (4 October 1934) (Passant on 'Theory of the Modern State'); 1932–1933 (1 October 1932), 21 (Passant on 'Representative Government in Europe since 1789'); 1934–1935 (4 October 1934), 90 (Passant on 'The Political Background of National Socialism'); 1935–1936 (4 October 1935), 90; 1936–1937 (3 October 1936), 91; 1937–1938 (7 October 1938), 88; 1938–1939 (4 October 1939), 87; (Passant on 'Germany: Social and Political Theory and Institutions, 1871–1919').

[74] William Beveridge, Letter to F. Oakeshott, 21 July 1924, Beveridge Papers, British Library of Political and Economic Science, London School of Economics: Beveridge/2B/23/5/150, folio 7. See Michael Oakeshott Archives, British Library of Political and Economic Science, London School of Economics: Notebook 2/1/3 (1922), folios 25, 62–3; Notebook 2/1/5 (1923), folio 96; Notebook 2/1/6 (1924), folio13.

[75] Michael Oakeshott, 'On Peace with Germany' (1943) in Oakeshott, *What Is History?*, 175.

the Second World War but rejected the idea that the 'Germans are more wicked than the rest of human nature'.[76] His argument about the construction of distinctions between theories of politics, normative political philosophy and a synthetic analysis of the theory of the state also mirrored the well-established and German-dominated field of *Allgemeine Staatslehre.*

Towards the end of his junior research fellowship application, Oakeshott noted the central distinction between *Politik* and *Staatslehre* drawn from Johann Kaspar Bluntschli's three-volume work, *Lehre vom Modernen Staat.* He presented it as one of the more focussed ways of trying to reconcile a philosophy of the state and self as unified and unitary but separable in terms of politics and law, or *Politik* and *Recht.* The claim he made was that the state ultimately rests on metaphysical principles and simply must be understood in terms of its most general purpose.[77] From this point, the particular dimensions of his twofold narrative of the history of political thought could be reprised as a story about the vocabularies of theory and practice in political self-understanding drawn from post-medieval Europe. What that history showed, apart from a distinction between an activist and a simply legal state, is that the distinctive quality of the modern European state lies in its continued attempt to try to ground either a theory of natural or unnatural (commercial or adventitious and utilitarian) sociability with or without a social contract.[78] For most, even Kant, this came down to a choice between an austere Hobbism or a wider political theology. Many have noted Oakeshott's avowed interest in Augustine as his guide to such matters.[79]

The 'character' of politics and state focussed on pursuit of government in an era of 'modernity', lay in a contrast originating in the sixteenth

[76] Herbert Butterfield, 'Reflections on the Predicament of Our Time', *Cambridge Journal*, 1 (1947), 5, 12f.

[77] Michael Oakeshott, 'A Discussion of Some Matters Preliminary to the Study of Political Philosophy' (1925) in Oakeshott, *Early Political Writings*, 39–140, at 87ff, 135: 'A political philosophy founded upon no metaphysical prolegomenon, or upon one fundamentally in error, is doomed not to propagate truth, but falsehood'. For the publishing history of Bluntschli's ultimately three-volume *Staatslehre*, see Adolph Loening, 'Vorrede', in J. K. Bluntschli, *Lehre vom Modernen Staat, Erster Teil, Allgemeine Staatslehre*, 6th edn. (Stuttgart: J. G. Cotta, 1886), xi.

[78] Michael Oakeshott, 'The Emergence of the History of Thought' (1967) in Oakeshott, *What Is History?*, 345–72.

[79] See, e.g., Elizabeth Campbell Corey, *Michael Oakeshott on Religion, Aesthetics and Politics* (Columbia, MO: University of Missouri Press, 2006), Chapter 2, esp. 32; see also Oakeshott, *Lectures in the History of Political Thought*, 492f.

century – firstly, between languages of state and the morality of individuality, and secondly, between languages of state and a collectivist or productivist morality based on utility. The latter genealogy runs from Francis Bacon to the nineteenth-century socialists via cameralism and the rise of statistics that underpinned its notion of good governance (*Gute Policey*). It culminates in the welfare state.[80] Oakeshott's wider history also incorporated the divine right of kings, a Protestant challenge in the form of an updated Calvinism and the government of the saints (where magistracy trumps divine right) and a claim about how Marxist analyses of the proletariat render it analogous to the Calvinist elect. It was a similar claim to that which Leo Strauss had made about Hobbes, presenting him as the theorist of radical enlightenment and proto-Marxism in early writings, and subsequently in a book written in Cambridge whilst a Rockefeller-funded student at Sidney Sussex, supported by Ernest Passant and Ernest Barker. Oakeshott reviewed Strauss's book very favourably upon its first appearance.[81] The implications he wished to draw from his genealogy of modernity were, nevertheless, quite different. Although he transposed Strauss's claim about the Hobbesian sources of modern Marxism into those of a proletariat-elect, analogous to Calvinism, he elsewhere noted that 'our political theory, it seems, is still under the domination of the categories of these seventeenth century thinkers, [he was referring here to Hobbes, as discussed by Otto Gierke] categories which we all recognize to be unsatisfactory but which nobody has yet shown us how to replace.'[82] Ernest Barker's elaboration of the principle of group personality, in part inspired by Hobbes and Gierke in tandem, was not an option that Oakeshott himself found particularly attractive as a way out of these categories of political theory.

For Oakeshott, then, it was right to say that the modern state emerged when *jurisdictio* (or matters of law) was supplemented by *gubernaculum*

[80] Ibid., 419–22.

[81] See Leo Strauss, 'Hobbes's Critique of Religion' (1933–1944) in G. Bartlett and S. Minkov (eds.), *Hobbes's Critique of Religion and Related Writings* (University of Chicago Press, 2011), 24, 25, 28, 115; Leo Strauss, 'Some Notes on the Political Science of Hobbes' (1932), *Hobbes's Critique of Religion*, 154; Leo Strauss, *The Political Philosophy of Hobbes* (1936) (University of Chicago Press, 1952), 138, on Hobbes' 'paradoxical' morality and 'utopian' politics; Michael Oakeshott, 'The Political Philosophy of Hobbes' (1937), in Luke O'Sullivan (ed.), *The Concept of a Philosophical Jurisprudence* (Exeter, UK: Imprint Academic, 2007), 145–6.

[82] Oakeshott, *Lectures in the History of Political Thought*, 439; Oakeshott, 'Review of Otto von Gierke, *Natural Law and the Theory of Society, 1500–1800*' (1934) in Oakeshott, *Philosophical Jurisprudence*, 97ff, at 99.

(or matters of state), allowing the state to deal with the exceptional situation.[83] Strauss noted the importance of this separation for ancient and modern constitutionalism when reviewing the work of C. H. Mcilwain.[84] Further, this meant that 'governing' was supplemented by 'ad hoc' decisions about *utilitas publica* at a time when rulers embodied their realms, and their subjects were objects of princely policy.[85] Modern political theory is, for Oakeshott, a reflection upon the state that emerged out of this conjuncture, and politics is an *explicandum*, an Aristotelian fact of experience, focused upon it. But he thought that conventional histories of political thought missed this point entirely.[86] They were 'no better than scrap books of deceptively similar intellectual adventures'.[87] The history of political thought is not and cannot be a cumulative or iterative enterprise because it is part of a philosophy of politics, but which is a special application of philosophical theory to the field of practice. Furthermore, this means that a genuine philosophy of politics is literally self-defeating, because philosophy aims at the totality of experience, and politics is only one of the many forms that attempt to arrest that experience over time. This means, in a sentence that could stand as an epigraph to Oakeshott's writings on the subject, 'in philosophy, and consequently in a philosophy of politics, the criterion is never conformity with our ordinary view of the matter.'[88]

This was precisely what Oakeshott's first course of lectures in Cambridge had suggested, spending three quarters of his time explaining just how difficult it is to think philosophically about anything and finally concluding that political philosophy itself is literally impossible as philosophy, even though the most coherent and profound attempts to think about a philosophy of politics come from those writers who entertain general philosophical explanations of our practice.[89] Illustrations of this came from Aristotle and Augustine, Hobbes and Spinoza, Rousseau and

[83] Oakeshott, *Lectures in the History of Political Thought*, 321; Oakeshott, 'Political Thought as a Subject of Historical Inquiry' (1980) in Oakeshott, *What Is History?*, 417f.

[84] Leo Strauss, *What Is Political Philosophy?* (University of Chicago Press, 1959), 271.

[85] Oakeshott, *Lectures in the History of Political Thought*, 321.

[86] Oakeshott, 'Emergence of the History of Thought' in Oakeshott, *What is History?*, 397–401.

[87] Oakeshott, 'Political Thought as a Subject of Historical Inquiry', *What Is History?*, 419; see Oakeshott, Notebook 19 (1966), folio 1: 'Much of modern European "political thought", so-called, belongs, not to the history of political reflection, but to the history of dreams. It is a set of, often banal, variations on the theme: *Schlaraffenland*.'

[88] Oakeshott, *Early Political Writings*, 135.

[89] Martyn P. Thompson, 'Oakeshott on the History of Political Thought' in Franco and Marsh (eds.), *Companion to Oakeshott*, 197, at 199ff, offers wider reflection.

Hegel.[90] So, too, was St. Paul exemplary for Oakeshott, once even calling him 'perhaps the greatest political philosopher'.[91] In general, therefore, the history of thinking about politics is a history of thinking about ways in which the vocabularies of political thought and practice have come together, particularly in Europe. This is a theme dominating his entire work, and in explaining European uniqueness, Oakeshott began to think about the rise of political science itself. Self-conscious reflection on political science began with the practical experience of the Greeks and their attempts to deal with diversity, but it developed into a relationship between experience and reflection and provided the structure for his lectures on the history of political thought, which he delivered for decades. Politics emerges out of communal diversity, imaginable alternatives, legitimate authority and ultimately the state. It thereby refuses easy categorization.

What Oakeshott's account led him to was the rejection of consent and contract theories of political obligation, and a different focus on political authorization as the processes through which power becomes moralized across time and space. It appeared in an early formal publication, 'The Historical Element in Christianity', as well as elsewhere in his youthful writings, and culminated in a defence of patriotism as a form of 'sociality', a perfect union within a civil association.[92] This early movement or relationship between morality and politics in modern Europe through authorization, experience and sociality would register fully with his later accounts of collectivism versus individualism. This, in turn, provided his taxonomy of conventional authors, where the individualism of Hobbes, Spinoza, Hegel, Burke, Montesquieu, Hume, Smith, Kant, Bentham and Mill was contrasted with the 'mass man' of modern representative democracy, heir to Baconian productivism, common good morality and lacking individual capacity.[93] Contemporary Fabianism here was simply an updated form of German cameralism, and therefore provided another neat way of subverting his opponent Laski. Although Laski had sought to

[90] Oakeshott, *Early Political Writings*, 126f, 224f; Oakeshott, *Experience and Its Modes*, 344, 350, 354.

[91] Oakeshott, 'Cambridge Study of Politics', 48.

[92] Michael Oakeshott, 'The Historical Element in Christianity' (1928) in Oakeshott, *Religion, Politics, and the Moral Life*, 63–73, 64–8; see Oakeshott, 'Authority of the State', 75f, 84–7; Oakeshott, 'Some Remarks on the Nature and Meaning of Sociality' (1925) in Oakeshhott, *Religion, Politics, and the Moral Life*, 46–62, esp. 59–62; Oakeshott, *Lectures in the History of Political Thought*, 449f, 456, 465f.

[93] Oakeshott, 'Masses' in Oakeshott, *Rationalism in Politics*, 376.

ground his political pluralism upon a different reading of German-inspired associational life, for Oakeshott, that just meant his account was another form of productivism or rationalism.[94]

Taken singly, these two strands of modern political thinking, with their contrasting intellectual genealogies of reason of state and political prerogative, suggest that politics as associational practice is either about necessity or about welfare. For instance, Ciceronian reason of state, updated through the *salus populi* demands of writers from Hobbes to Kant in particular, was necessary to the morality of individualism. Conversely, safety, public health, prosperity, abundance and welfare lay behind the morality of collectivism. Both, though, were component parts of the vocabulary of the modern European state.

The individualists, Oakeshott wrote, rejected the 'Pelagianism of the politics of faith' but did not move into a self-defeating politics of scepticism, rather unlike modern republicanism for example. Oakeshott's critique of republicanism was that it remained far too trusting in the centralization of power for the sake of the common good, because such centralization was antithetical to a politics of civil association predicated upon the desirability of diffusing power.[95] The point here is that to think that any single technical instrument of state authorization will avoid all problems and readily solve the problems of welfare is simply to relapse into a politics of faith. To avoid the dilemma, it seems to me that Oakeshott was compelled to re-describe reason of state simply as the normal politics of a civil association properly understood, and to recognize that much contemporary politics was itself (in his terms) a rejection of this idea, which made it in fact a form of anti-politics. Oakeshott's counter-narrative of the intellectual history of the state seen simply as *universitas*, or enterprise association, is a genealogy of this process of neutralization and de-politicization, and it operates in a similar way to that outlined by Schmitt.

Thus, the State has *Place* (territory), *Personification* (ruler and land), is an *Association* (not a medieval community) and has certain sense of *Solidarity* (which can be cultivated through exclusion or toleration).

[94] Oakeshott, *Lectures in the History of Political Thought*, 476ff. For a wider discussion, see David Runciman, *Pluralism and the Personality of the State* (Cambridge University Press, 1997), Chapter 9.

[95] Michael Oakeshott, *The Politics of Faith and the Politics of Scepticism* (New Haven, CT: Yale University Press, 1996), ed. Timothy Fuller, 83f: 'Of all the follies of the politics of scepticism, the strangest is that which appears in the history of modern republicanism'. See Oakeshott, *Vocabulary of a Modern European State*, 17ff.

Clarifying the state in historical terms, then, required a distinction between *Potestas* and *Potentia*, or Sovereignty, and Oakeshott was well aware of the exceptional increase in sovereignty that adhered to the modern state.[96] In conventional fashion, this derives from its monopoly of legitimate violence, bureaucracy, territorial border control, efficient tax systems, continuous diplomacy and technological advances ultimately grounded in war. On this reading, the formation of the state in war looks like the very model of the state as an enterprise association. Oakeshott's recourse to Hobbes, though, presented a counterpoint to this sort of state-making practice. His focus was on Hobbes as an exponent of political philosophy, which for Oakeshott is a very particular enterprise, as has already been suggested.[97] Indeed, one might think that Oakeshott, who was otherwise sharply critical of the work of Quentin Skinner on the foundations of modern politics, could usefully agree with him on the extent to which Hobbes as the theorist of the civil association was also the theorist of counter-revolution, a counter-revolution to the idea of the state as *universitas.*[98] Thus, when Oakeshott moved to discuss the rise of the modern state, tracing the development of personal rule by the prince to rule by the recognizably modern state as legislative person, he made the case that 'modern European political thought may be understood as the play of the modern European intellect around the experience of living in a "state"'. Thus, to understand it as a practice means that we cannot engage in the exercise in tracing foundations, but must consider 'experience itself translated into the general idiom of ideas'.[99] As he would later reiterate:

[96] Oakeshott, *Lectures in the History of Political Thought*, 368–72 (emphasis in original).

[97] See Michael Oakeshott, 'Hobbes' (1935) in Oakeshott, *Philosophical Jurisprudence*, 110, originally published in *Scrutiny*. So too was his attack on Bentham, which is the only extant record of his critical views of utilitarianism, although he had regularly given sixteen lectures in the Michaelmas and Lent terms in Cambridge between 1930 and 1935. See Michael Oakeshott, 'The New Bentham', *Scrutiny*, 1 (1932), 114; Faculty of History Lecture List, *Cambridge University Reporter*, 1930–1931 (1 October 1930), 75 (Oakeshott on 'The Philosophical Background of Political Thought in the 19th Century'); 1931–1932 (9 October 1931), 83 (Oakeshott on 'The Philosophical Background of Utilitarian Political Thought'); 1933–1934 (2 October 1933), 58 (Oakeshott on 'Utilitarianism'); 1934–1935 (4 October 1934), 90 (Oakeshott on 'Utilitarianism' in Michaelmas term, 'Hegel and Marx' in Lent); 1935–1936 (4 October 1935), (Oakeshott on 'Utilitarianism')

[98] Oakeshott, *Lectures in the History of Political Thought*, 471, 476, 480–1, 483, 486–489. Cf. Quentin Skinner, *Hobbes and Republican Liberty* (Cambridge University Press, 2008); Oakeshott, 'Review of Quentin Skinner, *The Foundations of Modern Political Thought*' (1980) in Oakeshott, *Vocabulary of a Modern European State*, 287.

[99] Oakeshott, *Lectures in the History of Political Thought*, 389–90.

> The use of the word 'state' to identify the emergent associations of modern Europe may be recognized as a masterpiece of neutrality; it revealed nothing about what might be thought to be the character of the associates or the condition (*l'estat*) they shared.[100]

If Hobbes's counter-revolution undercut both princely and republican sources of politics, then the practice of Hobbes' statecraft was also counter-revolutionary. He became once again the theorist of anti-war and thereby the proponent of the civil condition. For some, this makes Hobbes a theorist of anti-politics, but for Oakeshott, this made Hobbes the preeminent theorist of politics as a predicament or human condition, to be dealt with through prudence and practice. If this is right, the force of Oakeshott's claim about what the history of political thought is and what it can do becomes clearer. As he suggested, '[W]hat writers like Hobbes, or Locke, or Rousseau, or Bentham were doing was not inventing a concept, but seeking a more profound understanding of the experience of living under a government which was recognized to have the sort of authority it was recognized to have'. This means that the diversity of meaning that lies behind modern political concepts is a counterpart to the 'ambivalence of the modern European character'. Philosophical reflection on politics is then a form of 'self-anatomy', a diagnosis of the practical forms of associational life under the modern state.

Our modern vocabulary of the state often focusses on it as an artificial rather than a 'real' personality because of the predominance of a language derived from the arguments of writers such as Hobbes that are pressed into service as political theory rather than political philosophy. And because the most influential attempts to think about the limits to political action under the state tend to come from political theory, Oakeshott was forced to consider why. He answered that the success of political theory was that it routinely offered a 'crib', or a rough guide, for how to think politically. This is why Machiavelli, Locke, Bentham and Marx are more powerful in the political imagination than, say, Hobbes, Spinoza or Augustine, but also why they do not have political philosophies to offer.[101] The contrast between the enterprise and the civil association in

[100] Oakeshott, *On Human Conduct*, 233.

[101] Oakeshott, *Vocabulary of a Modern European State*, 11, on Locke's 'questionable enterprise of recommending a political position in the idiom of "general ideas"'. See Oakeshott, 'Rationalism in Politics', 149, on Locke's 'crib' in the *Second Treatise* as a product of political inexperience and Marxism generally as an entirely illusory attempt to escape from such inexperience; see also Oakeshott, *Lectures in the History of Political Thought*, 394–5, 449–50.

Oakeshott's work therefore also seems to overlay a distinction between the civil association as political philosophy and the enterprise association either as political theory, or as anti-politics. Even if this overlay is not quite right, the twin strands of the vocabulary of the modern European state present a genealogy that backs up the claim, as does Oakeshott's distinction more generally between political philosophy and political theory, a distinction also upheld by Carl Schmitt and Leo Strauss.

Reconfiguring reason of state

If Oakeshott's distinction between civil and enterprise association mirrored the account of neutralizations and de-politicizations offered by Schmitt, both found their fulcrum in a critique of contemporary liberalism. The ambiguity surrounding arguments about the political or anti-political nature of the modern state was, for both, an ambiguity indicative of liberalism itself. Its apparent attempt to bracket in advance what sort of politics one should have, or to pre-commit constitutionally to basic rights and duties, for example, was anathema to both Oakeshott and Schmitt.[102] In Oakeshott's case his rather whimsical rejections of post-war social democratic welfarism in British politics have long cast him as a rather grey political writer. Yet, for both Oakeshott and Schmitt, the ultimate grounds for thinking about authority (and hence experience itself), are to be found externally to secular politics. For Schmitt, this required an account of a truly Catholic vision of representation. For Oakeshott, it required a different metaphysics of experience, one grounded in an Augustinian-inspired recognition of the fallen nature of man. To understand the ways in which modern politics was part of a wider secularizing process, chipping away at the ultimately metaphysical foundations of real authority, both sought recourse in Hobbes. It is perhaps why Schmitt, for example, was stung so sharply by Leo Strauss's pertinent critique of his attempt to ground a political anti-liberalism in Hobbes, both because Strauss found Hobbes to be a liberal in turn, and because the ultimate foundations of Strauss's political theology were located in non-Christian sources, sources outside the preferred range of reference (and attack) of both Schmitt and Oakeshott.[103] Nevertheless, Schmitt doubtless agreed with Oakeshott that 'the pedigree

[102] Duranti, 'Totalitarianism', *passim.*

[103] Leo Strauss, 'Notes on Carl Schmitt, *The Concept of the Political*' (1932) in H. Meier (ed.), *Carl Schmitt and Leo Strauss: The Hidden Dialogue* (University of Chicago Press,

of all modern European States is unquestionably medieval.'[104] Indeed, to understand that pedigree and to engage in sophisticated judgement about it required deep study in the history of political thought, and this was the subject that engaged the attention of both men from the beginning to the end of their very long lives.

In his reading from the later 1920s and early 1930s, alongside various Germanic themes, Oakeshott was also thinking explicitly about the Aristotelian foundations of practical reasoning. He thought judgement and action as central to his account of the various modes of experience, and their 'arresting' by particular forms of conduct. The jotting down of these notes, written up on the back of Cambridge History Tripos examination papers from 1930, formed a central part of his account in *Experience and Its Modes*. In the same notebook folder in his archive are notes on German historicism, hermeneutics, Kant and Hegel, Montesquieu and Locke, as well as Aristotle and Plato, a clearly detailed and careful set of reading notes that went into his subsequent teaching and research.[105] These seem to be early versions of what became his *Morality and Politics in Modern Europe* lectures. Soon after these early notes, his thoughts began to crystallize and focussed on the understanding of modern political doctrines. Like theories or ideologies, they attempt to arrest experience and capture it in authority words and as simplifications. They attempt to '*fix* a civilization'. Such doctrines are modern, and although the 'Liberal Democratic doctrine' was the 'oldest of our doctrines', Oakeshott wrote, it only had its roots in the nineteenth century.[106]

The legacy for modern 'ideological politics' of these doctrines is a 'style of politics which springs from attributing to principles a certain character'. This assumes that concepts such as 'justice' or 'liberty' are fixed and determinate in character. Oakeshott countered, suggesting instead that

1995), trans. J. Harvey Lomax, 91–120. David Boucher's contribution to this volume (Chapter 6) considers the radical implications of Strauss's account for both Oakeshott and Schmitt when thinking about contemporary crises of the democratic state.

104 Oakeshott, *Lectures in the History of Political Thought*, 360.

105 Oakeshott, Notebook 2/1/17 (n.d.), folio 18; Notebook 2/1/19 (1966), folio 15; Notebooks 2/1/3 and 2/1/17, with numerous paper-clipped bundles of A4 size notes on Dilthey and *Geisteswissenschaft*, Hegel, Kant, Montesquieu, which are written up as 'Character of Modern Politics'; there are further extensive notes on Harrington, Locke, Aristotle, Adam Smith and so on.

106 Michael Oakeshott, 'The Social and Political Doctrines of Contemporary Europe' (1939) in Oakeshott, *What Is History?*, 149, at 154, 157; see also Luke O'Sullivan, 'Introduction' in Oakeshott, *What Is History?*, 21f.

only if we think about how principles are 'apt to emerge' can we learn to think about our contemporary problems through them. Thus, even if modern representative democracy were a 'Rip van Winkle of social and political doctrine', it is the doctrine under which the 'majority of *civilized* mankind still live'.[107] Unlike more complex forms of Catholicism and more brutally destructive types of fascism and National Socialism, even liberal democracy seemed to have something worth defending during times of extreme crisis. By clarifying the emergence of reason of state as the practical and experiential politics of the civil condition, Oakeshott offered an illustration of how this might be defended and understood as the 'diverse representations of our civilization'.[108] And although both Oakeshott and Schmitt were shrill, perhaps even intransigent, in their criticisms of contemporary forms of what they thought of as ideological anti-politics, both were resolute in thinking that the best response to the ideological crisis of the modern nation-state was to seek to understand that crisis historically. Focussing on the use made of political ideas, without assuming that those ideas have a fixed or stable meaning for all time, could offer a guide to the nature of political experience and judgement in times of crisis. Indeed, only a very few have offered more powerful or provocative reflections about what the history of political thought might be or what it might offer in this regard, and their construction of an historical challenge to understanding contemporary politics is one that remains central to any serious understanding of our own world.[109]

[107] Michael Oakeshott, 'Conduct and Ideology in Politics' (1955) in Oakeshott, *What Is History?*, 248, 250–2; Michael Oakeshott, *The Social and Political Doctrines of Contemporary Europe* (1939) (New York: Cambridge University Press, 1950), xvif (emphasis added).

[108] Oakeshott, 'Social and Political Doctrines', 159.

[109] Oakeshott, 'Conduct and Ideology' in Oakeshott, *What Is History?*, 252f.

9

The rules of the game

Stochastic rationality in Oakeshott's rule-of-law theory

ERIKA A. KISS

> [W]hen dealing with human actions, in so far as these can be allotted to different categories, we must be able to define a standard against which these too can be measured. Now insofar as we act simply as human beings, we possess a capacity to act – a 'virtue', if we understand this in a general sense – and according to this we judge people to be good or bad. In so far as we act as human beings who are citizens, we have the law, by whose standards we can describe a citizen as good or bad; in so far as we act as human beings who are Italians, there are certain very simple features of manners and appearance and speech, by which the actions of the people of Italy can be weighted and measured. But the most noble actions among those performed by Italians are proper to no one Italian city, but are common to them all; and among these we can now place the use of the vernacular that we were hunting above, which has left its scent in every city but made its home in none.
>
> *Dante*[1]

Oakeshott claims in *On Human Conduct* that the theoretical understanding of the rule of law has been led astray 'because the theorists of law have laid so many false trails':

> The most difficult feature of the civil condition to identify and get into place has been law . . . It is made difficult also because the theorists of law have laid so many false trails (for example, misidentifying it as a 'command' and as instrumental to the achievement of substantive satisfactions), and have usually been so much more concerned with the so-called 'sources' of law, with contingent beliefs about its authority, and with its so-called 'purpose' than with what it is.[2]

[1] Dante, *De Vulgari Eloquentia* (Cambridge University Press, 1996), trans. and ed. S. Botterill, 1.16.3–5.

[2] Michael Oakeshott, *On Human Conduct* (Oxford University Press, 1975), 58.

Oakeshott thus positions himself radically against many conventional accounts of the rule of law: he does not accept that law is a command and that law is to be followed in order to achieve results, even if this result is the higher end of prosperity or peace. This indeed is an unusual theoretical position, which Oakeshott desperately tries to clarify in an awkwardly put argument that takes up one third of *On Human Conduct* (which, in fact, as a whole is dedicated to his theory of the rule of law). This long introduction argues that only embarking on Oakeshott's own kind of intellectual adventure will lead to an adequate understanding of the civil condition without explaining it away[3] in the manner of analytical philosophy or the so-called social sciences (with psychology and sociology singled out in particular for his criticism). Oakeshott's strenuous efforts to clarify his position, however, only seem to have led to further frustration and what he perceived as profound misunderstandings of his arguments, as his uncharacteristically petulant response to his critics demonstrates.[4]

In fact, the problem with the awkward first part of *On Human Conduct* might be simply that Oakeshott, by trying too hard, has abandoned his usual style of elegant nonchalance. He could not keep to his maxim, which recommends an exercise of agency in which 'the energy of pursuit is prudentially mixed with *nonchaloir* in respect of the outcome.'[5] In the spirit of this maxim, this chapter recalls a (tongue-in-cheek) theory from Oakeshott's juvenilia in order to elucidate Oakeshott's highly original and indeed still misunderstood account of the rule of law – and also more freely to explore some of its implications. The early piece in question, co-authored with his friend Guy Griffith,[6] intimates the concept of the genuine gambler who precisely exercises the kind of agency in which purposiveness is overwritten by *nonchaloir* in respect of outcomes. Gambling as a metaphor is used almost interchangeably with 'unconditional adventure' in Oakeshott's oeuvre to illustrate the particular mentality required for liberal education, genuine conversation and – as argued in *On Human Conduct* – both for the ideal mode of civil conduct and for its theorizing.

3 Ibid., 101.

4 Michael Oakeshott, 'On Misunderstanding Human Conduct: A Reply to My Critics', *Political Theory*, 4 (1976), 353.

5 Oakeshott, *On Human Conduct*, 71.

6 Guy Griffith and Michael Oakeshott, *A Guide to the Classics or How to Pick the Derby Winner* (London: Faber & Faber, 1936).

Gambling, or wagering, in Oakeshott's work refers to an epistemologically relaxed mode of intellectual engagement which is somewhat unconcerned with outcomes. And it is this mode, I argue, which it is crucial to grasp to make sense of Oakeshott's peculiar, but, I would argue, also normatively highly promising, account of the rule of law and his correlating theory of enterprise versus civil association. In this chapter, this relaxed intellectual engagement is referred to with a term that at first might seem rather unusual: 'stochastic rationality'. I shall contrast stochastic rationality with the epistemologically rigorous and purely purposive rationality unmixed with *nonchaloir*, which Oakeshott opposed throughout his work, though for different reasons at different times. Furthermore, I shall examine Oakeshott's distinction between civil and enterprise association as one between postulates of stochastic and purposive rationality, respectively.

Oakeshott himself does not use the particular expression 'stochastic rationality', but he articulates its contours negatively as the counterpart of instrumental rationality. Aristotle, however, uses the ancient Greek verb *tugkhano* – which is the etymological root of our word 'stochastic' – to make a distinction between the everyday intellectual engagement of the people who try and err and guess and gamble as best as they can, often enough hitting upon (*tugkhano*) the truth in the process, and the intellectual elite (experts), who calculate in order to get it exactly right and in order to achieve some goal instrumentally.

Aristotle claims in his *Metaphysics* that it is crucial to know which topics require what kind of epistemological treatment ranging from perfectly diligent to completely lax. His *Rhetoric* introduces enthymeme (the rhetorical argument) which is the lax counterpart of the epistemologically strict syllogism. Within enthymemic reasoning, Aristotle differentiates several types according to how lax they are. It is easy to see that, in fact, there are gradations of epistemological diligence, from an ideal of perfectly analytical engagement to the one as nonchalant as our intellectual engagement while dreaming. The expressions 'adventure', 'voyage', 'gambling' and 'dreaming' are used by Oakeshott to describe the difference of stochastic rationality from its epistemologically diligent counterpart, that is, instrumental rationality.

While his ideas are highly original, Oakeshott himself refers to his book, *On Human Conduct* – in which he elucidates his ideas about the rule of law – as a theory of a 'somewhat Aristotelian cast'.[7] The most

[7] Oakeshott, 'On Misunderstanding Human Conduct', 356.

important reason for calling his theory of law Aristotelian could be their common emphasis on the particular kind of rationality – 'stochastic rationality' – which both thinkers connect with the kind of intellectual engagement involved in civil conduct (even though neither gives it a specific name). Aristotle describes the rhetorical competence to produce persuasion in the vocabulary of gambling: 'hitting upon (*tugkhano*) the truth', which is usually translated as 'to make a good guess'.

The obscure but rational conduct hidden in the shadow economy of the mind postulated by the condition of stochastic rationality significantly contributes to civil conduct. The *nonchaloir* of stochastic rationality has a moral and an epistemological dimension. *Nonchaloir* in the moral sense corresponds to non-instrumental conduct and epistemologically to a wagering (i.e., guessing, approximating, intuiting) intellectual conduct. The importance of stochastic rationality is that it enables the immature and those without the enlightenment of formal education 'to hit upon truth'.

Simply being native to a vernacular language provides a cognitive edge that can compensate for the lack of mature, formally, reflectively and diligently acquired competence. A good example to illustrate this point is the comparative advantage of small children in language acquisition not despite but because of their naturally lax epistemological engagement of trial and error. Vernacular competence (the competence to learn informally, stochastically) therefore ensures equal access to the conversation of humankind and to the rule of law for those (to use a Kantian term) in the state of minority and not only for those who are in the state of majority. Oakeshott's insistence that civil understanding is not learned with epistemological diligence but is still as good as if it were might be inspired by Aristotle's claim that 'the true and the approximately true are apprehended by the same competence; it may also be noted that men have a sufficient natural instinct for what is true, and usually do arrive at the truth.'[8]

As Dante's lines quoted earlier, written in the first years of the fourteenth century, testify, the analogy between the rule of the civic and the linguistic law had been explored long before the modern linguistic turn of philosophy. In fact, long before Dante, Socrates and his sophist opponent agreed in *Protagoras* that civic virtue is acquired like a native language, without formal instruction. More precisely, they agreed that it seems possible to acquire civic virtue in the vernacular mode directly through

[8] Aristotle, 'Metaphysics' in *The Complete Works of Aristotle* (Princeton University Press, 1984), ed. Jonathan Barnes, 1355a14–18.

acquiring one's native language without formal and specialized learning. It is Aristotle who first reflected theoretically on the fact that the epistemological condition of democracy is the acknowledgement of this competence of acquiring adequate enough knowledge without epistemological diligence. He thereby emancipates rhetorical persuasion as an epistemologically valid way 'to hit upon truth' and makes it the discursive mode of law, politics and the liberal arts.

Aristotle's three branches of rhetoric in modernized terms – aesthetic (epideictic), judicial (forensic) and political (deliberative) – model the correspondence among the arts, the law and the state as all three hinge upon rhetorical persuasion. Bad (i.e., propagandistic, dogmatic, sentimental) art, law conceived of as policy and the telocratic state operate via purposive rhetorical persuasion within the frame of instrumental rationality. Genuine art, authentic law and nomocracy operate via genuine rhetoric that is via the capability (or imagination, in Oakeshott's terminology) of seeing all the possible means of persuasion without pursuing one definite line of persuasion, that is, not teleologically but rather stochastically.

Aristotelian epistemology, which does not recognize any hierarchy between vernacular-vulgar learning and formal-expert-elite learning, is the counterfoil of the epistemology of the Enlightenment articulated clearly in Kant's manifesto, *What Is Enlightenment?* Kant's imperative to know everything for oneself makes epistemological diligence the criterion sorting the *cives* in the state of maturity from the human beings who are in a state of immaturity. From the point of view of democratic theory, however, the Kantian hierarchy between human beings in the state of maturity versus human beings in the state of minority is a step back from the Aristotelian epistemology, which insists on the universally homogeneous condition of human competence for learning, be it lax or diligent, stochastic or analytical.

Oakeshott is firmly within the frame of Aristotelian epistemology, which allows for the trial-and-error approach to access the rules of living together linguistically as well as in terms of civility. I claim that stochastic rationality is also and predominantly at work in the way people learn their native language starting from birth – and that for this very reason Oakeshott could argue that *cives* 'learn' the rule of law the same way they learn a vernacular language. In fact, Oakeshott argues that the rule of law *is* a vernacular language. As a consequence, in Oakeshott's scheme, there are no 'experts' of civil conduct – we all 'learn' it by observing adverbial qualifications in the appropriate manner, the same way we learn a language and observe its rules in the appropriate manner. It follows, then, that for Oakeshott, the human condition as a competence of self-expression and self-enactment, which is both universally and at the same time particularly expressed through the vernacular practices of an association, is a sufficient criterion for citizenship.

Language learners eventually develop a *Sprachgefühl*; *cives*, Oakeshott suggests, eventually need an appropriate *Rechtsgefühl* (feeling for the rule of law). As with a vernacular language, the rule of law will not prescribe what has to be said, and sometimes things can be said that nobody had ever thought could be said in the language at all; as with gambling, we do not know what the outcomes will be – we can just wager as best as we can, using our judgement. In this sense, Oakeshott's theory of the rule of law poses a radical challenge to anyone who associates the rule of law with certainty, predictability, or, for that matter, bases the rule of law on some kind of instrumental rationality (law for the purpose of peace, prosperity, etc.).

I argue that Oakeshott uses the notion of *Rechtsgefühl* (through his analogy between vernacular language and the rule of law) to criticize a game-theoretical approach to the rule of law. He insists that the rule of law is not stochastic in the sense of a chess or cricket game, whose system of rules is invented in a more or less arbitrary fashion, but as a vernacular-language game, whose rules are like those of a natural language. A vernacular-language game is imbedded in heterogeneous vernacular practices based upon the kind of stochastic conduct that relies on a historically acquired and analytically obscure feeling for stochastic approximation. Analytical (including game-theory) approaches to the rule of law – Oakeshott argues – are based upon the false assumptions of finiteness, commensurability and the concept of mathematical probability as opposed to real-life likelihood. Consequently, these approaches are unable to address the phenomena of *Rechtsgefühl* and the inherent condition of uncertainty– all they can do instead is to explain it away.

At the same time as Oakeshott contrasts a simple game in the ordinary sense with the language game of the rule of law, he also draws an analogy between the rule of law and the linguistic art of poetry on the basis of the work of the stochastic *Rechtsgefühl and Sprachgefühl*, respectively. He suggests that the rule of law requires the same sensitivity for nuances from its examiner as literature does from its critic. Relating Oakeshott's account of the rule of law to a proper understanding of vernacular language and to literature, I suggest in this chapter, helps us to grasp what is truly original in this account; it also invites further normative and empirical investigation as to whether Oakeshott's theory does perhaps a better job than conventional ones to elucidate the rule of law as a lived reality.[9]

***

In *On Human Conduct*, Oakeshott strikes an intellectual pose uncharacteristic of him, which could be easily taken for the kind of *superbia* (an hubristic confidence over one's abilities) he constantly draws attention to as the main vice of modern philosophy and science. The book claims that law has not been theorized properly because, at best, the uncertainty inherent in it is explained away by analytical calculations of probability. Law should be theorized – Oakeshott argues – as a performance of the *ars artium* of agency, that is, the art of human conduct (moral self-disclosure and self-enactment).[10] Accordingly, Oakeshott draws a sharply analytical line to demarcate where the analytical approach must stop when theorizing law. This line is between calculable probability and incalculable likelihood. He writes that

> probability in the strict sense of distributional uncertainty of a factor in a finite series of commensurables, plays no part in the deliberations of actions. Likelihood may be guide to life, but not probability.[11]

Apprehending likelihood – that is, to see a persuasive case about strange things or strangers appearing as familiar, as well as familiar things or familiars appearing as strange or strangers – is the ability to metaphorize, according to Aristotle. In terms of citizenship, the *cives* have to be able to see the familiar quality (in respect of the law) in what is in fact not familial or not from one's own tribe, and vice versa they have to be able to see their familial and tribal fellows as strangers in respect of the law. The contingency involved in civic and legal relationships therefore is not probabilistic but rather based upon likelihood, which is incalculable and conditioned upon the ability to metaphorize (to apprehend likelihood).

[9] For intensive discussion of these ideas, I thank David Dyzenhaus, John S.Brunero and Jan-Werner Müller.

[10] 'Moral conduct is agents related to each other in the acknowledgement of the authority of a practice composed of conditions which because of their generality attract to itself the generic name, "practice": morality, *mos*. A morality is the *ars artrium* of conduct; the practice of all practices; the practice of agency without further specification' (Oakeshott, *On Human Conduct*, 60).

[11] Ibid., 44.

Metaphorizing, Aristotle claims, cannot be taught, which does not mean that its competence cannot be acquired through learning in the mode of stochastic rationality. Rather, it means that its acquisition cannot be guaranteed through the epistemologically diligent way of formal teaching. Consequently, it is impossible to teach a machine how to metaphorize meaningfully. Analytically simulated stochastic rationality (such as game theory) can model likelihood in form of calculated probability only by explaining it away, to use Oakeshott's expression. Only natural, vernacular stochastic rationality can apprehend likelihood, form genuine civic and legal conduct and make genuine metaphors.

The other side of the fact that the apprehension of likelihood cannot be taught is that it is impossible to give an account of it by externalizing its rules in the analytical fashion. This is because there is no traditional explanation for the particular congruence of the contingent elements of a likelihood: neither causal nor functional, neither utilitarian nor teleological. 'They touch'[12] contingently by virtue of a particular kind of human conduct. Just like metaphors can be taken to be simply false in the ordinary sense, a genuine law, if taken in the ordinary sense as a command, can also be said to be badly constructed. Law as a command will not be able to instruct clearly or provide an unambiguous line to follow:

> A criminal law, which may be thought to come nearest to forbidding actions, does not forbid killing or lighting a fire, it forbids killing 'murderously' or lighting fire 'arsonically'; and these adverbs are narrowly specified terms of the evidence required to substantiate or to rebut the considerations alleged.[13]

Legal utterances, just like metaphors, are formulated in relations of contingency. It is this contingent nature which explains why law in Oakeshott's understanding cannot give specific commands. While it is possible to command the performance of a specific conduct, one cannot command one to perform this conduct in a specific style. I can command someone to sing but cannot command: 'Sing elegantly!' One cannot simply follow such a command either because adverbials cannot become definite ends of intentions. (Exceptions are the adverbials that are not truly modal but adverbials of measurement such as 'loudly' or 'fast'.) Legal and poetic utterances of the human condition exhibit an interminable indeterminacy on the one hand and, on the other, a particular

[12] Ibid., 104. [13] Ibid., 58.

(even unique) exercise of the art of agency. It is the style of the performance of the rule of law and of poetry that account for their authority, not their content.

The English expression 'the rule of law' becomes perplexing when scrutinized closely: it has an oddly self-referential structure, since 'rule' and 'law' are synonyms in the common use of English. Yet, is this repetition a result of a mere mistake (as in an unintended stutter) or that of a careful articulation of a self-referential conduct in the manner of 'art for art's sake' and 'education for education's sake' or, in this case, 'law for law's sake' and 'legality for legality's sake'?

Oakeshott chooses to take the circularity of the expression to be a sign of precision, the precise articulation of a demand for non-instrumental conduct. His claim is that the expression means literally what it says:

> [T]he expression 'the rule of law', taken precisely, stands for a mode of moral association exclusively in terms of the recognition of the authority of known, non-instrumental rules (that is, laws) which impose obligations to subscribe to adverbial conditions in the performance of the self-chosen actions of all who fall within their jurisdiction.[14]

There are two metaphors hidden in Oakeshott's definition of the rule of law just quoted, which he will make explicit and clear especially in the 1983 essay: (1) the rule of law is like a game, and (2) the rule of law is like social tissue. The first quality explains the stochastic, probabilistic (wager-like) character of the rule of law. The second quality, Oakeshott argues, makes the rule of law not just a simple game but rather a vernacular (or language) game. It is a game that is performed by the civil association in such a way that in their performance the rule of law is being created while simultaneously the rule of law is creating the specific conditions of the association, most importantly, its non-purposiveness. The fact that the performance of the rule of law is like a game ensures that its performer cannot shake the responsibility of being creative: the following of the rules is not mechanical but stochastic, that is, wager-like.[15] The fact that it is a vernacular game, that is,

[14] Michael Oakeshott, 'The Rule of Law' in Oakeshott, *On History: And Other Essays* (Totowa, NJ: Barnes and Noble Books, 1983), 119.

[15] An analogy for this distinction is following a recipe by measuring the weight of ingredients as well as the time and temperature of cooking exactly as opposed to taking a guess and approximating all these quantities according to a sense developed by repeated experience of cooking the dish. This example shows that vernacular practice is naturally but not necessarily accompanied by stochastic rationality.

that the rules are like the social tissue of the association, ensures obligation without external coercion.

David Dyzenhaus is right in pointing out that Oakeshott 'did not say precisely why he took this form of association to be moral or what it means for a law to be non-instrumental',[16] although precision is not what one should expect from Oakeshott on human matters, which, for him, are always of indefinite character. Still, Oakeshott's work provides the most acute analytical breakdown of what intrinsic standard is in the context of law. Oakeshott chooses an unusual strategy in investigating the concept of intrinsic standard – which is what 'law as social tissue' refers to – by avoiding any reference to values. He does not make it entirely clear why he avoids talking about values. The reason, only implied by Oakeshott, might be that intrinsic values are in fact invaluable because they cannot be externalized and reified and thereby made available for assessment. This would explain Oakeshott's insistence on using the expressions 'adverbial qualification' or 'modes'.

The nominal term 'value' reifies and thereby distorts the quality of being intrinsic to something: it supposes that we could take what is internal in and out when, in fact, being intrinsic is a mode of being characterized by inextricability. Oakeshott attempts to define intrinsic measure as a modal category (like the tuning of a musical instrument) by avoiding the nominal phrasing and characterizing it in terms of adverbial qualifications. Therefore, he shifts the discourse from value (a nominal category) to conduct whose qualifications are not nominal but adverbial. His sharp focus on the adverbial qualifications of human conduct is a highly original idea and proves most productive in the philosophical investigation of the problem of intrinsic standard as well as the problem of non-coercive rule following. One of the most frequently occurring adverbial qualifications in Oakeshott's theory is 'incidental'.

According to Oakeshott, the internal standard provided by the rule of law is 'strict yet unexacting';[17] its rules are not commanding or coercive but rather guiding; its outcomes are not consequences determined in a cause-effect pattern but produced incidentally. Therefore, the rule of law is not compatible with utilitarian justifications, that is to say, it cannot be recommended as useful because it is unable to deliver desired (useful) ends in a reliable manner.

[16] David Dyzenhaus, 'Dreaming the Rule of Law', in this volume (Chapter 10).
[17] Oakeshott, 'The Rule of Law', 148.

> Many writers who have undertaken to *recommend* this vision of a state [civic association, that is, governance according to the rule of law] have sought its virtue in what they present as a consequence, something valuable which may be enjoyed as the outcome of this mode of association. And some have suggested that its virtue is to be instrumental to the achievement of 'prosperity' understood as the maximum continuous satisfaction of the wants of the associates.[18]

The continuation of this long passage reveals the most original bent of Oakeshott's philosophy:

> But the more discerning apologists (recognizing the inconsistency of attributing the virtue of a non-instrumental mode of association to its propensity to produce, promote or even encourage a substantive condition of things) have suggested that its virtue is to promote a certain kind of 'freedom'. But this is misleading.[19]

After making a distinction between utilitarian and non-utilitarian conceptions of the rule of law, Oakeshott goes a step further by making another sharp distinction between proponents of justifications of non-purposive conduct versus his own Socratic-style apology for non-purposive conduct. Non-purposive conduct (such as obliging the rule of law, learning for learning's sake or art for art's sake) is impossible to justify because justifications refer to some external end. Moral freedom cannot be posited as the external end of the rule of law or the liberal arts or the free market because freedom cannot be a product determined by a conduct. This sharp distinction between so-called higher ends and internal ends runs through all of Oakeshott's philosophical investigations. Oakeshott denies the possibility of any consistent justifications of liberal education or the free market or the rule of law on the basis that they pursue and fulfil the higher end of moral freedom since 'freedom does not follow as a consequence' of any of these; rather, 'it is inherent in [their] character'. Moral freedom is not in the service of satisfying individual wants in the utilitarian manner. Moral freedom, however, is also not in the service of the so-called higher ends of peace and prosperity, society or market.

> But this 'freedom' does not follow as a consequence of this mode of [civic] association; it is inherent in its character. And this is the case also with other common suggestions: that the virtue of this mode of association is its consequential 'peace' (Hobbes) or 'order'. A certain kind of 'peace' and 'order' may, perhaps, be said to characterize this mode of association, but not as consequences.[20]

[18] Ibid., 161. [19] Ibid. [20] Ibid.

If freedom does not follow as a consequence, then it is not produced in a chain of cause and effect but is an unplanned, un-purposeful, incidental by-product of a human conduct. Purposeful conduct can also have incidental outcomes, such as the damage to the environment in the pursuit of the external end of prosperity. Incidental outcomes, however, are the blind spot of purposeful conduct because of this kind of conduct's compulsive orientation toward external, definite ends. Self-referential, non-purposive conduct, which does not predetermine a cause-effect path for itself to follow, can only result in incidental outcomes. Being mindful of incidental possibilities weakens the fixed and focussed compulsion to reach a definite end, but the adventurous act of wager will replace this weakened compulsion with an unfocussed and flexible compulsion to proceed 'blindly', stochastically among likelihoods.

On the one hand, non-instrumental conduct is adventurous, that is, epistemologically lax, because it proceeds in the boundless sea of uncertainties without a plan. On the other hand, not having a fixation on a definite end affords it a cognitive edge over teleological conduct because non-purposive conduct has a heightened awareness of incidental outcomes, even if this awareness has no analytical clarity. This heightened awareness is a state of mind of being able to expect the unexpected, or even unpredictable, incident is like the state of mind of wagering, or stochastic rationality. While purposive conduct is facilitated by an epistemologically diligent, analytical rationality, non-purposive conduct is made possible by an epistemologically lax, stochastic rationality.

Let us return now to Oakeshott's youthful work on wager. Oakeshott and Griffith's guide to the classics is, of course, not about Plato, Dante or Shakespeare but the classic English horse races, first and foremost the Derby, which the authors at one point assert is the heir of European Antiquity.[21] Not all horse races are classic, we learn in the first pages, only the ones which have historically acquired a certain style. And only the classic ones allow a 'rule of law'–like character, stable in their style and impersonal enough to bet on with the help of the guide. Moreover, not all gambling is genuine gambling. According to Oakeshott, gambling does not simply consist in going to the races and following the procedures of placing a bet but in performing all that while at the same time

[21] T. S. Eliot mentions this book on how to bet on the Derby in his famous 1944 lecture 'What is a classic?' Curiously, both Eliot, characterizing the classic, and Oakeshott, characterizing the rule of law, claim that these phenomena are typically but not exclusively European.

observing the 'adverbial qualifications' of genuine gambling. Not unlike the proper manner of observing the rule of law, or the mind's activity in the poetic mode, or in the state of dreaming, genuine gambling lies in not having purposeful or prudential considerations relating to ends external to their activities.

The idea that there is a mode or, in other words, an adverbial of intellectual engagement that is neither purposeful in terms of practical outcome nor in terms of a conclusive outcome of reasoning runs through Oakeshott's entire oeuvre and gives it an appearance of quixotic idealism. Oakeshott, however, emphasized that while non-instrumentality as an adverbial (a mode) of conduct is real,[22] one cannot realistically expect it to be actualized unmixed with other adverbials, with other qualifications: a conduct might have both an internal and various external (two birds with one stone) ends at the same time. A student may study for its own sake in a liberal arts college as well as enjoy benefits external to her education such as student discounts in museums or the opportunity to meet other young people or, for that matter, a future job. The non-purposive manner of human conduct manifested in genuine gambling and analyzed playfully but thoroughly in the juvenilia on the Derby returns in the 1956 essay, 'The Voice of Poetry in the Conversation of Mankind':[23]

> Conversation is not an enterprise designed to yield an extrinsic profit, a contest where a winner gets a prize, nor is it an activity of exegesis; it is an unrehearsed intellectual adventure. It is with conversation as with gambling, its significance lies neither in winning nor in losing, but in wagering.[24]

Gambling for gambling's sake is a non-instrumental activity: its success lies not in winning but in the observance of the adverbial qualifications of wagering itself. Obliging internal standards, however, cannot be assessed in a positive manner of measurement to external standards. The small book, *A Guide to the Classics or How to Pick a Derby Winner*, is not really a 'how-to' book but rather an attempt to specify the adverbial qualifications of gambling itself, including an argument on why a technical 'how-to' attitude is just as inappropriate as the attitude of getting tips from

22 Oakeshott, answering his critics, says about his concept of civil association that '[i]t is no more an ideal type than the kitchen sink' (Oakeshott, 'On Misunderstanding Human Conduct', 356).
23 Michael Oakeshott, 'The Voice of Poetry in the Conversation of Mankind' in Oakeshott, *Rationalism in Politics and Other Essays* (Indianapolis, IN: Liberty Press, 1991), 488.
24 Ibid, 490.

your great aunt's dream, as the book explains. But how can we tell apart genuine gambling from the instrumental kind?

The first sentence of the guide to the classics sets up a minimal pair that fleshes out the difference between instrumental and genuine gambling:

> Nearly 2000 years ago the poet Ovid wrote: *Ne te nobelium fugial certamen equorum* – Never miss a good race meeting; and Ovid, like most poets, knew what was what. It is true that he intended this maxim primarily for lovers, and that when Ovid went to the races he went not to watch the horses but to watch the girls; but the advice is a good advice for all that, and indeed Ovid is a conspicuous example of a man who does the right thing for the wrong reason.[25]

Doing the wrong thing for the right reason or the right thing for the wrong reason is only possible if our conduct could admit both an internal and an external measure, that is, both an end in itself (which cannot be pursued but only be revealed in the adverbial qualifications of our conduct) and a possible external end which can be pursued and can serve as a transparent measure of accountability.

To take the example quoted earlier, if the lover heeds Ovid's recommendation and attends the race only in order to get the girl, he abides the rule of law not for its own sake but rather in order to pursue a chosen end. Oakeshott defines *telocracy* as a form of governance that might discharge its obligation to laws only in order to be able to reach its chosen ends. As Oakeshott says in his London School of Economics lectures on the history of political thought, '*telocracy* does not necessarily mean the absence of law. It means only that what may roughly be called "the rule of law" is recognized to have no independent virtue, but to be valuable only in relation to the pursuit of the chosen end.'[26] Therefore, the rule of law – when taken 'roughly' and not precisely – can be followed for instrumental reasons, in order to achieve an end that lies beyond the internal end of following the law. Similarly, you can go to the Derby for the wrong – instrumental – reason, namely, not to wager for its own sake but instead planning to win the girl (or the money, for that matter). The manner of your gambling will have no provable effect on the external success of winning, while only the non-instrumental manner of conduct can fulfil the internal end of gambling. Moreover, the successful fulfilment of an internal end is independent of any external outcome because

[25] Griffith and Oakeshott, *Guide to the Classics*, 1.

[26] Michael Oakeshott, *Lectures in the History of Political Thought* (Exeter, UK: Imprint Academic, 2006), ed. Terry Nardin and Luke O'Sullivan, 474.

it is guaranteed by the self-referential structure of the non-instrumental conduct. Since successful fulfilment of internal ends does not depend on any external outcome, courses of action pertaining to internal versus external ends do not compete with each other for external success: the operation can be successful (according to the internal standard) even if the patient dies (external end).

Law can also admit both internal and external ends, but justice can only be served according to the internal standard of the rule of law. The external end of law might feel like justice, but in fact, this feeling is the satisfaction of retribution, a transactional as opposed to a non-instrumental adverbial quality. Let me evoke Socrates' trial to illustrate this point, even if it is not one of Oakeshott's examples. Socrates claims that he fulfils the internal standard of Athenian law by obeying the law that puts him to death: justice is served even when the external outcome is a false sentence.[27] Justice itself (not law) has only an internal standard, which is fulfilled by Socrates' conduct of obeying the rule of law he has previously consented to as a citizen. Socrates' seemingly eccentric teaching that no injustice can happen to the just man is the central quality of the rule of law, which demands 'the recognition of the authority of known, non-instrumental rules'[28] in a conduct that is measured only by its own internal standard: the success of just conduct is self-referential. Socrates is aware of the gamble involved in going to the Athenian court, which his *daimon* (the voice of his stochastic rationality) made him avoid up to this point. Socrates' acceptance of the conditions of genuine wager, by not pursuing 'justice' as an external end, ensures the success of justice enfolding intrinsically in his conduct during his trial. Socrates' eccentric moral teaching to dedicate life to internal as opposed to external success is dramatized in his trial in which living up to the internal standard of his life comes to mean sacrificing it in order to reinforce the morality (and the rule of law) of his city. He is confident that his eccentricity will be recognized as the very centre of the public morality of Athens soon after his death.

Given that your gambling itself does not in fact determine the success of winning, but observing the qualifications of non-instrumental gambling *is* the successful fulfilment of the internal end of gambling, you might say that the more rational choice is to gamble genuinely rather than

[27] Plato, 'Apology' in *The Collected Dialogues of Plato* (Princeton University Press, 1989), ed. Edith Hamilton and Huntington Cairns.

[28] Oakeshott, 'The Rule of Law', 136.

instrumentally.[29] This way you at least have the self-referential success guaranteed, while your chances of winning are not diminished by it. The only reason why the rationality of this wager is overlooked is that internal success has no clear external signs to prove one's claim for reward and, therefore, generally it is not acknowledged as a value.

Education can also admit both internal and external ends. You can study the same curriculum in the truly liberal arts manner for learning's sake or as a means to get a job. Liberal arts college education is often advertised as the better instrument to achieve external success than the straightforwardly instrumental education, which is like arguing that, statistically, genuine gambling for gambling's sake brings more success than instrumental gambling. The real argument for liberal education, however, is that it is your best bet because it can determine success in something (the fulfilment of its own internal end) that instrumental education excludes by definition, while neither kind of education can determine who, in fact, will get the job. It is impossible to discern the difference between betting on a horse as part of a plan to win and betting on a horse for the sake of the wager itself just by looking at the procedure or the outcome of the wager. Planning and wagering can only be distinguished by the different adverbial qualifications of the different conducts.

So it seems that in affairs of the state, which are indefinite by nature, the better gamble is to gamble rather than to calculate with a definite end in mind. The Finnish state, for example, successfully gambles with a sizeable per cent of Finland's gross domestic product by giving it to its citizens who are caretakers of pre-school-aged children without a hint of any incentive on how to spend it. There is a gamble in trusting the Finnish citizen not to spend this money frivolously, but a gamble whose incidental outcome seems to have proven to be the total eradication of child poverty, a superb educational system and superb economic productivity, more than worth the risk. There is no positive way to prove whether the current Finnish government is acting in the *mentality* of planning, but *de facto* they do gamble by giving direct agency to parents to decide how to use a considerable percentage of the available tax revenue.

The adverbial qualifications of planning are such that it is future oriented going from mental purpose through the means of betting to the pursued end of the prize while shunning the present. (An analogy for

[29] This can be recognized as the argument of Pascal's wager.

this is making your child work very hard in kindergarten because your plan is for her to go to a good college a dozen years later and you believe that her hard work at five is a means to your desired end in the future.) The adverbial qualifications of a genuine wager for its own sake, on the other hand, favour the present and shun the future. In the Derby, it would mean a mentality in which the present activity of betting is enjoyed by savouring the momentum of the wager and the state of indeterminacy with its complex play of possible incidents as opposed to preposterously and narrow-mindedly 'pursuing' the desired result enfolding in the race. The gambler who wagers with the adverbial qualifications of planning experiences the outcome of the race either as a frustrating failure in producing the desired end or as a success in determining the desired end. Both the frustration and the satisfaction are based upon the false and hubristic thought that the outcome of the race was determined by the act of betting. The genuine gambler, on the other hand, experiences the outcome of the bet as an incidental by-product of the coincidence of the act of wager and the horse race. Here, there is neither frustration nor pleasure over the instrumental loss or gain, only the pleasurable savouring of the self-referential act of wager while all the possibilities of the future outcome are still up in the air.

Lawfulness in the rough sense is not absent in the instrumental conduct, but the rule of law (taken in the precise sense in which Oakeshott uses it) certainly is. The rule of law in the rough sense is not completely self-referential because it uses the law as a means to an end, even if as a means to a so-called higher end. The unique character of Oakeshott's philosophy lies in his analytical distinction between the purposive and non-purposive adverbial qualifications of human conduct and, moreover, in his recognition that so-called higher ends are still instrumental. Planning the unplanned is still planning.[30] As Luke O'Sullivan points out, for Oakeshott, 'the relevant political distinction was not between left and right but between those who would "plan and impose a way of life upon a society" and those who "not only refuse to hand over the destiny of a society to any set of officials but also consider the whole notion of planning the destiny of a society to be both stupid and immoral",[31] Nomocratic governance is an unrehearsed adventure, while governance

[30] 'A plan to resist all planning may be better than its opposite, but it belongs to the same style of politics' (Oakeshott, *Rationalism in Politics*, 26).

[31] Luke O'Sullivan, 'Michael Oakeshott on European Political History', *History of Political Thought*, 21 (2000), 132, 137.

in the telocratic style is planning the destiny of a society, that is, laden with the hubris of social engineering.

The difference between the telocratic and the nomocratic obligation to law can only be captured in terms of style, in the different adverbial qualifications of their characteristic conduct, but not in terms of accountability. From the point of view of assessment *telocracy* or *nomocracy*, either obeys the law or not. In case they do, the possible difference (whether they oblige the law as a means to an end or for the sake of allowing solely the law to rule) cannot be positively accounted for. Yet David Dyzenhaus is right in pointing out that according to Oakeshott's theory, when *telocracy* uses the rule of law instrumentally, it still has a civilizing effect[32] – as if the values intrinsic to the rule of law would incidentally rub off on the telocratic state even if used for the wrong reason. The act of wager used as a means to an end still obliges the rules of wagering procedurally, if only with the wrong adverbial qualification (planning-ly), and could eventually change the mentality of planning into genuine wagering.[33] The current Finnish government might gamble strategically (planning-ly) with a sizeable per cent of the country's gross domestic product, but their law based upon the practice of trusting and being trusted is changing the quality of the association on the scale of enterprising to civil through the exercise of trust. It is quite obvious that the social contract between American citizens and the U.S. government would not make it possible to 'gamble' with the taxpayers' money in the Scandinavian manner. An enterprise society in the direct mode of planning would want to implement transparent mechanisms of accountability and guarantees for enforcement at every level of legislation rather than relying on trust. 'In this *mode* of association' – says Oakeshott – 'there is nothing whatever to correspond to the expression "the rule of law": there is only Purpose, Plan, Policy and Power.'[34]

When a *telocracy* gambles with the adverbial of planning (only to win), it does so by simulating the state of mind of wager. However, simulating the state of mind pertaining to wager can only be done by an acknowledgement of randomness and what follows from it: the impersonality and neutrality law requires. The mentality of the genuine gambler, however, is not a simple acknowledgement of arbitrariness but a sense

[32] Dyzenhaus, 'Dreaming the Rule of Law,' in this volume (Chapter 10).

[33] See Pascal's recommendation to follow the rules of religion even if you are unable to make the genuine wager.

[34] Oakeshott, 'The Rule of Law', 125.

developed in the vernacular practice of the game that makes the act of wager a leap of faith based upon an historically conditioned sense as opposed to a truly random choice. The cognitive leap in the genuine wager is a stochastic act of cognition with different adverbial qualifications from those of the mechanically simulated stochastic rationality that operates not as a leap of faith backed by an unenlightened historical sense but as a calculated suspension of instrumental rationality for an ultimately instrumental reason. The adverbial qualification of the genuine, not calculated, stochastic rationality is its being intrinsically embedded in a (re)current vernacular practice.

> As a practice, the civil condition is an enactment of human beings; a continuous, not a once-and-for-all enactment. And what is enacted and continuously re-enacted is a vernacular language of civil understanding and intercourse; that is, some historic version of what I have called the language of civility.[35]

Here Oakeshott explicitly qualifies the adverbial of the vernacular stochastic conduct as 'historical'. The epistemologically lax leap of the genuine wager falls back on an historically developed sense informing habits of conduct, about which Oakeshott writes in 'Tower of Babel':

> Custom is always adaptable and susceptible to the *nuance* of the situation. This may appear a paradoxical assertion; custom, we have been taught, is blind. It is, however, an insidious piece of misobservation: custom is not blind, it is only 'blind as a bat.'[36]

In the context of law, the historical sense, which is 'only 'blind as a bat', is a feeling for the law that informs both civil conduct and the theorist of the rule of law. The blind bat in fact has the advantage of superb navigation in the dark. Oakeshott does not only point to a more or less mystical *Rechtsgefühl*. After drawing a sharp analytical line between calculable probability and real-life 'likelihood of uncertainties',[37] he does not fall silent but keeps philosophizing, only in a different manner, that of the sceptic.

Oakeshott's definition of the rule of law can only make sense from the perspective of his scepticism. In a possible world of certainties, we would not need the rule of law. What we would need instead is either experts or technocrats leading us to these certainties in an accountable, reliable,

[35] Ibid., 120. [36] Oakeshott, 'The Tower of Babel' in *Rationalism in Politics,* 471.
[37] Oakeshott, *On Human Conduct*, 44.

epistemologically diligent but fundamentally undemocratic and illiberal manner or God leading us according to His inscrutable plans. Since all human affairs are uncertain (and even admit opposites), we need the rule of law to protect us from the claims of certainties and truths. An epistemology that postulates certainties corresponds to a morality that demands either the epistemologically diligent pursuit of truth or the faith in the dogma of divine revelation. Oakeshott's entire oeuvre can be interpreted as his resistance to the increasing dominance of instrumental rationality as a morality, for which he thought both the idealizing morality of Christianity and the modern march of enlightened science were responsible. His juvenilia of a guide to how to gamble fits into his general warning about the hubris of the Enlightened Man and his recommendation of the unrehearsed adventures of the *homo ludens*.

10

Dreaming the rule of law

DAVID DYZENHAUS

> *Leviathan* has passed for a book of philosophy and a book about politics, and consequently it has been supposed to interest only the few who concern themselves with such things. But I believe it to be a work of art in the proper sense, one of the masterpieces of the literature of our language and civilization. . . . We are apt to think of a civilization as something solid and external, but at bottom it is a collective dream. . . . What a people dreams in this earthly sleep is its civilization. And the substance of this dream is a myth, an imaginative interpretation of human existence, the perception (not the solution) of the mystery of human life.
>
> Michael Oakeshott[1]

In 'The Rule of Law', Michael Oakeshott says that 'the expression "the rule of law", taken precisely, stands for a mode of moral association exclusively in terms of the recognition of the authority of known, non-instrumental rules (that is, laws) which impose obligations to subscribe to adverbial conditions in the performance of the self-chosen actions of all who fall within their jurisdiction.'[2]

Oakeshott did not say precisely why he took this form of association to be moral or what it means for a law to be non-instrumental. Nor did he explain exactly how something can be 'self-chosen' and subject to obligation, though the thought seems to be something like this: it is up to you whether to perform a certain action, but if you do, you are obliged to abide by the conditions the authority has legislated for performing that action.

It does, however, seem clear that the association's morality has to do with the way in which it makes possible a politically valuable kind of

For discussion, I thank the participants at the conference at the London School of Economics in 2013 and the audience at a Cardozo Law Faculty Workshop. I also thank Arie Rosen, Johan Olsthoorn, Lars Vinx and Jacob Weinrib for written comments on drafts of this chapter.

[1] Michael Oakeshott, '*Leviathan* – A Myth' in Oakeshott, *Hobbes on Civil Association* (Berkeley: University of California Press, 1975), 150.

[2] Michael Oakeshott, 'The Rule of Law' in Oakeshott, *On History and Other Essays* (Indianapolis, IN: Liberty Fund, 1999) 129, 148.

liberty – civil liberty or the liberty of the subjects of a state who live under an order of public laws, though Oakeshott emphasized that such '"freedom" does not follow as a consequence of this mode of association; it is inherent in its character.'[3] So he does suggest a necessary link between the rule of law and liberty and thus presents what we can think of as a liberal account of the rule of law, despite the fact that he was anxious at all times to insist that his account was formal, that is, not driven by any *telos* or substantive end.

These ideas are not novel in Oakeshott's thought. He had fully elaborated them in 1975 in *On Human Conduct*,[4] and the theme of the connection between authority, law and liberty is central to his discussion of Roman political thought in his *Lectures in the History of Political Thought*, given at the London School of Economics in the 1960s.[5] The novelty lies in what Richard Friedman, in my view, the most sensitive expositor of Oakeshott's legal theory, calls a 'startling innovation in his interpretation of what natural law is all about in and for Hobbes'.[6] Friedman has in mind Oakeshott's claim that Hobbes' laws of nature are 'no more than an analytic breakdown of the intrinsic character of law, what I have called the *jus* inherent in genuine law which distinguishes it from a command addressed to an assignable agent or a managerial instruction concerned with the promotion of interests'.[7] As Friedman explains, the claim is an innovation because in earlier writings Oakeshott had understood natural law on 'the vertical model of a higher law whose function is to provide standards for judging the content of man-made laws'.[8]

Oakeshott's essay is virtually ignored in debates within philosophy of law. On the one hand, it must seem too positivistic to the critics of legal positivism in its insistence that law's authority is a matter of compliance with formal procedures for enacting positive law, as well as in its apparent endorsement of legal positivist accounts of the rule of law, notably, when Oakeshott said that the vision of the rule-of-law state he was

[3] Ibid., 175.

[4] Michael Oakeshott, *On Human Conduct* (Oxford University Press, 1975), Chapter 2.

[5] Michael Oakeshott, *Lectures in the History of Political Thought* (Exeter, UK: Imprint Academic, 2006), ed. Terry Nardin and Luke O'Sullivan, esp. Lecture 3, 237.

[6] Richard Friedman, 'Michael Oakeshott and the Elusive Identity of the Rule of Law' in Corey Abel and Timothy Fuller (eds.), *The Intellectual Legacy of Michael Oakeshott* (Exeter, UK: Imprint Academic, 2005) 160, 175. See also Richard Friedman, 'What Is a Non-Instrumental Law?', *Political Science Review* 21 (1992), 81–98.

[7] Oakeshott, 'The Rule of Law', 172–3. [8] Ibid.

elaborating 'hovers over the reflections of many so-called "positivist" modern jurists'.[9] In addition, Oakeshott clearly rejects versions of natural-law arguments that seek to find the standards of *jus* in something external to *lex*, thus abandoning questions of the authenticity or authority of *lex* 'in favour of "rightness" as the ground of moral obligation'.[10] With Hobbes, Oakeshott regarded such a stance, one that would make the issue of authority or authenticity 'redundant',[11] as a 'recipe for anarchy', since it amounts to the claim he rejects, following Hobbes, that 'the voice of "conscience" [is] . . . the voice of *jus*.'[12]

But, on the other hand, his position must appear too naturalistic to positivists in its insistence that the rule of such law constitutes a genuine kind of *moral* association, for that insistence seems to commit Oakeshott to the idea that H. L. A. Hart describes as 'repugnant to the whole notion of morality' – 'the idea of a moral legislature with competence to make and change morals, as legal enactments make and change law'.[13] I shall suggest later that the perplexing place of Oakeshott when we try to situate him in contemporary debates in philosophy of law indicates precisely why his essay might well be the most important contribution on its topic since, say, the Second World War.

I suspect that the same sorts of perplexity account for the fact that scholars who give an account of Oakeshott's views on law tend to regard this essay as little more than a further meditation on the character of 'the civil condition' in *On Human Conduct* and hence miss what Friedman regards as the startling innovation.[14] In addition, the claim and the analysis that follows it might well seem to provide, or at least go some considerable way towards doing so, a rationalist or instrumentalist

[9] Ibid., 175. [10] Ibid., 146. [11] Ibid., 147. [12] Ibid., 169.

[13] H. L. A. Hart, *The Concept of Law*, 2nd edn. (Oxford University Press, 1994), 177.

[14] Moreover, this idea combined with his emphasis on the authority of law as residing in formal procedures for enactment of *lex* must appear to undermine the claims to authority of custom and tradition, including the common law, and hence, the idea seems in serious tension with Oakeshott's general critique of rationalism for its blindness to such claims. Consider that in the essay on law in the most recent collection of Oakeshott's writings, the author pays no attention to this element in Oakshott's account of the rule of law: Steven Gerencser, 'Oakeshott on Law' in Paul Franco and Leslie Marsh (eds.), *A Companion to Michael Oakeshott* (University Park, PA: Penn State Press, 2012), 312. He is not alone. Martin Loughlin, in his magisterial *Foundations of Public Law* (Oxford University Press, 2010), 331, says that Oakeshott 'offers us what is probably the most rigorous and coherent account of the concept of the rule of law as a foundation of public law'. But in his close reading of Oakeshott at 324–32, he does not mention this remark. See my 'The End of the Road to Serfdom?', *University of Toronto Law Journal*, 63 (2013), 310, 324–6, for criticism of Loughlin on this point.

solution to a puzzle that Oakeshott articulated in all his attempts to provide an account of the role of law in making possible a civil condition – the relationship between law and a standard of rightness, *lex* and *jus*. This is so because in his innovative move, Oakeshott seems to endorse the Hobbesian idea that the *lex naturalis* is composed of 'maxims of rational conduct', the 'necessary causal conditions of peaceful association'.[15] And this suggests that the rule of law is the instrument of achieving the *telos* of peace and that the principles of natural law are rationally derived means to achieving that end.

I shall try to show that Oakeshott did provide at least the sketch of a solution to the puzzle of the rule of law – the relationship between *lex* and *jus* – one which makes sense of Hobbes' thought that *jus* is no more than action in conformity with right, that is, in conformity with the law. The sketch of that relationship goes as far as one can to bringing to the surface the content of the collective civilizational dream Oakeshott portrayed in the text for a radio talk in 1947 from which the epigraph to this chapter is taken. To go further would be to go into a kind of institutional detail that Oakeshott perhaps thought beyond the scope of a philosophical inquiry into the rule of law.

But the limits set by this kind of inquiry do not preclude uncovering problems that require a certain kind of institutional solution, nor do they preclude reference to substantive political ideals, as long as the ideals figure in the inquiry as formal features of the *explanandum*. I shall argue in the latter regard that the substantive political ideal is peace, but not peace in the sense of any effectively imposed order; rather, it is the kind of order that makes it possible for free and equal individuals to live peaceably together. Whether that ideal is itself desirable is not, however, a question that the inquiry seeks to answer – it is merely the ideal that holds together the other formal features that figure in the *explanandum* – *lex*, *jus*, and *auctoritas* or authority – and so it has a proper place in a formal theory, in which the central idea is the non-instrumentality of law. Law's non-instrumentality resides in the way it makes possible interaction between individuals in which their actions are 'self-chosen'.

That our collective civilizational dream is of the rule of law might seem rather dreary to many, as Oakeshott acknowledged when he said that

[15] See Gerencser, 'Oakeshott on Law', and in the same volume, Noel Malcolm, 'Oakeshott and Hobbes', 217. Malcolm, in contrast to Gerencser, does see the importance of this passage to understanding Oakeshott's legal theory, though in his view it leads to a kind of rationalism that Oakeshott generally rejects.

Hobbes' version of the myth might appear 'an unduly disenchanted interpretation of the mystery of human life' to those whose dream it replaced – that of a providentially-ruled 'destiny of man'.[16] However, in that same talk, itself more a work of art than of philosophy, Oakeshott said that the 'myth of our civilization' depicted by Hobbes 'recalls man to his littleness, his imperfection, his mortality, while at the same time recognizing his importance to himself' and thus that Hobbes conveyed the same kind of idea as 'the literature of Existentialism is doing today with an exaggerated display of emotion and a false suggestion of novelty'.[17]

The rule of law holds out the promise of deliverance from the natural state where each rules himself but is at the same time subject, or at least potentially subject, to the arbitrary rule of others so that the natural state is one of absolute liberty that is worthless because of the threat of conflict such liberty engenders. However, deliverance might not seem to amount to much. It might be to a civil state which, on a description that Hobbes appears to revel in at times, substitutes a condition in which one is subject to the arbitrary rule of all others – the war of one against all – for a condition in which all are subject to the arbitrary rule of one person – the sovereign. And while subjection to the 'lusts, and other irregular passions' of a person who has 'unlimited power' might seem 'obnoxious', Hobbes suggests that such subjection is always better than the 'dissolute condition of masterlesse men', the condition of the state of nature.[18]

But, as Oakeshott helps us to see, civil society is not only a state where all have security but also one where each enjoys liberty under an order of public laws. This is the achievement of the rule of law and the concrete manifestation of the civilizational dream. Its description requires a move from the register of art to that of philosophy and thus to a register of rational argument, but not to a particular form of rational argument, one which directly subordinates all maxims of action to one end. As Oakeshott said in 'The Rule of Law', the character of a state in terms of the rule of law was for those who tried to articulate it in the seventeenth century 'something less than the promise of the fulfilment of the dream of being, at last, ruled by incontestable "justice", and something more than the mere extrapolation of a current tendency'.[19]

[16] Oakeshott, '*Leviathan* – A Myth', 153. [17] Ibid., 154.
[18] Thomas Hobbes, *Leviathan* (Cambridge University Press, 1997), ed. Richard Tuck, 128.
[19] Oakeshott, 'The Rule of Law', 169.

Oakeshott, or so I shall argue, puts in place the basis of an account of legality in which Hobbes effects a radical break with the past in conceiving of the principles of natural law as entirely secularized, formal principles that are constitutive of a form of civil association in which sovereignty inheres in an artificial, that is, legally constituted, person. Natural law is reconceived as principles of legality that make intelligible to the members of a political society the claim that they are under a prior obligation to obey the laws made by a body or person the authenticity of which can be checked formally. This person or body need not be a parliament because what matters from the legal perspective is not the political constitution of the body but that it is legally constituted. The innovation adds that there is more to authenticity than validity – there are also the formal attributes of legality or *jus*.

The puzzle: but authority and not truth makes law

Carl Schmitt considered Hobbes to be the central figure in the civilizational story of the West and thought that the most significant sentence in Hobbes' work that explained this place was from the Latin version of *Leviathan*: '*Sed Authoritas non Veritas facit Legem*'.[20] Oakeshott had the same view of Hobbes and also regarded the claim that authority and not truth makes law as the animating idea in the establishment of the modern state. However, unlike Schmitt, Oakeshott did not think that the idea that authority makes law reduces law to the commands of the powerful.

In order to understand Oakeshott's argument, we need to notice that the idea that authority makes law might seem ambiguous between what appear to be two rather different claims. The first is that law is an artefact produced by an authority in the sense that if we want to know what the law of a jurisdiction is, we should find out what its official procedures are for making law; we will then know that all that is produced in accordance with those procedures is the law of that jurisdiction. The second is that whatever counts as law in a jurisdiction has authority in the sense of making a justified or legitimate demand on those subject to it.

[20] See, e.g., Carl Schmitt, *Political Theology: Four Chapters on the Concept of Sovereignty* (Cambridge, MA: MIT Press, 1988), trans. George Schwab, 33–5. This spelling of *auctoritas* is given in Thomas Hobbes, *Leviathan, Volume 2 of the Clarendon Edition, The English and Latin Texts* (Oxford, UK: Clarendon Press, 2012), ed. Noel Malcolm, 431.

But this ambiguity arises mainly because of the hold of legal positivism on our thought with two consequences. Firstly, we tend to assume that political and legal philosophy are distinct endeavours. Secondly, we tend to adopt John Austin's slogan, 'The existence of law is one thing; its merit or demerit another',[21] the view that legal duty and moral duty coincide only contingently or, in more traditional terms, that *de facto* legal authority does not imply *de jure* authority.

Hobbes did not see any ambiguity because he took political and legal philosophy to be one continuous endeavour to explain why law made by an authority in the first sense has authority in the second sense. In other words, *lex* is always *justa*, which is an affirmation, not a denial, of the natural-law slogan, *lex injusta non est lex*,[22] for if law is always just, there can be no such thing as an unjust law, precisely the standard interpretation of Hobbes, despite his many assertions that the sovereign can act inequitably.[23] The question is what the standards for justice are.

Oakeshott had grappled with just this issue when he sought to trace the relationship between *jus*, *lex* and *auctoritas* in the third of his lectures on Roman political thought. There, he argued that *lex*, a statute made in accordance with a 'known process', was the means the Romans discovered for emancipating themselves 'from the rule of ancient custom'.[24] They thus confined their reflection about law to the processes for making law with the exception of one 'speculative idea' taken from the Greeks, who set themselves the task of understanding the relationship between 'law' and 'justice' or the law of nature. The puzzle for them was how law could be legitimate, because made in the proper way, and yet unjust.

To solve this puzzle, the Romans saw the need to appeal to a law not made by men, which then required appeal to a law 'embedded in the operation of the universe' or made by 'a providential god'. But Oakeshott also claims that the Romans 'clung to the idea of legality' because 'they

[21] Quoted in H. L. A. Hart, 'Positivism and the Separation of Law and Morals', *Harvard Law Review*, 71 (1958), 591, 596.

[22] As it happens, at the point in *Leviathan* where Hobbes makes this striking claim, he is not strictly speaking concerned with the issues set out in the text to this note but with denying any claim by the writers of books of 'Moral Philosophy' to be a source of law's authority; in the English version: 'The Authority of writers, without the Authority of the Commonwealth, maketh not their opinions Law, be they never so true' (Hobbes, *Leviathan*, Chapter 26, 191).

[23] For example, ibid., Chapter 26, 192–3.

[24] Oakeshott, *Lectures in the History of Political Thought*, 244.

could think of *no* other way of criticizing the justice of current legal rules than by measuring them against other and higher legal rules, the rules of the laws of nature'.[25] He adds that it was in 'virtue of the high value the Romans placed upon legality . . . that the Roman *civitas* became and was what may be called a civil association. That is, a set of private persons joined in the recognition of a law to which they, all alike, owed obedience.'[26] This idea was, in turn, connected with the ideas of *auctoritas*, or authority, and *libertas*, or 'freedom', in that the three ideas come together since the Romans knew 'themselves to be joined in the common recognition of the authority of a law'.[27]

But quite how this common recognition gave rise to liberty, other than as a contrast with slavery or as a reference to the fact that Rome was founded in a 'free act', is not clear from Oakeshott's account, nor what role the law of nature/legality could play in all this.[28] Moreover, there is no answer forthcoming in his three last lectures, on authority and obligation, as these lectures – a tour of modern European thought on this topic – reveal the inadequacies of the various proposed solutions, though Oakeshott clearly remains intrigued by the influence of the idea in European thought that it is the procedural legitimacy of statutes that endows them with authority/legitimacy.[29]

This way of approaching the problem makes the legitimacy or authority of law a matter of compliance with procedures, whereas the issue of the justice of the enacted law or *lex* will depend on its correspondence, not with procedures, but with higher legal rules or *jus*. But, if the source of *jus* is divine, what we get is a set of moral rules that are imposed from above, a kind of natural law that is both vertical and substantive, and in a disenchanted or secular world, secular legitimacy is pitted against the versions of substantive natural law that are in contest with each other. The myth of secularism displaces the myth of a providential deity, but then, as Schmitt argued, the myth might find itself prey to a contest of conflicting myths: an anarchic condition of warring social groups each with its own claim to moral authenticity and that share only their denial that laws are legitimate merely because they have been enacted in accordance with recognized procedures.[30]

[25] Ibid., 244–5 (his emphasis). [26] Ibid., 246. [27] Ibid., 251. [28] Ibid., 247–51.

[29] Ibid., 426–68, and see 429, 455, and 466 for references to procedural legitimacy.

[30] Carl Schmitt, *The Leviathan in the State Theory of Thomas Hobbes: Meaning and Failure of a Political Symbol* (Westport, CT: Greenwood Press, 1996), trans. George Schwab and Erna Hilfstein.

Schmitt sets out a two-pronged critique of what we can think of as liberal legalism, whose twentieth-century representative he takes to be Hans Kelsen. First, liberal legalism implodes because the idea of standards of justice internal to legality is incoherent, with the result that justice either gets wholly externalized, and thus becomes the property of a plurality of competing ideologies, or remains wholly internal, in which case it is reduced to being a property of validity. Indeed, Schmitt seems to suppose that the incoherence arises because liberalism has to embrace both options: because justice is reduced to being a property of validity, law becomes seen as a mere instrument of power, with the result that competing interest groups will compete to make the law the instrument of their particular conception of justice.[31] Secondly, these problems arise out of liberalism's failed attempt at myth making.

Oakeshott had a different approach, one which seeks to solve the puzzle which he found in his 'Lectures on Roman Law', in which he gestured at an idea of higher law that is not vertical in nature and higher only in the sense that it is not man-made. In so doing, he indicated a possibility that is different from both procedural legitimacy and compliance with a substantive morality, that is, formality, an attribute of law that comes about because to be law, artefacts must be more than validly produced; they also must be legal.

The full exposition of this idea comes in 'The Rule of Law'. There, Oakeshott says of association in terms of the rule of law that it, firstly, 'postulates a distinction between *jus* and the procedural considerations in respect of which to determine the authenticity of a law. Secondly, it recognizes the formal principles of a legal order which may be said to be themselves principles of "justice"'.[32] He seems thus to put in place two kinds of formality – on the one hand, the formal procedural criteria of the rule of law that pertain to the recognition of valid law and, on the other, the formal attributes of the rule of law that pertain to its *jus*.

However, his most explicit description of legality criteria is in his discussion of 'The Civil Condition' in *On Human Conduct* in the part where he sets out what the idea of the authority of the civil condition or *respublica* 'categorially excludes'.[33] Firstly, authority cannot be attributed to the *respublica* on account of what it achieves, for example, peace and order, nor on the basis of common conformity, for both peace and order

[31] See, e.g., Carl Schmitt, *Constitutional Theory* (Durham, NC: Duke University Press, 2008), ed. Jeffrey Seitzer.

[32] Oakeshott, 'The Rule of Law', 151.

[33] Oakeshott, *On Human Conduct*, 152.

and common conformity are made possible by recognition of its authority; hence any such attribution would be viciously circular.[34] Second, the authority of *respublica* does not lie in social purpose, approved moral ideals, a common good or general interest, or a justice 'other than that which is inherent in *respublica*'. Thus, Oakeshott concluded that the attribution of authority is nothing more than the 'acknowledgement of *respublica* as a system of moral (not instrumental) rules'.[35]

However, in a note, Oakeshott remarks, in a clear, albeit unreferenced allusion to American legal theorist Lon L Fuller,[36] that included in that which is 'inherent in *respublica*' is

> of course, not merely *lex* justified (i.e., validated) in terms of *lex* but the other attributes intrinsic to association in terms of non-prudential rules, such as: the quality of legal subjects; rules not arbitrary, secret, retroactive or awards to interests; the independence of judicial proceedings (i.e., all claimants or prosecutors, like defendants, are litigants); no so-called 'public' or 'quasi-public' enterprise or corporation exempt from common liability for wrong; no offence without specific prescription; no penalty without specific offence; no disability or refusal of recognition without established inadequacy of subscription; no outlawry, etc., etc.: in short, all that may be called the 'inner morality' of a legal system.[37]

In other words, for the rules to be acknowledged as such, that is, as a system of *moral* or *non-instrumental* rules, these rules must have attributes that go beyond the Kelsenian idea that rules are legal because they are the valid products of recognized procedures; they must also display these (and perhaps other) attributes.

This note foreshadows the radical innovation in Oakeshott's account of civil authority, for until this point in the analysis it had seemed the case that it is necessary and sufficient for a rule to have authority that it is the valid product of a recognized procedure. The procedure itself has to be the reason for our acknowledgement, not any benefits – for example, peace – that might be secured as a result of the acknowledgement. But, from the note, it seems to be the case that if the procedures produced a

[34] Ibid. [35] Ibid., 153.

[36] See Lon L. Fuller, *The Morality of Law*, rev. edn. (New Haven, CT: Yale University Press, 1969).

[37] Oaheshott, *On Human Conduct*, note 1, 153. Oakeshott adds to this note that there is 'no place in civil association for so-called "distributive justice"; that is the distribution of desirable substantive goods'. Not only can *lex* not be a 'rule of distribution of this sort', but 'civil rules have nothing to distribute'. I will come back to this qualification in the text that follows.

rule that affronted the 'inner morality' of a 'legal system', the rule would not be fit for acknowledgement as authoritative unless Oakeshott at this point saw a difference between the claim that the attributes are 'inherent in *respublica*' and the claim that they are 'inherent in *lex*'. This would amount to the difference between, on the one hand, a law that was perfectly legal because it had been validly produced but unjust from the perspective of the morality of civil association and, on the other, a law that failed to be law despite its compliance with criteria of validity because it lacked the attributes of legality. The latter option states that the fact that a rule complies with criteria of validity makes the rule a candidate to be recognized as authoritative but points out that there are further criteria – the criteria of legality – that have to be met. It would follow that a secret rule, or a law that was immunized against judicial review, 'etc., etc.' would not count as an authoritative rule, which is to say as a valid rule of the legal system.

Of particular significance, I think, are the first and last items on the list: 'the quality of legal subjects' and 'no outlawry', and when Oakeshott gives a shorter version of the list in 'The Rule of Law', these two items figure prominently on it as the last two items:

> rules not secret or retrospective, no obligations save those imposed by law, all associates equally and without exception subject to the obligations imposed by law, no outlawry, and so on.[38]

The 'quality' of the legal subject, which I take to be a consideration described only a little more elaborately in 'all associates equally and without exception subject to the obligations imposed by law', is clearly linked to his claim of the repugnance of outlawry to the inner morality of law, that is, to the practice of declaring a fugitive from justice to be beyond the law so that the fugitive was stripped of legal status – the status of a *persona*.[39]

A *persona* for Oakeshott is, firstly, a person abstractly or formally conceived as 'related to others in terms of distinct and exclusive conditions' and, secondly, as having the character common to relationships

[38] Ibid., 152–3.

[39] See H. Erle Richards, 'Is Outlawry Obsolete?', *Law Quarterly Review*, 18 (1902), 207, and for recent treatments, Larry May, 'Magna Carta: The Interstices of Procedure, and Guatanamo', *Case Western Reserve Journal of International Law*, 42 (2009), 91, and Jane Y. Chong, 'Targeting the Twenty-First-Century Outlaw', *Yale Law Journal*, 122 (2012), 724. As all three essays show, outlawry was tamed by judges who subjected it to procedural constraints, thus protecting liberty.

between 'intelligent agents' – 'what they have seen fit to require of themselves and one another'.[40] His inquiry is thus into the question, 'What is the character of the mode of relationship whose conditions are man-made laws?'[41] And as I will now show, despite some hesitation, Oakeshott, in turning in 'The Rule of Law' to Hobbes for the radical innovation highlighted by Friedman, adopts the claim that the attributes are inherent in *lex*. This makes questions about law's authority or authenticity still a formal matter, but compliance with criteria of validity no longer seems sufficient for authority because there also has to be compliance with legality.

Oakeshott frames the question this essay is seeking to answer as 'how human beings might acquire the condition of being *obligated* to observe the prescriptions of an *humanus legislator*'.[42] He takes Hobbes to be one of the few who not only addressed exactly this question but also saw that it had to be addressed in recognition of a prior relationship of obligation between sovereign and subject.[43] And he finds most significant in Hobbes his insistence 'that the rule of law stands for a moral (not a prudential) relationship', which entails in part that it does not determine actions but '"the measure of the good and evil of actions"',[44] a claim which I will come back to later. Hobbes, that is, does not regard the sovereign (as Bentham and Austin were to) as causing subjects to act in a certain way by issuing commands to which sanctions attach but as putting in place public standards which subjects are obliged to take into account when choosing how to act.

In his discussion of Hobbes, Oakeshott suggests that Hobbes managed to provide an 'imperfect' but 'less shaky' formulation of the rule of law than is to be found in the writings later jurists – 'a state ruled by *lex*, the authority of which lies in its *jus*'. For Hobbes, a state is an association 'ruled exclusively by law'. 'Such a state . . . is composed of *personae* related solely in terms of their obligation to observe in all their self-chosen conduct certain non-instrumental (that is, moral or procedural) conditions prescribed by a sovereign legislative office expressly authorized to deliberate, make and issue such prescriptions which constitute the *lex* of the association.'[45] It follows, says Oakeshott, that

> Authentic *lex* cannot be *injus*. This does not mean that the legislative office is magically insulated from making 'unjust' law. It means that this

[40] Oakeshott, 'The Rule of Law', 130–1. [41] Ibid., 131. [42] Ibid., 162.
[43] Ibid., 163. [44] Ibid. [45] Ibid., 171.

> office is designed and authorized to make genuine law, that it is protected against indulging in any other activity and that in a state ruled by law the only 'justice' is that which is inherent in *lex*.[46]

Oakeshott, however, seems unsure what to make of this claim. First, even its most abstract institutional implications are unclear, for example, what to make of the fact that the legislative office is both not 'insulated' from making 'unjust' law and yet 'protected' from doing so. For example, if we were to suppose that it is to the judiciary that we should look for such protection, Oakeshott seems quickly to squash that thought in insisting that *jus* 'has no room for ... either a so-called Bill of Rights (that is, alleged unconditional principles of *jus* masquerading as themselves law), or an independent office and apparatus charged with considering the *jus* of a law and authorized to declare a law to be inauthentic if it were found to be "unjust"'.[47] His understanding of the separation of powers is as strictly formal as the rest of his legal theory. Legislators deliberate the desirability of changes to the law. But the judge's 'task is to relate a general statement of conditional obligation to an occurrence in terms of what *distinguishes* it from other occurrences. Deliberation, here, is an exercise in retrospective casuistry.'[48]

Secondly, and more generally, Oakeshott seems unsure of the status of the claim. He said that there 'are some considerations that are often characterized as *jus* but which are inherent in the notion, not of a just law, but of law itself' and that these amount to conditions that 'distinguish a legal order and in default of which whatever purports to be a legal order is not what it purports to be'.[49] 'It is only', he added, 'in respect of these considerations and their like that it may perhaps be said that *lex injusta non est lex*.'[50] He also said, again perplexingly, that the 'only "justice" the rule of law can accommodate is faithfulness to the formal principles inherent in the character of *lex*: non-instrumentality, indifference to persons, and interests, the exclusion of *privelege* and outlawry, and so on'.[51]

These reflections leave intact the puzzle of the relationship between *lex* and *jus*. One could conclude from them that there is no moral quality to *lex* that comes from its conformity with certain formal attributes – from the fact that law to be such has to be legal.

46 Ibid. 47 Ibid., 156.

48 Ibid., 156–7 (his emphasis). In note 6 on 157, he speaks of the 'Dworkinesque judge' who 'usurps the office of legislator'.

49 Ibid., 152. 50 Ibid., 153. 51 Ibid., 173.

However, Oakeshott seems to envisage three possibilities about the morality of the rule of law: (1) the *jus* inherent to *lex* (the inner morality), (2) the substance inherent in the form (i.e., peace), and (3) the character of the rules relating civil authority and civil obligation.

The first is that when we have the rule of law, a kind of moral deliberation is made possible about *jus* in that the agents may consider 'the propriety of the conditions prescribed in a particular law'[52]: 'a form of moral discourse not concerned generally with right and wrong in human conduct, but focussed narrowly upon the kind of conditional obligations a law may impose'.[53] It is Hobbes' failure to appreciate this aspect of the rule of law that is, according to Oakeshott, the major problem in his account of the state as an association in terms of the rule of law.[54] Hobbes is right not to identify *jus* with 'a supposedly universal inherently just Natural Law or a set of fundamental Values', for example, a Bill of Rights, because not only does the rule of law have no need of such notions, but 'when invoked as the conditions of the obligation to observe the conditions prescribed by *lex*, they positively pervert the association: they are the recipe for anarchy.'[55] Oakeshott adds that the '*jus* of *lex* cannot be identified simply with its faithfulness to the formal character of law' since to 'deliberate the *jus* of *lex* is to invoke a particular kind of moral consideration',[56] which he elaborates by saying that 'the prescriptions of the law should not conflict with a prevailing educated moral sensibility', one that is capable of distinguishing between conditions of the kind that should be imposed by law, that is, 'justice' in contrast with 'virtue' and 'good conduct'.[57] Hence, it appears that *jus* of the conditions is a

> combination of their absolute faithfulness to the formal character of law and to their moral-legal acceptability, itself a reflection of the moral-legal self-understanding of the associates which (even when it is distinguished from whatever moral idiocies there may be about) cannot be expected to be without ambiguity or internal tension – a moral imagination more stable in its style of deliberation than in its conclusions.[58]

The second possibility is the relationship between the rule of law and values such as freedom and peace. In regard to freedom, Oakeshott notes that Hobbes identifies a category of 'civil rights' or 'liberties'. But these, Oakeshott says, 'turn out not to signify conduct and considerations which *lex* should, in justice, recognize and protect; they represent

[52] Ibid., 153. [53] Ibid., 156. [54] Ibid., 173. [55] Ibid. [56] Ibid. [57] Ibid., 174.
[58] Ibid.

conduct in respect of which *lex* has not in fact prescribed conditions: the circumstantial silence of the law which may at any time properly be broken.'[59] And he insists that the virtue of the rule of law is 'not to promote a certain kind of "freedom"'. Rather, it

> denotes a certain kind of 'freedom' which excludes only the freedom to choose one's obligations. But this 'freedom' does not follow as a consequence of this mode of association; it is inherent in its character.[60]

And the same, he says, is true of "peace" and "order". 'A certain kind of "peace" and "order" may, perhaps be said to characterize this mode of association, but not as consequences.'[61]

Thirdly, the particular rules are themselves moral in kind because they impose obligations on conduct that apply regardless of the particular ends that the *personae* seek. They are not, however, merely moral because the obligations are authenticated through a public procedure:

> [T]he distinctive quality of civil freedom, the recognition given in *civitas* to moral agency, springs from civil association being rule and relationship in terms of authority and obligation ... It is relationship in terms of a system of *lex* which prescribes, not satisfactions to be sought or actions to be performed, but moral conditions to be subscribed to in seeking self-chosen satisfactions and in performing self-chosen actions.[62]

In my view, all three possibilities are right, but the relationship between them has to be appreciated in order to see why *lex* might be thought necessarily to have a moral quality to it, and here, both Hobbes and F. A. Hayek are helpful.

Hobbes and Hayek on the quality of civil liberty

There are two places where, as I interpret *Leviathan*, Hobbes held views rather different from those Oakeshott attributed to him, and these views are, as I will argue, pertinent to an elaboration of the relationship that Oakeshott sought to disinter between *lex* and *jus*. The first has to do with Oakeshott's claim that Hobbes failed to appreciate that the rule of law makes possible a certain kind of moral deliberation, and the second is that civil liberty is for Hobbes no more than the space where the individual has freedom to act because the law is silent as to his or her obligations.

[59] Ibid., 171–2. [60] Ibid. [61] Ibid. [62] Oakeshott, *On Human Conduct*, 157–8.

It is true that Hobbes discourages moral deliberation of a certain sort. He insists that it would be irrational for the subject to claim that a law is unjust since he argues that the subjects are the authors of the sovereign's laws, and one cannot be unjust to oneself. In addition, he is generally allergic to public deliberation about justice since subjects should take justice to be no more than compliance with the law, and in any case, they are ultimately the authors of the law since they authorize the sovereign to make it, and one cannot be unjust to oneself. But Hobbes clearly sees that the rule of law require a kind of constrained moral deliberation – the deliberation by subordinate judges involved in interpreting enacted law. Such deliberation is moral because Hobbes regards judges as under a duty to interpret the law in the light of their understandings of the laws of nature, which he regards as the 'true and onely Moral Philosophy. For Morall Philosophy is nothing else but the Science of what is *Good*, and *Evill*, in the conversation and Society of man-kind.'[63]

My claim here is not that Hobbes regarded judges as entitled to invalidate a law that seems to conflict with one or more of the laws of nature, only that judges are obliged to interpret any enacted law as if the sovereign intended it to comply with natural law and, further, that Hobbes clearly regards a law that cannot be so interpreted as legally as well as morally problematic.[64] Entailed in this understanding of adjudication is that a subject is entitled to challenge an enacted law on the basis that its 'literal' interpretation does not comply with natural law in the hope that a judge will find that there is a way to interpret the law so that its meaning is more consistent with the laws of nature. The subject must take the judge's interpretation as definitive, though it has no force beyond the parties to the matter, as Hobbes is firmly opposed to any doctrine of precedent.[65] But the point remains that the laws of nature condition the content of the subject's obligations in so far as the text of the enacted law relevant to the matter permits and until such point as the sovereign overrules his subordinate judge.

[63] Hobbes, *Leviathan*, 110.

[64] Though, as I have pointed out, Hobbes does think that laws that are perfectly valid are void when they purport to grant away any of the essential rights of sovereignty; see David Dyzenhaus, 'Hobbes on the Authority of Law' in David Dyzenhaus and Thomas Poole (eds.), *Hobbes and the Law* (Cambridge University Press, 2012), 186, 205–6, referring to the right of 'judicature'; Hobbes, *Leviathan*, 125.

[65] Hobbes, *Leviathan*, 193–4.

The morality at stake is internal to *lex* – 'The Law of Nature, and the Civill Law, contain each other, and are of equall extent.'[66] And deliberation about it is not about morality at large. It is about how best to understand the conditions of interaction that the sovereign has prescribed in his public laws in terms that live up to the assumption that judges must adopt: that all his law is intended to serve the interests of subjects viewed abstractly, as *personae* equal before the law.

However, those interests are not confined to abstract equality. They include liberty, the second issue where Oakeshott's account of Hobbes in 'The Rule of Law' could do with some refinement in order to appreciate that the kind of liberty that is constituted by a regime of public laws or *publica lex* is akin to the kind of liberty defended by contemporary republicans in terms of an ideal of freedom as non-domination.[67]

Hobbes begins Chapter 21 of *Leviathan,* 'Of the Liberty of Subjects', by saying that freedom is the 'absence of . . . external Impediments of motion'. He goes on to define a free man as 'he, that in those things, which by his strength and wit he is able to do, is not hindered to doe what he has a will to do'.[68] And it seems from this chapter, and from elsewhere in *Leviathan*, that the point of entering the civil condition is to establish a sovereign who will enact laws that restrain the radical liberty of the state of nature so that individuals can interact on terms set by the sovereign rather than by other individuals. Hence, the liberty an individual has in civil society is the liberty that one has through the 'silence' of the law 'to act according to his own discretion',[69] the same kind of liberty one had in the state of nature, but now restricted by the law so that individuals can safely act on their desires within the restricted space.

[66] Ibid., 185.

[67] The claim that Hobbes set out a view of freedom as non-domination will strike contemporary republicans as absurd, since they regard *Leviathan* as a polemic against the republicans of his day. See Philip Pettit, 'Liberty and Leviathan', *Politics, Philosophy, and Economics*, 4 (2005), 131; Quentin Skinner, *Hobbes and Republican Liberty* (Cambridge University Press, 2008). For an account of Oakeshott as committed to this kind of republican ideal, see David Boucher, 'Oakeshott, Freedom and Republicanism', *British Journal of Politics and International Relations*, 7 (2005), 81, and for an account of Hobbes in similar terms, see Lars Vinx, 'Hobbes on Civic Liberty and the Rule of Law' in Dyzenhaus and Poole, *Hobbes and the Law,* 145.

[68] Hobbes, *Leviathan*, 146 (emphasis removed from the definition).

[69] Ibid., 152. Hobbes continues: 'As for the other Lyberties, they depend on the Silence of the Law. In cases where the Soveraign has prescribed no rule, there the Subject hath the Liberty to do, or forbeare, according to his own discretion. And therefore such Liberty is in some places more, and in some lesse; and in some times more, in other times lesse, according as they that have the Soveraignty shall think most convenient.'

This sketch is mistaken in one fundamental respect and also does not capture the full complexity of Hobbes' views on the liberty of the subject.[70] While Hobbes calls the civil law of the sovereign 'Artificiall Chains', he says that they are in 'their own nature but weak', though he adds that they may 'be made to hold, by the danger, though not by the difficulty of breaking them'.[71] The chains are not physical bonds of the sort that can literally restrict liberty but rather obligations that subjects recognize as such because they understand that they are under a prior obligation of obedience to the sovereign. Fear of sanctions for disobedience is not the basis for obedience and cannot restrict liberty since fear is not an external impediment. However, it is still important that those who do not understand their obligation to the sovereign are motivated by fear of sanctions so that those who do understand have the security that permits them to follow the law without making themselves prey to others.

Notice that the idea of being able to act at one's discretion does share something with the liberty one has in the state of nature since it is the liberty to act on the basis of one's desires. But while natural liberty is constrained only by physical obstacles and thus not by legal obligations, this kind of liberty is constituted rather than constrained by legal obligations, since legal obligations cannot constrain in the literal way that Hobbes conceives of external impediments to individual motion triggered by desire. Moreover, it is a liberty I have even when there are such external impediments, for even if I am physically obstructed from doing something that I desire to do and that the law permits me to do through its silence, that obstruction does not take away the permission but merely prevents me from exercising it. I still have the liberty, even though I cannot execute my desire to use it. It would thus be a mistake to think of civil liberty as a residue of natural liberty. Rather, it is the freedom of the subject to act on his or her own desires through subscribing to the conditions set out by the law.

[70] Note that this view cannot also properly account for what Hobbes calls the 'true Liberty of a Subject', that is, those things 'which though commanded by the Soveraign, he may nevertheless, without Injustice, refuse to do' and which consists in the freedom of the subject to resist the commands of the sovereign when these threaten his survival or require him to do something dishonourable that is unnecessary to the state's end; ibid., 150. In my view, this kind of situation is a limit situation, in that it indicates a point where the individual is no longer in a reciprocal sovereign-subject relationship but in a power relationship or, better, a stand-off of the sort found between individuals in the state of nature.

[71] Ibid., 147.

Civil liberty thus has two aspects to it – what we can think of as a negative aspect, the freedom to do as we desire, and a positive aspect, the conditions that make it possible for us to do as we desire. On this view, the criminal law is not best understood as commands to subjects backed by threats but as setting out the conditions to which subjects have to subscribe in order to interact on peaceful terms with each other. Notice also that the liberty to enter into contracts and the liberty to own property not only permit the exercise of a discretion but also create the very possibility of exercising a special kind of discretion, one which permits one to attach legal consequences to one's actions.[72]

Now the first aspect could be cast as a kind of negative freedom and the second as a kind of positive freedom. This would be a little misleading since in both cases there is a positive element in that the law makes action possible and a negative element in that action is left to the subject's discretion. Hence, civil liberty, or freedom under an order of public laws, makes possible liberties that require legal constitution even if the substantive ends for which they are used are at the discretion of the subjects. And it is, in my view, this kind of non-instrumental law, one that makes possible civil interaction between subjects, that Hobbes has in mind when he offers the following account of the function of law in civil society:

> For the use of Lawes, (which are but Rules Authorised) is not to bind the People from all Voluntary actions; but to direct and keep them in such a motion, as not to hurt themselves by their own impetuous desires, rashnesse, or indiscretion; as Hedges are set, not to stop Travellers, but to keep them in the way.[73]

If I am right that Hobbes sees law as constitutive of civil liberty, it might appear difficult to make sense of his remarks to the effect that law is a restraint, notably, as he says in Chapter 26 of *Leviathan*, a

> Restraint ... without the which there cannot possibly be any Peace. And Law was brought into the world for nothing else, but to limit the natural liberty of particular men, in such manner, as they might not be hurt, but assist one another, and joyn together against a common Enemy.[74]

[72] See Hobbes, *Leviathan*, 148: 'The Liberty of a Subject, lyeth therefore only in those things, which in regulating their actions, the Soveraign hath prætermitted: such as is the Liberty to buy, and sell, and otherwise contract with one another; to choose their own aboad, their own diet, their own trade of life, and institute their children as they themselves think fit; & the like.'

[73] Ibid., 239–40. [74] Ibid., 185.

However, Hobbes also says in Chapter 21 that it is absurd to clamour for liberty from the law if it is natural liberty that men have in mind. His argument on this point is in part that to clamour for such liberty – for exemption from the law – is to demand a return to the state of nature in which 'all other men may be masters of their lives'.[75] It is this thought that lies behind the claim that if one lives under an order of public laws, whether made by an absolute monarch or democratic assembly, 'the Freedome is still the same'.[76] But Hobbes' argument is not only about the precariousness of life in the state of nature – the 'dissolute condition of masterlesse men';[77] it is also about what we give up in not having a sovereign who rules us through public laws. That is, going beyond the security provided by the sword of the sovereign, we give up on the institution by law of civil liberty, which makes it possible to act on our desires and also to attach legal consequences to some of them in ways that are important to us as creatures who wish so to act.

For Hobbes, then, the point of individuals consenting to live under the authority of an all-powerful sovereign is to move from the natural condition in which the only freedom they can enjoy is a worthless pre-political freedom to the civil condition in which they enjoy civil liberty. However, this point requires not only that the sovereign have a monopoly on political power but also that when he exercises that power, he does so through law, by putting in place an order of public laws. With such an order in place, subjects will find that the law does more than leave to them a secure space in which to act on their desires – to exercise discretionary liberty. The law also constitutes the spaces of civil liberty, which are unavailable in the absence of law and which are put in individuals' discretion, thus permitting civil interaction.

Civil liberty, then, does not consist in a freedom from physical obstacles because the bonds of the law are not such obstacles. Rather, the bonds of the law create civil liberty, and as long as that is what the laws do, they will create the same quality of liberty, even though the space they make for the exercise of discretion by subjects will vary greatly across both time and area. The quality of civil liberty is thus more important for Hobbes than the quantity, and that a universal quality is secured, even though quantity will vary according to sovereign will, is important to understanding why for Hobbes sovereign rule is not arbitrary in the way his republican critics allege, despite the fact that their charge against him

[75] Ibid., 147. [76] Ibid., 149. [77] Ibid., 128.

is accurate that he wishes to argue that it is absurd to demand freedom from the law, whatever its political provenance, because freedom, considered qualitatively, is the same in any civil condition.[78]

Republicans thus fail to appreciate that Hobbes' argument turns on an account of legal order, or of a political society under the rule of law, in which the fact of the rule of law secures liberty for those subject to it. Indeed, Hobbes' argument is not even, in my view, best understood, as contemporary republicans think, as directed against their position. Rather, it is directed against a version of anarchism that claims that 'whatsoever a man does, against his Conscience is Sinne', from which it would follow, according to Hobbes, that no one would 'dare to obey the Soveraign Power, farther than it shall seem good in his own eyes'.[79] If anything, his argument points to a tension in the republican position in so far as republicans seem unable to decide between the view that freedom is constituted by law and this version of anarchism.

Hayek set out a similar conception of freedom almost exactly four centuries later in *The Constitution of Liberty*, though his references to Hobbes in this work consistently put Hobbes on the wrong side of the argument.[80] In his best-known essay on the rule of law – 'Planning and the Rule of Law' – in his polemic against collectivism, *The Road to Serfdom*,[81] Hayek presented a view of the virtue of the rule of law that it provided determinate points for individuals which permitted them to make plans for their own lives, confident that the state would not disrupt their plans. This view ruled out extensive redistributive efforts by the welfare state on an epistemic rather than a normative ground. Hayek's objection was based not on the inherent wrongness of taxation but on the claim that any large-scale efforts at redistribution required the establishment of an extensive administrative state, which made individual planning difficult since such plans would be subject to unpredictable exercises of discretion by administrative officials. In other words, the state had to avoid large-scale planning and stick to a regime of general laws in order to enable the epistemic conditions for successful individual planning. It was this idea which led Oakeshott to comment that a 'plan to resist all

[78] I will not deal here with those places in Hobbes' works where he seems to give the sovereign a prerogative power to act without legal authorization or even against the law. For discussion, see Thomas Poole, 'Hobbes on Law and Prerogative' in Dyzenhaus and Poole, *Hobbes and the Law*, 68.

[79] Hobbes, *Leviathan*, 223.

[80] For example, F. A. Hayek, *The Constitution of Liberty* (London: Routledge, 1990), 181.

[81] F. A. Hayek, *The Road to Serfdom* (University of Chicago Press, 1994).

planning may be better than its opposite, but it belong to the same style of [rationalist] politics'.[82]

Some ten years later, though, Hayek resorted, like Oakeshott, to a more normative account of the rule of law, finding his inspiration in Roman political and legal thought for his conception of the law of liberty. Hayek now claimed Cicero as the 'main authority for modern liberalism' because he had provided 'many of the most effective formulations of freedom under law', in particular, the idea 'that there is no conflict between law and freedom and that freedom is dependent upon certain attributes of the law, its generality and certainty, and the restrictions it places on the discretion of authority'.[83] Moreover, Hayek relied on exactly the contrast between slavery and freedom so central to Roman and republican thought. His *The Constitution of Liberty* is presented as an exercise in the recovery of the 'original meaning' of freedom, which he takes to be summed up in the 'time-honored phrase' – 'independence of the arbitrary will of another'.[84] Finally, Hayek is clear that while there is an important question about 'how many courses of action are open to a person', this is a 'different question' from the one that should be the primary focus of political and legal philosophy. This is the question of

> how far in acting he can follow his own plans and intentions, to what extent the pattern of his conduct is of his own design, directed towards ends for which he has been persistently striving rather than towards necessities created by others in order to make him do what they want. Whether he is free or not does not depend on the range of choice but on whether he can expect to shape his course of action in accordance with his present intentions, or whether somebody else has power so to manipulate the conditions as to make him act according to that person's will rather than his own.[85]

For Hayek, then, the kind of liberty that one has under an order of public laws is not freedom from the law because it is freedom constituted by the law, and its value depends, as I argued is the case for Hobbes, not on its extent or quantity but on its quality.

In this same book, Hayek suggests that there is much to be learnt from Schmitt, especially from his *Constitutional Theory*, in regard to the fact that 'the law of liberty must possess certain attributes.'[86] Hayek thus

[82] See Michael Oakeshott, 'Rationalism in Politics' in Oakeshott, *Rationalism in Politics and Other Essays* (Indianapolis, IN: Liberty Fund, 1991), 26.

[83] Hayek, *The Constitution of Liberty*, 166–7. [84] Ibid., 12. [85] Ibid., 13.

[86] Ibid., 205, and note 1, 484–6, at 485.

seems to be suggesting that Schmitt helps us to appreciate that the rule of law should not be confused with the requirement of 'mere legality in all government action' since that confusion leads to the claim that a government acts under the rule of law simply because a law has given it 'unlimited power to do as it pleased'. The rule of law is more than mere legality and 'more than constitutionalism': 'it requires that all law conform to certain principles.'[87]

But even if Schmitt helps us with this appreciation, the point of his help is to get us to see that that we cannot have what we appreciate. It does not suffice in this regard to point out that while liberal legalism did implode in late Weimar, it enjoyed a resurgence after the Second World War, with the manifesto for its resurgence Hayek's *The Road to Serfdom*, and hence to claim that with the collapse of the totalizing myths of Nazism and fascism, and then of communism, Schmitt's challenge has been answered by history. Schmitt's challenge would survive the judgement of history if what we have is a mere myth, one that permits us to dream of the rule of law while in our waking lives we move in a world that Schmitt best describes, save for the fact that it is not in danger of imminent implosion.

Indeed, Schmitt's challenge becomes even sharper when we note that Oakeshott and Hayek regarded democracy with some suspicion, if not hostility, as did Hobbes. In addition, while Hayek regarded considerations of distributive justice as having a restricted place in the civil condition, Oakeshott was prone to lapidary and unsupported assertions that they had no place at all. In *On Human Conduct*, he asserted that such a '"distribution" of substantive benefits or advantages requires a rule of distribution and a distributor in possession of what is to be distributed, but *lex* cannot be a rule of distribution of this sort, and civil rulers have nothing to distribute'.[88] And he repeated this thought in the magnificent peroration to 'The Rule of Law': 'the rule of law bakes no bread, it is unable to distribute loaves and fishes (it has none).'[89]

Finally, since neither Oakeshott nor Hayek, and certainly not Hobbes, thought that judges could legitimately strike down valid laws on the basis that the laws lacked the attributes of *jus*, all three seem to concede that a democratic legislature has the authority to use the form of *lex* to create an administrative state dedicated to redistribution. Such a state might lack the attributes of *lex* on Oakeshott's list from *On Human Conduct* and

[87] Ibid., 205. [88] Oakeshott, *On Human Conduct*, 153, note 1.
[89] Oakeshott, 'The Rule of Law', 178.

thus be an affront to the rule of law, but its laws would still have authority. Still one has to ask why Oakeshott supposed that redistribution must offend against the rule of law if the state could redistribute through rules that are appropriately enacted, public, prospective, clear, applicable to all and so on. And it is to that question which I now turn.

Conclusion

In his essay, 'Oakeshott and Hobbes', Noel Malcolm comments that Oakeshott's attraction to Hobbes is in his thought that Hobbes had an 'account of the nature of a political community as something constituted by a web of mutual understandings and mutual commitments of a particularly open-ended and unconditional kind'. [90] Hence, in 'Oakeshott's eyes, Hobbes was an archetypal non-rationalist in politics because he had a rich understanding of the non-instrumentality of the state'.[91] And Malcolm says that Hobbes was in fact 'non-teleological and anti-teleological and therefore an opponent of one type of "rationalist" thinker, the type that assumes that reason can intuit supreme values or goals, and that the aim of politics is to construct a state and a society that will fulfill them'.[92]

However, as Malcolm also points out, this requires a view of the state as not existing to 'solve problems; it existed, rather, to be the condition of civilized life'.[93] Oakeshott's answer to the question of how such a state differs from standard versions of the neutral liberal state is to be found, Malcolm suggests, in 'the concept of law', that is, in the central idea of 'The Rule of Law', where the argument is that '[o]nly a state where authority remains fully non-instrumental can maintain a full and proper concept of law.'[94] Malcolm says further that Oakeshott's claim that 'the laws of nature are no more than an analytic break-down of the intrinsic character of law . . . the *jus* inherent in genuine law' is his 'most extreme claim about Hobbes'.[95]

Malcolm's point here is that Hobbes derived these laws from the substantive aim of peace, itself driven by the substantive end of self-preservation.[96] He recognizes that this is an end that is 'hardly substantive' as it does not tell individuals what to do once it is secured, but he still regards it as too substantive to fit into Oakeshott's austere non-instrumentalism.[97] Oakeshott was not, however, altogether consistent

[90] Malcolm, 'Oakeshott and Hobbes', 222. [91] Ibid. [92] Ibid., 223. [93] Ibid., 228.
[94] Ibid. [95] Ibid. [96] Ibid. [97] Ibid., 228–9.

here. Recall that he seemed to endorse the Hobbesian idea that the *lex naturalis* is composed of 'maxims of rational conduct', the 'necessary causal conditions of peaceful association'. And this suggests that the rule of law is the instrument of achieving the *telos* of peace and that the principles of natural law are rationally derived means to achieving that end.

In my view, this tension can be dissolved once one sees that it is produced by an implausible distinction. Consider Oakeshott's remark that '*telocracy* does not necessarily mean the absence of law. It means only that what may roughly be called "the rule of law" is recognized to have no independent virtue, but to be valuable only in relation to the pursuit of the chosen end.'[98] This remark is made in the context of a state that finds the rule of law useful for achieving its ends and thus merely instrumental.

However, there is no obvious inconsistency in the thought that there are two aspects to an account of the rule of law, the 'external' justification of why we should want that rule and the 'internal' account of its intrinsic character.[99] Only the external justification can explain why the rule of law has any virtue, though it should be noted that the external and internal are not sealed off from one another. Suppose, as I think is the case for Hobbes, that the external justification is that the rule of law secures a certain kind of peace, the peace that makes it possible for individuals not only to interact with another but also to interact on terms of equality and liberty. One should then expect that those same terms will figure as part of the internal account of the *jus* of *lex*.

In addition, the remark presupposes that a *telocratic* state could govern using the rule of law. However, if the rule of law is in place, those subject to the law will have what is characteristic of the rule of law – civil liberty of the sort that makes it possible for them to regard the law as prescribing the conditions for their self-chosen acts. It does not matter that the state regards the rule of law as a mere instrument because it turns out that governing through the rule of law imposes a discipline on government so that the rule of law is far from merely instrumental.[100] It would then be consistent for a government that recognizes the independent virtue of the rule of law to set out deliberately to achieve through law certain

[98] Oakeshott, *Lectures on the History of Political Thought*, 472.
[99] See John Rawls, 'Two Concepts of Rules' in Rawls, *Collected Papers* (Cambridge, MA: Harvard University Press, 1999), ed. Samuel Freeman, 20.
[100] That is, the point of the allegory of King Rex in Fuller's, *The Morality of Law*, 33–8.

substantive ends, including the ends involved in setting up an extensive welfare state. Tensions will arise, but a rule-of-law order is committed to resolving them by subjecting government to the discipline of the rule of law. Indeed, Oakeshott's analysis of the modern state becomes implausible if it amounts to a covert and radical libertarianism that dresses a 'Tea Party' political agenda in philosophical garb. Rather, we should take his account at face value as pointing out an ineliminable tension that we have to try constantly to eliminate in favour of the rule-of-law side.

Finally, it is not the case that for the rule of law to exert this kind of discipline, judicial review based on what Oakeshott unkindly called the 'moral idiocy' of an entrenched bill of rights is required. All one needs is the hard work done by lawyers in developing the modern law of judicial review in administrative law to see that the purposes of an administrative state can be rendered consistent with *jus* as long as the state purports to govern through *lex*.[101]

This kind of work is for the most part unexciting, but it is work that attempts to show that the *jus* in *lex* makes it possible for individuals who recognize, on the one hand, their littleness, their imperfection and their mortality and, on the other, their importance to themselves to live peaceably together under the conditions of liberty made possible by an order of public laws. Moreover, that it is unexciting is a good thing. As I have argued elsewhere, the more boring the administrative law of a jurisdiction is, the healthier it is on the scale of human dignity, where dignity is understood as the formal equality of individuals before the law.[102]

Once we see this, we can also recognize three related aspects of the power of our myth. Firstly, it is a myth that subverts all other myths since it eschews all reference to providence or to the fabric of the universe and requires a justification to mere mortals. They are the little men, or free and equal individuals, who are important to themselves in that they suppose that their judgements as to the ends of their own lives should be given priority. But, secondly, they regard, as Hobbes suggested, the public laws of their sovereign as a kind of 'public conscience' since they recognize that they must subordinate private conscience to the law if they

[101] This point is the main theme of a most illuminating review article of Loughlin's *Foundations of Public Law*: Mark Walters, 'Is Public Law Ordinary?', *Modern Law Review*, 75 (2012), 894.

[102] See my 'Dignity in Administrative Law: Judicial Deference in a Culture of Justification', *Review of Constitutional Studies*, 17 (2012), 87.

are to enjoy the conditions that make the exercise of private conscience possible. Such subordination requires that subjects be in awe of the sovereign. But, since the sovereign is no more than the 'soul'[103] of the artificial person – the state – that the individuals themselves have created, the person they must be in awe of if they are to have peace and liberty under an order of public law is their artifice. What they should be in awe of, therefore, is themselves.[104]

[103] Hobbes, 'The Introduction' in *Leviathan*, 9.

[104] See Oakeshott, '*Leviathan* – A Myth', 153: 'The destiny of man is ruled by no Providence, and there is no place in it for perfection or even for lasting satisfaction. He is largely dependent upon his own inventiveness; but this, in spite of its imperfection, is powerful enough to create a civilized life out of the very fears and compulsions that belong to his nature and circumstance.'

11

What, if anything, is wrong with Hayek's model constitution?

JAN-WERNER MÜLLER

> If politics is the art of the possible, political philosophy is the art of making politically possible the seemingly impossible.
>
> F. A. Hayek[1]

> All political theories assume, of course, that most individuals are very ignorant. Those who plead for liberty differ from the rest in that they include among the ignorant themselves as well as the wisest.
>
> F. A. Hayek[2]

Friedrich von Hayek is often suspected of being at best an ambivalent friend of democracy. Some have gone further in their suspicions and thought him a more or less secret supporter of dictatorship (albeit a liberal one). Indeed, Hayek did explicitly claim in the *Constitution of Liberty* that 'a democracy may well wield totalitarian powers, and it is conceivable that an authoritarian government may act on liberal principles.'[3] Infamously, he told a Chilean newspaper in 1981 that 'personally, I prefer a liberal dictator to democratic government lacking in liberalism.'[4] Already in 1962 he had sent a copy of *The Constitution of Liberty* to Portuguese dictator Antonio Salazar (once called by *TIME* magazine the 'dean' of European dictators and in fact the dictator who lasted the longest in twentieth-century Europe); in an accompanying note, Hayek expressed the hope that the book would assist Salazar 'in his endeavour to design a constitution which is proof against the abuses of democracy'.[5]

[1] Friedrich von Hayek, *The Constitution of Liberty* (University of Chicago Press, 1978), 114.
[2] Ibid., 30. [3] Ibid., 103.
[4] Quoted in Andrew Farrant, Edward McPhail and Sebastian Berger, 'Preventing the "Abuses" of Democracy: Hayek, the "Military Usurper" and Transitional Dictatorship in Chile?', *American Journal of Economics and Sociology*, 71 (2012), 513.
[5] Ibid.

Shocking words at first and perhaps also at second sight. However, such concerns about potential deformations and 'abuses' of democracy also need to be understood in historical context. Hayek was on one level merely articulating a liberal, self-consciously post-totalitarian sensibility that was widespread among Western political theorists in the 1950s and 1960s. Many accepted Jacob Talmon's claim that democracy could take a totalitarian form (and that the first thinker who had espoused such a form of democracy had been Rousseau).[6] Many also would have agreed with Hayek's claim – typical of Cold War liberals – that democracy had at best an instrumental value: it was the only peaceful – and hence best – means of removing undesirable rulers, but it had no intrinsic worth.[7] As Hayek put it, 'however strong the general case for democracy, it is not an ultimate or absolute value and must be judged by what it will achieve. It is probably the best method of achieving certain ends, but not an end in itself.'[8] Thinkers such as Isaiah Berlin agreed with Hayek that there was no necessary connection between liberty and democracy and that a benevolent despotism might secure more liberty (understood strictly as non-interference) than an illiberal 'democratism'.

Such concerns were not merely articulated by theorists on the sidelines of politics: as I have argued elsewhere, elites in post-war Western Europe erected a political order that was based on the supposed lessons of the political catastrophes of the mid-twentieth century – and that could be said to have embodied a number of typically Hayekian concerns about democracy. Elites drew the conclusion – rightly or wrongly – that the cataclysmic events of the 1930s and 1940s could be traced to irresponsible (and, ultimately, irrational) 'masses'; more specifically, they held that totalitarianism itself had been based on an ideal of unconstrained collective subjects, whether the Nazi *Volksgemeinschaft* or the homogeneous Soviet people as conceived under Stalinism.[9] Hence, the post-war

[6] J. L. Talmon, *The Origins of Totalitarian Democracy* (London: Secker & Warburg, 1955).

[7] Hayek claimed that '[d]emocracy is the only method of peaceful change that man has yet discovered.' See ibid., 107. On cold war liberalism and its central tenets, see my 'Fear and Freedom: On "Cold War Liberalism"', *European Journal of Political Theory*, 7 (2008), 45.

[8] Hayek, *The Constitution of Liberty*, 106.

[9] For this conception of totalitarianism, see D. D. Roberts, *The Totalitarian Experiment in Twentieth-Century Europe: Understanding the Poverty of Great Politics* (New York: Routledge, 2006); see also my *Contesting Democracy: Political Ideas in Twentieth-Century Europe* (New Haven, CT: Yale University Press, 2011); and Michael Geyer and Sheila Fitzpatrick (eds.), *Beyond Totalitarianism: Stalinism and Nazism Compared* (New York: Cambridge University Press, 2009).

order came to be based on a deep distrust of popular sovereignty – and even parliamentary sovereignty. After all, it had been unconstrained parliaments such as the German Reichstag and the French National Assembly which had formally handed all power over to leaders such as Hitler and Marshall Pétain.[10] Constraining any direct influence of 'the people' and securing the liberal-democratic order through non-elected and electorally unaccountable institutions – a prime example being constitutional courts[11] – these came to be the chief characteristics of a model that I have termed 'constrained democracy'.[12] This model was eventually also adopted by countries which in the early post-war period had still suffered under dictatorships: Spain and Portugal in the 1970s and most Central and Eastern European countries after 1989.[13]

While some Hayekian anxieties are clearly present in this conception of constrained democracy, one can be forgiven for thinking that in his later writings Hayek went considerably further in trying to constrain democracy, particularly in his three volumes entitled, *Law, Legislation, and Liberty*. The 'model constitution' he proposed in the last of these has been widely criticized, even if Hayek himself went out of his way to claim that he was a genuine friend of democracy – just one who was worried that the pathologies of actually existing Western democracies in the 1960s and 1970s would lead to a disenchantment with democracy altogether and hence a desire to return to authoritarianism. He was anxious that in what he called a new democratic 'household state', 'a majority of takers ... decide what they will take from a wealthier minority.'[14] He also insisted that 'the old liberal is in fact a much better friend of democracy than the dogmatic democrat, for he is concerned

[10] See also Peter Lindseth, 'The Paradox of Parliamentary Supremacy: Delegation, Democracy, and Dictatorship in Germany and France, 1920–1950s', *Yale Law Journal*, 113 (2004), 1341.

[11] Of course, in some European countries, constitutional court judges are elected – they are simply not elected by citizens directly. However, none of them are accountable through elections.

[12] See Müller, *Contesting Democracy*, and also Jan-Werner Müller, 'The Triumph of What (if Anything)? Political Ideologies and Political Institutions in Twentieth-Century Europe', *Journal of Political Ideologies*, 14 (2009), 211.

[13] One could speak of an ideal type of 'non-ideal circumstances', where constraints of popular and even parliamentary sovereignty are justified, because the demos – deep down – knows that it has reasons to distrust itself, and because democratic institutions are too new to have proven to be in truly 'good working order'. See Jeremy Waldron, 'The Core of the Case against Judicial Review', *Yale Law Review*, 115 (2006), 1348.

[14] Hayek, *The Constitution*, 289.

with preserving the conditions that make democracy workable.'[15] But this particular 'old liberal', while claiming to mount a rescue operation for democracy properly understood, also confessed to being 'no longer certain that the name democracy can still be freed from the distaste with which increasing numbers of people for good reasons have come to regard it, even though few yet dare publicly to express their disillusionment'.[16]

What, then, to make of the model constitution and Hayek's conception of democracy more broadly? As I have argued earlier, *historically* it is difficult to claim that his ideas constituted a fundamental break with post-war trends in political thinking – even if he was willing to go much further than the actual architects of post-war Western Europe's constitutions (as well as most self-confessed Cold War liberals). And normatively (and also empirically), as I shall argue in the first half of this chapter, the model constitution presents a significantly more profound challenge to much contemporary liberal-democratic thought than is usually acknowledged. To be sure, for defenders of some strong form of majoritarianism and, more broadly, of maximizing popular input into the political system, it will be a relatively straightforward matter to reject Hayek's conception as fundamentally undemocratic.[17] Equally, for all those inclined to argue that the right regularly to vote is owed to all citizens as a matter of basic respect, Hayek's highly restrictive understanding of democracy will seem obviously problematic. For many others, though, things will not be quite so straightforward: for them, the challenge will (and should) be that Hayek's model simply radicalizes the application of principles that many liberals (as well as many republican political theorists) are willing to accept in general: the need to 'depoliticize' democracy in certain policy areas, the benefits of a 'mixed constitution' and a form of checks and balances and, not least, the legitimacy of limiting popular input through restricting the franchise.[18]

[15] Ibid., 117.

[16] Friedrich von Hayek, *Law, Legislation and Liberty*, vol. 3: *The Political Order of a Free People* (University of Chicago Press, 1979), 139.

[17] See, e.g., Richard Bellamy, 'Republicanism, Democracy, and Constitutionalism', in Cécile Laborde and John Maynor (eds.), *Republicanism and Political Theory* (Oxford, UK: Blackwell, 2008).

[18] See, e.g., Philip Pettit, 'Depoliticizing Democracy', *Ratio Juris*, 17 (2004), 52–65. To his credit, Pettit has since disavowed the language of 'depoliticization' in *On the People's Terms: A Republican Theory and Model of Democracy* (New York: Cambridge University Press, 2013). See also Nadia Urbinati, 'Unpolitical Democracy', *Political Theory*, 38 (2010), 65.

To be sure, large-scale disenfranchisement might not seem so obviously part of the contemporary liberal political imagination – but this is partly because existing practices of restricting the franchise on grounds of age and mental ability are often considered unproblematic (if they are given any thought at all).[19] In other areas where the vote is restricted in some countries – most controversially, prisoner disenfranchisement but also, more particularly, disenfranchisement on the basis of electoral fraud and 'uncitizenly conduct' – there remains a sense that one might still find reasonable arguments on both sides.[20] What used to be called 'civil death' in former times is at first sight a shocking idea for observers today – but effectively it continues to be practiced in many countries, most notably in some American states.[21] We might vigorously affirm the all-subjected principle – but virtually nowhere does anyone live up to it (of course, the same is true – only more so – for the all-affected principle).[22]

It seems, then, that Hayek was not actually arguing for new political principles; he was just trying to make a wider (and more radical) application of existing liberal principles politically possible – very much in line with his conception of political philosophy as 'the art of making politically possible the seemingly impossible'. Put differently, if many liberals are initially inclined to reject the model constitution, they ought to be honest enough with themselves to realize that this rejection should lead them to re-examine some of their own principles (in particular, a deep distrust of majoritarianism and a certainty that we can disenfranchise some citizens on grounds of maturity or even judgements of moral character). Or is it possible to find fault with the model constitution *without* simply adopting an outright majoritarian position or falling back on an uncompromising affirmation of the intrinsic value of democracy?

In this chapter, I shall first briefly reconstruct Hayek's case for a particular kind of 'democracy-saving' constitution. I shall also point to some of the less obvious underlying assumptions of Hayek's model and draw out some of its implications. I then proceed to discuss common criticisms of Hayek's constitution and explain why they can rather easily

[19] Philippe Van Parijs, 'The Disenfranchisement of the Elderly, and Other Attempts to Secure Intergenerational Justice', *Philosophy and Public Affairs*, 27 (1998), 292.

[20] For arguments surrounding the Hirst case – now of European-wide fame – see Susan Easton, 'Electing the Electorate: The Problem of Prisoner Disenfranchisement', *Modern Law Review*, 69 (2006), 443.

[21] Ludvig Beckman, *Frontiers of Democracy: The Right to Vote and Its Limits* (New York: Palgrave, 2009).

[22] Ludvig Beckman, 'Democratic Inclusion, Law and Causes', *Ratio Juris*, 21 (2008), 348.

be rebutted from within the Hayekian framework (without radically deviating from a number of liberal assumptions). I shall then proceed to argue that the best reasons for rejecting the model constitution are furnished by none other than Hayek himself: it is partly what we know from experience about the modern state and partly what we know we cannot possibly know – our understanding of our own ignorance – that should lead us to reject the model constitution.[23] More specifically, I will suggest that Hayek's constitution failed to incorporate the two instrumental uses of democracy that he himself directly (or sometimes more indirectly) endorsed: democracy as the best way to remove undesirable power-holders and democracy as a means to detect actual opinions or judgements dispersed across society. Note that this latter criticism will not depend on a factual (and sometimes crypto-normative) claim that modern societies are necessarily characterized by deep moral and political disagreements or on a controversial philosophical position such as value pluralism.[24] The point is that without wide and deep democratic consultation, we will not even know whether there is disagreement and how serious it is. I want to suggest at the end of the chapter that this finding has wider implications for how we think about democracy and political conflict.

The model constitution revisited

Hayek's model constitution relies on a fundamental distinction: that between law and legislation. The former, he argued, refers to universal, non-instrumental rules of just conduct; the latter designates acts of government that allow government to have a particular 'direction'. The tragedy of modern political life, according to Hayek, consists in the fact that a single institution – the sovereign legislature – began to conflate the two. In an assessment that remarkably paralleled Michael Oakeshott's, Hayek lamented that law had come to be understood as instrumental; moreover, the supposed legitimacy of giving direction or 'instructions' to government had led to the coercion of citizens in the name of an ideal of

[23] This is not quite the same as Oakeshott's well-known criticism of Hayek having offered a rationalist plan to resist all planning (Hayek, in any case, might not have objected to the association with a rationalist 'style'). The point is that the scheme Hayek proposes makes it exceedingly difficult to detect certain kinds of knowledge.

[24] Compare Richard Bellamy, '"Dethroning Politics": Liberalism, Constitutionalism and Democracy in the Thought of F. A. Hayek', *British Journal of Political Science*, 24 (1994), 419.

all subjects having to follow a particular direction or achieve a particular collective purpose (a point that very much resembles Oakeshott's claim about modern European states turning into enterprise associations).[25]

Hayek's response was to separate law and legislation by entrusting two different institutions with their respective formulation. The Legislative Assembly was charged with working out just rules of conduct; the Governmental Assembly was actually to govern, that is, formulate and pursue policies, but always within the bounds set by universal rules of just conduct (again, the comparison with Oakeshott is illuminating: government, for Hayek, resembles Oakeshott's individual citizens who have to subscribe to universal, non-instrumental rules when they choose and then pursue their aims – or, in Oakeshott's parlance, adventures – in life).

Hayek had no qualms about the Governmental Assembly being subject to regular elections, with parties competing for power by formulating programs (which, according to Hayek, would mainly appeal to citizens' material interests). The actions (and composition) of the Legislative Assembly, however, were not to reflect citizens' interests – rather, the Legislative Assembly was to base itself on citizens' opinions about just conduct. Its members were to revise existing law in light of changing opinions and sometimes formulate new law in response to novel challenges – while presumably pursuing the intimations of a particular polity's legal tradition and its conceptions of justice. The emphasis on new challenges is important here: Hayek was explicit that regulations, as required, for instance, by new technologies, would have to be formulated in the Legislative Assembly; it was not for government to decide whether its overall direction might mandate regulation to satisfy particular interests (or values, for that matter).[26] And neither the Legislative Assembly nor the Governmental Assembly was allowed to delegate tasks such as health and safety regulations to administrative agencies (and thereby license arbitrary decisions by the bureaucracy).[27]

[25] Michael Oakeshott, *On Human Conduct* (1975) (Oxford, UK: Clarendon Press, 2003).

[26] This is not a trivial point, especially in light of the fact that Hayek was such a fervent advocate of technological and material progress – the faster the better. Curiously, he at one point even saw the primary value of democracy not in providing a stable framework for growth but in its own dynamic aspect. He claimed that 'it is in its dynamic, rather than in its static, aspects that the value of democracy proves itself' (Hayek, *The Constitution*, 109).

[27] Already in Hayek's time – but even more so today – this seems highly unrealistic. No matter how wise the members of the Legislative Assembly, it is impossible to see how they

Hayek proposed a peculiar method for selecting the members of the Legislative Assembly. Only citizens aged forty-five were supposed to be eligible to vote, and they would have to vote for a member of their own generation to serve a fifteen-year term. One-fifteenth of the assembly would be replaced each year.[28] Hayek justified this method with the claim that by age forty-five electors had for sure reached a certain political maturity – and that, by the same time, potential candidates would have had enough time to demonstrate their capacities.[29] Candidates were not allowed to belong to parties; they would not have to face any election after the first one ever again; and the state was to find ways of making them financially independent. Without qualms, Hayek admitted that he wished to re-create something like the nineteenth-century liberal class of notables or *Honoratioren* – independent citizens of leisure, free from partisan, let alone petty material, interests so as to focus solely on the common good and the long-term flourishing of the polity.[30]

In case of conflicts between the two bodies, a constitutional court was to determine whether one of the assemblies had overstepped their mandate – and thereby also build up case law that would render the distinction between law and legislation ever clearer. There was to be no bill of rights; the codification of rights could never adequately ensure protection from arbitrary interference (but the restriction that law would have to be based solely on universally shared rules of just conduct could).[31] Clearly, the constitutional court would have to have the last word in this arrangement, but it would itself be constrained by the specifications of the constitution and, in particular, the rules about the unchangeable division

would not have to give out some control to experts when it comes to, for instance, regulation of novel technologies.

[28] This might strike many as an outlandish idea, but it is worth pointing out that in some advanced industrial countries the median age right now actually is forty-five, while in some countries the median *voter* is exactly forty-five years old (Van Parijs gives the example of Belgium in the mid-1990s; presumably it has crept up since).

[29] As Hayek put it, 'The whole would thus mirror that part of the population which had already gained experience and had had an opportunity to make their reputation, but who would still be in their best years.' See Hayek, *Political Order*, 113.

[30] To put the contrast differently, the Governmental Assembly gives free rein to the rational pursuit of interests; the Legislative Assembly relies on its members' role identification. Or, another possible contrast, the former contains delegates or, at the most, deputies; the latter is filled with trustees.

[31] Again, a striking resemblance with Oakeshott – though the latter was, of course, not only dismissive of a bill of rights but also of any kind of judicial review. See Michael Oakeshott, 'The Rule of Law' in Oakeshott, *On History and Other Essays* (Totowa, NJ: Barnes and Noble Books, 1983), 119.

of labour between the Legislative and Governmental Assemblies (and the clause that mandated all laws to be uniform and universal rules of just conduct).[32]

Let us be clear as to what the ideal result of this scheme was supposed to be: for Hayek, it secured both liberty and justice (while at the same time abolishing sovereignty). A government constrained by rules determined by the Legislative Assembly would not be in a position to coerce individual citizens in the name of values which they could not recognize as their own. In this sense, freedom from arbitrary interference was assured. Coercion in the name of shared conceptions of just conduct could not possibly be experienced as arbitrary or unlicensed interference – after all, law in Hayek's sense was based on universally agreed understandings of just conduct and would ensure that citizens' expectations would match and not conflict.[33] By definition, then, law also assured justice – because law proper would have to reflect these understandings of just conduct, which could be thought of as the outcome of an evolutionary process, as well as the 'exigencies of a going order'.[34]

I think it is fair to say that Hayek himself understood that for all its apparent simplicity, the model constitution was a highly demanding one – and demanding of citizens in the first place. Deep disagreement about justice would make the very idea of the Legislative Assembly finding just rules of conduct that citizens would universally recognize seem wildly utopian. Furthermore, a lack of trust among citizens would render the notion that everyone would have only one shot at electing and being elected to the Legislative Assembly highly unattractive.[35] After all, why accept something like a dictatorship of the middle-aged when generations could be expected to have very different forms of lived experience and hence very divergent values? Why trust someone who has lived a completely different kind of life and drawn moral conclusions from it that seem utterly alien to you? There is nothing, one might say, like generational

[32] This kind of court would be closer to Kelsen's original vision of a constitutional court: it would decide conflicts between separated powers; it would not effectively make policy choices in the name of value judgements. This latter role would effectively be performed by the Legislative Assembly in Hayek's scheme. See Theo Öhlinger, 'The Genesis of the Austrian Model of Constitutional Review of Legislation', *Ratio Juris*, 16 (2003), 206.

[33] Friedrich A. Hayek, *Law, Legislation and Liberty*, vol. 1: *Rules and Order* (University of Chicago Press, 1983), 94–123.

[34] Ibid., 118.

[35] Trust might be re-described as being content with being virtually represented if one does not happen to be forty-five years old.

differences to make what John Rawls famously called the burdens of judgement even heavier. And, not least, there is the problem of what one might call a very peculiar civic psychology where in one set of elections men and women can think mainly of their selfish interests and in another set of elections – albeit only an election along the lines of one man, one vote, just one time – men and women are expected to choose the great and the good on a purely non-partisan, selfless basis.[36]

Hence, Hayek suggested a positively Rousseauean scheme which would render individual citizens more responsible and the polity as a whole more homogeneous. He proposed that everyone would be inducted into clubs (clubs resembling Rotary to some extent) in order to discuss and better understand civic affairs. By the time they had reached age forty-five – after almost thirty years of deliberation without consequences, so to speak – citizens would almost be guaranteed to have the level of 'maturity' Hayek deemed appropriate. Since he suspected that political club life, even for the most civically devoted, might take too many evenings, he thought of an additional incentive. Men and women would join the clubs at an age when they were also looking for suitable marriage partners. As Hayek put it, 'clubs of contemporaries might well be formed either at school-leaving age or at least when each class entered public life, say at the age of 18. They would possibly be more attractive if men of one age were brought together with women two years or so younger.'[37] But would clubs, even if they effectively also functioned as marriage markets, be enough to ensure political 'maturity' and judgement – especially when in their regular form of participation, that is to say, voting for the Governmental Assembly, men and women were encouraged, or at least given free rein, to think of their narrow self-interest?

[36] Even though the Legislative Assembly at first sight appears to be like a judicial body – making it an obvious target of criticism for all theorists in principle opposed to judicial review – in fact, things are potentially far worse than 'government by supreme court judges'; after all, judges do have a lifetime of training in law (and often, *de facto*, in politics; in some countries, such as Germany, it is not even uncommon for politicians with an appropriate legal background to join the Constitutional Court). But the successful candidates for Hayek's Legislative Assembly might just happen to be people with a track record of success in life that makes them admirable to many voters but ill-suited to discerning shared political understandings of justice. Keeping out people who have experience in politics – that is, with partisanship – exacerbates this danger. To put it bluntly, one could imagine a Legislative Assembly filled with Berlusconis.

[37] Hayek, *Political Order*, 117.

There was a further difficulty to which the Rousseauean scheme did not really respond. Elections to the Governmental Assembly are explicitly allowed to mobilize partisan passions and self-interest. Everyone above a certain minimum age will get to participate. But then it is unclear what government can actually do: for instance, it cannot pass regulations to respond to new technological or economic challenges. It also cannot increase taxes, but presumably it can shift existing funds around (and also alter the 'rules for the organization of the services of government', which simply seems to mean restructuring the bureaucracy).[38] It can do things that may count as instrumental, but presumably they cannot be formulated as rules that apply only to some. What, in short, could count as legislation that would somehow reflect a distinct direction for a country – and yet respect the constraints of Hayek's model constitution and eliminate administrative discretion and discrimination among citizens? Not much perhaps – and yet 'government' (unlike in Oakeshott's thought, one might add) explicitly raises the expectation of 'giving direction' and 'getting particular things done', even if it never ought to amount to something like 'running a country'.[39] The overall scheme promises citizens the capacity to direct policy, but in the end, it only appears to offer something like a democracy without choices or, put differently, without any sense of collective direction.[40]

One could add further to these somewhat speculative concerns and queries about Hayek's conception. Rather than doing so, I now would like to turn to two common criticisms of the model constitution. I shall argue that initially these might seem quite plausible but that they do not prove fatal to Hayek's scheme, as Hayekians have at least somewhat credible answers ready. My point here is not that all the responses to them which one can generate from Hayek's thought are necessarily convincing. It is rather that, ultimately, an even tighter case against the

[38] Hayek, *Law, Legislation and Liberty*, vol. 1, 132. [39] Ibid., 131.

[40] These are no hypothetical scenarios at all. To take two examples from recent European history: EU intervention in potential accession states has often amounted to 'democracy without choices'; some plans for a EU Political Union that follow a broadly speaking neo-liberal/ordo-liberal line of thought are based on the idea of setting economic and financial choices in stone – but making them legitimate by allowing European peoples to vote for the European Commissioners who will be responsible for implementing and supervising them. See Ivan Krastev, 'The Balkans: Democracy without Choices', *Journal of Democracy*, 13 (2002), 39, and my 'Europe's Perfect Storm: The Political and Economic Consequences of the Eurocrisis' in *Dissent* (Fall 2012).

model constitution can be presented on the basis of Hayek's own insights into the instrumental uses of democracy.

Criticizing the model constitution: two false starts

Why would men and women choose the model constitution in the first place when it leads to the disenfranchisement of a significant part of the population (most of the time for almost everyone, as far as the Legislative Assembly is concerned, and for some permanently, if they are already over forty-five at the time of the adoption of the constitution)? The underlying assumption of this line of criticism is, of course, that people would never accept any reversal of the process of extending the franchise.[41] Nothing less than universal suffrage will do in the modern, more or less liberal-democratic world, and nobody would consent to anything like a rollback of the franchise.

Yet, from a Hayekian perspective, two answers suggest themselves to this point: first of all – and this is, above everything else, what Hayek himself had in mind when he wrote in the 1970s – conditions could deteriorate to such an extent that people are willing to make a fresh start with a different kind of democracy.[42] And, if they believe Hayek, they would actually be returning to a form that already existed once before: the rule of law *cum* limited democracy in Britain prior to *circa* 1914 (when, in Hayek's eyes, the Lords supposedly checked the proper development of the common law and the Commons held the purse strings), except that in the new version there would be no restrictions based on gender (everyone would get to vote once for the Legislative Assembly and more often for the Governmental Assembly, of course).[43] Thus, Hayek's

[41] This argument is advanced, for instance, in Adam Tebble, *Hayek* (London: Continuum, 2010).

[42] Hayek claimed he was providing nothing less than 'an intellectual emergency equipment which will be available when we have no choice but to replace the tottering structure by some better edifice rather than resort in despair to some sort of dictatorial regime. Government is of necessity the product of intellectual design. If we can give it a shape in which it provides a beneficial framework for the free growth of society, without giving to any one power to control this growth in particular, we may well hope to see the growth of civilization continue.' See Hayek, *Political Order*, 152.

[43] As Hayek put it, '[W]e have no right to assume that the particular forms of democracy which have worked with us must also work elsewhere. Experience seems to show that they do not. There is, therefore, very reason to ask how those conceptions which our kind of representative institutions tacitly presupposed can be explicitly put into such constitutions.' See ibid, 108.

vision might not be so unrealistic after all: in times of crisis, it is not the radically new or the perfect rationalist scheme option that wins out, but what can actually be presented as tried and tested.[44]

Secondly, there have, of course, been many instances – even quite recently – when people effectively voted to narrow their future political choices. Choosing parties that promise to make a central bank independent is an obvious example; voting to join the European Union in a referendum is another. One can have serious doubts about some of the underlying models of 'self-binding' or 'other-binding'[45] – but one cannot deny, it seems to me, that they have gained real traction even in popular political consciousness and that we have enough empirical examples of effective self-disenfranchisement for the sake of some greater good (usually economic growth, of course; see the two preceding examples). In short, then, it is simply not very convincing to say that the model constitution could never be enacted because it is so obviously contrary to any conceivable constituent power's interests.

Still, one might say that for people to disenfranchise themselves completely, as far as law in the specific Hayekian sense is concerned (except for the one shot at elections at age forty-five), is to violate the intrinsic, or constitutive, value of democracy. Never mind whether people would ever vote for it or not – the model constitution is contrary to a widely shared understanding that citizens are owed equal respect by the state and that this respect is, among other things, best expressed by giving them a political voice on a regular basis (thereby – supposedly – ensuring something like equality of political effect). This, one might further hold, is a *sine qua non* of any modern, liberal-democratic form

[44] Or, for that matter, no option 'wins out' in a clear-cut manner at all, and instead, democracies muddle through crisis after crisis. Such muddling through is perfectly compatible with the conservative, Burkean and evolutionary strand in Hayek's thought; the model constitution, on the other hand, is clearly part of the rationalist strand of Hayek's theorizing. On democracies, crises and muddling through, see now David Runciman, *The Confidence Trap: A History of Democracy in Crisis from World War I to the Present* (Princeton University Press, 2013).

[45] This thought has come under much criticism recently – including by Jon Elster, who made it influential in the first place. While one can indeed question the notion of 'self-binding', cases such as joining the EU are actually a matter of 'wanting to be bound by others' – and clearly renouncing the power to unbind oneself, short of jumping the (EU) ship altogether. See the chapter 'Ulysses Unbound: Constitutions as Constraints' in Jon Elster, *Ulysses Unbound: Studies in Rationality, Precommitment, and Constraints* (New York: Cambridge University Press, 2000), 88–174; for the original theory, see Jon Elster, *Ulysses and the Sirens: Studies in rationality and irrationality* (Cambridge University Press, 1979).

of legitimacy and also the only way for citizens to have a secure sense of their own individual dignity as participants in a long-term scheme of social cooperation. They might not wish to participate – but they want to be sure that they could, if they so desired (and they would want everybody else to be sure and know that everybody else knows that they are secure in their participation rights).

From a Hayekian perspective, two answers seem available to respond to this criticism. Firstly, it remains the case that nobody is entirely disenfranchised (with the possible exception of those over forty-five at the time of the introduction of the model constitution – though, of course, they would still get to elect members of the Governmental Assembly). Hayek might have argued that giving one vote in a lifetime only increases the value of that vote – who would want to miss it; who would not take it seriously?

Secondly, Hayek hinted that what really mattered about democracy were not necessarily democratic institutions in a strict sense (such as an equal and frequent vote). Somewhat like Alexis de Tocqueville, he also understood democracy as a mentality, a set of *moeurs* that ensured mutual respect and dignity among citizens. In *The Constitution of Liberty*, he distinguished explicitly between a 'democratic spirit' – what he called 'the principle of equality' in 'rules of moral and social conduct' – on the one hand, and democratic institutions, on the other.[46] So the Hayekian might conclude that a society under the model constitution could very well be characterized by a modern spirit of equal respect and what more recently has been called 'civic dignity', even if everyone under forty-five was also officially deemed deficient in political 'maturity'.[47] So what grounds, then, are there left for criticizing the model constitution?

What *is* wrong with the model constitution

There are two criticisms of the model constitution which I claim no Hayekian could reasonably reject. The first has to do with the very instrumental use of democracy which Hayek explicitly endorsed: removing bad rulers. The second relies on the quintessentially Hayekian insight into the fact that knowledge, including tacit knowledge, is widely dispersed in society, with the result that no 'epistocracy' – no matter how

[46] Hayek, *The Constitution of Liberty*, 85.
[47] Josiah Ober, 'Democracy's Dignity', *American Political Science Review*, 106 (2012), 827.

wise or well resourced – could have access to all such social knowledge.[48] Let me explicate these criticisms in turn.

A widely accepted finding in the empirical political science literature is that only broad democratic empowerment can ultimately lead to functional states and, more particularly, accountable elites who do not simply treat the state as their temporary (or even permanent) property.[49] Another way of putting this is to say that a citizenry needs to be able to contest elites' decisions and, in the worst-case scenario, be capable of popular resistance.[50]

The problem with Hayek's scheme is not that it provides no means of resistance – very few constitutions do[51]; rather, the fatal flaw consists in the fact that it envisages no way to contest the decisions of the Legislative Assembly at all (which, of course, also puts in place an authoritative, incontestable framework within which the government is allowed to change direction, after having been so instructed by the people via the legislature). The only way to reverse law would be for several age cohorts to vote for candidates who would be explicitly committed to overturning law that had been deemed undesirable (which, in Hayek's model, would have to mean not universal and/or not just in some substantive sense and/or failing systematically to match citizens' expectations). Of course, the Hayekian could counter that this is precisely the point: it would take time for a society to form a genuine consensus that laws did in fact not reflect shared understandings of justice; laws should not be rapidly overturned in line with partisan majorities and their potentially highly skewed notions of justice.

But this reply will not do. Especially when combined with Hayek's insistence that societies should progress rapidly (in material and technological terms), the notions that, for instance, sophisticated forms of regulation would have to be left in place for a fairly long time, even if they are widely experienced as dysfunctional or unjust, seems highly implausible. Of course, one could again counter that the members of the Legislative Assembly would themselves come to see that what they had decided does not work (whether morally or practically) – yet the

48 David Estlund, *Democratic Authority: A Philosophical Framework* (Princeton University Press, 2007).

49 Two popular recent examples are Daron Acemoğlu and James A. Robinson, *Why Nations Fail* (New York: Random House, 2012) and Francis Fukuyama, *The Origins of Political Order* (New York: Faber, Straus and Giroux, 2011).

50 Pettit, *On the People's Terms*.

51 Article 20 of the German Basic Law is an interesting exception here.

whole point of a constitution, especially one that, like Hayek's, promises nothing less than the abolition of sovereignty, is that citizens do not have to put all their trust in one assembly of the great and the good and then just hope for the best, as far as their 'probity, wisdom, and judgment' (Hayek) are concerned.[52] Hayek's scheme, it seems, fails by its own standards.

Let me shift to the second line of criticism: perhaps Hayek's most important contribution to social and political thought – widely accepted even by those who reject the political and legal conclusions he drew from it – was the insight that central planning has to founder practically, since it could never properly take account of the widely dispersed knowledge in society. It would also necessarily be unjust, since central planning would have to be based on a distinct prioritization of certain values, when there were likely to be widely divergent judgements of value across a modern society.[53] One can debate to what extent different institutional arrangements might be better or worse at gaining knowledge from and about society (and the value judgements of its members in particular); what can hardly be denied, however, is Hayek's central insight that a state in general will always have trouble 'seeing' a society properly, given the difficulties of accessing local and, in particular, tacit knowledge.[54] This, of course, explains the importance of prices as signalling devices and the superiority of the market over state planning.

The question, then, is how exactly the members of the Legislative Assembly can gain knowledge of society's conceptions of what constitutes just conduct. In Hayek's own view, these conceptions can undergo significant transformations; it will not be obvious what law – in the special Hayekian sense – would have to be in response to new technological developments but also in response to changing *moeurs* or even what he called 'that higher, superindividual wisdom which, in a certain sense, the products of spontaneous social growth may possess'.[55]

Hayek made it plain that members of the Legislative Assembly would have to exercise judgement in discerning such wisdom; put differently, they cannot mechanically apply rules or existing 'models' of justice. The

[52] Hayek, *Political Order*, 113.

[53] Unlike Berlin, Hayek tended to treat value pluralism like a social fact more than like a conceptual truth.

[54] James C. Scott, *Seeing Like a State: How Certain Schemes to Improve the Human Condition Have Failed* (New Haven, CT: Yale University Press, 1998).

[55] Hayek, *The Constitution*, 110.

Legislative Assembly needs to be properly *responsive*; yet by design it is not in any clear sense *representative* (reflecting only the choices of the mature forty-five-year-olds), unless the electorate in their votes somehow already reflects all of society's judgements of what constitutes just conduct.[56] Put simply, a wider franchise and more frequent elections would allow a more accurate signalling of changing conceptions of just conduct.

No doubt one could argue that elections are actually not the obviously best source of what might be called democratic signalling of considered judgements of just conduct. A lively public sphere where serious arguments about justice can be debated; surveys that ask sophisticated questions about what constitutes right conduct; and devices such as 'minipublics', deliberative polls, and so on – these could all remedy what prima facie is by his own standards a glaring epistemological deficit in Hayek's scheme. However, all of them are still selective: not everyone gets access to the media – for that is what the public sphere is, of course, under contemporary conditions – and what one might call 'detection devices' of actual judgements in the form of 'minipublics' and so on can only ever involve a few citizens. None of them can match elections where a wide variety of candidates and parties ideally represent distinct judgements of justice among which all citizens can choose. This no doubt involves a risk – a risk of choosing ill-conceived ideas about law – and that risk could perhaps be lessened by restricting the franchise. But then again, as Hayek pointed out, '[F]reedom granted only when it is known beforehand that its effects will be beneficial is not freedom.'[57] And, arguably, the franchise, granted only when it is known beforehand that its effects will be beneficial, is not proper democracy.

Of course, these problems would disappear if one could reliably designate 'knowers' and certified competent judges of just conduct.[58] But Hayek's own insistence that we cannot know certain things other than by somehow receiving signals from each and every individual blocks this possibility.[59] To be sure, his Rousseauean scheme for shaping a

[56] For the difference between responsive and indicative representation, see Pettit, *On the People's Terms*. One might say that the Legislative Assembly could actually turn out to be more an indicative than a responsive representative assembly, not least because there is no need to face re-election.

[57] Hayek, *The Constitution*, 31.

[58] Estlund, *Democratic Authority*.

[59] Putting this differently again, virtual representation of interests might be conceivable, but virtual representation of individual considered judgements is not. Compare also Frank Michelman, 'Conceptions of Democracy in American Constitutional Argument: Voting Rights', *Florida Law Review*, 41 (1989), 443.

homogeneous political (and moral) culture makes it more likely that citizens will converge on judgements of just conduct – but the point is that this cannot be known for sure (and, in any case, it is somewhat unlikely: Hayek himself seemed to suggest in *The Road to Serfdom* that under modern conditions something like value pluralism would necessarily characterize society).[60] The institutionalized civic schizophrenia – thinking of selfish interests in frequent elections and the common good in a once-in-a-lifetime vote – might make this convergence even more difficult, as might the possibility of different generations forming judgements against the background of very different life experiences. Again, it is not pre-determined that generational conflict will make law (in the Hayekian sense) illegitimate – the point is that without democracy, we cannot even know whether it might or it already does.

Concluding remarks: democracy, disagreement and uncertainty

In this chapter I have tried to show how Hayek's model constitution can be criticized on Hayekian grounds, invoking the instrumental uses of democracy as removing power-holders and as aggregating widely dispersed knowledge and considered judgements in society. The latter use is not only relevant in case of deep disagreement or persistent value pluralism among a population. The point is that without elections, we cannot even know whether there is profound disagreement or not (again, surveys and debates in the public sphere cannot fully substitute for elections as 'democratic detection devices' of agreement or disagreement; arguably only political parties mobilize citizens broadly, systematically structure political choices and, not least, bring out latent disagreement when it appears to be to their electoral advantage).[61] Hence, there is

[60] Otherwise there would not have been such a problem with planners imposing plans and hence, according to Hayek, certain controversial value choices which those subject to planning might simply not share, without in any sense being unreasonable or clinging to exotic life plans. If all values were compatible and commensurable, planning still might be highly inefficient and hold back the material progress of society as a whole – but it would not have created the particular moral (and, in a sense, irresolvable) challenge Hayek identified in his *Road to Serfdom* (University of Chicago Press, 2007).

[61] This is, of course, a highly ambiguous point. Parties can increase polarization by artificially deepening disagreements – but they can also strengthen a sense that involvement in politics is worthwhile precisely because clear-cut choices are on offer. For a comprehensive normative account of what is good about parties and partisanship, see Nancy Rosenblum, *On the Side of the Angels: An Appreciation of Parties and Partisanship* (Princeton University Press, 2008).

never an argument for dispensing with democracy[62] on the grounds that it is only in the face of deep disagreement that we need democracy.[63] Without democracy, we cannot be certain about the existence of as well as the levels of disagreement, or agreement, for that matter.

Of course, one does not need to accept only broadly speaking Hayekian criticisms. Arguably, the intrinsic or constitutive value of democracy – one citizen, one vote, not just once – is the strongest position from which to oppose Hayek's radical limit of the franchise for his Legislative Assembly. Implicitly to judge everyone under forty-five as immature and everyone over forty-five as too old to make decisions with consequences they might not live to see (or suffer) is to deny a basic form of civic respect or dignity. And this denial cannot be compensated by a general 'democratic spirit' prevailing in society, even if, like Hayek, one finds such a thing desirable.

Still, the model constitution should continue to disturb us for a number of reasons: firstly, one might say that a sense of the intrinsic value of democracy is shared by fewer and fewer citizens themselves today. Witness the declining voter turnout virtually across the West in recent decades. Of course, this is on one level too hasty an interpretation of steadily lower participation in elections; the reason behind it may well be that citizens think that actual democracies fail to accord them respect and dignity. But it could also be – and this seems a more plausible interpretation – that they have lost faith in the very instrumental uses of democracy: they think that in contemporary democracies one can change the people at the top but not the policies coming from the top; hence, they would think that individual judgements and opinions simply do not matter in what is already a democracy without choices.[64]

There is a further, perhaps even more worrying aspect of why the model constitution might yet come into its own. The arguments for the two instrumental uses of democracy would weaken significantly if

62 All of which is not to even broach questions about the value of voting and, more broadly speaking, the 'wisdom of the crowds' in actual political problem solving. See Jeremy Waldron, 'The Wisdom of the Multitude: Some Reflections on Book 3, Chapter 11 of Aristotle's Politics', *Political Theory*, 23 (1995), 563, and Hélène Landemore and Jon Elster (eds.), *Collective Wisdom: Principles and Mechanisms* (New York: Cambridge University Press, 2012).

63 See also Laura Valentini, 'Justice, Disagreement and Democracy', *British Journal of Political Science*, 43 (2012), 177.

64 See Peter Mair, *Ruling the Void: The Hollowing-Out of Western Democracy* (New York: Verso, 2013).

the following scenarios were to become plausible: firstly, room for anything resembling law-making in the Hayekian sense could be drastically reduced if polities choose to constitutionalize large areas of policy.[65] This is probably not a proposal that could ever truly succeed in practice – decisions would still have to be taken about the application of supposedly unchangeable laws – but it could lessen the need for regular elections as a means to remove misbehaving power holders.[66]

The other scenario involves ever more refined forms of predictive analysis – through 'big data' crunching, for instance – so that citizens need less and less consciously to signal preferences and judgements. In other words, we can already know what they think, what they want and, in general, how they judge. This might still turn out to be a fatal conceit in individual cases – but with a large enough number of citizens, the predictions will be accurate enough. Who, then, needs democracy as a detection device? And who would not see the model constitution as a relief from irrational partisan politics and the burdens of involving oneself in politics and wasting too many evenings?

[65] Examples of such a tendency would be the 2012 Hungarian 'Fundamental Law' and, to a lesser extent, the attempt to constitutionalize economic policy making in the Eurozone (by incorporating 'debt brakes' in national constitutions, for instance).

[66] Of course, misbehaviour is always a possibility – but here something like the institution that Hayek envisaged for sanctioning grossly misbehaving members of the Legislative Assembly might be enough.

12

Hayek and the state

CHANDRAN KUKATHAS

> There exists, under modern conditions, no single society to which an individual normally belongs, and it is highly desirable that this should not be so.[1]

In the index to *The Constitution of Liberty* there is no entry under the rubric 'state', unless one includes the instruction 'see Government'. A search for references to the state in Hayek's writings generally would yield little. The same would be true of a browse through John Rawls's work – indeed, *A Theory of Justice* makes no reference to the state in the index because nowhere in its 538 pages is the idea discussed. Yet the reasons for the omission in Hayek's case are interestingly different, for he was throughout his intellectual career troubled by the idea of the state, and his failure to theorize systematically about it reveals a great deal not only about his political philosophy but also about the distinctive place he holds in contemporary political thought. My purpose in this chapter is to explain the place of the state in Hayek's thinking and to draw out what we might learn from an engagement with his thought in this matter. My thesis is that we find in Hayek's political philosophy an important departure from received ways of understanding political order – one that goes against the trend of political thinking over the 500 years since the emergence of the modern state. The Rawls of *A Theory of Justice* saw no need to mention the state because he was working within a framework that had accepted completely a state-centric conception of political order. Hayek declined to pay substantial attention to the state in his political theory because he ended up offering an understanding of political order that in effect repudiated the state as the fundamental institution governing human society.

To show this is not a straightforward matter. Hayek's political ideas are elaborated over a substantial array of works and also evolve over the course of nearly half a century. Not only does he change his mind on

[1] F. A. Hayek, *Law, Legislation and Liberty* (London: Routledge, 1982), vol. III, 140.

some questions, but he also presents arguments and conclusions that at times seem incompatible, if not flatly inconsistent. My contention is that there are within Hayek's thought two conflicting tendencies. One operates on the assumption that we need to reform and liberalize the institutions of the modern state in order to protect liberty and uphold the rule of law. The other perceives that liberty and the rule of law cannot prevail unless we get away from a state-centric understanding of political order. It is the latter understanding that presents Hayek's distinctive contribution to political theory. In what follows, I will attempt to demonstrate this by tracing the development of Hayek's thought. My hope is that by this genealogical method I will be able to explain how, out of the intellectual struggles of a thinker who claimed to be doing no more than re-stating the basic principles of liberalism, emerges a distinctive and radical theory of political order.

The origins and development of Hayek's political theory

Hayek began his intellectual career in the early 1920s as an economist by profession and a socialist by political inclination. His economic studies, over time, eroded his socialist convictions, while his observation of the growing popularity of socialist ideas turned him from an economist into a more broadly political thinker. The confluence of two political developments in the 1930s was of decisive importance. The first was the emergence and example of the Soviet Union, which offered to socialists everywhere a model of the planned economy that looked worthy of emulating. The second was the rise of National Socialism in Germany, which Hayek, as an Austrian now settled in London, viewed with great alarm. Hayek's initial response to the growing infatuation with central planning was largely a technical one. Partly in collaboration with Ludwig von Mises, he edited and wrote a number of works demonstrating why socialist economic planning was incapable of achieving its purported ends: socialism of a certain kind was simply impossible. His response to the rise of Hitler was a more impassioned one, as he began to argue that Nazism needed to be exposed for what it was, since German citizens in particular had been kept in the dark about its true nature. By the time Britain was once again at war, Hayek had reached the conclusion that Europe, and indeed civilization itself, was endangered by a deeper tendency of which the developments in the Soviet Union and Germany were simply particular manifestations. That tendency was the growing inclination of intellectual and political elites to think that the whole of society could and ought to be brought under collective control and direction.

Hayek's first substantial statement elaborating this concern was *The Road to Serfdom*. The main purpose of the book was to warn that central planning would require a centralization of power, that the centralization of power necessarily brought with it an increase in the scope and extent of power of those wielding it and a concomitant diminution of the power of others and that since it was in the nature of things that those attracted to power were invariably among the worst elements of society, we could only expect the concentration of power to produce a system of rule by those we would least like to see in positions of dominance. Most importantly, Hayek wanted to draw attention to the danger that the rise of a regulatory state would sap the spirit of independence, for people would in time grow used to their fetters and eventually not mind them at all.

These concerns lie at the heart of Hayek's political theory and are the considerations that shaped his subsequent theoretical writings. He came to think that the popularity of socialism's methods required a response in the form of a re-statement and defence of liberalism, which socialists had in some cases disparaged and in others appropriated as a doctrine that was perfectly compatible with their own. The question was what to present as essential to liberalism if it was to be distinguished from socialism. Hayek's conclusion, implicit in the work that followed, was that a liberal society was one governed not by command but by law. The problem addressed by *The Constitution of Liberty* was how to present the ideal of a society under the rule of law and to establish the scope of government operating within its framework. Here, Hayek faced both a theoretical and a strategic question. The strategic issue arose out of his concern to construct a statement of the liberal credo that would attract broad support and provide an alternative to the doctrines whose totalitarian proclivities he feared. This meant crafting a theory that would find friends among conservative liberals, on the one hand, and 'socialist' liberals, on the other. The theoretical problem was to elaborate a doctrine that achieved this without loss of coherence or commitment to the liberal core.

To achieve this, Hayek adopted the assumption that the defence of liberalism required an account of the principles of a constitutional state or, to borrow a formulation to which Hayek made occasional reference, a *Rechtsstaat*. If the worry was the danger of the exercise of arbitrary power by bad men (in an *Obrigkeitsstaat*), surely what was the most desirable alternative was a system of rule not by individuals with the right to command but by laws informed by justice. *The Constitution of Liberty* thus presented an account of the theoretical foundations of a state operating under the rule of law, coupled with an elaboration of the proper scope of government policy under a constitutional order. Two problems arose. The first was internal to the project, since the very idea of the rule of law serving as a meta-principle of constitutionalism was not easy to articulate or defend. Law certainly could guide and constrain, but could it *rule* in any meaningful sense, given that the interpretation and execution of the laws are, inescapably, acts of human will? If it could not, the political ideal of the rule of law was only a metaphor or a slogan rather than a serious possibility.[2] The second was that focussing on the role and limits of the state, even a *Rechtstaat* or constitutional state, required doing something that Hayek was otherwise loath to do: putting the state at the centre of an understanding of political order.

What developed as a consequence in *The Constitution of Liberty* was a treatise on the principles of a liberal political order, which also discussed in detail the role and limits of government action across a range of policy areas from housing to labour market regulation to environmental protection but which offered no theory of the state. It is worth dwelling on this point. Hayek offered in this work a statement of liberal principles that not only would supply a justification of a particular kind of political order but also would serve as a guide to public policy.[3] It was important, he thought, that we become clear on the political principles which inform the workings of the state and that policy be shaped or pursued consistently with such principles rather than on the basis of expediency. He was not, Hayek insisted, a conservative 'prepared to be dragged along a path not of his own choosing'.[4] But of the nature of the state whose development he seemed keen to see guided by the principles and policies he advanced, he said almost nothing. To the extent that he did, it was in part by way of a rejection of the formulations of Carl Schmitt and others for whom the state represented that structure which subsumed the whole of society and

[2] See Martin Louglin, *The Foundations of Public Law* (Oxford University Press, 2010), 312–3.

[3] I do not wish to exaggerate this latter point because Hayek made it clear that it was the role of the political philosopher to serve as a critic of institutions and policy rather than as a functionary whose only concern was to work out what was best within the limits of the immediately feasible or politically possible.

[4] 'Why I Am Not a Conservative', postscript to F. A. Hayek, *The Constitution of Liberty* (London: Routledge and Kegan Paul, 1976), 398.

regulated its workings. Yet, while he rejected their formulations of the idea of a state, he declined to offer any of his own.

What Hayek was rejecting was any conception of political order that threatened to bring together state and society. To do so would be to encourage an understanding of political order according to which society could legitimately be shaped and controlled by the collective as a whole and by those able to secure the power to speak and act on its behalf. To think about the state in this way, as far as Hayek was concerned, was to think in totalitarian terms. He was most explicit about this fear in his 1966 essay, 'The Principles of a Liberal Social Order', in which he wrote

> The progressive displacement of the rules of just conduct of private and criminal law by a conception derived from public law is the process by which existing liberal societies are progressively transformed into totalitarian societies. This tendency has been most explicitly seen and supported by Adolf Hitler's 'crown jurist' Carl Schmitt who consistently advocated the replacement of the 'normative' thinking of liberal law by a conception of law which regards as its purpose the 'concrete order formation'.[5]

Yet, while he was forthright in revealing what he did not like about such formulations of the notion of the state, his own account of the state is nowhere to be found.

What is it that might account for this? One explanation, offered by William Scheuerman, is that Hayek's understanding of the state owed much to Schmitt in so far as both saw government activity as highly discretionary. Both recognized that such discretionary intervention in society could only mean that the state was governed not by the rule of law but by the agents who possessed the authority to exercise sovereign power. Schmitt welcomed this because he wanted the state to act decisively to strengthen the political community and shape it by reinforcing concrete values. But Hayek abhorred such a possibility and so longed for a return to an earlier kind of state whose non-interventionist and neutral character was more consistent with the rule of law. For Schmitt, the rule of law was an impossibility given the reality of the state as a political community; for Hayek, it could only be secured under the right kind of state.[6] Scheuerman's analysis is an especially insightful one

[5] F. A. Hayek, *Studies in Philosophy, Politics and Economics* (London: Routledge and Kegan Paul, 1967), 169.

[6] William Scheuerman, 'The Unholy Alliance of Carl Schmitt and Friedrich A. Hayek', *Constellations*, 4 (1997), 172.

which identifies some of the serious difficulties Hayek faced to the extent that he wished at one and the same time to advocate the rule of law and yet have a government that could intervene in some aspects of society but not in others.[7] Nonetheless, while this examination of Hayek's affinities with Schmitt is revealing of important tensions in Hayek's work, it is off the mark to the extent that it suggests that, in the end, Hayek longed for a return to a nineteenth-century liberal-neutral state. If anything, something like the reverse is true: confronted by the difficulties that beset his understanding of a political order under the rule of law, he pushed out in a very different, more radical direction in *Law, Legislation and Liberty*. In the end, Hayek never quite sorts out the problems that set him on this path. But the effort is instructive, for it reveals what is distinctive about Hayek's liberalism and suggests a very different way of thinking about political society.

Law, Legislation and Liberty

Although presented as a supplement rather than an alternative to *The Constitution of Liberty*, Hayek's trilogy is not only a more original work (as he himself thought it was) but also one that is built upon an effort of rethinking the fundamental nature of order in human affairs.[8] Here, Hayek returned to the concerns that prompted him to write *The Road to Serfdom*, but he does not, as Scheuerman intimates, try to return to some imaginary nineteenth-century liberal theory of the neutral state. Instead, he asks some very fundamental questions about the nature of human reason and the possibility of its exercise to create a social order that might best serve human purposes. The result is a conception of order that offers even less scope for the development of a theory of the state as the state itself diminishes in importance as an institution and as a concept.

The key to understanding this development is Hayek's notion of 'the Great Society', which he introduces as an idea related to the theory of the 'Open Society' but which is a term that serves a very different

[7] Scheuerman's objection here is that Hayek unjustifiably criticizes interventions that establish a welfare state. Libertarians of various stripes, on the other hand, have criticized Hayek for admitting such an extensive role for government not just by permitting a minimal welfare state but by elaborating functions which it might also perform elsewhere.

[8] Hayek, *Law, Legislation and Liberty*, Preface to the consolidated edition, xix.

purpose to Popper's. In Volume II of *Law, Legislation and Liberty*, Hayek asserts that a 'Great Society has nothing to do with, and is in fact irreconcilable with "solidarity" in the true sense of unitedness in the pursuit of common goals.'[9] He has already suggested that a free society was a pluralistic society without a common hierarchy of ends.[10] Now he was insisting that such a society did not need to share any deep commitments or bind its members together to establish a form of social unity. Solidarity did not matter, for it was of no particular value either instrumentally or in itself. Human beings inhabited a world in which they were in fact members of numerous societies and had the capacity to relate to, as well as an interest in interacting with, people from more than one group or collective. To the extent that all were connected in a single type of order, they were members of a *catallaxy*: an undirected and uncontrolled realm of mutual co-operation given existence by the very possibility of friendship and exchange.

In this conception of order, the state is of limited significance. This is not because states do not exist or because they are without consequence. Hayek does devote considerable attention to the matter of the tasks governments can usefully perform and also considers the problem of constitutional design. But, in addressing the question of the basis of order, he declines to take the state as the framework within which order is to be understood. In effect, he treats the state as an *empirical* phenomenon rather than as a *philosophical* construction. In this regard, he operates in a very different way from other contemporary liberal theorists such as Rawls, who theorize assuming a closed society.[11] Hayek has no use for such an assumption because he has determined that the best way to understand social order is to recognize that it is the unintended outcome of the evolution of human beings who come over time to interact with one another less and less through processes that bind them in solidaristic units but increasingly through indirect connections that require little sense of shared commitment or commonality. Philosophically speaking, human beings lived not in states but in an 'abstract order'. Empirically speaking, of course, they were almost everywhere members of states, but this membership was not what was most important for trying to understand the way in which they related to one another.

[9] Ibid., 111. [10] Ibid., 109.

[11] John Rawls is the most explicit about this. See John Rawls, *Political Liberalism*, 2nd edn. (New York: Columbia University Press, 1996).

To understand the significance of this, we need to look more closely at the notion of an *abstract order*. Hayek constructs this term because he wishes to account for what he calls the 'extended order of human cooperation'. The extended order is an abstract order. An abstract order is one governed by abstract rules of just conduct. Abstract rules of just conduct are so-called because when they come into dispute, the issue is settled by appealing to other rules that share some abstract features with the present issue. Disputes thus are settled without any appeal to, or agreement about, the importance of the particular aims pursued by the disputing parties.[12] The persistent application of abstract rules over time produces an abstract order which, as a whole, serves no particular end but which nevertheless facilitates the peaceful pursuit of diverse ends. The nature of the extended society as an abstract order has to be explicitly recognized, however, because it must be understood that this order is *not* a community.

In saying this, Hayek in effect embraces a position that Carl Schmitt thought was implicit in liberalism and the source of its weakness. In its tendency to extend rights of membership to outsiders, and so failing to distinguish clearly between friends and enemies, the liberal state ran the risk of destroying the political unity that made its existence possible and eventually succumbing to internal or external enemies who were more united political forces.[13] To avert this danger it was important that the boundaries of the natural political unit that was the nation coincide with the boundaries of the state. The problem with liberalism, according to Schmitt, is that it is unable to create the requisite political identity because of its faith in the possibility of human co-operation through exchange, deliberation and compromise. As a consequence, it is simply unable to constitute any form of political community.

Hayek explicitly denies the importance of political community and repudiates the idea that the pursuit of solidarity or social unity is necessary or desirable. Indeed, he bemoans this tendency in the development of modern liberalism, which had from time to time succumbed to the lure of nationalist sentiment. Hayek had already voiced this concern in the 1930s when he first criticized John Stuart Mill for arguing in his *Considerations of Representative Government* that '[i]t is in general a necessary condition of free institutions that the boundaries of

[12] Hayek, *Law, Legislation and Liberty*, 15.
[13] Carl Schmitt, *The Concept of the Political* (University of Chicago Press, 2007), ed. George Schwab, 69–79.

government should coincide in the main with those of nationalities.'[14] For Hayek, Mill accepted more of nationalist doctrines than was compatible with his liberal program. Acton, however, saw more clearly that liberty required diversity rather than uniformity – or even consensus. He recognized that 'the combination of different nations in one State is as necessary a condition of civilized life as the combination of men in society' and that 'this diversity in the same State is a firm barrier against the intention of the Government beyond the political sphere which is common to all into the social department which escapes legislation and is ruled by spontaneous laws.'[15] Diversity was the bulwark of resistance to social organization. Now, in *Law, Legislation and Liberty*, Hayek began to draw out the implications of his long-standing unease about nationalism. A liberal social order was not an order bounded by the state, nor was it one marked by any form of deep social unity.

It is in this context that we should understand Hayek's well-known repudiation of social justice. Social justice makes sense as a political ideal within a closed community of like-minded people but cannot coherently be pursued across an abstract order of people who interact with and relate to one another not because they share particular deep ethical commitments but in spite of the fact that they do not. Hayek has no objection to government recognizing among its responsibilities the task of establishing a welfare safety net for the poor and even suggests that as societies grow wealthier they might provide for the indigent more generously. But establishing such an arrangement as a matter of justice would require also settling upon a common ethical framework that simply cannot exist across the abstract order that is the extended order of human co-operation.

The plausibility, if not plain correctness, of Hayek's assessment in conceptual terms is clearly suggested by the fact that a number of thinkers have argued that the pursuit of social justice requires a commitment to social unity. David Miller has argued consistently for recognition of the importance of nationality on the grounds that social justice can only be sustained within a community with certain shared values.[16]

14 Quoted in F. A. Hayek, 'The Economic Conditions of Interstate Federalism' in *Individualism and Economic Order* (University of Chicago Press, 1980), 270 note. This essay was first published in the *New Commonwealth Quarterly*, 5, no. 2 (September 1939), 131.

15 Lord Acton, in *The History of Freedom and Other Essays*, quoted in Hayek, 'The Economic Conditions of Interstate Federalism', 270.

16 David Miller, *On Nationality* (Oxford University Press, 1996).

Brian Barry also, in various writings that include a vigorous critique of multiculturalism, makes clear the need for a liberal community of shared egalitarian commitments if social justice is to be established. Most famously, John Rawls developed a theory of political liberalism that argued explicitly that political order had to be founded on a shared understanding of social justice that alone could supply the social unity that would make for long-run stability. All are preoccupied to some degree with the problem of how to secure a community's political existence – confronting a challenge Schmitt argued liberalism was by its very nature unable to meet.

Hayek's theory accepts that liberal principles cannot secure any kind of political unity, for in his view liberalism has no such aspiration, but rather than address it as a problem, he, in effect, embraces it as a virtue. The challenge is to articulate a conception of a liberal order that is not bounded by the state but which nonetheless acknowledges the existence of states and accounts for their operation.

Liberal internationalism

Hayek first tackled this problem indirectly when he grappled with the issue of nationalism, well before his re-formulation of liberalism in *Law, Legislation and Liberty*. The result was his theory of inter-state federalism as a solution to the problem of national conflict. The idea of a federation of states he saw as in certain ways the implication or outcome of the development of liberalism. But the immediate impetus for the elaboration of the theory in Hayek's case was the fate of post-war Germany, which was a subject that preoccupied him well before the Allies' victory. It would be necessary, he thought, for Germany to be placed under Allied control but also important that Germans be discouraged from regaining an attachment to the idea of a central state. This meant cultivating in Germany some kind of commitment to liberal institutions. The way to do this would be to give German states the option of joining a federation of European states as a way of escaping the ignominy of foreign occupation. In the course of time, Hayek thought, they might become a part of a much more comprehensive European federation which included France and Italy.[17] The idea would be to so 'entangle' the states with their

[17] F. A. Hayek, 'A Plan for the Future of Germany', first published, with the subtitle 'Decentralization Offers Some Basis for Independence', in *The Saturday Review of Literature*, 23 June 1945, 7–9, 39–40. This reference is to the reprinted essay in *The*

non-German neighbours that they would become 'far from anxious once again to merge their individuality in a highly centralized Reich'.[18]

Crucially, Hayek thought, federation would have to involve not only political union but also economic union. Political union would abrogate national sovereignty, while economic union would mean the elimination of barriers to trade and the reduction of conflict between interests tied to group identity. The problem with central economic planning is that it was only possible if there was agreement on substantive values, and this was not possible where there is diversity. Planning required the suppression of diversity. Federation, he thought, offered a way of maintaining a diversity of values by placating the demand for unification.[19]

At the same time, however, Hayek also thought that for this project to succeed, it was vitally important that there be within a liberal political order some shared commitment to certain values. There needed to be some kind of awareness of and attachment to liberal ideas, notably of toleration and freedom, though it was no less important that people did not associate such values with their own societies rather than with good societies generally.

Yet, here an important problem arises. If it is important for the survival of liberalism that liberal ideals are not only understood but also accepted or embraced – internalized – how is this to be achieved without turning liberalism into just another sectarian doctrine, albeit one that is represented as a universal norm? To put the matter slightly differently, if political society takes it upon itself to inculcate values that are deemed vital to its survival, what is to say that it will not simply end up promoting sectional values or the values of particular interests, which are asserted to be of universal worth, and suppressing diverse minority standpoints. Is the idea of a liberal state even a coherent one if the aspiration is for some kind of political order whose concern is to accommodate diverse values?

This is a problem that Hayek has not been alone in facing. Most famously, John Rawls was confronted with this issue when his *Theory of Justice* was criticized as incapable of being embraced by anyone not

Collected Works of F. A. Hayek, vol, 4: *The Fortunes of Liberalism: Essays on Austrian Economics and the Ideal of Freedom* (University of Chicago Press, 1992), ed. Bruce Caldwell, 226.

18 Ibid.

19 See the discussion in my 'Hayek and Liberalism' in Edward Feser (ed.), *The Cambridge Companion to Hayek* (Cambridge University Press, 2006), 201.

already committed to a particular and very narrow range of values. His was a liberalism for liberals who accepted the ideals of individuality and autonomy commonly associated with the thought of John Stuart Mill and Immanuel Kant. Rawls responded to this critique by conceding that the theory he had crafted was indeed more limited in its reach than he had initially hoped. His re-working of his view in *Political Liberalism* suggested that the most he hoped to do was to offer a statement of the liberal ideal as one that could appeal only to those within a particular modern Western political tradition – and possibly only within the American tradition at that. Rawls aimed in his later writings to craft a theory of justice that might serve as a statement of principle that could be embraced by a diversity of people within a political tradition by expressing the terms under which they could live as a single people within a closed society. Rawls constructed a theory that was in effect an account of the foundations of the modern American *Rechtsstaat*.

Confronting the same problem, Hayek took a different path. While Rawls backed away from his original aspirations to develop a widely applicable theory, Hayek moved in a more international direction. What he sensed was that it was not possible to defend the *Rechtsstaat* without retreating to the kind of nationalist position he saw as the main threat to the idea of a liberal political order.

The difficulty was how to theorize about a liberal political order and to defend liberal political ideas without closing the borders to exclude those who did not share the same deep commitments to particular values? In *Law, Legislation and Liberty*, we see Hayek grappling with the various problems in which this difficulty finds particular expression: how do we understand the nature of order, what is the place of justice within it, and what does this understanding mean for the democratic ideal?

It would be too much to suggest that Hayek reaches a complete resolution of the problem. What is instructive, however, is his engagement with it, for the tensions that become apparent show us something about the dilemma confronting political theorists now. The thought by which he is guided is that it is 'very misleading to single out the inhabitants or citizens of a particular political unit as the prototype of a society'.[20] Moreover, it is important that we resist the growing tendency to equate state with society, not only politically but also sociologically. The state does not subsume society, either empirically or conceptually.

20 Hayek, *Law, Legislation and Liberty*, vol. III, 140.

Society is at once continuous to the degree that all human activity is a part of an 'extended order of cooperation' and also composed of numerous smaller self-generating structures – societies – people develop. The state, as 'the organization of the people of a territory under a single government', will contain numerous societies but is itself at the same time merely one organization within an extended society.

The task facing people as a practical matter, and political theorists as contributors to the understanding of the nature of the practical task, is how to deal with the tendency of the state to expand and absorb society. This is a question of how to contain the power of the state or the power of those who will exert control over individuals and groups within society in the pursuit of their own particular ends. For Hayek, then, the problem is not one of how we can secure the legitimacy of the state, maintain some form of unity or articulate some kind of understanding that will reconcile us with the political arrangements by which we are governed. His concern is the more immediate one of how to contain power – and political power in particular.

Now Hayek is not the first thinker to evince this concern. Even Rawls, while he does not devote much attention to problem, expresses a worry about the 'oppressive use of state power'. But what Hayek comes to think is that the problem of political power cannot be resolved institutionally. This is not to say that institutional mechanisms are unimportant or irrelevant, for there can certainly be better or worse rules, procedures or legal and political structures. Indeed, Hayek considers a range of topics in this regard from the content of education policy to the ideal constitution.[21] The major point he tries to make, however, is that power is not readily contained by such mechanisms when the broader tendency is towards the dominance of the territorial state.

What is disconcerting about this conclusion is that it is, at least for anyone sympathetic to Hayek's concerns, a very pessimistic one. While *The Constitution of Liberty* was a programmatic work, given both to the articulation of principles and to the supply of solutions to practical policy questions, the conclusions reached by Hayek in his later works suggest that there is no programme. And, indeed, this is so, for once one concedes that institutional solutions are not to be found, elaborating a systematic programme has little point.

[21] See his 'Model Constitution' Chapter 17 in Hayek, *Law, Legislation and Liberty*, vol. III, 105–27, and Jan-Werner Müller's contribution to this volume (Chapter 11).

Conclusion

How, then, are we to understand Hayek's contribution to political theory and to our grasp of the nature of political order in the modern world? In the early Hayek in some ways what we saw was an optimistic attempt to address the problem of how to respond to the challenge he saw posed by totalitarian ideals. The answer was a re-statement of the guiding principles of liberalism to encourage others to take up the task of supporting the liberal state, understood as a political order in which government operated under the rule of law. The Hayek we see at the end of his career is much more the political realist who has come to recognize the limitations of institutional solutions and is much more deeply sceptical about the possibility of a limited state. This Hayek elaborates and defends liberalism in very different terms. Liberalism is no longer a state ideology, but a theory of the free society that transcends political boundaries.

The theory is not one that repudiates the state, nor is it even one that is indifferent to the issue of political reform. But it is one that suggests that for as long as a state-centric perspective is embraced political theory – and practice – will head down the wrong path. The *Rechtsstaat* may have been a noble ideal, but it was doomed to failure. In the end, the state cannot limit itself, and if we are at all concerned by this, we need to think about the problem very differently.

13

Local and global knowledge in the administrative state

ADRIAN VERMEULE

How should the administrative state be organized from the epistemic point of view? The institutions of the administrative state must aggregate both preferences and judgements. The preference-aggregation side of the ledger is the subject of extensive literatures in law and economics, public choice, political economy and positive political theory. Theorists of preference aggregation in regulatory and administrative institutions study the industrial organization of Congress, the White House and the agencies; lobbying, litigation and other forms of individual and collective action; and a range of other activities undertaken by rational agents whose preferences differ from those of other agents, whether or not their beliefs differ as well.

By contrast, the epistemic organization of the administrative state is relatively *terra incognita*, with useful exceptions in the literatures on political economy and industrial organization.[1] On the epistemic side, the main issue is not the aggregation of conflicting preferences but the aggregation of diverse judgements. Information must be generated, aggregated and deployed by executive officials, administrative agencies and other actors who share important fundamental preferences but who have differing beliefs and thus have different derived preferences over policies. The breadth of the topic is daunting; I will examine only one of the major fault lines that structures debates about the epistemic capacities of administrative agencies and the administrative state more generally.

At issue is the conflict, tension or trade-off between *local and global knowledge*.[2] Across a variety of controversies, I will suggest, the same

For helpful comments, thanks to Sabeel Rahman, Emma Rothschild, Cass Sunstein, participants in the conference on 'Law, Liberty and State' at the London School of Economics, and participants in the Harvard Seminar on Law and Politics. Thanks also to Samantha Goldstein for excellent research assistance.

[1] See sources cited below.

[2] For these terms, see M. J. Holian, 'Understanding the M-Form Hypothesis', *Journal of Industrial Organization Education*, 5 (2010), 3.

issue can be discerned in varying forms, whether explicitly or implicitly. Proponents of local knowledge, often taking their cue from Friedrich Hayek's work, argue that the scope of the administrative state or its internal organization within that scope should be arranged so as to privilege context-specific knowledge about particular economic or regulatory problems, especially tacit or practical knowledge. Proponents of global knowledge, among whom the best known may be Justice Stephen Breyer of the United States Supreme Court, argue for a kind of synoptic technocratic rationality that implies an expansive scope for the administrative state and, within that scope, attempts to maximize the epistemic coordination of regulatory approaches across different agencies and different subject matters.

I will examine the trade-off between local and global knowledge at two levels. The first is the scope of the administrative state's regulatory jurisdiction; this is the large-scale question of government versus markets which is central to the Hayekian program. The second level is the internal organization of the regulatory bureaucracy within the area committed to the administrative state's regulatory jurisdiction. Here, the industrial organization literature, as we will see, has adapted Hayekian questions to new settings. These two levels – the scope of the administrative state and its internal organization – parallel a conventional distinction in the industrial organization literature between the scope of firms and the internal structure of firms.

The framing and analysis of these two questions is meant to have value independent of the answers I will offer. However, once the trade-offs are stated and evaluated, I go on to suggest that the Hayekian arguments for local knowledge fare poorly at both levels. At the level of the scope of the administrative state, the Hayekian position emphasizes the benefits of local knowledge and adaptation to the contingencies of time and place, but it overlooks or downplays a major trade-off: centralized synoptic regulation is indispensable for *epistemic coordination.* Spill-overs, externalities and lost opportunities for economic synergy may arise not only because of conflicts of interest and problems of collective action but also for epistemic reasons: actors with thick localized information may be myopic about what other actors are doing. Consequently, a major role for synoptic national regulation is not (only) command and control but epistemic co-ordination and the creation of common knowledge – measures for generating and sharing information that dispel the local myopia of market actors.

Furthermore, even setting this trade-off aside, Hayek and many of his successors overlook that markets are just one institutional arrangement for aggregating local information. The administrative state itself can and actually does embody a range of institutions for aggregating thick local knowledge, including the tacit practical knowledge whose importance Hayek underscored. Congress itself is a summation of representatives with local knowledge of dispersed constituencies, while the administrative agencies often incorporate actors with industry- or area-specific skills and information. The administrative state deploys far more than abstract or statistical technocratic expertise; rather, it has developed a *representative bureaucracy* devoted to the gathering and exploitation of local knowledge.

At the second level, the internal organization of the bureaucracy, the argument for local knowledge underscores that front-line agencies may have more issue-specific expertise and tacit practical knowledge than centralized reviewing institutions, such as the Office of Information and Regulatory Affairs (OIRA), can ever possess; centralized reviewers must always be boundedly informed. Yet, line agencies are also boundedly informed on other dimensions, as the very context specificity of their expertise makes them prone to overlook synergies and spill-overs across agencies and regulatory areas. The result is a problem of epistemic coordination among the regulators. This problem can be solved in principle either through centralized top-down coordination by a body such as OIRA or through decentralized bottom-up coordination by agencies interacting horizontally. Under a realistic assessment of the conditions of the American administrative state, however, top-down epistemic coordination will prove the superior approach. OIRA aggregates and coordinates dispersed information – information that is dispersed around the bureaucracy rather than society – and does so in a manner that cannot be replicated by horizontal coordination among agencies given background features of the federal government.

When both the scope and organization of the administrative firm are considered simultaneously in light of the knowledge problem, it becomes clear that certain combinations of views are inconsistent. We will see that Hayekians attempt to justify, on free-market grounds, the creation of a central planner for regulation – a synoptic overseer of the bureaucracy. I will suggest that such a justification rests on inconsistent premises about local knowledge and thus fails. Yet, there is no inconsistency in believing, on epistemic grounds, both that the administrative state should have a robust scope and that an OIRA-style centralized synoptic coordinator is necessary to oversee the bureaucracy; I will press this combination of views instead.

The first part of this chapter examines the scope of the administrative state and the trade-off between local knowledge and centralized epistemic coordination; a principal claim is that Hayekian arguments for a constrained administrative state overlook the ability of non-market institutions to aggregate local and tacit knowledge. The second part examines the internal organization of the bureaucracy and claims that under realistic conditions, at least in the American administrative state, the trade-off between global or synoptic coordination and local knowledge will have to be resolved by a centralized coordinating body such as OIRA. The third part brings the two halves of the discussion together by asking whether a theoretically consistent Hayekian may justify OIRA-style centralized oversight of the bureaucracy as a measure for protecting the dispersed local knowledge generated by free markets. In my view, this approach is logically untenable, although a robust role for OIRA is justifiable on other grounds. A brief conclusion follows.

The scope of the administrative state

Assumptions

The first question involves the scope of the administrative 'firm' – the area of regulatory jurisdiction that the administrative state will oversee. From an epistemic standpoint, the scope of the administrative state should be chosen so as to aggregate information and judgements in whatever way optimally promotes commonly agreed-upon ends. To get traction on these questions, we will need to make some simplifying assumptions.

First and foremost is the assumption that there *are* commonly agreed-upon ends somewhere in the picture. In some domains, there are not, of course; it is value conflict all the way down. In other domains, however, the questions about the performance of the administrative state are questions about how well agencies and the executive branch generally pursue social goals admitted by nearly everyone to be valid and whose ranking vis-à-vis other goals may be widely shared as well. Even where there is disagreement about goals, there is typically unanimous agreement that goals should be pursued in the most cost-effective manner possible, so the choice of efficient means is a matter of common interest even if goals are contested.

Here two points are important. Firstly, Hayekians, in contrast to more radical libertarians and anarchists, do not deny the existence of commonly agreed-upon ends,[3] although they believe that the administrative state does a poor job of promoting those ends. Secondly, observed disagreement among political or economic actors or even bitter conflict among such actors does not at all entail that there is any conflict of fundamental or bedrock preferences. Strictly epistemic differences arising from differing information or beliefs – beliefs about causal processes, means-ends judgements and the like – may produce deep disagreements about optimal policies. Derived preferences – preferences for particular policies – may diverge because of differences in beliefs, even if relevant actors share deep or fundamental preferences in a given area.

Some legal assumptions are also necessary to frame the issue. I assume that, as a first approximation, Congress may (1) regulate any aspect of the national economy and (2) delegate to the executive branch jurisdiction over anything which it could regulate directly. Both assumptions abstract from an elaborate body of constitutional law, which respectively establishes the bounds of Congress' regulatory powers and the limits of its ability to delegate power to the executive. However, it is conventional wisdom among constitutional lawyers that both bodies of doctrine are impressively capacious; barring unusual circumstances,[4] Congress may regulate any and all economic matters either directly[5] or indirectly through administrative delegation.[6]

Finally, I assume that the alternative to national regulation is 'the market'. This assumption is made strictly to engage Hayekian arguments against the administrative state that rest on an opposition between 'government' and 'markets'. In federal systems such as that of the United States, of course, the opposition is somewhat misleading. A third alternative is federalism – regulation by states and localities, which holds out the promise of being decentralized but not market based. Absent some constitutional restriction, state governments can regulate even if the

[3] F. A. Hayek, *The Road to Serfdom* (University of Chicago Press, 1944), 60.

[4] One such circumstance is 'inaction' on the part of regulated actors. See *Nat'l Fed'n of Indep. Bus.* v. *Sebelius*, 132 S.Ct. 2566, 2587 (2012) (under Commerce Clause, Congress lacks power to justify regulation by citing the effects of individual 'inaction').

[5] See, e.g., *Gonzalez* v. *Raich*, 545 U.S. 1, 26 (2005) (application of the Controlled Substances Act, which criminalizes the manufacture, distribution or possession of marijuana, to intrastate growers and users of marijuana for medical purposes did not violate Commerce Clause).

[6] See, e.g., *Whitman* v. *Am. Trucking Ass'ns*, 531 U.S. 457, 473–76 (2001) (Clean Air Act's grant of authority to EPA to set pollution standards at level 'requisite to protect public health' was not unconstitutional delegation).

national government cannot or will not, so the market can be constrained by state regulation as well as federal; indeed, in a number of domains, federal regulation attempts to clear away state regulation or to impose national uniformity in order to reduce legal uncertainty or to unshackle markets.

However, absent national regulation, there is some class of activities that states cannot effectively regulate because economic actors with mobile assets enjoy low costs of exit; in the extreme cases, no state can regulate more than does the least-regulatory jurisdiction (the 'race to the bottom'). And activities by market actors in one state may affect both market actors and regulators in other states, as in the case of pollution. These inter-state spill-overs imply some irreducible role for national coordination and regulation, so it is not entirely misleading to contrast national regulation with markets. In any event, I mean to bracket questions of federalism; the simplifying assumption allows me to more cleanly identify two problems with Hayekian arguments from local information. Those problems would also arise in many cases in which state rather than federal regulation is contrasted with markets, so bracketing questions of federalism does not seriously distort the substantive issues.[7]

Trade-offs: local and global knowledge

Hayek's 1945 paper, 'The Use of Knowledge in Society',[8] argues quite brilliantly that central planning suffers from two problems, not one. Most obvious is the problem of incentives, created by the self-interest of the planner. Thus, undergraduates are prone to say that a genuinely benevolent dictator would be the best of all possible worlds in politics, but Hayek argues that even a benevolent dictatorial planner would fail due to inadequate information.

Hayek's main argument runs this way: the central planner may call upon experts who possess specialized technical information, usually embodied in statistical form, but economic actors possess dispersed, disaggregated information about the 'particular circumstances of time

[7] I also bracket here the contrast between administrative regulation and common-law decision making. For an epistemic analysis of the common law and common-law constitutionalism, including an assessment of Hayek's views, see Adrian Vermeule, *Law and the Limits of Reason* (Oxford University Press, 2010).

[8] F. A. Hayek, 'The Use of Knowledge in Society', *American Economic Review*, 35 (1945), 519.

and place'.[9] This sort of information about a myriad of rapidly changing variables is indispensable for on-going adjustments in a relentlessly dynamic economy; this is the Austrian side of Hayek. Crucially, the information takes the form of tacit practical knowledge, knowing how rather than knowing that. The key feature of this sort of information is that it cannot be transmitted to the planner, at least not at sufficiently low cost or in a sufficiently timely manner; according to Hayek, it is 'knowledge of the kind which by its nature cannot enter into statistics and therefore cannot be conveyed to any central authority in statistical form'.[10] Thus, the planner, no matter how many experts he or she has on tap, will be unable to supply plans or even regulations that are sufficiently well adapted to the ever-changing localized problems of the economy. As a shorthand, I will call this highly contextualized and non-transmissible type of knowledge 'local knowledge'; James Scott uses the Greek term *metis*.[11]

Hayek is aware that market actors need to coordinate their behaviours with one another and that the flip side of local knowledge is a kind of informational parochialism or myopia. '[T]he "man on the spot" cannot decide solely on the basis of his limited but intimate knowledge of the facts of his immediate surroundings. There still remains the problem of communicating to him such further information as he needs to fit his decisions into the whole pattern of changes of the larger economic system.'[12] Thus, there is a need for coordination across local contexts and local knowers, but as I will discuss more extensively in the second part of this chapter, coordination need not entail centralization; there can

[9] Ibid., 521.

[10] Ibid., 524. In other words, '[Hayek's] claim is not merely that information is widely dispersed and therefore hard to acquire. Rather, it is impossible to acquire' ('Friedrich Hayek', by David Schmidtz, in *Stanford Encyclopedia of Philosophy*; available at http://plato.stanford.edu/entries/friedrich-hayek/). However, that the central planner cannot acquire the information does not entail that there is no information to be acquired. Thus, I think it is wrong to say that 'the problem has a deeper level. The problem is not merely lack of *access* to information; rather, the information does not exist.' Idem. That interpretation is inconsistent with Hayek's idea that market competition is a *discovery* procedure; see note 13. On Hayek's picture, the planner's dilemma is precisely that a certain category of real information forever hovers just out of reach.

[11] James C. Scott, *Seeing Like a State: How Certain Schemes to Improve the Human Condition Have Failed* (New Haven, CT: Yale University Press, 1999), 311. For distinctions among various forms of tacit knowledge and expertise, see Harry Collins, *Tacit and Explicit Knowledge* (University of Chicago Press, 2010); Harry Collins and Robert Evans, *Rethinking Expertise* (University of Chicago Press, 2007).

[12] Hayek, 'The Use of Knowledge in Society', 524–5.

be decentralized coordination. Hayek puts his faith in horizontal rather than vertical coordination – in coordination achieved through a myriad of decentralized interactions rather than through top-down commands. Market competition is a 'discovery procedure' that gives each actor the information necessary to adjust his or her plans to those of others.[13]

For Hayek, the critical mechanism that produces informational coordination in markets is the price system. On this view, prices are a kind of summary statistic which impounds a bewildering array of variables, drawn from many localized decisions, and conveys them in useful form to other localized decision makers. The effects of any given actor's decisions on other actors, and vice versa, are communicated through prices, and this suffices to dispel the myopia of locally adaptive agents who have thick knowledge of their own circumstances but limited informational horizons.

The problems with this view are manifold. Firstly, under a range of conditions, prices will supply highly misleading information about the real cost of resources; a stock example is monopoly, in which the monopolist sets prices above marginal cost and thus, in effect, sends a distorted signal about the social cost of the goods the monopolist supplies. Hayek therefore allows that regulation to curb monopoly is valid,[14] but this opens the door to other arguments that real costs diverge from perceived costs as embodied in prices. Secondly, even where there are no problems of externality or monopoly, genuine coordination problems may arise, an example being the choice of 'compatibility standards' for products and technology.[15] In such problems, there exists more than one mutually beneficial equilibrium for market actors; prices will not tell the actors which equilibrium to adopt. Thirdly, as emphasized by Karl Popper, administrative experimentation and intervention – Popper's 'piecemeal social engineering' – is precisely what generates new information and allows agencies to learn by doing. On this view, even if Hayek's diagnosis is correct, his prescription is backwards; profound ignorance about complex social and economic processes itself counsels in favour of (constrained) intervention and experimentation by regulators rather than in favour of free-market liberalism.[16] At a minimum,

[13] F. A. Hayek, 'Competition as a Discovery Procedure', *Quarterly Journal of Austrian Economics*, 5 (2002), 9.

[14] F. A. Hayek, *Law, Legislation and Liberty* (University of Chicago Press, 1981), vol. III, 85.

[15] P. Bolton and J. Farrell, 'Decentralization, Duplication and Delay', *Journal of Political Economy*, 98 (1990), 804.

[16] See C. L. Kerstenetsky, 'Hayek and Popper on Ignorance and Intervention', *Journal of Institutional Economics*, 3 (2007), 33.

there is no epistemic warrant for a global presumption either for or against regulatory intervention and experimentation; intervention has informational benefits as well as risks of unintended consequences and unexpected costs, so interventions should be judged locally on their particular merits.

Finally – and this is the most general problem of all – it has been shown that as long as information is costly, no market can be fully informationally efficient, even in principle.[17] In simplified terms, the reason is that market actors will have incentives to acquire costly information only if they can profit from it. But if they can, then – precisely on Hayekian grounds – their information will be transmitted via the price system to competitors who may profit as well, even though they have not made costly investments in information. Anticipating this free-rider problem, no one may invest in information, but if this occurs, then everyone has incentives to do so – and so forth. In other words, the costliness of information creates a free-rider problem that has no general equilibrium solution, implying that markets for information are intrinsically unstable. The more efficient the price system becomes at conveying information, the worse the free-rider problem becomes, the less efficient the price system will be and so on in a circle. Hayek's appeal to the price system to give an informational rationale for free markets is in this sense self-defeating.

The upshot is that decentralized coordination through the price system cannot, even in principle, fully substitute for centralized coordination through governmental institutions. There is a real trade-off between local knowledge and adaptation, on the one hand, and epistemic coordination which attempts to take a broader synoptic overview of firm behaviour and of the economy generally, discerning spill-overs, externalities and opportunities for synergies across enterprises which go unnoticed by locally myopic actors. The administrative state is a very large institutional mechanism for pursuing epistemic coordination and managing the resulting trade-offs.

To be clear, nothing in this account limits the administrative state to operating through command-and-control regulation. Coordination often may be pursued through essentially informational measures.[18] The

[17] See S. J. Grossman and J. E. Stiglitz, 'On the Impossibility of Informationally Efficient Markets', *American Economic Review*, 70 (1980), 393.

[18] See R. B. Ahdieh, 'The Visible Hand: Coordination Functions of the Regulatory State', *Minnesota Law Review*, 95 (2010), 278.

problem with Hayekian agents with thick local knowledge, on this account, is not that they are selfish (although they may be) but that they are locally myopic; they may overlook opportunities for cooperation with other agents and fail to understand how coordinating their behaviours with those of other agents could make all better off. Given these problems, agencies may pursue measures that collect globally relevant information and provide it to local agents, better enabling them to coordinate their behaviours with those of others. Indeed, in Hayekian vein, agencies often may be able to invent and deploy summary statistics that impound a great deal of global information about the behaviours of whole economic sectors or industries.

A key example of this technique is the promulgation, by agencies or quasi-public bodies, of various types of standards: voluntary industry standards which convey information to firms about the behaviours of other firms or technical standards where uniformity lowers the costs of cooperation and exchange among firms (the modern equivalent of uniform weights and measures). It has been shown that under plausible conditions, committees that promulgate standards – either regulatory commissions or quasi-public bodies such as the American National Standards Institute – will be more likely to produce widespread coordination than will decentralized action by 'market leaders' who attempt to start a bandwagon of subsequent imitation by other firms.[19] Centralized standard-setting measures amount to *central planning without coercion*, at least without the sort of ad hoc and discretionary administrative coercion that Hayek feared would undermine the rule of law.[20]

Thus, there are real trade-offs between the benefits of local adaptation and the benefits of global synoptic coordination, especially epistemic coordination. Although Hayek was right that coordination does not logically entail centralization, the mechanism of decentralized coordination on which he relied – the price system – will not do the trick; absent any other candidate for a mechanism of decentralized coordination, the administrative state has important coordinating functions that require agencies to collect and provide synoptic information. I return to these points in the second part of this chapter, where, as we will see, the same

[19] J. Farrell and G. Saloner, 'Coordination through Committees and Markets', *RAND Journal of Economics*, 19 (1988), 235. The basic intuition is that the market mechanism suffers from 'the incompatible adoption that often happens if two or more firms try to lead the bandwagon'. Ibid., 237.

[20] F. A. Hayek, *The Constitution of Liberty* (University of Chicago Press, 1960), 149–50.

trade-off between global and local knowledge is critical to the internal organization of the administrative state.

Nonmarket aggregation of local knowledge

The foregoing provides an external critique of the Hayekian argument for local knowledge, but there is an internal critique as well. Let us put aside the trade-off between coordination and local adaptation and suppose that local adaptation is a good that should be strictly maximized. Even on this assumption, there is an important lacuna in the Hayekian argument. The market is just one possible institutional mechanism for generating and then aggregating local knowledge. One cannot simply posit the importance of local knowledge and then conclude to the superiority of market mechanisms; rather, one must carry out an even-handed institutional comparison between, or among, the institutional possibilities. In particular, I will suggest, the institutions of the regulatory state themselves can be, and have been, justified in part as mechanisms for aggregating local knowledge.[21]

Although it is not essential to my argument here, I believe that Hayek himself overlooked this point. As of 1945, Hayek repeatedly juxtaposed decentralized coordination through the price system, on the one hand, to 'the single mind' of 'the planner', on the other. But, of course, a single mind cannot encompass dispersed local knowledge. Hayek has here built his thesis on a particular kind of nirvana fallacy, comparing the worst-possible version of one institutional arrangement to the best-possible version of another. We might even dub this the Hayek fallacy: a

[21] For earlier statements of this point, see K. S. Rahman, 'Conceptualizing the Economic Role of the State: Laissez-Faire, Technocracy, and the Democratic Alternative', *Polity*, 43 (2011), 283. ('The same knowledge-aggregating properties that Hayek attributes to the decentralized market as a mechanism for decision-making may well be present in democratic decision-making, since each individual can register his own impressions through the democratic process.'); Adrian Vermeule, 'The Hayek Fallacy', *OUPblog*, 9 December 2008, http://blog.oup.com/2008/12/the-hayek-fallacy. For an analogous claim that the institutions of the Athenian democracy successfully aggregated local knowledge, see Josiah Ober, *Democracy and Knowledge: Innovation and Learning in Classical Athens* (Princeton University Press, 2010), 95–6. For a more general suggestion that democratic institutions do better than markets at aggregating dispersed knowledge because democratic institutions 'simultaneously giv[e] each perspective the opportunity to challenge any other feasible perspective', see James Johnson and Jack Knight, *The Priority of Democracy: Political Consequences of Pragmatism* (Princeton University Press, 2012), 260–1.

comparison between an informationally rich decentralized market and an informationally impoverished regulatory apparatus.[22] Regulatory institutions are far from perfect aggregators of information, and no one would claim otherwise; I shall expand upon their imperfections in what follows. But the right comparison is between informationally imperfect regulatory institutions and an informationally imperfect market. As we have seen, markets are necessarily imperfect aggregators of information as long as information is costly; the problem is structural, not contingent or remediable.[23]

Whatever the logical and causal problems with Hayek's argument, however, I want to focus on the affirmative case that the institutions of the administrative state themselves aggregate dispersed information and local knowledge through a variety of mechanisms. I will begin with a set of classical justifications for legislative representation and then move to the administrative state proper, in which delegation of power from legislatures to bureaucracies is the principal means of policymaking.

Legislatures and representation. Let me begin with one of the classical justifications for legislative representation. On this view, urged both by Publius and the Antifederalists in the founding era, a major function of representation is precisely to aggregate 'local information'[24] – Hayek's 'knowledge of people, of local conditions, and special circumstances'. Responding to the argument that federal representatives will make poorly informed decisions about taxation due to 'want of a sufficient knowledge of local circumstances', Publius asks, '[c]annot the like knowledge be obtained in the national legislature from the representatives of each State? And is it not to be presumed that the men who will generally be sent there will be possessed of the necessary degree of intelligence to be able to communicate that information?'[25]

The problem of obtaining local knowledge was central to several questions of constitutional design in the founding era. One of the major debates during the ratification process centred on the House of Representatives and its representation ratio, capped by the constitutional text

22 See Vermeule, 'The Hayek Fallacy'. Hayek acknowledges *en passant* that the price system in imperfect (Hayek, 'The Use of Knowledge in Society', 527) but never conducts a systematically even-handed comparison between informationally imperfect markets and informationally imperfect regulatory processes.

23 Grossman and Stiglitz, 'On the Impossibility of Informationally Efficient Markets'.

24 James Madison, 'The Federalist No. 58' in C. Rossiter (ed.), *The Federalist Papers* (New York: Penguin, 1961), 356, 360.

25 Alexander Hamilton, 'The Federalist No. 36', ibid., 217, 218.

at no more than one representative for every 30,000 inhabitants.[26] Anti-federalists held, as Publius put it, that the representation ratio of the House was too small, so '[the representatives] will not possess a proper knowledge of the local circumstances of their numerous constituents.'[27] Far from rejecting the normative premise of the argument, Publius embraces it and devotes a whole paper to arguing that the federal representatives actually will bring to their tasks an adequate degree of local knowledge. 'The representatives of each state will not only bring with them a considerable knowledge of their respective districts; but will probably in all cases have been members . . . of the state legislature, where all the local information and interests of the state are assembled, and from whence they may easily be conveyed by a very few hands into the legislature of the United States.'[28]

There is no logical inconsistency between this argument and Publius's better-known defence of representation and elections as a selection mechanism that 'refine[s] and enlarge[s] the public views'[29] – yielding a set of representatives who possess a kind of synoptic understanding of the public good of the whole polity. The latter argument suggests that federal representatives will be well positioned to promote synoptic coordination, but Publius also thinks they will be well positioned to aggregate local information. The argument is cast in the alternative, and the alternatives are not logically exclusive. It is fair, however, to discern a pragmatic trade-off between the two aims of synoptic understanding of the federal law-making system as a whole, on the one hand, and local knowledge, on the other, in so far as time is a scarce resource and the time spent by federal legislators on acquiring one type of knowledge is time not spent on acquiring the other.

So far, we have seen that a leading justification for representation in *The Federalist* emphasizes the local character of the knowledge held by representatives, although Publius is candid that the benefits of local information trade off against other goods. A closely related idea, one not prominent in Publius's argument, emphasizes the dispersed or decentralized character of the knowledge held by representatives. One of the most piercing critics of representative democracy, Carl Schmitt,

[26] U.S. Constitution, Article I, §2, clause 3 ('The number of Representatives shall not exceed one for every thirty Thousand, but each State shall have at Least one Representative').

[27] James Madison, 'The Federalist No. 55' in *The Federalist Papers*, 341.

[28] Madison, 'The Federalist No. 56', ibid., 346, 348.

[29] Madison, 'The Federalist No. 10', ibid., 77, 82.

distilled the classical liberal account of representation by arguing explicitly that representation aggregates dispersed information. As Schmitt put it, 'Parliament is . . . the place in which particles of reason that are strewn unequally among human beings gather themselves and bring public power under their control.'[30] It might be backwards to say that Schmitt's terms are explicitly Hayekian; although we have no information on the transmission of this particular idea, the channel of influence between the two thinkers seems to have run generally from Schmitt to Hayek.[31] Hayek's conception of dispersed information in competitive markets ultimately may derive from Schmitt's conception of dispersed information in representative government.

Representative bureaucracy. A great and neglected theorist of the American administrative state, John A. Rohr, agreed with the Antifederalists that the framers plausibly erred by choosing an excessively low representation ratio in Congress, particularly in the lower and more populist legislative chamber.[32] The House has an exceedingly low ratio in historical and comparative perspective; capped by the Constitution at one representative per 30,000 citizens,[33] it currently stands much lower, at around one per 700,000.[34] It is an open question whether representatives of that sort may plausibly be viewed as possessing thick local knowledge; let us suppose that such a claim would be implausible. The general problem is that in large modern representative democracies, with high representation ratios, the local-knowledge justification for legislative institutions becomes ever more attenuated. Sheer scale dilutes the 'local information' that both Madison and the Antifederalists valued. Likewise, assuming that economic and social conditions change more rapidly today than in the founding era, the balance struck by Publius between local knowledge and global knowledge may be askew; the legislative terms chosen by the framers may be too long in current conditions, even if they were optimal when chosen.

30 Carl Schmitt, *The Crisis of Parliamentary Democracy* (Cambridge, MA: MIT Press, 1988), 35.

31 William E. Scheuerman, *Carl Schmitt: The End of Law* (Lanham, UK: Rowman and Littlefield, 1999), 209–24.

32 John A. Rohr, *To Run a Constitution: The Legitimacy of the Administrative State* (Lawrence, KS: University Press of Kansas, 1986), 44.

33 U.S. Constitution, Article I, §2, clause 3.

34 'America Needs a Larger Congress', National Public Radio, 24 January 2011, www.npr.org/2011/01/24/133184399/Op-Ed-America-Needs-A-Larger-Congress.

Nonetheless, Rohr suggested, the administrative state has generated – whether by happenstance, evolutionary adaptation or intentional institutional design – a second-best set of institutions that at least partially compensate for the high representation ratios and slow informational updating of modern legislatures. The main mechanism is delegation from legislatures to 'representative bureaucracy',[35] an idea drawn from the literature on public administration. Although representative bureaucracy comes in a bewildering variety of shapes and sizes, one version of the idea is that administrative institutions may themselves build right into their structure and procedures a kind of representation that brings local knowledge into the regulatory enterprise.

Under the Administrative Procedure Act of 1946, the main mechanism for incorporating the information held by the public and by affected groups into administrative policy making is 'notice-and-comment rule making', under which agencies issue a notice of proposed regulation, receive and consider comments by any interested person and then issue a final decision with a published rationale that is supposed to take the comments into account.[36] Notice-and-comment rule making, however, has both detractors and defenders. The main issues in debate are whether agencies take comments into account at all or instead merely pretend to do so, and if they do, whether the process of commenting is dominated by well-organized and well-funded groups with high stakes who swamp the efforts of public-interest groups and a diffuse citizenry.[37] In the limit, the dominance of well-funded interests may result in a form of 'epistemic capture', in which agencies act with a marked bias in favour of industry and other regulated parties not because of corrupt motivations but because the information agencies receive is itself skewed.

Given these problems, scholars such as Jody Freeman have in effect taken up Rohr's theme by studying alternative administrative mechanisms which in some way promise to create representative bureaucracy. In various forms of 'collaborative governance', agencies develop rules and policies through 'negotiated rule making' among multiple

[35] See Rohr, *To Run a Constitution*, 45. [36] See 5 U.S.C. §553(c).

[37] For relatively optimistic views of public participation in notice and comment, see Steven P. Croley, *Regulation and Public Interests* (Princeton University Press, 2007); M. Cuellar, 'Rethinking Regulatory Democracy', *Administrative Law Review*, 57 (2005), 411. For relatively pessimistic views, see C. Coglianese, 'Citizen Participation in Rulemaking: Past, Present and Future', *Duke Law Journal*, 55 (2006), 943; J. W. Yackee and S. W. Yackee, 'A Bias Towards Business? Assessing Interest Group Influence on the U.S. Bureaucracy', *Journal of Politics*, 68 (2006), 128.

stakeholders.[38] The list of stakeholders may include representatives of trade and industry, public-interest groups which represent the interests of a diffuse citizenry, state and local regulators and other affected parties. Although part of the justification for collaborative governance is straightforward interest representation through bargaining, another major justification is epistemic and points to the deep understanding of the particulars of the regulatory problems – the local knowledge – that stakeholders possess. 'The collaborative claim that problem solving [through collaborative governance] tends to produce higher-quality rules rests upon the belief that unanticipated or novel solutions are likely to emerge from face-to-face deliberative engagement among knowledgeable parties ... [Accordingly, i]n addition to the federal agency, likely members of a negotiated rule-making committee include representatives from the regulated industry, trade associations, labor organizations, public interest groups, and state and local governments.'[39]

Beyond negotiated rule making, Congress sometimes enacts mandates that create structural forms of representative bureaucracy, built right into agencies' composition or procedure. The Advisory Commission on Childhood Vaccines within the Department of Health and Human Services (HHS), created by statute to advise the HHS secretary on vaccine-related problems, comprises 'health experts, members of the general public (two of whom have children who have suffered vaccine-related injury or death), lawyers, and officials from relevant agencies'.[40] The Dodd-Frank Act that reformed financial regulation created an 'Investor Advisory Committee, which is tasked with advising the [Financial Stability Oversight Council] on regulatory reforms to protect investors. The Committee is comprised of a mix of representatives of various stakeholder interests, such as state governments, senior citizens, and pension funds, in addition to relevant experts.'[41] Likewise, 'the financial reform act includes a provision to establish a Municipal Securities Rulemaking Board, comprised of experts and representatives of brokers, investors, and the general public, to set standards for municipal securities

[38] See J. Freeman, 'Collaborative Governance in the Administrative State', *UCLA Law Review*, 45 (1997), 33; 5 U.S.C. §561 *et seq.* (Negotiated Rulemaking Act).

[39] Ibid., 22–3, 38.

[40] A. Vermeule, 'The Parliament of the Experts', *Duke Law Journal*, 58 (2008), 2269.

[41] K. S. Rahman, 'Envisioning the Regulatory State: Technocracy, Democracy, and Institutional Experimentation in the 2010 Financial Reform and Oil Spill Statutes', *Harvard Journal on Legislation*, 48 (2011), 577.

advisors.'[42] In all these examples, technocratic experts, whose knowledge Hayek impeached as excessively general and abstract, are accompanied and complemented by actors with thicker industry-specific practical and local knowledge.

Crisis and delegation. The recurrent major crises of the era since 1914 underscore that the administrative state may itself be capable of aggregating and organizing local knowledge even more rapidly than the market. For these purposes, crisis may be defined as a condition that increases the optimal rate of policy adjustment. In a crisis, policy must be modified and updated more rapidly than in normal times. The increase in the optimal rate of policy adjustment militates in favour of delegation to hierarchical bureaucracy and in favour of enhanced executive power; counter-intuitively, markets adjust too slowly to changing circumstances, and legislatures are even worse in this regard. I will support these claims with a point about the rate of adjustment in markets, a point about legislatures and the speed of policy change and a point about delegation to bureaucracies as a response to rapidly changing circumstances.[43]

Hayek claimed that the price system adjusts more rapidly than a central planner and thus enables an endless dance of mutual adjustment by economic actors; he suggests, in other words, that decentralized coordination works more quickly under rapidly changing conditions than does centralized coordination. This is in principle a testable hypothesis, and it is hardly obvious that Hayek is correct. Decentralized coordination plausibly requires *more* time to reach an equilibrium than does centralized coordination, which is why greater urgency implies greater benefits from centralization.[44] In the Second World War, across political regimes of different types, '[e]verywhere the price mechanism came to be regarded as a method of allocating resources which was too slow and too risky.'[45] The solution, across regimes, was bureaucratic coordination of the generation and distribution of resources.

What about legislatures? Publius addresses the speed of adjustment to changing circumstances when discussing the optimal length of the term for federal representatives in the House. In constitutional design, the

42 Ibid.

43 For a full treatment, see Eric A. Posner and Adrian Vermeule, *The Executive Unbound: After the Madisonian Republic* (Oxford University Press, 2011).

44 Bolton and Farrell, 'Decentralization, Duplication and Delay', 805.

45 Ibid. [quoting A. S. Milward, *War, Economy and Society, 1939–1945* (Berkeley: University of California Press, 1977), 99].

speed with which legislatures can acquire updated information about changes in local circumstances is determined, and constrained, by the length of the legislative term and the frequency of elections. As to these issues, Publius affirms the value of relatively frequent elections as a means of supplying representatives with updated local information, yet he also praises synoptic knowledge of the operation of the whole federal law-making system. The former implies a shorter legislative term and more frequent elections; the latter, a longer legislative term and less frequent elections. The resulting optimization problem has no pinpoint solution, but the trade-off curve plausibly has an internal maximum; Publius argues that the Constitution's two-year term for the House strikes a sensible balance.[46]

This is fine as far as it goes, but it does not get at the main question, which is whether legislatures are capable of keeping up with the necessary pace of policy change in crises. Publius, through Hamilton, famously argued that speed of policy adjustment requires an energetic executive.[47] But even this argument was offered in an environment in which legislative agendas were far less constrained than they are today and in which the capacities of the administrative bureaucracy – as opposed to the presidency per se – were childish compared to those of the modern administrative state. The severely impacted agenda of the modern legislature implies that delegation to a hierarchically organized bureaucracy is the main way in which government will be able to react to crises. A major justification for administrative policy making is that agencies respond more quickly to changing conditions than do legislatures,[48] and part of what allows them to do so is the power to issue ad hoc, situation-specific orders rather than the general rules that Hayek preferred.

Hayek feared the abuse of power that ad hoc administrative orders make possible. A leading model,[49] however, illustrates a competing consideration which is usually decisive in practice: delegation to the executive should increase during crises, despite the increased risk of abuse, when and because the benefits are greater still. The more serious

[46] See generally Madison, 'The Federalist No. 53', *The Federalist Papers.*

[47] See generally Hamilton, 'The Federalist No. 70', ibid.

[48] J. E. Shuren, 'The Modern Regulatory Administrative State: A Response to Changing Circumstances', *Harvard Journal on Legislation*, 38 (2001), 292. ('[T]he modern basis for regulatory administrative agencies is to provide a more effective mechanism for the federal government to respond to changing conditions.').

[49] See P. Aghion, A. Alesina and F. Trebbi, 'Endogenous Political Institutions', *Quarterly Journal of Economics*, 119 (2004), 565.

the crisis, the greater is the anticipated benefit if the executive uses its enhanced discretion to adopt utility-improving policies. Some level of executive abuse is the necessary by-product of other goods; hence, the risk of abuse should be optimized, not strictly minimized.

To be sure, the main Hayekian comparison is between 'government' or 'the planner' and markets, not between legislatures and the presidency or bureaucracy.[50] But because the administrative state has developed a mechanism – delegation to the executive and to agencies – that speeds up the pace of governmental response, the government-to-markets comparison is more favourable to government on the dimension of rapidity of adjustment than it would otherwise be. In so far as Hayekians emphasize the speed of adjustment to changing conditions, delegation to bureaucracies is itself part of the solution. And judging by the experience of the Second World War, the more extreme the crisis, the more bureaucratic adjustment will emerge as the only feasible option.

Let me sum up the claims so far. It is a cartoonish oversimplification to claim that the administrative state relies upon abstract technocratic knowledge, whereas the market relies upon local practical or tacit knowledge (*metis*). Critics who say things of this sort are unfamiliar with the actual institutions of the administrative state, which are variegated and complex and which contain far more in the way of novel institutional forms than is dreamt of in the critics' philosophy. The administrative state itself builds in mechanisms which generate, aggregate and exploit local knowledge and which adjust rapidly to crises and changing circumstances. Even if there are no trade-offs between the generation and exploitation of local and global knowledge so that local knowledge is a good which should be strictly maximized, the choice between markets and administration on epistemic grounds is far more difficult than the Hayekian argument implies.

[50] In the American administrative state, there are second-decimal issues about whether delegation runs to the presidency per se, to the 'executive agencies' who are generally under the president's legal control, or to the 'independent agencies' who are to some degree exempt from the president's legal control. Legal scholars have spilled much ink on these questions, but the choice is not material for my thesis here. The Hayekian argument for markets cannot be squared with extensive regulatory aggregation of local knowledge, whether conducted through presidential institutions or through the administrative bureaucracy. In the second part of this chapter, I discuss the organization of bureaucratic authority in detail.

The organization of the bureaucracy

I turn now from the boundaries of the governmental firm – the scope of the administrative state vis-à-vis the market – to the internal organization of the bureaucracy given an administrative state of a certain scope. Suppose that the legislature delegated some domain of jurisdiction to the administrative state. Conditional on the assignment of that set of regulatory tasks, how should the bureaucracy be organized? I will suggest that the trade-off between local and global knowledge is central here as well. As we will see, however, although the questions are partly inspired by the Hayekian concern with dispersed local knowledge, the answers need not be Hayekian at all, in so far as the relevant variables and trade-offs counsel in favour of a more centralized administrative state than Hayekians might find desirable.

One might, of course, also come at the problem the other way around, by asking what tasks ought to be assigned to the bureaucracy, conditional on a certain internal organization. I will pursue the first formulation because it poses questions that have explicitly been analyzed in epistemic and Hayekian terms in the literature on industrial organization, which may usefully be arbitraged into the bureaucratic setting, *mutatis mutandis*. Although most of my examples and concrete details will come from the American administrative state, I believe that the trade-offs are universal and that similar questions arise in the organization of any advanced industrial democracy.

Synoptic or contextual regulation

A major fault line in the theory of the American administrative state involves the question of whether regulation should be synoptic or contextual. These are my terms rather than banners carried by the participants in the debates themselves, yet I hope that they capture the core of the disagreements in a way that hooks up with neo-Hayekian analyses of the administrative state. An example is James Scott's *Seeing Like a State*, which contrasts the synoptic regulation characteristic of high-modernist administration with local knowledge and *metis*, or tacit practical knowledge which central experts find it costly to acquire. Quite obviously, the contrast between synoptic and contextual regulation is a highly stylized one, whereas in reality there is a continuum between the two extremes, and everything is a matter of degree.

Synoptic regulation: Justice Breyer and OIRA. In the American debates, a leading proponent of synoptic regulation is Justice Stephen Breyer of the United States Supreme Court. In academic writings, Breyer has championed an approach to risk regulation that in effect requires regulators who possess global knowledge.[51] On this view, regulation should achieve an overview of all socially or economically relevant risks, should attempt to arrange them in order of priority and should regulate them just to the point at which the net social costs of regulation are equal to the benefits, but no more. The antithesis of synoptic regulation is uncoordinated, socially wasteful regulation by a myriad of myopic agencies and bodies. A decentralized regulatory apparatus of this sort will suffer from three major problems: 'tunnel vision', a kind of obsessive myopia in which agencies attempt to eliminate the last 10 per cent of the particular risk within their jurisdiction, even if the costs of doing so far exceed the benefits; 'random agenda selection', in which uncoordinated agencies devote resources to regulating risks on grounds other than a ranking of expected social benefits; and 'inconsistency', in which uncoordinated agencies regulate similar risks differently or different risks similarly.[52] Breyer's institutional prescription is a centralized overseer – a coordinating body perched atop the American administrative state, composed of politically insulated technocrats and charged with attempting a global assessment of the relative priorities of various risks.

The closest real analogue to Breyer's council of technocrats is a powerful body called the Office of Information and Regulatory Affairs (OIRA).[53] On paper, OIRA is merely a body subordinate to the Office of Management and Budget (OMB), itself a division of the Executive Office of the President. Yet, a bipartisan series of presidential orders – starting with President Reagan and continuing through President Obama – has given OIRA broad powers to coordinate and oversee regulation by the line agencies, such as the Environmental Protection Agency.[54] OIRA

[51] See, e.g., Stephen G. Breyer, *Breaking the Vicious Circle: Toward Effective Risk Regulation* (Cambridge, MA: Harvard University Press, 1993), 59–61.

[52] Ibid, 11–22.

[53] Breyer's proposed body differs from OIRA in at least one critical respect: the members of Breyer's body would have to follow a 'rotating career path' that would take them through posts at several line agencies in order to give them 'practical experience'. In this respect, Breyer aims to leaven the synoptic overview with practical knowledge. OIRA has no such mandatory career path for its staff.

[54] See *Federal Regulation*, Executive Order No. 12,291, 46 *Fed. Reg.* 13,193 (17 February 1981) (Reagan); *Regulatory Planning and Review*, Executive Order No. 12,866, 58 *Fed.*

requires agencies to submit annual regulatory plans, with a view to coordinating the agendas of different agencies, but its most salient and controversial power is that it reviews major rules proposed by agencies to ensure that the quantified social benefits – defined in economic willingness-to-pay terms – exceed the quantified social costs. Although, in theory, OIRA also may issue informal requests or more formal 'prompt letters' that nudge agencies to promulgate regulations where regulation would produce net social benefits, in practice, the main effect of OIRA review is probably de-regulatory or anti-regulatory, blocking proposals by line agencies whose quantified net benefits cannot be demonstrated to be positive. I will return to this point later in this section.

Viewed in its best light, OIRA is a centralized mechanism for aggregating and coordinating information that is dispersed around the bureaucracy. Through formal review and informal consultation, OIRA draws together packets of information scattered through the line agencies and attempts to piece them together into a comprehensive picture of inter-related risks and their relative priority. There is a separate question – to be taken up shortly – about whether epistemic aggregation and coordination of this sort might be accomplished through decentralized mechanisms; for now, the point is just that epistemic coordination is the major good that OIRA supplies.

Contextual regulation: OIRA's critics. If Justice Breyer is the most visible proponent of synoptic, highly centralized and coordinated regulation, there is an array of critics who call for more contextual, decentralized forms of regulation, entrusted principally to the line agencies which specialize in particular regulatory problems. Although the resulting debates are multi-faceted, a prominent strand is epistemic. The critics suggest that OIRA intervention often makes things worse, rather than better, because OIRA lacks contextualized local knowledge about particular regulatory domains and problems. In one account, evaluations of OIRA's work by the personnel of line agencies

> are almost uniformly negative ... In one midlevel [agency] employee's opinion, 'they [OMB personnel, i.e., OIRA] don't know what they are talking about, and they don't care.' One EPA analyst complained that OMB analysts spend too little time with any single regulation to become sufficiently educated to contribute much to the agency's analytical efforts. Agency officials frequently observe that OMB analysts lack sufficient

Reg. 51,735 (30 September 1993) (Clinton); *Improving Regulation and Regulatory Review*, Executive Order No. 13,563, 76 *Fed. Reg.* 3,821 (18 January 2011) (Obama).

> expertise to understand highly technical questions that often arise in agency rulemaking. [One agency's] scientists, for example, note that OMB analysts often 'venture their opinions on items of industrial hygiene and epidemiology when they are not qualified to be giving opinions.' Addressing OMB's attempt to affect agency carcinogen policies, Congressman John Dingell complained about OMB's 'extensive effort to second-guess the scientific and technical judgments of federal agencies in the highly complex area of cancer risk assessment.'[55]

The main thrust of these critiques is that OIRA is under-specialized. The downside of its purportedly comprehensive vision and comprehensive agenda planning, across different agencies and regulatory risks, is that OIRA analysts may not understand particular risks in context. To some degree, OIRA might attempt to solve its under-specialization problem in either of two ways: (1) soliciting comments from line agencies during the OIRA review process or (2) expansion which internalizes subject-specific expertise, perhaps by hiring experts in relevant domains. The first is a routine feature of OIRA's decision making, and as for the second, an OIRA administrator in the George W. Bush administration, John Graham, hired experts in a range of disciplines.[56]

Even in principle, however, neither approach can provide a complete solution because part of line agencies' context-specific knowledge is practical, tacit and non-transmissible. The problem is Hayekian: part of what agencies know they learn by doing in the course of implementing congressional or presidential commands on the front line.[57] The tacit practical knowledge of line agencies is a form of *metis*, knowing how rather than knowing that, and will by the nature of the case be inaccessible to experts in OIRA, no matter how technically specialized, who have not themselves worked through the myriad complexities of implementing general statutory commands and policies. No amount of meetings between line agencies and OIRA personnel or hiring of new OIRA personnel will convey this tacit local knowledge to the centre. Neither communication with OIRA nor internalization of expertise within OIRA can fully substitute for the local knowledge of line agencies.

55 T. O. McGarity, *Reinventing Rationality: The Role of Regulatory Analysis in the Federal Bureaucracy* (Cambridge University Press, 2005), 281.

56 J. D. Graham, P. R. Noe and E. L. Branch, 'Managing the Regulatory State: The Experience of the Bush Administration', *Fordham Urban Law Journal*, 33 (2006), 968.

57 See S. Gailmard and J. Patty, *Learning While Governing: Expertise and Accountability in the Executive Branch* (University of Chicago Press, 2012).

It follows that there is a genuine trade-off between the benefits of synoptically rational priority setting and coordination, on the one hand, and local knowledge, on the other. A structurally analogous trade-off is recognized in the literature on team theory and the industrial organization of firms.[58] The trade-off can be analyzed either in incentive terms or in epistemic terms or both; in its epistemic aspect, the trade-off is sometimes traced explicitly to Hayek and in effect restates the trade-off between local and global knowledge. 'Decentralized organizations have a natural advantage in adapting decisions to local conditions, since the decisions are made by managers with the best information about those conditions. However, such organizations also have a natural disadvantage since the manager in charge of one division is uncertain about the decisions made by others.'[59] The debate over synoptic versus contextual regulation, over global knowledge of the risk-regulation agenda and global priority setting versus localized problem-specific expertise and practical knowledge, sounds in exactly these terms. Despite the pretensions of both camps, neither can claim the mantle of full rationality or true expertise; rather,

> bounded rationality affects both decentralized and centralized decision making. In a centralized setting, bounded rationality manifests itself in a 'one size fits all' policy. In a decentralized setting, bounded rationality manifests itself as a lack of awareness of synergies [across subdivisions].[60]

Mutatis mutandis, the same holds for the organization of the risk-regulation bureaucracy. Although synoptic regulators such as Breyer emphasize the failures of line agencies to set globally rational priorities in risk regulation, contextual critics argue that OIRA's decision procedures, particularly quantified cost-benefit analysis based on willingness to pay, amount to a one-size-fits-all approach that sometimes ignores the full complexity of local regulatory problems.

[58] See, e.g., R. Alonso, W. Dessein and N. Matouschek, 'When Does Coordination Require Centralization?', *American Economic Review*, 98 (2008), 145; M. Aoki, 'Horizontal vs. Vertical Information Structure of the Firm', *American Economic Review*, 76 (1986), 973; P. Bolton and J. Farrell, 'Decentralization, Duplication, and Delay', *Journal of Political Economy*, 98 (1990), 820; L. Garicano, 'Hierarchies and the Organization of Knowledge in Production', *Journal of Political Economy*, 108 (2000), 897.

[59] Alonso, Dessein and Matouschek, 'When Does Coordination Require Centralization?', 146.

[60] Holian, 'Understanding the M-Form Hypothesis', 6.

Coordination: vertical or horizontal?

Given this large-scale trade-off between local and global knowledge in risk regulation, can we make any progress on the design of the regulatory bureaucracy? As the team theory and firm organization literature also emphasizes, it is a mistake to state the trade-off as pitting the benefits of coordination against the benefits of local adaptation or tailoring. Coordination may be accomplished through centralized oversight or else through decentralized mechanisms. Just as Hayek argued that the price system might bring about decentralized coordination of economic activity, so too it is possible that lateral communication between or among line agencies might bring about decentralized coordination of risk-regulation agendas and priorities. Indeed, assuming that agencies have common fundamental preferences, the greater the benefits of inter-agency coordination, the greater is the incentive for line agencies to coordinate horizontally.[61]

So the real trade-off is between centralized coordination through an OIRA-style oversight body and decentralized coordination through various mechanisms of inter-agency collaboration and communication. The devices and mechanisms available for this purpose are myriad, ranging from simple talk between agency officials to the relatively formal 'memorandum of understanding' which sets forth the agencies' priorities, jurisdiction or cooperative agenda. Of course, some mix of centralized and decentralized coordination will almost certainly be optimal in any given regulatory environment; it is unlikely that either of the extremes, total centralization or total decentralization, will prove desirable. But the desirable set of arrangements may well be skewed in one direction or another in any given environment.

To get traction on these questions, we need to identify the conditions under which a relatively more or less centralized regulatory bureaucracy will prove to be optimal. (Or, if 'optimal' is too ambitious, we may think in terms of marginal or incremental movements from the status quo; given some extant organization of the regulatory bureaucracy, would we want to nudge it towards greater centralization or the opposite?) The industrial organization literature teems with models, some of which focus on trade-offs between local and global knowledge, some on incentive

[61] J. Freeman and J. Rossi, 'Agency Coordination in Shared Regulatory Space', *Harvard Law Review*, 125 (2012), 1184 (describing mechanisms of horizontal coordination that 'seek to draw on the specialized knowledge of different agencies to produce net gains').

compatibility and some that attempt to combine the two questions by endogenizing the incentives for actors in the bureaucracy to acquire information.[62] Limiting myself as far as possible to the epistemic side of these questions, I will attempt to distil and extract some common themes from the models and offer a list of variables that push in one direction or the other. When all is said and done, I believe, the American administrative state is distinctly unpromising terrain for decentralized coordination by line agencies.

Duration in office and turnover of personnel. As emphasized by a pioneering study of vertical and horizontal coordination in American and Japanese business firms,[63] horizontal coordination flourishes in the presence of long-standing informal relationships among actors in different divisions or offices. Relationships of this sort reduce the costs of communication, allow repeated interactions which support long-term commitments and engender trust and deepen horizontal knowledge across units. In a stylized contrast, Japanese firms typically display low inter-firm mobility but high intra-firm mobility on the part of workers, who may stay at a single firm for a whole career but move frequently among the firm's internal units; American workers show the opposite pattern. The Japanese pattern encourages informal horizontal relationships and thus supports horizontal coordination across divisions and units, while the American pattern hampers informal relationships and thus supports vertical coordination by firm management.

Even a passing familiarity with the American administrative state suggests that low duration in office and high turnover make the horizontal coordination model inapposite. Although the civil service is staffed by career employees, most line agencies have several layers of political appointees at the top, who serve for a few years and then return to the private sector or go on to an unrelated government post.[64] The American administrative state is under-professionalized in comparative perspective, and given the role of political appointment to leadership posts, the chiefs of line agencies typically have little chance to form enduring relationships of repeated cooperation and trust. All this raises the costs

62 For an overview of the literature on incentives to acquire information, with particular applications to public institutions, see M. C. Stephenson, 'Information Acquisition and Institutional Design', *Harvard Law Review*, 124 (2011), 1422.

63 Aoki, 'Horizontal vs. Vertical Information Structure of the Firm'.

64 A. J. O'Connell, 'Vacant Offices: Delays in Staffing Top Agency Positions', *Southern California Law Review*, 82 (2009), 914.

of horizontal or decentralized communication and thus raises the costs of horizontal transmission of local knowledge[65]; thus, top-down coordination of regulatory priorities through an overseer such as OIRA becomes relatively more attractive.

Spillovers and communication costs. Suppose that the risks agencies regulate are highly inter-related. To the extent that this is so, the action of any particular agency may have large spill-over effects on the work of other agencies, yet the first agency may not realize this because its knowledge is local. In an epistemic framework, the spill-over issue is not or not mainly that one agency fails to internalize the costs that it is inflicting on other agencies; the issue is that the agency producing spill-overs is myopic and is unaware of the effects of its behaviour.[66]

Just as 'externalities' arise from the transaction costs of bargaining,[67] so too spill-overs arise from the costs of communication. The smaller the costs of horizontal communication between or among agencies, the easier it is for agencies to inform one another of these spill-overs and coordinate horizontally. This implies that the greater the number of agencies involved in regulating any particular risk, the higher are the costs of communication and the greater is the attraction of a centralized coordinator, who can act in part as a clearinghouse for information and in part can enforce bureaucracy-wide standards that reduce the informational load on line agencies.

Here too, structural characteristics of the American administrative state make a centralized coordinator attractive. For reasons good and bad, Congress has parcelled out regulatory jurisdiction to a staggering variety of agencies, many of which have overlapping jurisdiction to regulate the very same risk or else risks that are causally and scientifically inter-related.[68] In the response to the *Deepwater Horizon* oil spill in the Gulf of Mexico, over a dozen U.S. federal agencies played a role, 'making

[65] '[R]apid turnover is an obstacle for learning and professionalism.' Tocqueville asserted that '[i]n America, men remain in power for but an instant before fading back into a crowd.' Hence, '[i]t is very difficult for American administrators to learn from one another' [Jon Elster, 'Conclusion' in Hélène Landemore and Jon Elster (eds.), *Collective Wisdom: Principles and Mechanisms* (Cambridge University Press, 2012), 401 (citing and quoting Alexis de Tocqueville, *Democracy in America* (New York: Library of America, 2004), 237–8)].

[66] Holian, 'Understanding the M-Form Hypothesis', 7–9.

[67] R. H. Coase, 'The Problem of Social Cost', *Journal of Law and Economics*, 3 (1960), 1.

[68] Freeman and Rossi, 'Agency Coordination in Shared Regulatory Space', 1134; J. E. Gersen, 'Overlapping and Underlapping Jurisdiction in Administrative Law', *Supreme Court Review*, 2006 (2007), 208.

decision making slow, conflicted and confused' and producing an overall 'lack of coordination'.[69] The relevant agencies included the Environmental Protection Agency, the Coast Guard, the National Oceanic and Atmospheric Administration, the Minerals Management Service, and the list goes on; the jurisdiction of these agencies is defined in cross-cutting terms. This is not the sort of issue for which OIRA review is relevant, but it illustrates in extreme form the chronic problem that communication costs increase exponentially as the network of related agencies and inter-related risks becomes ever more dense.

Asymmetrical bureaucracies. Another determinant of the relative costs of vertical and horizontal coordination is the presence or absence of symmetry across bureaucratic units. Symmetry can be defined either in terms of size, in terms of organizational form and procedures or in terms of the timing of decisions; asymmetrical organizations are ones in which units are of unequal size, in which units are structured differently and make decisions through very different procedures or in which one unit moves first and the other follows rather than the two units engaging in simultaneous decision making.

In a leading model of the trade-offs between centralized and decentralized coordination, asymmetries tend to push in favour of centralization.[70] Although that model gives a mix of epistemic and non-epistemic reasons, there is a straightforward intuition that asymmetries will generally make informational coordination more difficult. Other things being equal, larger organizations and first-mover organizations will generally prove more myopic in the local-knowledge sense both because their own problems and organizational imperatives will loom larger and because the first mover will necessarily have less information than will the second mover about which policies have been adopted and what effects those policies produce. Generally speaking, the more unlike coordinating units are, the higher are the costs of transmitting information among them and the less the leadership of one will understand the problems of the other.

If this intuition holds, then the American administrative state is singularly unpromising terrain for horizontal coordination. The American bureaucracy is characterized by exorbitant variability and heterogeneity of size, scale, function and institutional organization. Its bewildering alphabet-soup of agencies and its menagerie of agency forms imply that

[69] I. Urbina, 'In Gulf, It Was Unclear Who Was in Charge of Rig', *New York Times*, 5 June 2010, www.nytimes.com/2010/06/06/us/06rig.html?pagewanted=all.

[70] Alonso, Dessein and Matouschek, 'When Does Coordination Require Centralization?'.

very often unlike will have to coordinate with unlike, resulting in miscommunication and coordination failures. An obvious answer is bureaucratic consolidation and reorganization, which is occasionally tried, with mixed results. But, conditional on the current welter of agencies persisting, the high costs of horizontal communication among unlike entities implies the need for some centralized coordinator.

Overall, I believe that extant models of the trade-offs between centralized and decentralized communication imply a robust role for centralized oversight of the American administrative state. None of these considerations enable to us to make pinpoint prescriptions about how centralized that oversight ought to be or what form it ought to take; abstract considerations of the sort I have adduced cannot tell us whether a body such as OIRA is a good idea or what the precise bounds of its authority ought to be. But they can tell us, at a minimum, that conditional on assuming no large-scale simplification of the American bureaucracy and no large-scale retrenchment of its delegated regulatory jurisdiction, fully decentralized coordination is a deeply unpromising strategy. As Breyer and the other proponents of synoptic regulation argue, the problem of locally myopic agencies does imply a need for centralized oversight – although the analytical path needed to reach this conclusion is different from the one which Breyer and other synoptic regulators usually follow. Whatever its failings, OIRA aggregates and deploys information which is dispersed around the bureaucracy; plausibly, decentralized or horizontal coordination among agencies cannot accomplish the same ends.

A central planner to protect free markets?

I conclude by attempting to bring the two parts of the discussion together. The distinction between the scope of the governmental firm, on the one hand, and its internal organization, on the other, has the effect of pitting two Hayekian premises against one another. In the modern administrative state, a centralized overseer of the bureaucracy is an indispensable protector of free markets, yet the same local-knowledge arguments that Hayekians deploy to support market freedom in the first place also may be deployed to undermine centralized oversight of the regulators.

Hayekians seek to protect the market from unnecessary regulatory intervention by agencies in the name of local knowledge, dispersed information and decentralized coordination by economic actors. The principal way to do this would be to limit the delegated regulatory jurisdiction of the agencies altogether, as discussed in the first part of this chapter. Yet, given the large-scale delegation of regulatory jurisdiction to line agencies – an entrenched feature of the American administrative state – some Hayekians argue for a centralized overseer of the bureaucracy, a guardian of the regulatory guardians. The overseer might apply cost-benefit analysis or instead some other decision procedure, but its main aim will be to take a synoptic perspective that cuts across regulatory domains, coordinates risk-regulation priorities and agendas with a view to social welfare and corrects for the myopia of line agencies which becomes obsessed with their regulatory missions and thereby over-regulate.

For concreteness, let me focus on an article by Susan Dudley, the administrator of OIRA in the second term of the George W. Bush administration.[71] Dudley's principal concern is that line agencies are charged with 'single-issue missions' that structure their 'perspectives' and cause them to suffer from Breyer's 'tunnel vision'.[72] By contrast, Dudley says that the value of OIRA lies in its 'cross-cutting perspective and its focus on understanding tradeoffs and consequences'.[73] For Dudley, the main risk of agency myopia is over-regulation of the market, and the promise of OIRA's synoptic perspective is to check over-regulation. She explicitly invokes Hayek in order to warn against 'substituting the judgment of government regulators for the decentralized wisdom of crowds'.[74] Her peroration asks,

> [H]ow can we overcome this fatal conceit [a Hayekian catchphrase][75] and raise awareness of the Hayekian insight that decentralized market processes are better able than centralized government to focus dispersed

[71] S. E. Dudley, 'Lessons Learned, Challenges Ahead', *Regulation*, 32 (2009), 6. In other cases, the same tension appears, although it is less patent. See, e.g., P. Noe, 'Analyzing the Destruction of Human Capital by Regulations', *Administrative Law Review*, 63 (2011), 203 (citing Hayek to show that the 'decentralized marketplace' has more 'dispersed knowledge' than the government, while also urging more centralized oversight of line agencies by OIRA or by Congress); J. Rauch, 'Mitch Daniels on How Libertarians Can Govern', *The Browser*, 4 July 2010 (interview with Mitch Daniels, former head of OMB and governor of Indiana) (quoting Daniels: 'I guess that, if you say, correctly, that this job involves overseeing necessary regulatory activity, that mentality came in some part from books like Hayek's.') (available at http://old.thebrowser.com/interviews/mitch-daniels-on-how-libertarians-can-govern).

[72] Dudley, 'Lessons Learned, Challenges Ahead', 8. [73] Ibid. [74] Ibid., 11.

[75] See F. A. Hayek, *The Fatal Conceit: The Errors of Socialism* (University of Chicago Press, 1991).

information – information that no one individual (not even a regulator) can obtain – and convey it efficiently to market participants?[76]

But this combination of views suffers from a latent tension. The Hayekian argument from local and tacit knowledge that Dudley uses to support OIRA's role as a check on over-regulation, and (indirectly) as a defender of free markets, is the very same argument that line agencies, and the critics who support them, urge against centralized oversight by OIRA. In this line of criticism, OIRA is itself the synoptic regulator which relies on abstract technocratic expertise to issue general guidelines and to set system-wide priorities. And, in the critics' view, OIRA does poorly because it suffers from the very same informational deficits that afflict 'the planner' in Hayek's argument: no matter how well motivated, OIRA lacks the local, partly tacit and practical knowledge of particular regulatory problems which would be needed to make optimal decisions.

The hidden pre-condition for this tension to arise is that OIRA usually intervenes to block putatively myopic agencies from creating new regulations which hamper free markets. In principle, OIRA might also nudge agencies to intervene where welfare-enhancing regulation is called for. OIRA occasionally employs the device of 'prompt letters' which nudge line agencies to regulate where the apparent benefits of regulation exceed the apparent costs. Yet, there is broad consensus that in practice OIRA rarely does this;[77] agencies do not lie awake worrying that OIRA will force them to regulate where they do not want to. Dudley and other Hayekians want an OIRA which is vigilant to weed out 'unnecessary'[78] regulation but rarely discuss the opposite case.

The logical implication of their views is a centralized synoptic overseer of the bureaucracy – a sort of *Hayekian central planner of regulation.* The patent tension in this ideal is not a contingent peculiarity of Dudley's argument which might be corrected. Rather, it is a structural problem for Hayekians, who must come to terms with the existence of a massive regulatory bureaucracy and who will have to decide whether the

[76] Dudley, 'Lessons Learned, Challenges Ahead', 11.

[77] See N. Bagley and R. L. Revesz, 'Centralized Oversight of the Regulatory State', *Columbia Law Review*, 106 (2006), 1277.

[78] See, e.g., C. C. DeMuth and D. H. Ginsburg, 'White House Review of Agency Rulemaking', *Harvard Law Review* 99 (1999), 1075 ('We all know that a government agency charged with the responsibility of defending the nation or constructing highways or promoting trade will invariably wish to spend "too much" on its goals.'); Dudley, 'Lessons Learned, Challenges Ahead', 6.

local-knowledge argument for protecting markets from unnecessary regulation can be squared with the global-knowledge argument for a centralized regulatory overseer.

For my part, I do not think the two halves of Dudley's view can be reconciled. The most promising approach would be a second-best argument: the Hayekian ideal is a genuinely free market, but conditional on the creation of a massive regulatory bureaucracy, a centralized overseer which in effect constrains unnecessary regulation is the attainable second best. The problem with this justification is that it is ideological, in the sense that it treats the same *causal* argument differently depending on the political valence of the context in which the argument arises. If one subscribes to the original Hayekian argument that decentralized tacit knowledge justifies a robust regime of free markets, then one ought also to agree with OIRA's critics that decentralized line agencies will enjoy a comparative informational advantage – relative to the centralized overseer – on the question of which regulations are actually necessary. Valid second-best arguments, like other arguments, must rest on consistent causal premises, and it is hardly obvious that the Hayekian justification for a centralized regulatory overseer satisfies this minimal-validity condition.

This is a point about the consistency of Hayekian *justifications* for the centralized overseer. It is not an objection to the overseer itself, which is in my view justifiable on other grounds. It is perfectly consistent to believe both the following claims: (1) the benefits of centralized epistemic coordination in the economy as a whole and the ability of representative bureaucracies to generate local knowledge together imply a broad scope for the administrative state, and (2) the benefits of centralized epistemic coordination within the bureaucracy and the costs of horizontal coordination among agencies together imply a robust role for an OIRA-style overseer. Hayekians who desire a centralized overseer to defend free markets subscribe to point (2) but not point (1) – even though the argument for point (2) also implies support for point (1). A practical difference between these two (combinations of) views is that the non-Hayekian approach implies that OIRA 'prompt letters' to spur regulation might well be justifiable depending upon the circumstances, while on the Hayekian approach, such letters would always be suspect, absent special circumstances such as monopoly.

Conclusion

The distinction between local and global knowledge is essential for understanding both the scope of the administrative state and its internal organization; the epistemic organization of the administrative state ought to be a central agenda item for prescriptive legal and political theory. Hayek's views are directly relevant to these questions, but his views have also turned out to be largely untenable. The market is necessarily an imperfect aggregator of information, including local knowledge; on the other side of the ledger, the administrative state, although itself highly imperfect, amounts to a complex machine for aggregating and exploiting local and practical knowledge, both through democratic representation and through delegated policy making by representative bureaucracies. Given large-scale delegation, the trade-off between local and global knowledge and the high costs of horizontal coordination among agencies implies a robust role for centralized oversight of the bureaucracy by an institution such as OIRA. Paradoxically enough, free-market Hayekians applaud such an institution precisely because it is a centralized overseer whose effect is to protect markets from regulatory intervention. Whether this applause is theoretically consistent is at best unclear; I believe it to rest on shifting, inconsistent and ideologically inflected causal premises.

INDEX